Differential Equations in Applied Mathematics

Differential Equations in Applied Mathematics

Editor

Tianwei Zhang

MDPI

Basel • Beijing • Wuhan • Barcelona • Belgrade • Novi Sad • Cluj • Manchester

Editor
Tianwei Zhang
School of Mathematics
and Statistics
Yunnan University
Kunming
China

Editorial Office
MDPI
St. Alban-Anlage 66
4052 Basel, Switzerland

This is a reprint of articles from the Special Issue published online in the open access journal *Axioms* (ISSN 2075-1680) (available at: www.mdpi.com/journal/axioms/special_issues/applied_differential_equations).

For citation purposes, cite each article independently as indicated on the article page online and as indicated below:

Lastname, A.A.; Lastname, B.B. Article Title. *Journal Name* **Year**, *Volume Number*, Page Range.

ISBN 978-3-7258-0146-6 (Hbk)
ISBN 978-3-7258-0145-9 (PDF)
doi.org/10.3390/books978-3-7258-0145-9

Contents

Laurent Cairó and Jaume Llibre
Phase Portraits of Families VII and VIII of the Quadratic Systems
Reprinted from: *Axioms* **2023**, *12*, 756, doi:10.3390/axioms12080756 . . . . **1**

Yongyan Yang, Tianwei Zhang and Zhouhong Li
Boundary Controlling Synchronization and Passivity Analysis forMulti-Variable Discrete Stochastic Inertial Neural Networks
Reprinted from: *Axioms* **2023**, *12*, 820, doi:10.3390/axioms12090820 . . . . **19**

Zhongkai Guo and Liang Zhang
Global Dynamics of an Age-Structured Tuberculosis Model with Vaccine Failure and Nonlinear Infection Force
Reprinted from: *Axioms* **2023**, *12*, 805, doi:10.3390/axioms12090805 . . . . **40**

Marina Pireddu
A Proof of Chaos for a Seasonally Perturbed Version of Goodwin Growth Cycle Model: Linear and Nonlinear Formulations
Reprinted from: *Axioms* **2023**, *12*, 344, doi:10.3390/axioms12040344 . . . . **63**

Jimin Yu, Xiaoyu Qi and Yabin Shao
Asynchronous Switching Control of Discrete Time Delay Linear Switched Systems Based on MDADT
Reprinted from: *Axioms* **2023**, *12*, 747, doi:10.3390/axioms12080747 . . . . **88**

Kaihong Zhao
Solvability, Approximation and Stability of Periodic Boundary Value Problem for a Nonlinear Hadamard Fractional Differential Equation with ρ-Laplacian
Reprinted from: *Axioms* **2023**, *12*, 733, doi:10.3390/axioms12080733 . . . . **106**

Shumin Sun, Tianwei Zhang and Zhouhong Li
Weighted Pseudo-θ-Almost Periodic Sequence and Finite-Time Guaranteed Cost Control for Discrete-Space and Discrete-Time Stochastic Genetic Regulatory Networks with Time Delays
Reprinted from: *Axioms* **2023**, *12*, 682, doi:10.3390/axioms12070682 . . . . **119**

Alexander Khludnev
On the Crossing Bridge between Two Kirchhoff–Love Plates
Reprinted from: *Axioms* **2023**, *12*, 120, doi:10.3390/axioms12020120 . . . . **145**

Yujun Cui, Huiling Chen and Yumei Zou
Monotonically Iterative Method for the Cantilever Beam Equations
Reprinted from: *Axioms* **2023**, *12*, 178, doi:10.3390/axioms12020178 . . . . **159**

Kaihong Zhao
Probing the Oscillatory Behavior of Internet Game Addiction via Diffusion PDE Model
Reprinted from: *Axioms* **2022**, *11*, 649, doi:10.3390/axioms11110649 . . . . **175**

axioms

MDPI

Article

Phase Portraits of Families VII and VIII of the Quadratic Systems

Laurent Cairó [1] and Jaume Llibre [2,*]

1 Institut Denis Poisson, Université d'Orleans, Collegium Sciences et Techniques, Batiment de Mathématiques, Rue de Chartres BP6759, CEDEX 2, 45067 Orléans, France; lcairo85@orange.fr
2 Departament de Matemàtiques, Universitat Autònoma de Barcelona, 08193 Bellaterra, Spain
* Correspondence: jaume.llibre@uab.cat

Abstract: The quadratic polynomial differential systems in a plane are the easiest nonlinear differential systems. They have been studied intensively due to their nonlinearity and the large number of applications. These systems can be classified into ten classes. Here, we provide all topologically different phase portraits in the Poincaré disc of two of these classes.

Keywords: quadratic vector fields; quadratic systems; phase portraits

MSC: 34C05; 34A34; 34C14

1. Introduction and Statement of the Main Results

A *quadratic polynomial differential system* (or simply, a *quadratic system*) is a differential system of the following form:

$$\dot{x} = P(x,y), \qquad \dot{y} = Q(x,y), \tag{1}$$

where P and Q are real polynomials in variables x and y and the maximum degree of the polynomials P and Q is two.

At the beginning of the 20th century, the study of quadratic systems began. In [1], Coppel noted how Büchel [2], in 1904, published the first work on quadratic systems. Two short surveys on quadratic systems were published, i.e., by Coppel [1] in 1966 and by Chicone and Tian [3] in 1982.

In recent decades, quadratic systems were intensively studied and many good results were obtained, see references [4–6]. In the second reference, one can find many applications for quadratic systems. Although quadratic systems have been studied in more than one thousand papers, we do not have a complete understanding of these systems.

In [7], the authors prove that any quadratic system is affine-equivalent, scaling the time variable, if necessary, to a quadratic system of the form

$$\dot{x} = P(x,y), \qquad \dot{y} = Q(x,y) = d + ax + by + \ell x^2 + mxy + ny^2,$$

where $\dot{x} = P(x,y)$ is one of the following ten:

$$\begin{array}{llll}
\text{(I)} & \dot{x} = 1 + xy, & \text{(VI)} & \dot{x} = 1 + x^2, \\
\text{(II)} & \dot{x} = xy, & \text{(VII)} & \dot{x} = x^2, \\
\text{(III)} & \dot{x} = y + x^2, & \text{(VIII)} & \dot{x} = x, \\
\text{(IV)} & \dot{x} = y, & \text{(IX)} & \dot{x} = 1, \\
\text{(V)} & \dot{x} = -1 + x^2, & \text{(X)} & \dot{x} = 0.
\end{array}$$

Roughly speaking, the Poincaré disc is the disc centered at the origin of $\mathbb{R}^2$ and the radius, where the interior of this disc is identified with the whole plane $\mathbb{R}^2$ and its boundary

Citation: Cairó, L.; Llibre, J. Phase Portraits of Families VII and VIII of the Quadratic Systems. *Axioms* **2023**, *12*, 756. https://doi.org/10.3390/axioms12080756

Academic Editor: Tianwei Zhang

Received: 30 June 2023
Revised: 22 July 2023
Accepted: 26 July 2023
Published: 1 August 2023

circle $\mathbb{S}^1$ is identified with the infinity of the plane, $\mathbb{R}^2$. This is due to the fact that in the plane, we can go to infinity in as many directions as points on the circle $\mathbb{S}^1$. For more details on the Poincaré compactification, see Section 2.2; for the definition of topologically equivalent phase portraits in the Poincaré disc, see Section 2.3.

We note that quadratic system X has straight lines with constant $x =$ coordinates formed by orbits, and the conic $Q(x,y) = 0$ is filled with equilibrium points, so the phase portraits are trivial. On the other hand, quadratic systems IX does not contain any equilibrium points, thus making this quadratic system a subclass of the so-called chordal quadratic system. The phase portraits of these systems in the Poincaré disc have been completely studied in [7]. Thus, the aim of this paper is to classify the different topological phase portraits in the Poincaré disc of the classes of quadratic systems VII and VIII, i.e., of systems

$$\dot{x} = x^2, \qquad \dot{y} = d + ax + by + \ell x^2 + mxy + ny^2, \tag{2}$$

and

$$\dot{x} = x, \qquad \dot{y} = d + ax + by + \ell x^2 + mxy + ny^2, \tag{3}$$

respectively.

Our main result is as follows:

Theorem 1. *The following two statements hold:*

(a) *The family of quadratic systems* VII *has* 27 *topologically different phase portraits in the Poincaré disc.*

(b) *The family of quadratic systems* VIII *has* 25 *topologically different phase portraits in the Poincaré disc.*

Statements (a) and (b) of Theorem 1 are proved in Sections 3 and 4, respectively.

The paper is organized as follows. In Section 2, we present the basic results of equilibrium points and the Poincaré compactification. In Sections 3 and 4, we first study the local phase portraits of the finite equilibrium points, and then explore the local phase portraits of the infinite equilibrium points. Finally, we analyze the phase portraits of quadratic systems (2) and (3) in the Poincaré disc, respectively.

2. Preliminary Definitions

The study of the phase portraits of quadratic systems always begins with the study of the finite and infinite equilibria of the local phase portraits, followed by the study of their separatrix connections and limit cycles.

In this section, we introduce the basic notations and definitions that we use for the analysis of the finite and infinite equilibrium points of the local phase portraits.

2.1. Equilibrium Points

A point $q \in \mathbb{R}^2$ is said to be an *equilibrium point* of a polynomial differential system (1) if $P(q) = Q(q) = 0$. If the real parts of these eigenvalues (of the linear part of system (1)) are non-zero, the equilibrium point, q, is considered a *hyperbolic* equilibrium point and its possible phase portraits are well known; for instance, see Theorem 2.15 of [8]. If only one of the eigenvalues of the linear part of system (1) at equilibrium point q is zero, then q is considered a *semi-hyperbolic* equilibrium point, whose possible local phase portraits are also well known; see, among others, Theorem 2.19 of [8]. When both eigenvalues of the linear part of system (1) at equilibrium point q are zero, but the linear part is not identically null, then q is a *nilpotent* equilibrium point, and again, its local phase portraits are known; see, for instance, Theorem 3.5 of [8]. Finally, if the linear part of system (1) at equilibrium point q is entirely zero, then q is *degenerate* or q is *linearly zero*. The local phase portraits of such equilibrium points can be studied using the change of variables called blow-ups; see, for instance, [9].

2.2. Poincaré Compactification

Let $X = (P, Q)$ be the vector field defined by the polynomial differential system (1). Roughly speaking, the Poincaré compactification consists of creating a vector field $p(X)$ in a 2-dimensional sphere, $\mathbb{S}^2$, such that its phase portraits (in the open northern and southern hemispheres) is a copy of the phase portrait of the vector field X, and the equator of the sphere plays the role of the infinity of the phase portrait of X; for details, see [10], or Section 5 of [8]. In this way, we can study the orbits of the vector field X, which go to or come from infinity.

Let $\mathbb{S}^2 = \{x = (x_1, x_2, x_3) \in \mathbb{R}^3 : x_1^2 + x_2^2 + x_3^2 = 1\}$ be the *Poincaré sphere*. We denote by $T_x\mathbb{S}^2$ the tangent plane to $\mathbb{S}^2$ at a point $x \in \mathbb{S}^2$. We consider the vector field X defined on the plane $T_{(0,0,1)}\mathbb{S}^2$. Then the central projection $f : T_{(0,0,1)}\mathbb{S}^2 \to \mathbb{S}^2$ defines two copies of X in $\mathbb{S}^2$, one in the northern hemisphere and the other in the southern hemisphere. Obviously the equator $\mathbb{S}^1 = \{y \in \mathbb{S}^2 : y_3 = 0\}$ represents the *infinity* of $\mathbb{R}^2$. The projection of the closed northern hemisphere of $\mathbb{S}^2$ on $x_3 = 0$ under $(x_1, x_2, x_3) \longmapsto (x_1, x_2)$ is called the *Poincaré disc*, and it is denoted by $\mathbb{D}^2$. As $\mathbb{S}^2$ is a differentiable manifold, we define six local charts, $U_i = \{x \in \mathbb{S}^2 : x_i > 0\}$, and $V_i = \{x \in \mathbb{S}^2 : x_i < 0\}$ for $i = 1, 2, 3$; with the corresponding diffeomorphisms, $F_i : U_i \to \mathbb{R}^2$ and $G_i : V_i \to \mathbb{R}^2$ for $i = 1, 2, 3$ which are the inverses of the central projections from the tangent planes at points $(1, 0, 0)$, $(-1, 0, 0)$, $(0, 1, 0)$, $(0, -1, 0)$, $(0, 0, 1)$ and $(0, 0, -1)$, respectively.

We denote by (u, v) the value of $F_i(x)$ or $G_i(x)$ for any $i = 1, 2, 3$, so a few simple calculations (for $p(X)$) lead to the following formulae in the corresponding local charts (see Section 5 of [8]):

$$v^d\left(Q\left(\frac{1}{v}, \frac{u}{v}\right) - uP\left(\frac{1}{v}, \frac{u}{v}\right), -vP\left(\frac{1}{v}, \frac{u}{v}\right)\right) \quad \text{in } U_1,$$
$$v^d\left(P\left(\frac{u}{v}, \frac{1}{v}\right) - uQ\left(\frac{u}{v}, \frac{1}{v}\right), -vQ\left(\frac{u}{v}, \frac{1}{v}\right)\right) \quad \text{in } U_2,$$
$$(P(u, v), Q(u, v)) \quad \text{in } U_3,$$

where d is the degree of the polynomial differential system (1). The formulae for V_i are similar to the formulae for U_i with a multiplicative factor of $(-1)^{d-1}$. In the coordinates for $i = 1, 2$, points (u, v) of the infinity $\mathbb{S}^1$ satisfy $v = 0$.

2.3. Phase Portraits on the Poincaré Disc

The *separatrix* of $p(X)$ denotes all the orbits of the circle at infinity, the equilibrium points, the limit cycles, and the orbits that lie in the boundary of hyperbolic sectors, i.e., the two separatrices of a hyperbolic sector.

Neumann, [11], showed that the set of all separatrices $S(p(X))$ of the vector field, $p(X)$, was closed.

When there is an orientation preserving or reversing homeomorphism, which maps the trajectories of $p(X)$ into the trajectories of $p(Y)$, we can say that the two differential systems defined by $p(X)$ and $p(Y)$ in the Poincaré disc are *topologically equivalent*.

The *canonical regions* of $p(X)$ are the openly connected components of $\mathbb{D}^2 \setminus S(p(X))$. The set formed by the union of $S(p(X))$ plus one orbit chosen from each canonical region is called a *separatrix configuration* of $p(X)$. When there is an orientation preserving or reversing homeomorphism, which maps the trajectories of $S(p(X))$ into the trajectories of $S(p(Y))$, we can say that the two separatrix configurations, $S(p(X))$ and $S(p(Y))$, are *topologically equivalent*.

The next result is mainly due to work by Markus [12], Neumann [11], and Peixoto [13].

Theorem 2. *Phase portraits in the Poincaré disc of two compactified polynomial differential systems ($p(\mathcal{X})$ and $p(\mathcal{Y})$) with (finitely) many separatrices are topologically equivalent if and only if their separatrix configurations $S(p(\mathcal{X}))$ and $S(p(\mathcal{Y}))$ are topologically equivalent.*

3. Proof of Statement (*a*) of Theorem 1

3.1. Finite Equilibrium Points

We will determine the local phase portrait at the finite equilibrium points of the quadratic system (2).

Assume that $n \neq 0$. If $b^2 - 4dn > 0$, then the finite equilibrium points of system (2) are as follows:

$$p_{\pm} = \left(0, \frac{-b \pm \sqrt{b^2 - 4dn}}{2n}\right),$$

The eigenvalues of the Jacobian matrix of system (2) at $p_{\pm}$ are 0 and $\pm\sqrt{b^2 - 4dn}$. Thus, from Theorem 2.19 of [8], we have that p_+ and p_- are semi-hyperbolic saddle-nodes.

If $b^2 - 4dn < 0$, there are no finite equilibrium points.

If $b^2 - 4dn = 0$, then $d = b^2/(4n)$ and $p_+ = p_- = p = (0, -b/(2n))$. The Jacobian matrix of the differential system at p is

$$\begin{pmatrix} 0 & 0 \\ a - \dfrac{bm}{2n} & 0 \end{pmatrix}.$$

If $a - bm/(2n) \neq 0$, then this equilibrium point is nilpotent, and from Theorem 3.5 of [8], this equilibrium point is a saddle-node.

If $a = bm/(2n)$, the linear part of the differential system at the equilibrium point p is identically zero, and the differential system becomes a homogeneous quadratic differential system. Using the results by Date in [14], who classified the phase portraits of all the homogeneous quadratic systems, we can see that the phase portraits of system (3) when $(m-1)^2 - 4\ell n > 0$ are given in Figure 1, according to the sign of n, If $(m-1)^2 - 4\ell n = 0$, then the phase portraits of system (3) are given in Figure 2, determined by the sign of n. Finally, if $(m-1)^2 - 4\ell n < 0$, the phase portraits of system (3) are given in Figure 3, determined by the sign of n.

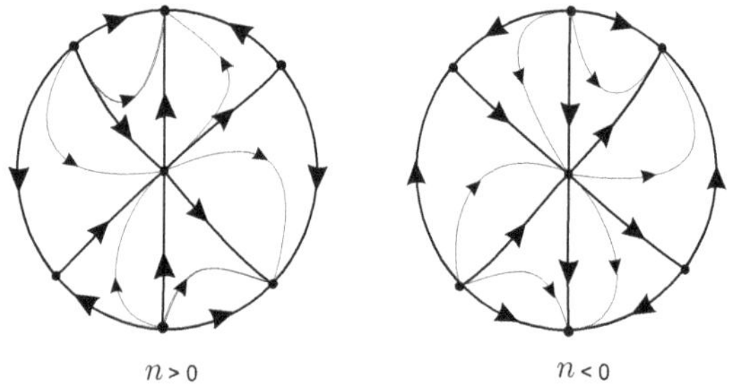

Figure 1. $(m-1)^2 - 4\ell n > 0$.

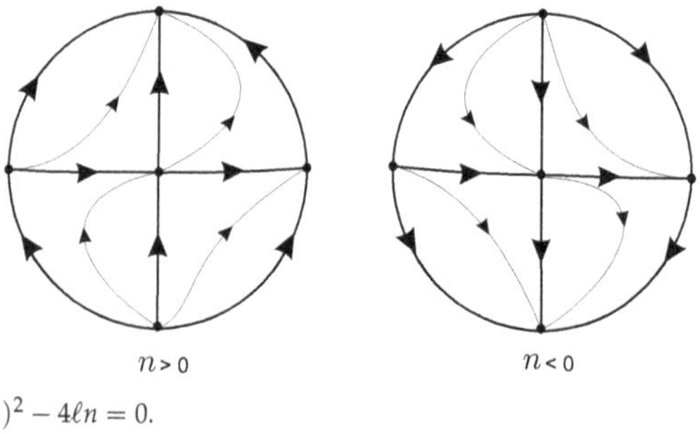

Figure 2. $(m-1)^2 - 4\ell n = 0$.

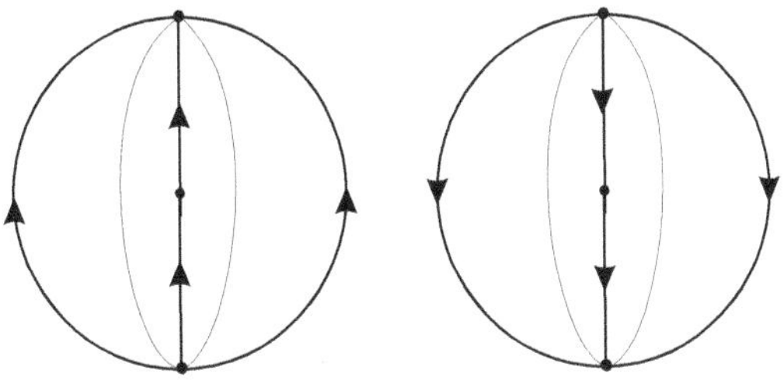

Figure 3. $(m-1)^2 - 4\ell n < 0$.

We assume that $n = 0$. In this case, if $b \neq 0$, there exists a unique equilibrium point, namely $q = (0, -d/b)$, and the eigenvalues of the Jacobian matrix at q are 0 and b. If $b \neq 0$, then q is a semi-hyperbolic saddle-node (by Theorem 2.19 of [8]). If $b = 0$ and $d \neq 0$, the differential system has no finite equilibria. If $b = d = 0$, then the system has a straight line filled with equilibria; we do not consider this kind of differential system because this case can be reduced to a linear differential system, involving the rescaling of the independent variable.

In summary, we proved the following proposition.

Proposition 1. *Assume that $n \neq 0$.*

(a) *If $b^2 - 4dn > 0$, the differential system* (2) *has two finite equilibria $p_\pm$ that are semi-hyperbolic saddle-nodes.*
(b) *If $b^2 - 4dn < 0$, the differential system* (2) *has no finite equilibria.*
(c) *$b^2 - 4dn = 0$.*
   (c.1) *If $a - bm/(2n) \neq 0$, the differential system* (2) *has one finite equilibrium point p that is a nilpotent saddle-node.*
   (c.2) *$a - bm/(2n) = 0$.*
      (c.2.1) *If $(m-1)^2 - 4\ell n > 0$, the phase portrait of the differential system* (2) *is topologically equivalent to the ones in Figure 1, determined by the sign of n.*
      (c.2.2) *If $(m-1)^2 - 4\ell n = 0$, the phase portrait of the differential system* (2) *is topologically equivalent to the ones in Figure 2 determined by the sign of n.*
      (c.2.3) *If $(m-1)^2 - 4\ell n < 0$, the phase portrait of the differential system* (2) *is topologically equivalent to the ones in Figure 3, determined by the sign of n.*

Assume that $n = 0$.

(d) *If $b \neq 0$, the differential system* (2) *has one finite equilibria q, which is a semi-hyperbolic saddle-node.*
(e) *If $b = 0$, then the differential system* (2) *has no finite equilibria if $d \neq 0$, and one straight line is filled with equilibria if $d = 0$.*

3.2. The Infinite Equilibrium Points in Chart U_1

System (2) in the local U_1 chart can be expressed as follows:

$$\dot{u} = \ell - u + mu + nu^2 + av + buv + dv^2, \qquad \dot{v} = -v. \tag{4}$$

Assume $n \neq 0$ the infinite equilibrium points are

$$P_\pm = \left(0, \frac{1 - m \pm \sqrt{(1-m)^2 - 4\ell n}}{2n}\right).$$

The eigenvalues of the Jacobian matrix at $P_\pm$ are $S_\pm = \left(-1, \pm\sqrt{(1-m)^2 - 4\ell n}\right)$. If they are real, then $(1-m)^2 - 4\ell n > 0$ and P_+ are hyperbolic saddles and P_- is a hyperbolic stable node. If $(1-m)^2 - 4\ell n = 0$, then $P_+ = P_- = P = (0, (1-m)/(2n))$. In this case, the Jacobian matrix can be expressed as follows:

$$\begin{pmatrix} 0 & a + \dfrac{b(1-m)}{2n} \\ 0 & -1 \end{pmatrix},$$

and the eigenvalues are -1 and 0, which means that the unique equilibrium point in chart U_1 is semi-hyperbolic, and from Theorem 2.19 of [8], is a semi-hyperbolic saddle-node.

Assume that $n = 0$. Then, the unique infinite equilibrium point in the local U_1 chart is $P = (-\ell/(m-1), 0)$, and the eigenvalues of the Jacobian matrix of system (4) at P are -1 and $m-1$. If $m \neq 1$, from Theorem 2.15 of [8], P is a hyperbolic saddle if $m > 1$ and a hyperbolic node if $m < 1$. If $m = 1$, there are no equilibrium points in U_1.

3.3. *The Infinite Equilibrium Point at the Origin of Chart U_2*

Studying the infinite equilibrium points in the local U_1 chart, we also studied the infinite equilibrium points in the local V_1 chart. Thus, we must see whether the origins of the local U_2 and V_2 charts are infinite equilibrium points or not.

System (2) in the local U_2 chart can be expressed as follows:

$$\begin{aligned} \dot{u} &= -u(n + (m-1)u + bv + \ell u^2 + auv + dv^2) = P(u,v), \\ \dot{v} &= -v(n + mu + bv + \ell u^2 + auv + dv^2) = Q(u,v), \end{aligned} \tag{5}$$

so the origin of U_2 is an infinite equilibrium point. The eigenvalues of the Jacobian matrix of system (5) at the origin are $-n$ with a multiplicity of two. Therefore, the origin is a hyperbolic stable node if $n > 0$, and an unstable node if $n < 0$.

If $n = 0$, then the Jacobian matrix of the system at the origin of the local U_2 chart is the zero matrix, and we need to make blow-ups in order to study its local phase portrait. Before conducting a vertical blow-up, we need to be sure that $u = 0$ is not a characteristic direction. If $u = 0$ is a characteristic direction, then u would be a factor of the polynomial $\Pi = vP_2(u,v) - uQ_2(u,v)$, where $P_2(u,v)$ and $Q_2(u,v)$ represent the terms of degree two in $P(u,v)$ and $Q(u,v)$. In our case, $\Pi = u^2 v$. Thus, $u = 0$ is a characteristic direction and, consequently, before conducting a vertical blow-up, we must perform a twist so $u = 0$ no longer acts as a characteristic direction. This is conducted through the change of variables $(u,v) \to (u_1, v_1)$, where $u_1 = u + v$, $v_1 = v$. By conducting this change of variables, the differential system (5) can be expressed as follows:

$$\begin{aligned} \dot{u_1} &= (1-m)u_1^2 - (b+2-m)u_1 v_1 + v_1^2 - \ell u_1^3 - (a-2\ell)u_1^2 v_1 + (a-d-\ell)u_1 v_1^2 \\ \dot{v_1} &= -m u_1 v_1 + (m-b)v_1^2 - \ell u_1^2 v_1 + (2\ell - a)u_1 v_1^2 + (a-d-\ell)v_1^3, \end{aligned} \tag{6}$$

Since $u_1 = 0$ is not a characteristic direction, we can conduct a vertical blow-up. This vertical blow-up is given by the change of variables $(u_1, v_1) \to (u_2, v_2)$, where $u_2 = u_1$, $v_2 = v_1/u_1$. Then, system (6) becomes

$$\begin{aligned} \dot{u_2} &= u_2^2(m - 1 + \ell u_2 + (b-m+2)v_2 + (a-2\ell)u_2 v_2 - v^2 - (a-d-\ell)u_2 v_2^2), \\ \dot{v_2} &= -u_2 v_2(-1+v_2)^2. \end{aligned}$$

Now, conducting the rescaling of the time with factor u_2, we obtain the system

$$\begin{aligned} \dot{u_2} &= u_2(m - 1 + \ell u_2 + (b-m+2)v_2 + (a-2\ell)u_2 v_2 - v^2 - (a-d-\ell)u_2 v_2^2), \\ \dot{v_2} &= -v_2(-1+v_2)^2. \end{aligned}$$

The equilibrium points of the previous system on $u_2 = 0$ are $(0,0)$ and $(0,1)$ (this is double). The eigenvalues of the Jacobian matrix at $(0,0)$ are -1 and $1-m$. Thus, the point $(0,0)$ is a hyperbolic stable node if $m > 1$, a hyperbolic saddle if $m < 1$, and for $m = 1$, a semi-hyperbolic saddle-node, according to Theorem 2.19 in [8]. The eigenvalues of the Jacobian matrix at $(0,1)$ are 0 and $-b$. Thus, the local phase portrait of the origin of the local U_2 chart is shown in Figure 4A when $n = 0$, $b > 0$, and $m > 1$.

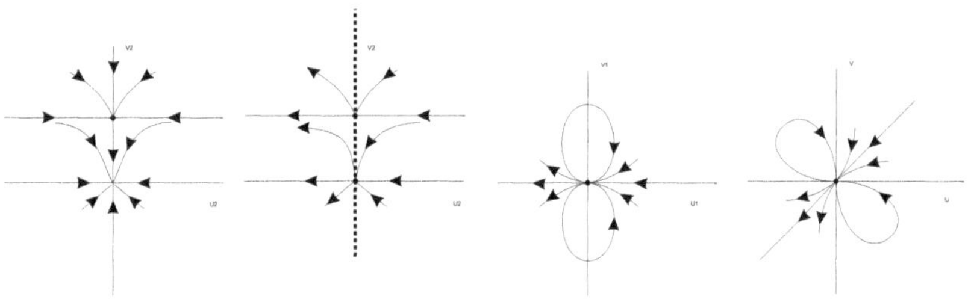

Figure 4. The sequences of blow-ups for obtaining the local phase portrait at the origin of the local U_2 chart when $n = 0$, $b > 0$, and $m > 1$.

Starting from Figure 4A, we obtain the local phase portrait at the axis $u_2 = 0$ of system (10); see Figure 4B. Going back through the vertical blow, taking into account the value of $\dot{u}_1|_{u_1=0} = v_1^2$, we obtain the local phase portrait at the origin of system (5) in Figure 4C. Finally, undoing the twist, we obtain the local phase portrait at the origin of the local U_2 chart, which is shown in Figures 4D and 5A.

Working in a similar way to the preceding case, conducting the convenient blow-ups and using Theorems 2.15 and 2.19 of [8], we obtain all the local phase portraits at the origin of the local U_2 chart in Figure 5. All the local phase portraits are the following

$n = 0$, $b > 0$ and $m > 1$ in Figure 5A;
$n = 0$, $b < 0$ and $m > 1$ in Figure 5B;
$n = 0$, $b > 0$ and $m < 1$ in Figure 5C;
$n = 0$, $b < 0$ and $m < 1$ in Figure 5D;
$n = 0$, $b > 0$, $m = 1$ and $l \neq 0$ in Figure 5E;
$n = 0$, $b > 0$, $m = 1$ and $l = 0$, then $v = 0$ is a straight line of the equilibrium points;
$n = 0$, $b < 0$, $m = 1$ and $l \neq 0$ in Figure 5F;
$n = 0$, $b < 0$, $m = 1$ and $l = 0$, then $v = 0$ is a straight line of the equilibrium points;
$n = 0$, $b = 0$, $d > 0$ and $m > 1$ in Figure 5G;
$n = 0$, $b = 0$, $d < 0$ and $m > 1$ in Figure 5H;
$n = 0$, $b = 0$, $d > 0$ and $m < 1$ in Figure 5I;
$n = 0$, $b = 0$, $d < 0$ and $m < 1$ in Figure 5J;
$n = 0$, $b = 0$, $d > 0$ and $m = 1$ in Figure 5K;
$n = 0$, $b = 0$, $d < 0$ and $m = 1$ in Figure 5L;
$n = 0$, $b = 0$ and $d = 0$, then $u = 0$ is a straight line of the equilibrium points.

3.4. The Global Phase Portraits

The preceding results of the finite and infinite equilibrium points allow us to obtain the global phase portraits quite easily, taking into account that the straight line $x = 0$ is invariant.

First, we consider the case satisfying the following conditions: $n > 0$, $b^2 - 4dn > 0$, and $(1-m)^2 > 4\ell n$. We can see that if $n > 0$, then there is a stable hyperbolic node at the origin of chart U_2. Since $b^2 - 4dn > 0$, there exist two real finite equilibrium points, p_+ and p_-, which are semi-hyperbolic saddle-nodes. Finitely, $(1-m)^2 > 4\ell n$ implies the existence of two infinite equilibrium points in chart U_1 (P_+ is a hyperbolic saddle and P_- a hyperbolic node). The local phase portraits at all these equilibrium points are shown in Figure 6. The tools for studying the phase portraits were employed for all possible configurations that appear in Figure 7.

$n > 0$, $b^2 - 4dn > 0$ and $(1-m)^2 > 4\ell n$ in Figures 7(1–4), but the phase portrait in Figure 7(2) appears by continuity between the phase portraits in Figure 7(1–3);
$n > 0$, $b^2 - 4dn > 0$ and $(1-m)^2 < 4\ell n$ from Figure 7(5);
$n > 0$, $b^2 - 4dn > 0$ and $(1-m)^2 = 4\ell n$ in Figure 7(6–8);
$n > 0$, $b^2 - 4dn < 0$, and $(1-m)^2 > 4\ell n$ in Figure 7(9);
$n > 0$, $b^2 - 4dn < 0$, and $(1-m)^2 < 4\ell n$ in Figure 7(10);
$n > 0$, $b^2 - 4dn < 0$, $(1-m)^2 = 4\ell n$ in Figure 7(11);
$n > 0$, $b^2 - 4dn = 0$, and $(1-m)^2 > 4\ell n$ from Figure 7(12,13);
$n > 0$, $b^2 - 4dn = 0$, and $(1-m)^2 < 4\ell n$ in Figure 7(14,15);
$n > 0$, $b^2 - 4dn = 0$, $(1-m)^2 = 4\ell n$ in Figure 7(16–20).

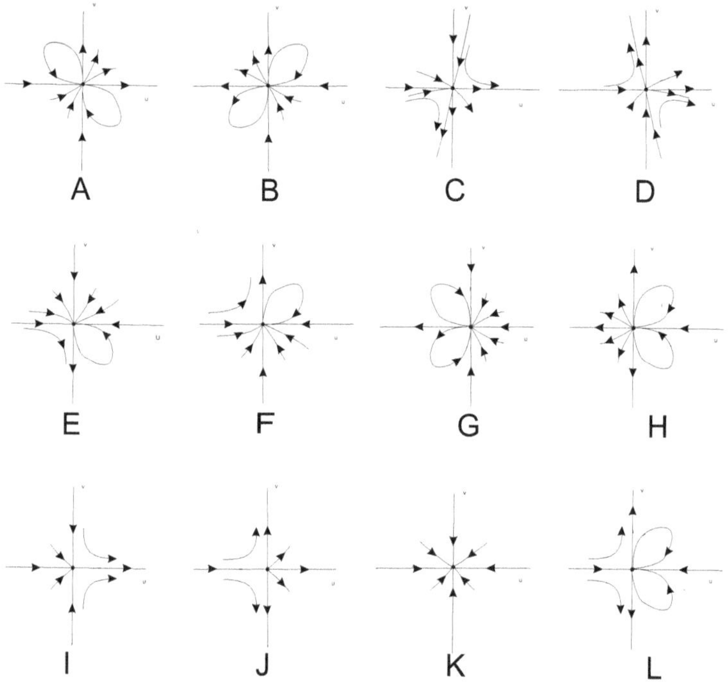

Figure 5. The distinct topological local phase portraits at the origin of the local U_2 chart.

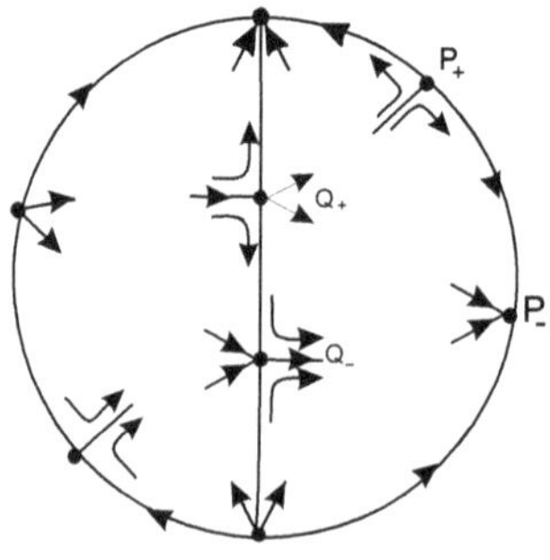

Figure 6. The local phase portraits at the finite and infinite equilibrium points for $n > 0$, $b^2 - 4dn > 0$ and $(1-m)^2 > 4\ell n$.

Phase portraits with $n < 0$ are symmetric with respect to the origins of the coordinates of the preceding eight cases.

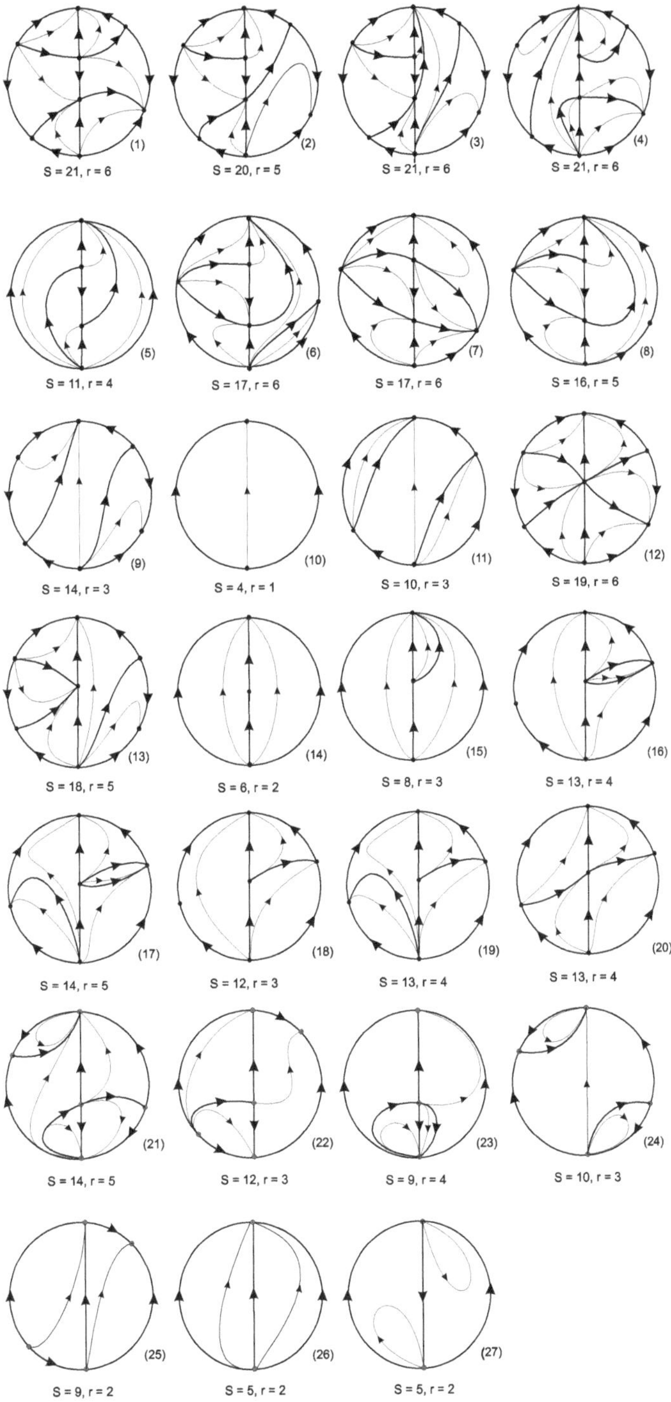

Figure 7. All the distinct topological phase portraits of quadratic system VII. Here, s (respectively, r) denotes the number of separatrices of a phase portrait in the Poincaré disc (respectively, canonical regions).

Now, we study the phase portraits when $n = 0$.
$n = 0, b > 0$ and $m > 1$ in Figure 7(21);
$n = 0, b > 0$ and $m < 1$ in Figure 7(22);
$n = 0, b > 0$ and $m = 1$ in Figure 7(23);

The cases with $b < 0$ are symmetric with respect to the origins of the coordinates of the preceding three cases.

$n = 0, b = 0, d > 0$, and $m > 1$ in Figure 7(24); The cases with $d < 0$ are symmetric with respect to the origins of coordinates of all the preceding cases.
$n = 0, b = 0, d > 0$ and $m < 1$ in Figure 7(25); The cases with $d < 0$ are symmetric with respect to the origins of coordinates of all the preceding cases.
$n = 0, b = 0, d > 0$ and $m = 1$ in Figure 7(26);
$n = 0, b = 0, d < 0$ and $m = 1$ in Figure 7(27).

Of course, from Table 1, the phase portraits with different numbers of separatrices and canonical regions are topologically distinct. Now, we shall see that the phase portraits with the same number of separatrices and canonical regions in Table 1 are also topologically different.

Table 1. Here, p.p. denotes the phase portrait in the Poincaré disc, s denotes the number of separatrices of the phase portrait, and r denotes the number of canonical regions of the phase portrait.

s	4	5	6	8	9	9	10	11	12
r	1	2	2	3	4	2	3	4	3
p.p.	10	26, 27	14	15	23	25	11, 24	5	18, 22
s	13	14	14	16	17	18	19	20	21
r	4	3	5	5	6	5	6	5	6
p.p.	16, 19, 20	9	17, 21	8	6, 7	13	12	2	1, 3, 4

Phase portraits 26 and 27 of Figure 7 are topologically different because phase portrait 27 has two elliptic sectors and phase portrait 26 has no elliptic sectors.

Phase portraits 11 and 24 of Figure 7 are topologically different because phase portrait 24 has two elliptic sectors and phase portrait 11 has no elliptic sectors.

Phase portraits 18 and 22 of Figure 7 are topologically different because phase portrait 18 has orbits starting at the origin of the local U_2 chart and ending at the origin of the local U_1 chart, and these kinds of orbits do not exist in phase portrait 22.

Phase portraits 16, 19, and 20 of Figure 7 are topologically different. First, phase portrait 16 has orbits starting at the origin of the local U_2 chart and ending at the origin of the local U_1 chart, and these kinds of orbits do not exist in phase portraits 19 and 20. Phase portrait 19 has a separatrix starting at the origin of the local U_2 chart and ending at an infinite equilibrium point in the local V_1 chart; this kind of separatrix does not exist in phase portrait 20.

Phase portraits 17 and 21 of Figure 7 are topologically different because phase portrait 21 has two elliptic sectors and phase portrait 17 has no elliptic sectors.

Phase portraits 1, 3, and 4 of Figure 7 are topologically different because the unstable separatrix of the lower equilibrium point on the straight line $x = 0$ contained in $x > 0$ has different ending infinite equilibrium points in the three phase portraits.

4. Proof of Statement (*b*) Theorem 1

4.1. Finite Equilibrium Points

We are going to analyze the equilibrium points of the quadratic system (3).

Assume that $n \neq 0$. The finite equilibrium points of system (3) are

$$p_{\pm} = \left(0, \frac{-b \pm \sqrt{b^2 - 4dn}}{2n}\right).$$

If $b^2 - 4dn > 0$, the eigenvalues of the Jacobian matrix of system (3) at $p_\pm$ are 1 and $\pm\sqrt{b^2 - 4dn}$. Thus, from Theorem 2.15 of [8], p_+ is a hyperbolic unstable node and p_- is a hyperbolic saddle. If $b^2 - 4dn = 0$, then $p_+ = p_- = p = (0, -b/(2n))$. The eigenvalues of the Jacobian matrix of system (3) at p are $1, 0$; therefore, by Theorem 2.19 of [8], p is a semi-hyperbolic saddle-node. Of course, if $b^2 - 4dn < 0$, there are no finite equilibrium points.

We assume that $n = 0$. In this case, if $b \neq 0$, there exists a unique equilibrium point, namely $p = (0, -d/b)$, and the eigenvalues of the Jacobian matrix at p are 1 and b. If $b > 0$, then p is a hyperbolic unstable node. If $b < 0$, then p is a hyperbolic saddle. If $b = 0$, there are no finite equilibrium points.

4.2. *The Infinite Equilibrium Points in Chart U_1*

System (3) in the local U_1 chart can be expressed as follows:

$$\dot{u} = \ell + mu + av + nu^2 + (b-1)uv + dv^2, \qquad \dot{v} = -v^2, \tag{7}$$

Assuming $n \neq 0$, the infinite equilibrium points are

$$P_\pm = \left(0, \frac{-m \pm \sqrt{m^2 - 4\ell n}}{2n}\right),$$

if $m^2 - 4\ell n > 0$. If $m^2 - 4\ell n = 0$, then $P_+ = P_- = P = (0, -m/(2n))$. The eigenvalues of the Jacobian matrix at $P_\pm$ are 0 and $\pm\sqrt{m^2 - 4\ell n}$). By Theorem 2.19 of [8], we obtain that $P_\pm$ are semi-hyperbolic saddle-nodes. The Jacobian matrix at P is

$$\begin{pmatrix} 0 & \dfrac{2an - bm + m}{2n} \\ 0 & 0 \end{pmatrix}.$$

If $2an + (1-b)m \neq 0$, then P is a nilpotent equilibrium point, and by Theorem 3.5 of [8], is a saddle-node. If $2an + (1-b)m = 0$, then P is degenerate. If we translate the equilibrium point P to the origin, it becomes a homogeneous quadratic system; the phase portraits have been classified by Date in [14]. It follows that if $b^2 - 4dn \geq 0$, we obtain that the local phase portrait at P on the Poincaré sphere is formed by two hyperbolic sectors separated by two parabolic ones, and infinity separates the two hyperbolic sectors, which have one separatrix at infinity. If $b^2 - 4dn < 0$, then the local phase portrait at P is a node, unstable if $n < 0$, and stable if $n > 0$.

Assume that $n = 0$. Then the unique infinite equilibrium point in the local U_1 chart is $P = (-l/m, 0)$, and the eigenvalues of the Jacobian matrix of system (7) at P are 0 and m. If $m \neq 0$, from Theorem 2.19 of [8], P is a semi-hyperbolic saddle-node. If $m = 0$, there are no infinite equilibrium points in the local U_1 chart.

4.3. *The Infinite Equilibrium Point at the Origin of Chart U_2*

Studying the infinite equilibrium points in the local U_1 chart, we have also studied the infinite equilibrium points in the local V_1 chart. Thus, we must see whether the origins of the local U_2 and V_2 charts are infinite equilibrium points or not.

System (3) in the local U_2 chart can be expressed as follows:

$$\begin{aligned} \dot{u} &= -u(n + mu + (b-1)v + \ell u^2 + auv + dv^2) = P(u,v), \\ \dot{v} &= -v(n + mu + bv + \ell u^2 + auv + dv^2) = Q(u,v), \end{aligned} \tag{8}$$

so the origin of U_2 is an infinite equilibrium point. The eigenvalues of the Jacobian matrix of the system at the origin are $-n$ with a multiplicity of two. Therefore, the origin is a hyperbolic node, stable if $n > 0$, and unstable if $n < 0$.

If $n = 0$, then the Jacobian matrix of the system at the origin is the zero matrix, and we need to make blow-ups in order to study the local phase portrait at the origin of U_2. Before conducting a vertical blow-up, we need to be sure that $u = 0$ is not a characteristic direction. If $u = 0$ is a characteristic direction then u is a factor of the polynomial $\Pi = vP_2(u,v) - uQ_2(u,v)$, where $P_2(u,v)$ and $Q_2(u,v)$ are the terms of the lowest degrees of $P(u,v)$ and $Q(u,v)$; in our case, $\Pi = uv^2$. Thus, $u = 0$ is characteristic direction; consequently, before conducting a vertical blow-up, we must conduct a twist so that $u = 0$ no longer acts as a characteristic direction. We accomplish this through the change of variables $(u,v) \to (u_1,v_1)$, where $u_1 = u + v$, $v_1 = v$. By making this change of variables, the differential system (8) can be expressed as follows:

$$\begin{aligned} \dot{u}_1 &= -mu_1^2 - v_1^2 + (1-b+m)u_1v_1 + (a-d-\ell)u_1v_1^2 - \ell u_1^3 + (2\ell - a)u_1^2v_1 \\ \dot{v}_1 &= -v_1\big(mu_1 + (b-m)v_1 + \ell u_1^2 + (a-2\ell)u_1v_1 + (d-a+\ell)v_1^2\big), \end{aligned} \tag{9}$$

The characteristic directions of this system are given by the polynomial $\Pi = (u_1 - v_1)v_1^2$, so $u_1 = 0$ is not a characteristic direction, and we can conduct a vertical blow-up. This vertical blow-up is given by the change of variables $(u_1,v_1) \to (u_2,v_2)$, where $u_2 = u_1, v_2 = v_1/u_1$. Then, system (9) becomes

$$\begin{aligned} \dot{u}_2 &= u_2^2\big(-m - \ell u_2 + (1-b+m)v_2 + (2\ell - a)u_2v_2 - v_2^2 + (a-d-\ell)u_2v_2^2\big), \\ \dot{v}_2 &= u_2(-1+v_2)v_2^2. \end{aligned} \tag{10}$$

Now, conducting the rescaling of the time with factor u_2, we obtain the system

$$\begin{aligned} \dot{u}_2 &= u_2\big(-m - \ell u_2 + (1-b+m)v_2 + (2\ell - a)u_2v_2 - v_2^2 + (a-d-\ell)u_2v_2^2\big), \\ \dot{v}_2 &= (-1+v_2)v_2^2. \end{aligned} \tag{11}$$

The equilibrium points of system (11) on $u_2 = 0$ are $(0,0)$, which is double, and $(0,1)$. The eigenvalues of the Jacobian matrix at $(0,0)$ are 0 and $-m$. Thus, $(0,0)$ is a semi-hyperbolic equilibrium point; by applying Theorem 2.19 of [8] to it, it is a saddle-node. The eigenvalues of the Jacobian matrix at $(0,1)$ are 1 and $-b$. Thus, this equilibrium point is hyperbolic, a saddle if $b > 0$, and an unstable node if $b < 0$; see Figure 8A, when $n = 0$, $m < 0$, and $b < 0$.

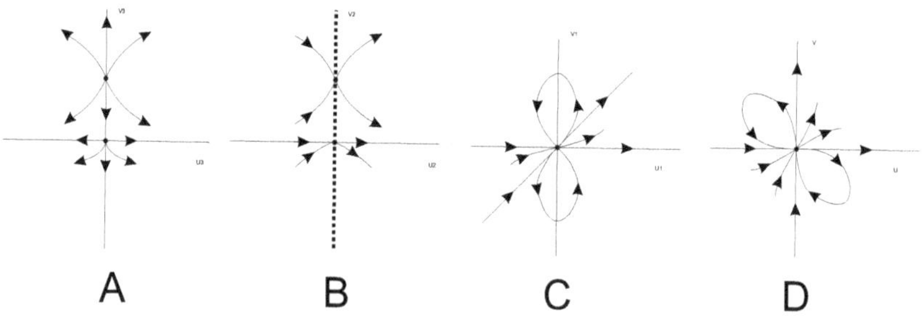

Figure 8. The sequences of blow-ups for obtaining the local phase portrait at the origin of the local U_2 chart when $n = 0$, $b < 0$, and $m < 0$.

From Figure 8A, we can see that the local phase portrait at the axis $u_2 = 0$ of system (10) is given in Figure 8B. Now, going back through the vertical blow-up and taking into account the value of $\dot{u}_1|_{u_1=0} = -v_1^2$, we obtain the local phase portrait at the origin of system (8) in Figure 8C. Finally, ending the twist, we obtain the local phase portrait at the origin of the local U_2 chart, which is shown in Figures 8D and 9A.

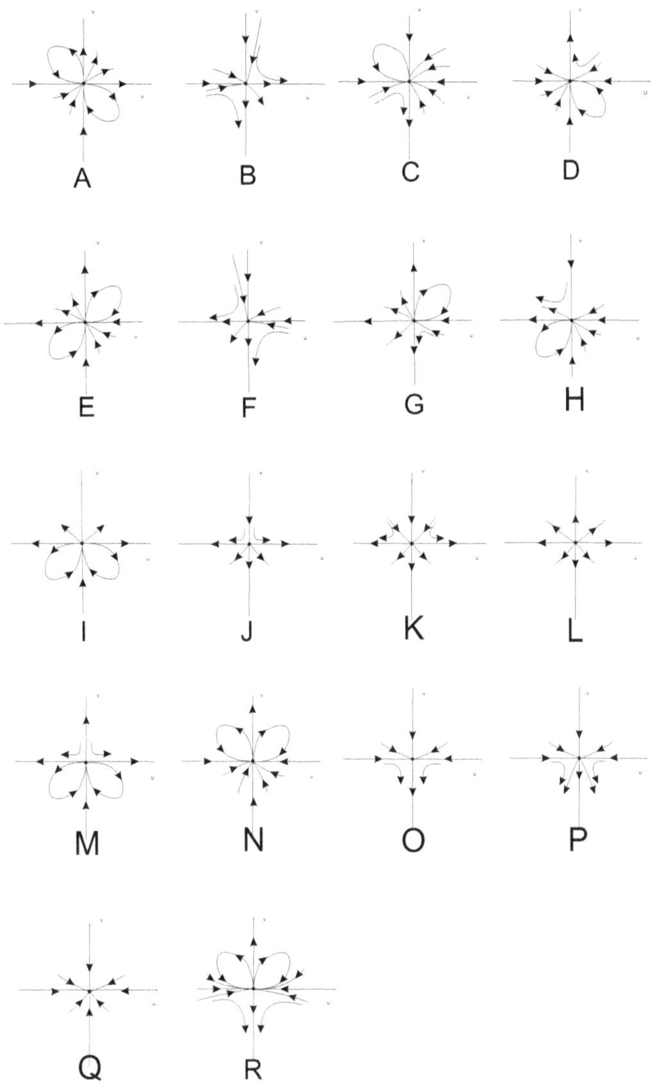

Figure 9. The distinct topological local phase portraits at the origin of the local U_2 chart.

Working in a similar fashion to $n = 0$, $b < 0$, and $m < 0$, i.e., performing the convenient blow-ups and using Theorems 2.15 and 2.19 of [8], we obtain all the local phase portraits at the origin of the local U_2 chart in Figure 9 for the following cases:

$n = 0$, $m < 0$ and $b > 0$ in Figure 9B;
$n = 0$, $m < 0$, $b = 0$, and $d < 0$ in Figure 9C;
$n = 0$, $m < 0$, $b = 0$ and $d > 0$, in Figure 9D;
$n = 0$, $m > 0$ and $b < 0$ in Figure 9E;
$n = 0$, $m > 0$ and $b > 0$ in Figure 9F;
$n = 0$, $m > 0$, $b = 0$ and $d < 0$ in Figure 9G;
$n = 0$, $m > 0$, $b = 0$ and $d > 0$ in Figure 9H;
$n = 0$, $m = 0$, $\ell < 0$ and $b < 0$ in Figure 9I;
$n = 0$, $m = 0$, $\ell < 0$ and $0 < b \leq \ell + 2$ in Figure 9J;
$n = 0$, $m = 0$, $\ell < 0$ and $b > \ell + 2$ in Figure 9K;

$n = 0, m = 0, \ell < 0, b = 0$ and $d < 0$ in Figure 9L;
$n = 0, m = 0, \ell < 0, b = 0$ and $d > 0$ in Figure 9M;
$n = 0, m = 0, \ell > 0, b < 0$ and in Figure 9N;
$n = 0, m = 0, \ell > 0$ and $0 < b \leq \ell + 2$ in Figure 9O;
$n = 0, m = 0, \ell > 0$ and $b > \ell + 2$ in Figure 9P;
$n = 0, m = 0, \ell > 0, b = 0$ and $d < 0$ in Figure 9Q;
$n = 0, m = 0, \ell > 0, b = 0$ and $d > 0$ in Figure 9R.

4.4. The Global Phase Portraits

The preceding results for the finite and infinite equilibrium points allowed us to obtain the global phase portraits quite easily, taking into account that the straight line $x = 0$ is invariant.

First, we consider the case satisfying the following conditions: $n > 0, b^2 - 4dn > 0$, and $m^2 > 4\ell n$. We have seen that $n > 0$ denotes a stable hyperbolic node at the origin of chart U_2, $b^2 - 4dn > 0$ indicates the existence of two real finite equilibrium points (p_+, which is a hyperbolic unstable node, and p_-, which is a hyperbolic saddle), and $m^2 > 4\ell n$ implies two infinite equilibrium points in chart U_1 (P_+ and P_-, which are nilpotent saddle-nodes). The local phase portraits at all these equilibrium points are shown in Figure 10.

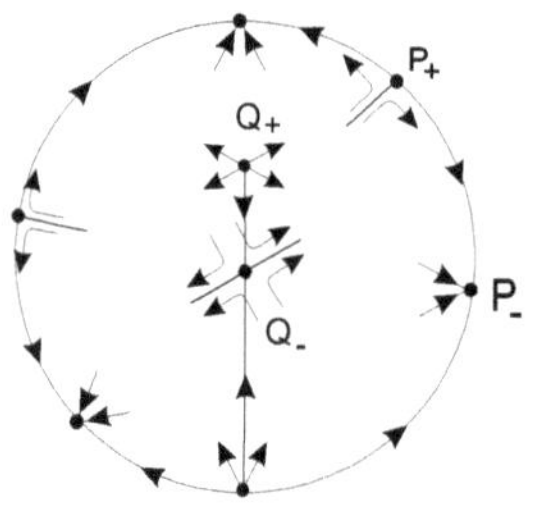

Figure 10. The local phase portraits at the finite and infinite equilibrium points for $n > 0, b^2 - 4dn > 0$, and $m^2 > 4\ell n$.

With the help of Mathematica, we proved that in order for the conditions $n > 0$, $b^2 - 4dn > 0$, and $m^2 > 4\ell n$ to hold, the parameters of the differential system (3) must satisfy one of the following conditions:

(i) $b < 0, d \leq 0, \ell < 0$ and $n > 0$;
(ii) $b < 0, d \leq 0, \ell \geq 0, n > 0$ and $m < -2\sqrt{\ell n}$;
(iii) $b < 0, d \leq 0, \ell \geq 0, n > 0$ and $m > -2\sqrt{\ell n}$;
(iv) $b < 0, d > 0, \ell < 0$ and $0 < n < b^2/(4d)$;
(v) $b < 0, d > 0, \ell \geq 0, 0 < n < b^2/(4d)$ and $m < -2\sqrt{\ell n}$;
(vi) $b < 0, d > 0, \ell \geq 0, 0 < n < b^2/(4d)$ and $m > -2\sqrt{\ell n}$;
(vii) $b = 0, d < 0, \ell < 0$ and $n > 0$;
(viii) $b = 0, d < 0, \ell \geq 0, n > 0$ and $m < -2\sqrt{\ell n}$;
(ix) $b = 0, d < 0, \ell \geq 0, n > 0)$ and $m > -2\sqrt{\ell n}$;
(x) $b > 0, d \leq 0, \ell < 0$ and $n > 0$;
(xi) $b > 0, d \leq 0, \ell \geq 0, n > 0$ and $m < -2\sqrt{\ell n}$;
(xii) $b > 0, d \leq 0, \ell \geq 0, n > 0$ and $m > -2\sqrt{\ell n}$;
(xiii) $b > 0, d > 0, \ell < 0$ and $0 < n < b^2/(4d)$;
(xiv) $b > 0, d > 0, \ell \geq 0, 0 < n < b^2/(4d)$ and $m < -2\sqrt{\ell n}$;
(xv) $b > 0, d > 0, \ell \geq 0, 0 < n < b^2/(4d)$ and $m > -2\sqrt{\ell n}$.

We proved that in cases (i), (ii), (iv), and (vii), and from (ix) to (xv), we could obtain phase portrait (1) of Figure 11; in cases (iii), (vi), and (viii) we obtain phase portrait (2) of Figure 11; finally, in case (v), we obtain the phase portrait that is symmetric to phase portrait

(2), with respect to the straight line $x = 0$. For instance, phase portrait (1) of Figure 11 is obtained when the parameters of system (3) are $d = a = 0$, $b = -1$, $\ell = -1$, $m = -3$, and $n = 1$; phase portrait (2) of Figure 11 is obtained when the parameters are $d = a = 0$, $b = -1$, $\ell = 1$, $m = 3$, and $n = 1$. Phase portrait (3) of Figure 11 exists by continuity, from phase portrait (1) to phase portrait (2).

We recall that the *separatrices* of a polynomial's differential system in the Poincaré disc are all orbits at infinity, the finite equilibria, and the two orbits at the boundary of a hyperbolic sector. Also, the limit cycles are separatrices but quadratic system VIII has no limit cycles. In a phase portrait of the Poincaré disc, if we remove all separatrices, the open components that remain are called the *canonical regions* of the phase portrait. For more details on the separatrices and canonical regions, see [11,12].

The tools used for studying the phase portraits of system (3) for $n > 0$, $b^2 - 4dn > 0$ and $m^2 > 4\ell n$ are used in the following cases, leading to the following results:

$n > 0$, $b^2 - 4dn > 0$, and $m^2 < 4\ell n$ in Figure 11(4);
$n > 0$, $b^2 - 4dn > 0$, $m^2 = 4\ell n$, and $2an + (1 - b)m > 0$ in Figure 11(5);
$n > 0$, $b^2 - 4dn > 0$, $m^2 = 4\ell n$, and $2an + (1 - b)m < 0$, in this case, the phase portrait is symmetric with respect to the straight line $x = 0$ of the phase portrait of the previous case;
$n > 0$, $b^2 - 4dn > 0$, $m^2 = 4\ell n$, and $2an + (1 - b)m = 0$ in Figure 11(6);
$n > 0$, $b^2 - 4dn < 0$, and $m^2 > 4\ell n$ in Figure 11(7);
$n > 0$, $b^2 - 4dn < 0$, and $m^2 < 4\ell n$ in Figure 11(8);
$n > 0$, $b^2 - 4dn < 0$, $m^2 = 4\ell n$, and $2an + (1 - b)m > 0$ in Figure 11(9);
$n > 0$, $b^2 - 4dn < 0$, $m^2 = 4\ell n$, and $2an + (1 - b)m < 0$; this case is a symmetric phase portrait with respect to the straight line $x = 0$ of the previous phase phase portrait;
$n > 0$, $b^2 - 4dn < 0$, $m^2 = 4\ell n$, and $2an + (1 - b)m = 0$ in Figure 11(10,11);
$n > 0$, $b^2 - 4dn = 0$, and $m^2 > 4\ell n$ from Figure 11(12–14);
$n > 0$, $b^2 - 4dn = 0$, and $m^2 < 4\ell n$ in Figure 11(15);
$n > 0$ $b^2 - 4dn = 0$, $m^2 = 4\ell n$, and $2an + (1 - b)m > 0$ in Figure 11(16,17);
$n > 0$, $b^2 - 4dn = 0$, $m^2 = 4\ell n$, and $2an + (1 - b)m = 0$ in Figure 11(18); The cases with $n < 0$ are symmetric with respect to the straight line $y = 0$ in all preceding cases;
$n = 0$, $m > 0$, $b > 0$ in Figure 11(19);
$n = 0$, $m > 0$, $b < 0$ in Figure 11(20);
$n = 0$, $m > 0$, $b = 0$, and $d > 0$ in Figure 11(21);
$n = 0$, $m > 0$, $b = 0$, and $d < 0$; this case has a symmetric phase portrait with respect to $y = 0$ in the previous case; Phase portraits of cases $n = 0$ and $m < 0$ are symmetric with respect to the straight line
$x = 0$ of the phase portraits of cases $n = 0$ and $m > 0$;
$n = 0$, $m = 0$, $b > 2 + l$, and $\ell > 0$ in Figure 11(22);
$n = 0$, $m = 0$, $b > 2 + l$, and $\ell < 0$; this case has a symmetric phase portrait with respect to the $y = 0$ axis;
$n = 0$, $m = 0$, $0 < b \leq 2 + \ell$, and $\ell \neq 0$ in Figure 11(23);
$n = 0$, $m = 0$, $b < 0$, and $\ell > 0$ in Figure 11(24);
$n = 0$, $m = 0$, $b < 0$, and $\ell < 0$; the phase portrait of this case is symmetric with respect to the straight line $y = 0$ in the previous phase portrait;
$n = 0$, $m = 0$, $b = 0$, $\ell > 0$, and $d < 0$ in Figure 11(25);
$n = 0$, $m = 0$, $b = 0$, $\ell < 0$, and $d > 0$; the phase portrait of this case is symmetric with respect to the straight line $y = 0$ in the previous phase portrait;
$n = 0$, $m = 0$, $b = 0$, $\ell > 0$, and $d > 0$; this case has the same phase portrait as Figure 11(8);
$n = 0$, $m = 0$, $b = 0$, $\ell < 0$, and $d < 0$; this case has the symmetric phase portrait with respect to the straight line $y = 0$ in the phase portrait of Figure 11(8).

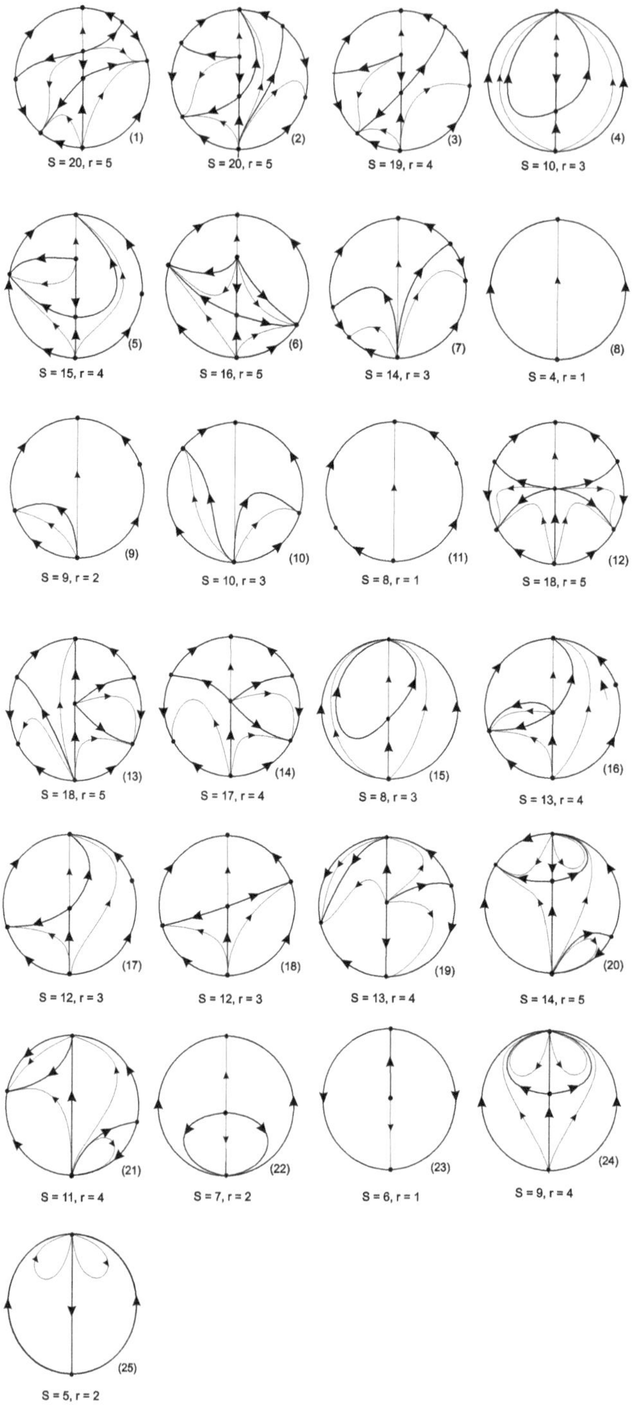

Figure 11. All distinct topological phase portraits of quadratic system VIII. Here, s (respectively, r) denotes the number of separatrices of a phase portrait in the Poincaré disc (respectively, canonical regions).

Of course, from Table 2, the phase portraits with different numbers of separatrices and canonical regions are topologically distinct. Now, we shall see that the phase portraits with the same numbers of separatrices and canonical regions in Table 2 are topologically different.

Table 2. Here, p.p. denotes the phase portrait in the Poincaré disc, s denotes the number of separatrices of the phase portrait, and r denotes the number of canonical regions of the phase portrait.

s	4	5	6	7	8	8	9	9	10	11
r	1	2	1	2	1	3	2	4	3	4
p.p.	8	25	23	22	11	15	9	24	4, 10	21
s	12	13	14	14	15	16	17	18	19	20
r	3	4	3	5	4	5	4	5	4	5
p.p.	17, 18	16, 19	7	20	5	6	14	12, 13	3	1, 2

Phase portraits 4 and 10 of Figure 11 are topologically different because phase portrait 4 has two finite equilibrium points and phase portrait 10 has no finite equilibrium points.

Phase portraits 17 and 18 (respectively, 16 and 19) of Figure 11 are topologically different because phase portrait 17 (respectively, 16) has two orbits going toward the origin of chart U_2, and such orbits do not exist in phase portrait 18 (respectively, 19).

Phase portrait 14 of Figure 11 has three pairs of infinite equilibrium points, while phase portraits 16 and 19 only have two pairs of infinite equilibrium points, so phase portrait 14 is different from phase portraits 16 and 19.

We note that phase portrait 13 in Figure 11 has three pairs of infinite equilibrium points, while phase portrait 20 only has two pairs, so these two phase portraits are topologically distinct.

Author Contributions: Methodology, L.C. and J.L.; Investigation, L.C. and J.L. Both authors have contributed equally to this paper. All authors have read and agreed to the published version of the manuscript.

Funding: This work has been realized thanks to the Agencia Estatal de Investigación grant PID2019-104658GB-I00, the H2020 European Research Council grant MSCA-RISE-2017-777911, AGAUR (Generalitat de Catalunya) grant 2021SGR00113, and by the Acadèmia de Ciències i Arts de Barcelona.

Informed Consent Statement: Not applicable.

Data Availability Statement: This paper has no data.

Conflicts of Interest: The authors declare no conflict of interest.

References

1. Coppel, W.A. A Survey of Quadratic Systems. *J. Differ. Equ.* **1966** 2, 293–304. [CrossRef]
2. Büchel, W. Zur topologie der durch eine gewöhnliche differentialgleichung erster ordnung und ersten grades definierten kurvenschar. *Mitteil. Math. Gesellsch. Hambg.* **1904**, *4*, 33–68.
3. Chicone, C.; Tian, J. On general properties of quadratic systems. *Am. Math. Mon.* **1982**, *89*, 167–178. [CrossRef]
4. Artés, J.C.; Llibre, J.; Schlomiuk, D.; Vulpe, N. *Geometric Configurations of Singularities of Planar Polynomial Differential Systems. A Global Classification in the Quadratic Case*; Birkhäuser: Basel, Switzerland, 2021.
5. Reyn, J. *Phase Portraits of Planar Quadratic Systems*; Mathematics and Its Applications; Springer: Berlin/Heidelberg, Germany, 2007; Volume 583.
6. Ye, Y.; Cai, S.L. *Theory of Limit Cycles*; Transl. Math. Monogr.; American Mathematical Soc.: Providence, RI, USA, 1986; Volume 66.
7. Gasull, A.; Li-Ren, S.; Llibre, J. Chordal quadratic systems. *Rocky Mt. J. Math.* **1986**, *16*, 751–782. [CrossRef]
8. Dumortier, F.; Llibre, J.; Artés, J.C. *Qualitative Theory of Planar Differential Systems*; Universitext; Springer: Berlin/Heidelberg, Germany, 2006.
9. Álvarez, M.J.; Ferragud, A.; Jarque, X. A survey on the blow up technique. *Int. J. Bifur. Chaos* **2011**, *21*, 3103–3118. [CrossRef]
10. González, E.A. Generic properties of polynomial vector fields at infinity. *Trans. Am. Math. Soc.* **1969**, *143*, 201–222. [CrossRef]
11. Neumann, D. Classification of continuous flows on 2-manifolds. *Proc. Am. Math. Soc.* **1975**, *48*, 73–81. [CrossRef]
12. Markus, L. Quadratic differential equations and non-associative algebras. *Ann. Math. Stud.* **1960**, *45* 185–213.

13. Peixoto, L.M.M. *Dynamical Systems*; University of Bahia–Acad. Press: New York, NY, USA, 1973; pp. 389–420.
14. Date, T. Classification and analysis of two-dimensional real homogeneous quadratic differential equation systems. *J. Differ. Equ.* **1979**, *21*, 311–334. [CrossRef]

axioms

MDPI

Article

Boundary Controlling Synchronization and Passivity Analysis for Multi-Variable Discrete Stochastic Inertial Neural Networks

Yongyan Yang [1,2], Tianwei Zhang [3,*] and Zhouhong Li [4]

1 Department of Mathematics, Puyang Petrochemical Vocational and Techenical College, Puyang 457001, China; pyyyyang@126.com
2 Department of Computer Science and Mathematics, Anyang University, Anyang 455131, China
3 Department of Mathematics, Yunnan University, Kunming 650091, China
4 Department of Mathematics, Yuxi Normal University, Yuxi 653100, China; mathzhli@163.com
* Correspondence: zhang@kust.edu.cn

Abstract: The current paper considers discrete stochastic inertial neural networks (SINNs) with reaction diffusions. Firstly, we give the difference form of SINNs with reaction diffusions. Secondly, stochastic synchronization and passivity-based control frames of discrete time and space SINNs are newly formulated. Thirdly, by designing a boundary controller and constructing a Lyapunov-Krasovskii functional, we address decision theorems for stochastic synchronization and passivity-based control for the aforementioned discrete SINNs. Finally, to illustrate our main results, a numerical illustration is provided.

Keywords: coupled networks; passivity-based control; stochastic synchronization; discrete spatial diffusion

MSC: 34D06, 68T07

check for updates

Citation: Yang, Y.; Zhang, T.; Li, Z. Boundary Controlling Synchronization and Passivity Analysis for Multi-Variable Discrete Stochastic Inertial Neural Networks. *Axioms* **2023**, *12*, 820. https://doi.org/10.3390/axioms12090820

Academic Editor: Fevrier Valdez

Received: 8 July 2023
Revised: 9 August 2023
Accepted: 15 August 2023
Published: 26 August 2023

1. Introduction

Neural networks (NNs) can be considered as complicated nonlinear models coupled with numerous internal nodes, and they are capable of offering an effective approach to solving many difficult tasks in the fields of engineering. Due to their huge potential in real-world applications, they have become a significant research topic over the last few decades and have garnered increasing interest in many areas of technology (please refer to refs. [1–7]). On the other hand, it is necessary to address practical problems by studying the dynamic properties of non-linear neural networks not only in the over-damped case but also under weakly damped conditions [8]. Hence, inertial neural networks (INNs), which can act as second-order differential systems, have been extensively studied. Additionally, numerous publications have addressed synchronization problems, including finite-time synchronization [9], nonfragile H_∞ synchronization [10], event-triggered impulsive synchronization [11], fuzzy synchronization [12], Mittag-Leffler synchronization [13], and others.

Passivity, as a specific form of dissipativity, constitutes a fundamental characteristic of physical problems. A system is considered passive when dissipative elements are present in the modeled system, and the accumulated energies remain lower than the external input over a certain time span. Consequently, passivity ensures internal stability of the systems. Due to its widespread applicability in mechanical and electrical systems, the concept of passivity has garnered increasing attention, leading to extensive studies on the passivity of nonlinear systems. In the literature [14], Zhou et al. discussed passivity-based boundary control for stochastic delay reaction-diffusion systems with boundary input-output. Padmaja and Balasubramaniam [15] analyzed passivity-based stability in fractional-order delayed gene regulatory networks. By leveraging Lyapunov-Krasovskii functionals, novel linear matrix inequality conditions were developed to guarantee certain levels of passivity performance in the networks. For further details on this topic, please consult the references [16–18].

Widely, NNs were implemented through IC in engineering applications; spatial diffusions invariably occur when electronic motion takes place in an inhomogeneous electromagnetic domain. Therefore, it is important to consider NNs that incorporate the impact of spatial diffusions. In recent years, greater attention has been devoted to NNs with spatial diffusions; please refer to papers [19–24]. Stochastic neural networks have received substantial attention in our everyday reality. Typically, actions of random networks are heavily time- and space-dependent. As a result, reaction diffusion must be taken into account. Relevant research topics are discussed in references [14,19,20,22,25,26], etc. While there have been reports on space-time discrete models [27–29] to date, the problems of synchronization and passivity-based control for discrete-time SINNs involving diffusions have not been explored.

It is well known that discrete systems,(DSs) can be utilized to simulate a wide range of phenomena, including biological dynamics and artificial NNs, among others. In many scenarios, it has been demonstrated that DSs outperform continuous systems. As a result, the theory of DSs holds significant importance; please refer to references [30–38]. Reports [35–38] have explored various types of discrete INNs. However, they have not focused on the effects of other variables, such as spatial variables. Addressing this gap, the present paper investigates the issues of stochastic synchronization and passivity-based control for time and space discrete SINNs by designing a novel boundary controller.

Our main contributions include the following:

(1) Establishment of a discrete space and time SINNs model, which complements the continuous cases in literature [22–24] and the discrete-time cases in literature [35–38].
(2) Unlike prior works in the literature [22–24], a controller is formulated at the boundary to achieve synchronization and passivity-based control of discrete space and time SINNs.

In what follows, Section 2 establishes the discrete space and time SINNs based on prior works in the literature [27,29]. Section 3 discusses synchronization and passivity-based control of the discrete SINNs. In Section 4, in order to illustrate our main results, a numerical illustration is provided. Finally, the conclusions and perspectives are described in Section 5.

2. Problem Formulation

2.1. SINNs in Discrete Form

Now, our primary focus is dedicated to the time and space discrete SINNs, as noted below

$$\begin{aligned}\Delta^2\mathbf{z}^{[\iota]}_{i,k+1} = {} & (e^{-D_\circ h}+e^{-Ih}-2I)\Delta\mathbf{z}^{[\iota]}_{i,k}+\frac{(I-e^{-D_\circ h})(I-e^{-Ih})}{D_\circ}\Bigg[M\Delta^2_{\hbar}\mathbf{z}^{[\iota-1]}_{i,k}-C\mathbf{z}^{[\iota]}_{i,k} \\ & +Af(\mathbf{z}^{[\iota]}_{i,k})+\alpha\sum_{j=1}^{N}b_{ij}\Gamma\left(\frac{\mathbf{z}^{[\iota]}_{j,k+1}-e^{-Ih}\mathbf{z}^{[\iota]}_{j,k}}{I-e^{-Ih}}\right)+\Xi g(\mathbf{z}^{[\iota]}_{i,k})w_{i,k}+\Lambda\gamma^{[\iota]}_{i,k}+J\Bigg], \quad (1)\end{aligned}$$

where $(\iota,k) \in (0,\ell)_{\mathbf{Z}} \times \mathbf{Z}_0$ and $\ell \in \mathbf{Z}_+$ (here, $\mathbf{Z}$ is the set of integral numbers, $\mathbf{Z}_0 := \{0,1,2,\ldots\}$ and $\mathbf{Z}_+ := \mathbf{Z}_0 \setminus \{0\}$), $\mathbf{z}_i = (\mathbf{z}_{i1},\ldots,\mathbf{z}_{in})^T \in \mathbb{R}^n$ is the state of node i; $i = 1,2,\ldots,N$; $\Delta^2\mathbf{z}_{i,k+1}^{[\cdot]} = \mathbf{z}_{i,k+2}^{[\cdot]} - 2\mathbf{z}_{i,k+1}^{[\cdot]} + \mathbf{z}_{i,k}^{[\cdot]}$, $\Delta\mathbf{z}_{i,k}^{[\cdot]} = \mathbf{z}_{i,k+1}^{[\cdot]} - \mathbf{z}_{i,k}^{[\cdot]}$ for $k \in \mathbf{Z}_0$;

$$\Delta_{\hbar}^2\mathbf{z}_{i,\cdot}^{[\cdot]} := \frac{\mathbf{z}_{i,\cdot}^{[\cdot+2]} - 2\mathbf{z}_{i,\cdot}^{[\cdot+1]} + \mathbf{z}_{i,\cdot}^{[\cdot]}}{\hbar^2},$$

$\hbar$ and h of less than 1 denote the space and time steps' length in order; $C = \mathrm{diag}\{c_1,c_2,\ldots,c_n\}$ and $D = \mathrm{diag}\{d_1,d_2,\ldots,d_n\}$ are constant positive definite matrices, $D_\circ = D - I$, I denotes n-order identity matrix; $M \in \mathbb{R}^{n\times n}$ with $|M| \neq 0$, A, Ξ and Λ are the connection weight n-order matrices; $\alpha > 0$ is the coupling strength, $\Gamma \in \mathbb{R}^{n\times n}$ is the inner coupling matrix, and $B = (b_{ij})_{N\times N}$ is the outer coupling configuration matrix satisfying $b_{ij} > 0\,(i \neq j)$ and $b_{ii} = -\sum_{j=1,j\neq i}^{N} b_{ij}$; $f(\cdot)$ and $g(\cdot)$ are n dimensional activation functions; $\gamma_i = (\gamma_{i1},\ldots,\gamma_{in})^T \in \mathbb{R}^n$ is the external input of the node i, $J \in \mathbb{R}^n$ is the external input; $w_{1,k},\ldots,w_{n,k}$, which are scalar mutually independent random variables on complete probability space $(\Omega,\mathcal{F},\mathbf{P})$, are $\mathscr{F}_k := \sigma\{(w_{1,q},\ldots,w_{N,q}) : q = 0,1,\ldots,k\}$-adaptive, independent of $\mathscr{F}_{k-1}$ and satisfy

$$\mathbb{E}w_{j,k} = 0, \quad \mathbb{E}w_{j,k}^2 = 1, \quad \mathbb{E}(w_{i,k}w_{j,k}) = 0\,(i \neq j), \quad \mathbb{E}(w_{j,k}w_{j,k'}) = 0\,(k \neq k')$$

for $k,k' \in \mathbf{Z}_0$, $i,j = 1,2,\ldots,N$. Hereby, $\mathbb{E}$ represents the expectation operator with respect to probability space $(\Omega,\mathcal{F},\mathbf{P})$. The INNs Equation (1) possesses the following controlled boundary conditions

$$\Delta_{\hbar}\mathbf{z}_{i,k}^{[\iota]}\Big|_{\iota=0} = 0, \quad \Delta_{\hbar}\mathbf{z}_{i,k}^{[\iota]}\Big|_{\iota=\ell-1} = \rho_{i,k}, \tag{2}$$

where $\Delta_{\hbar}\mathbf{z}_{i,k}^{[\cdot]} := \frac{1}{\hbar}(\mathbf{z}_{i,k}^{[\cdot+1]} - \mathbf{z}_{i,k}^{[\cdot]})$ and $\rho_{i,k}$ denotes the control input, $k \in \mathbf{Z}_0$, $i = 1,2,\ldots,N$. Further, the initial condition of the INNs Equation (1) is given by

$$\mathbf{z}_{i,0}^{\langle\iota\rangle} = \varphi_{i,0}^{\langle\iota\rangle}, \quad \Delta\mathbf{z}_{i,0}^{\langle\iota\rangle} = \tilde{\varphi}_{i,0}^{\langle\iota\rangle}, \quad \forall\iota \in [0,\ell]_{\mathbf{Z}}, \tag{3}$$

where $\varphi_{i,0}^{\langle\cdot\rangle}$ and $\tilde{\varphi}_{i,0}^{\langle\cdot\rangle}$ are $\mathscr{F}_0$-adaptive and $\mathscr{F}_1$-adaptive, respectively, $i = 1,2,\ldots,N$.

Let $\mathbf{z}_{i,k}^{[\iota]} = \mathbf{z}_i(\iota\hbar,kh)$ for $(\iota,k) \in [0,\ell]_{\mathbf{Z}} \times \mathbf{Z}_0$. So discrete space and time INNs Equation (1) provides a full discretization scheme for the following stochastic INNs with reaction diffusions

$$\begin{aligned}\frac{\partial^2\mathbf{z}_i(x,t)}{\partial t^2} &= -D\frac{\partial\mathbf{z}_i(x,t)}{\partial t} + M\frac{\partial^2\mathbf{z}_i(x,t)}{\partial x^2} - C\mathbf{z}_i(x,t) + Af(\mathbf{z}_i(x,t))\\ &\quad + \alpha\sum_{j=1}^{N} b_{ij}\Gamma\left(\frac{\partial\mathbf{z}_j(x,t)}{\partial t} + \mathbf{z}_j(x,t)\right) + \Xi g(\mathbf{z}_i(x,t))\frac{\mathrm{d}\mathbf{B}_i(t)}{\mathrm{d}t} + \Lambda\gamma_i(x,t) + J,\end{aligned} \tag{4}$$

where $(x,t) \in (0,L) \times [0,+\infty)$ with $L = \ell\hbar$, $\mathbf{B}_i$ is a one-dimensional Brownian motion on some complete probability space, $i = 1,2,\ldots,N$.

Recently, continuous-time INNs Equation (4) with reaction diffusions has been studied by a few authors (see refs. [21–24]) and the corresponding discrete networks have been discussed in reports [27,29]. The different approach of INNs Equation (1) is similar to those in refs. [27,29].

Hereon, INNs Equation (1) can be regarded as slaver networks and the isolated node $\mathbf{w} \in \mathbb{R}^n$ satisfies the master networks below

$$\begin{cases} \Delta^2 \mathbf{w}_{k+1}^{[\iota]} = (e^{-D_\circ h} + e^{-Ih} - 2I)\Delta \mathbf{w}_k^{[\iota]} + \dfrac{(I - e^{-D_\circ h})(I - e^{-Ih})}{D_\circ} \\ \qquad \times \left[M\Delta_\hbar^2 \mathbf{w}_k^{[\iota-1]} - C\mathbf{w}_k^{[\iota]} + Af(\mathbf{w}_k^{[\iota]}) + \Xi g(\mathbf{w}_k^{[\iota]}) w_{i,k} + J \right], \\ \Delta_\hbar \mathbf{w}_k^{[\iota]} \Big|_{\iota=0} = \Delta_\hbar \mathbf{w}_k^{[\iota]} \Big|_{\iota=\ell} = 0, \quad \forall (\iota, k) \in (0,\ell)_{\mathbf{Z}} \times \mathbf{Z}_0. \end{cases} \tag{5}$$

The initial condition of INNs Equation (5) is described as

$$\mathbf{w}_0^{\langle \iota \rangle} = \phi_0^{\langle \iota \rangle}, \quad \Delta \mathbf{w}_0^{\langle \iota \rangle} = \tilde{\phi}_0^{\langle \iota \rangle}, \quad \forall \iota \in [0,\ell]_{\mathbf{Z}}, \tag{6}$$

where $\phi_0^{\langle \cdot \rangle}$ and $\tilde{\phi}_0^{\langle \cdot \rangle}$ are $\mathscr{F}_0$-adaptive and $\mathscr{F}_1$-adaptive, respectively.

Let $\mathbf{u}_i = \mathbf{z}_i - \mathbf{w}$, then the error networks of INNs Equations (1) and (5) are described by

$$\begin{cases} \Delta^2 \mathbf{u}_{i,k+1}^{[\iota]} = (e^{-D_\circ h} + e^{-Ih} - 2I)\Delta \mathbf{u}_{i,k}^{[\iota]} + \dfrac{(I - e^{-D_\circ h})(I - e^{-Ih})}{D_\circ} \Bigg[M\Delta_\hbar^2 \mathbf{u}_{i,k}^{[\iota-1]} - C\mathbf{u}_{i,k}^{[\iota]} \\ \qquad + A\tilde{f}(\mathbf{u}_{i,k}^{[\iota]}) + \alpha \sum_{j=1}^{N} b_{ij} \Gamma \left(\dfrac{\mathbf{u}_{j,k+1}^{[\iota]} - e^{-Ih}\mathbf{u}_{j,k}^{[\iota]}}{I - e^{-Ih}} \right) + \Xi \tilde{g}(\mathbf{u}_{i,k}^{[\iota]}) w_{i,k} + \Lambda \gamma_{i,k}^{[\iota]} \Bigg], \\ \Delta_\hbar \mathbf{u}_{i,k}^{[\iota]} \Big|_{\iota=0} = 0, \quad \Delta_\hbar \mathbf{u}_{i,k}^{[\iota]} \Big|_{\iota=\ell-1} = \rho_{i,k}, \quad \forall (\iota, k) \in (0,\ell)_{\mathbf{Z}} \times \mathbf{Z}_0, \end{cases} \tag{7}$$

where $\tilde{f}(\mathbf{u}_i) := f(\mathbf{z}_i) - f(\mathbf{w})$ and $\tilde{g}(\mathbf{u}_i) := g(\mathbf{z}_i) - g(\mathbf{w})$, $i = 1,2,\ldots,N$. With the help of Equations (3) and (6), the initial condition for INNs in Equation (7) can be derived, as depicted by

$$\mathbf{u}_{i,0}^{\langle \iota \rangle} = \varphi_{i,0}^{\langle \iota \rangle} - \phi_0^{\langle \iota \rangle}, \quad \Delta \mathbf{u}_{i,0}^{\langle \iota \rangle} = \tilde{\varphi}_{i,0}^{\langle \iota \rangle} - \tilde{\phi}_0^{\langle \iota \rangle}, \quad \forall \iota \in [0,\ell]_{\mathbf{Z}}, i = 1,2,\ldots,N. \tag{8}$$

To study INNs Equation (1) effectively, let

$$\mathbf{u}_{i,k+1}^{[\iota]} = e^{-Ih}\mathbf{u}_{i,k}^{[\iota]} + \varepsilon(I - e^{-Ih})\mathbf{v}_{i,k}^{[\iota]}, \quad \forall (\iota, k) \in (0,\ell)_{\mathbf{Z}} \times \mathbf{Z}, \tag{9}$$

where $\varepsilon > 0$ is a controlling parameter, which can be adjusted freely, $i = 1,2,\ldots,N$. Then, the first equation in INNs Equation (7) is changed into

$$\begin{aligned} \mathbf{v}_{i,k+1}^{[\iota]} &= e^{-D_\circ h}\mathbf{v}_{i,k}^{[\iota]} + \frac{I - e^{-D_\circ h}}{D_\circ} \Bigg[M_\varepsilon \Delta_\hbar^2 \mathbf{u}_{i,k}^{[\iota-1]} + C_\varepsilon \mathbf{u}_{i,k}^{[\iota]} \\ &\quad + A_\varepsilon \tilde{f}(\mathbf{u}_{i,k}^{[\iota]}) + \alpha \sum_{j=1}^{N} b_{ij} \Gamma \mathbf{v}_{j,k}^{[\iota]} + \Xi_\varepsilon \tilde{g}(\mathbf{u}_{i,k}^{[\iota]}) w_{i,k} + \Lambda_\varepsilon \gamma_{i,k}^{[\iota]} \Bigg], \end{aligned} \tag{10}$$

$\forall (\iota, k) \in (0,\ell)_{\mathbf{Z}} \times \mathbf{Z}$, $C_\varepsilon = \varepsilon^{-1}(D - C - I)$, $M_\varepsilon = \varepsilon^{-1}M$, $A_\varepsilon = \varepsilon^{-1}A$, $\Xi_\varepsilon = \varepsilon^{-1}\Xi$, $\Lambda_\varepsilon = \varepsilon^{-1}\Lambda$, $i = 1,2,\ldots,N$.

The vector forms of INNs Equations (9) and (10) are written as

$$\begin{cases} \mathbf{e}_{u,k+1}^{[\iota]} = (e^{-Ih})_{\otimes}\mathbf{e}_{u,k}^{[\iota]} + \varepsilon(I - e^{-Ih})_{\otimes}\mathbf{e}_{v,k}^{[\iota]}, \\ \mathbf{e}_{v,k+1}^{[\iota]} = (e^{-D_{\circ}h})_{\otimes}\mathbf{e}_{v,k}^{[\iota]} + \left[\frac{(I - e^{-D_{\circ}h})M_{\varepsilon}}{D_{\circ}}\right]_{\otimes} \Delta_{\hbar}^{2}\mathbf{e}_{u,k}^{[\iota-1]} \\ \quad + \left[\frac{(I - e^{-D_{\circ}h})C_{\varepsilon}}{D_{\circ}}\right]_{\otimes} \mathbf{e}_{u,k}^{[\iota]} + \left[\frac{(I - e^{-D_{\circ}h})A_{\varepsilon}}{D_{\circ}}\right]_{\otimes} \mathbf{F}(\mathbf{e}_{u,k}^{[\iota]}) \\ \quad + \alpha\left[\frac{(I - e^{-D_{\circ}h})\Gamma}{D_{\circ}}\right]_{\otimes B} \mathbf{e}_{v,k}^{[\iota]} + \left[\frac{(I - e^{-D_{\circ}h})\Lambda_{\varepsilon}}{D_{\circ}}\right]_{\otimes} \gamma_{k}^{[\iota]} \\ \quad + \left[\frac{(I - e^{-D_{\circ}h})\Xi_{\varepsilon}}{D_{\circ}}\right]_{\otimes w_k} \mathbf{G}(\mathbf{e}_{u,k}^{[\iota]}), \\ \Delta_{\hbar}\mathbf{e}_{u,k}^{[\iota]}\Big|_{\iota=0} = 0, \quad \Delta_{\hbar}\mathbf{e}_{u,k}^{[\iota]}\Big|_{\iota=\ell-1} = \rho_k, \end{cases} \tag{11}$$

where

$$\mathbf{e}_u = (\mathbf{u}_1, \ldots, \mathbf{u}_N)^T, \quad \mathbf{e}_v = (\mathbf{v}_1, \ldots, \mathbf{v}_N)^T,$$
$$\mathbf{F}(\mathbf{e}_u) := (\tilde{f}(\mathbf{u}_1), \ldots, \tilde{f}(\mathbf{u}_N))^T, \quad \mathbf{G}(\mathbf{e}_u) := (\tilde{g}(\mathbf{u}_1), \ldots, \tilde{g}(\mathbf{u}_N))^T,$$
$$w = \mathrm{diag}(w_1, \ldots, w_N)^T, \quad \gamma = (\gamma_1, \ldots, \gamma_N)^T, \quad \rho = (\rho_1, \ldots, \rho_N)^T,$$

I_N denotes the N-order identity matrix. Hereby, $(A)_{\otimes} := I_N \otimes A$ and $(A)_{\otimes B} := B \otimes A$. In accordance with Equations (8) and (9), the initial condition of INNs Equation (11) is expressed by

$$\mathbf{e}_{u,0}^{\langle\iota\rangle} = \psi_0^{\langle\iota\rangle}, \quad \mathbf{e}_{v,0}^{\langle\iota\rangle} = \varepsilon^{-1}\left[(I - e^{-Ih})^{-1}\right]_{\otimes}\tilde{\psi}_0^{\langle\iota\rangle} + \varepsilon^{-1} I_N \otimes \psi_0^{\langle\iota\rangle}, \tag{12}$$

where $\iota \in [0, \ell]_{\mathbf{Z}}, i = 1, 2, \ldots, N$, $\psi_0^{\langle\cdot\rangle} = (\varphi_{1,0}^{\langle\cdot\rangle} - \phi_0^{\langle\cdot\rangle}, \ldots, \varphi_{N,0}^{\langle\cdot\rangle} - \phi_0^{\langle\cdot\rangle})^T$ and $\tilde{\psi}_0^{\langle\cdot\rangle} = (\tilde{\varphi}_{1,0}^{\langle\cdot\rangle} - \tilde{\phi}_0^{\langle\cdot\rangle}, \ldots, \tilde{\varphi}_{N,0}^{\langle\cdot\rangle} - \tilde{\phi}_0^{\langle\cdot\rangle})^T$. Throughout this article, supposing that

$$\sum_{\iota=1}^{\ell-1} \mathbb{E}\left\|\varphi_{i,0}^{\langle\iota\rangle}\right\|^2 < \infty, \quad \sum_{\iota=1}^{\ell-1} \mathbb{E}\left\|\phi_0^{\langle\iota\rangle}\right\|^2 < \infty, \quad \sum_{\iota=1}^{\ell-1} \mathbb{E}\left\|\tilde{\varphi}_{i,0}^{\langle\iota\rangle}\right\|^2 < \infty, \quad \sum_{\iota=1}^{\ell-1} \mathbb{E}\left\|\tilde{\phi}_0^{\langle\iota\rangle}\right\|^2 < \infty$$

for $i = 1, 2, \ldots, N$. Based on Equation (12), we have

$$\sum_{\iota=1}^{\ell-1} \mathbb{E}\left\|\mathbf{e}_{u,0}^{\langle\iota\rangle}\right\|^2 < \infty, \quad \sum_{\iota=1}^{\ell-1} \mathbb{E}\left\|\mathbf{e}_{v,0}^{\langle\iota\rangle}\right\|^2 < \infty. \tag{13}$$

The current discussion will establish a boundary controller to synchronize and passivity-based control the master INNs Equations (5) and slave INNs (1), which will be demonstrated in Section 3.

Hereon, we need the following assumption for activation functions.

(F) L_f and L_g are n-order matrices ensuring

$$[f(x) - f(y)]^T[f(x) - f(y)] \le (x - y)^T L_f (x - y),$$
$$[g(x) - g(y)]^T[g(x) - g(y)] \le (x - y)^T L_g (x - y), \quad \forall x, y \in \mathbb{R}^n.$$

2.2. Some Important Inequalities

Lemma 1 ([39]). *Let $X, Y \in \mathbb{R}^m$. Then $X^TY + Y^TX \le \alpha X^TX + \frac{1}{\alpha}Y^TY$ for any $\alpha > 0$.*

Lemma 2 ([40])**.** *If* $X : [0, \ell]_{\mathbf{Z}} \to \mathbb{R}^m$*,* $P \in \mathbb{R}^{m\times m}$*, one has*

$$\sum_{\iota=1}^{\ell-1} X_\iota^T P \Delta^2 X_{\iota-1} = X_\iota^T P \Delta X_{\iota-1}\Big|_1^\ell - \sum_{\iota=1}^{\ell-1} \Delta X_\iota^T P \Delta X_\iota.$$

Lemma 3 ([41,42])**.** *If* $X : [0, \ell]_{\mathbf{Z}} \to \mathbb{R}^m$*,* $P \in \mathbb{R}^{m\times m}$*,* $P \geq 0$*, and* $X_0 = 0$*, one has*

$$\nu_\ell \sum_{\iota=0}^{\ell} X_\iota^T P X_\iota \leq \sum_{\iota=0}^{\ell-1} \Delta X_\iota^T P \Delta X_\iota \leq \mu_\ell \sum_{\iota=0}^{\ell} X_\iota^T P X_\iota,$$

where $\mu_\ell = 4\cos^2 \frac{\pi}{2\ell+1}$ *and* $\nu_\ell = 4\sin^2 \frac{\pi}{2(2\ell+1)}$*.*

Lemma 4 ([41,43])**.** *If* $X : [1, \ell]_{\mathbf{Z}} \to \mathbb{R}^m$*,* $P \in \mathbb{R}^{m\times m}$*,* $P \geq 0$*, one has*

$$\kappa_\ell \sum_{\iota=1}^{\ell} X_\iota^T P X_\iota \leq \sum_{\iota=1}^{\ell-1} \Delta X_\iota^T P \Delta X_\iota + (X_1 + X_\ell)^T P (X_1 + X_\ell),$$

$$\sum_{\iota=1}^{\ell-1} \Delta X_\iota^T P \Delta X_\iota + \left[X_1 + (-1)^\ell X_\ell\right]^T P \left[X_1 + (-1)^\ell X_\ell\right] \leq (4 - \kappa_\ell) \sum_{\iota=1}^{\ell} X_\iota^T P X_\iota.$$

Using Lemma 3, we get

$$\sum_{\iota=0}^{\ell-2} \Delta_\hbar^2 \mathbf{e}_{u,k}^{[\iota]T} P \Delta_\hbar^2 \mathbf{e}_{u,k}^{[\iota]} \leq \frac{\mu_{\ell-1}}{\hbar^2} \sum_{\iota=0}^{\ell-1} \Delta_\hbar \mathbf{e}_{u,k}^{[\iota]T} P \Delta_\hbar \mathbf{e}_{u,k}^{[\iota]}, \quad \forall k \in \mathbf{Z}_0, \tag{14}$$

where P is defined as in Lemma 3.

3. Stochastic Synchronization and Passivity-Based Control

The slave INNs Equation (1) is said to be stochastically synchronized with the master INNs Equation (5) if the error vector networks Equation (11) achieves globally asymptotically stability in mean square, i.e.,

$$\lim_{k\to\infty} \sum_{\iota=1}^{\ell-1} \mathbb{E}\left\|\mathbf{e}_{u,k}^{[\iota]}\right\|^2 = 0 = \lim_{k\to\infty} \sum_{\iota=1}^{\ell-1} \mathbb{E}\left\|\mathbf{e}_{v,k}^{[\iota]}\right\|^2.$$

3.1. Stochastic Synchronization

Define

$$\rho_k = -\sum_{\iota=1}^{\ell-1} \Theta_\otimes \mathbf{e}_{u,k}^{[\iota]}, \quad \forall k \in \mathbf{Z}_0, \tag{15}$$

where $\Theta \in \mathbb{R}^{n\times n}$. Set $\mathcal{D} := \frac{I - e^{-D_\circ h}}{D_\circ}$.

Theorem 1. *Assuming that* **(F)** *is valid, and* $\varepsilon > 0$ *is given in advance,* $\mathcal{D}$ *and* M_ε *are nonsingular. The slaver INNs Equation (1) stochastically synchronizes with the master INNs Equation (5); in other words, model Equation (11) is globally mean-squared asymptotically stable if it has positive constants* λ_f, λ_g *and n-order matrices* $P > 0$*,* $Q > 0$*,* $H > 0$*,* $K > 0$ *such that*

$$\mathbb{O} := \begin{bmatrix} \mathbb{O}_{11} & \mathbb{O}_{12} & \mathbb{O}_{13} & \mathbb{O}_{14} & \mathbb{O}_{15} & \mathbb{O}_{16} \\ * & \mathbb{O}_{22} & \mathbb{O}_{23} & \mathbb{O}_{24} & \mathbb{O}_{25} & \mathbb{O}_{26} \\ * & * & \mathbb{O}_{33} & \mathbb{O}_{34} & \mathbb{O}_{35} & \mathbb{O}_{36} \\ * & * & * & \mathbb{O}_{44} & \mathbb{O}_{45} & \mathbb{O}_{46} \\ * & * & * & * & \mathbb{O}_{55} & \mathbb{O}_{56} \\ * & * & * & * & * & \mathbb{O}_{66} \end{bmatrix} < 0,$$

where

$$\mathbb{O}_{11} = -\frac{1}{\hbar} sym(C_\varepsilon K)_\otimes + \Big[e^{-Ih}Pe^{-Ih} - P\Big]_\otimes + \Big[C_\varepsilon \mathcal{D}Q\mathcal{D}C_\varepsilon\Big]_\otimes + \lambda_f(L_f)_\otimes + \lambda_g(L_g)_\otimes,$$

$$\mathbb{O}_{12} = \varepsilon\Big[e^{-Ih}P(I-e^{-Ih})\Big]_\otimes + \Big[e^{-D_\circ h}Q\mathcal{D}C_\varepsilon\Big]_\otimes^T + \alpha\Big[C_\varepsilon \mathcal{D}Q\mathcal{D}\Gamma\Big]_{\otimes B}, \quad \mathbb{O}_{13} = -\frac{1}{\hbar}(C_\varepsilon K)_\otimes,$$

$$\mathbb{O}_{15} = \Big[C_\varepsilon \mathcal{D}Q\mathcal{D}A_\varepsilon\Big]_\otimes, \quad \mathbb{O}_{25} = \Big[e^{-D_\circ h}Q\mathcal{D}A_\varepsilon\Big]_\otimes + \alpha\Big[A_\varepsilon^T \mathcal{D}Q\mathcal{D}\Gamma\Big]_{\otimes B}^T,$$

$$\mathbb{O}_{22} = -Q_\otimes + \varepsilon^2\Big[(I-e^{-Ih})P(I-e^{-Ih})\Big]_\otimes + \alpha sym\Big[e^{-D_\circ h}Q\mathcal{D}\Gamma\Big]_{\otimes B}$$
$$+2\Big[e^{-D_\circ h}Qe^{-D_\circ h}\Big]_\otimes + 2\alpha^2\Big[\Gamma^T\mathcal{D}Q\mathcal{D}\Gamma\Big]_{\otimes_{B^TB}},$$

$$\mathbb{O}_{33} = -H_\otimes, \quad \mathbb{O}_{44} = -sym\Big[C_\varepsilon\mathcal{D}Q\mathcal{D}M_\varepsilon\Big]_\otimes + \frac{4\mu_{\ell-1}}{\hbar^2}\Big[M_\varepsilon^T\mathcal{D}Q\mathcal{D}M_\varepsilon\Big]_\otimes + \frac{\hbar^2\ell}{\kappa_\ell}H_\otimes,$$

$$\mathbb{O}_{55} = -\lambda_f I_\otimes + 2\Big[A_\varepsilon^T\mathcal{D}Q\mathcal{D}A_\varepsilon\Big]_\otimes, \quad \mathbb{O}_{66} = -\lambda_g I_\otimes + \Big[\Xi_\varepsilon^T\mathcal{D}Q\mathcal{D}\Xi_\varepsilon\Big]_\otimes,$$

$\mathbb{O}_{14} = \mathbb{O}_{16} = \mathbb{O}_{23} = \mathbb{O}_{24} = \mathbb{O}_{26} = \mathbb{O}_{34} = \mathbb{O}_{35} = \mathbb{O}_{36} = \mathbb{O}_{45} = \mathbb{O}_{46} = \mathbb{O}_{56} = 0$. *Here* $sym(A) = A + A^T$. *The controller gain*

$$\Theta = \Big[\mathcal{D}Q\mathcal{D}M_\varepsilon\Big]^{-1} K.$$

Proof. Let us define a Lyapunov-Krasovskii function, which is described by

$$V_k = V_{1,k} + V_{2,k},$$

where

$$V_{1,k} = \sum_{\iota=1}^{\ell-1} \mathbf{e}_{u,k}^{[\iota]T}(I_N \otimes P)\mathbf{e}_{u,k}^{[\iota]}, \quad V_{2,k} = \sum_{\iota=1}^{\ell-1} \mathbf{e}_{v,k}^{[\iota]T}(I_N \otimes Q)\mathbf{e}_{v,k}^{[\iota]}, \quad \forall k \in \mathbf{Z}_0.$$

In the line with the first segment of the error networks Equation (11), we can derive

$$\begin{aligned} \mathbb{E}[\Delta V_{1,k}] &= \mathbb{E}\sum_{\iota=1}^{\ell-1} \mathbf{e}_{u,k+1}^{[\iota]T}(I_N \otimes P)\mathbf{e}_{u,k+1}^{[\iota]} - V_{1,k} \\ &= \mathbb{E}\sum_{\iota=1}^{\ell-1} \mathbf{e}_{u,k}^{[\iota]T}\Big[e^{-Ih}Pe^{-Ih} - P\Big]_\otimes \mathbf{e}_{u,k}^{[\iota]} + \varepsilon\mathbb{E}\sum_{\iota=1}^{\ell-1} sym\Big\{\mathbf{e}_{u,k}^{[\iota]T}\Big[e^{-Ih}P(I-e^{-Ih})\Big]_\otimes \mathbf{e}_{v,k}^{[\iota]}\Big\} \\ &+\varepsilon^2\mathbb{E}\sum_{\iota=1}^{\ell-1} \mathbf{e}_{v,k}^{[\iota]T}\Big[(I-e^{-Ih})P(I-e^{-Ih})\Big]_\otimes \mathbf{e}_{v,k}^{[\iota]}, \quad \forall k \in \mathbf{Z}_0. \end{aligned} \tag{16}$$

According to the second equation of networks Equation (11), we get

$$
\begin{aligned}
\mathbb{E}[V_{2,k+1}] &= \mathbb{E}\sum_{\iota=1}^{\ell-1} \mathbf{e}_{v,k+1}^{[\iota]T}(I_N \otimes Q)\mathbf{e}_{v,k+1}^{[\iota]} \\
&= \underbrace{\mathbb{E}\sum_{\iota=1}^{\ell-1} \mathbf{e}_{v,k}^{[\iota]T}\left[e^{-D_\circ h}Qe^{-D_\circ h}\right]_{\otimes}\mathbf{e}_{v,k}^{[\iota]}}_{\mathcal{U}_{1,k}} + \underbrace{\mathbb{E}\sum_{\iota=1}^{\ell-1} sym\left\{\mathbf{e}_{v,k}^{[\iota]T}\left[e^{-D_\circ h}Q\mathcal{D}M_\varepsilon\right]_{\otimes}\Delta_{\hbar}^{2}\mathbf{e}_{u,k}^{[\iota-1]}\right\}}_{\mathcal{U}_{2,k}} \\
&\quad \underbrace{+\mathbb{E}\sum_{\iota=1}^{\ell-1} sym\left\{\mathbf{e}_{v,k}^{[\iota]T}\left[e^{-D_\circ h}Q\mathcal{D}C_\varepsilon\right]_{\otimes}\mathbf{e}_{u,k}^{[\iota]}\right\}}_{\mathcal{U}_{3,k}} \\
&\quad \underbrace{+\mathbb{E}\sum_{\iota=1}^{\ell-1} sym\left\{\mathbf{e}_{v,k}^{[\iota]T}\left[e^{-D_\circ h}Q\mathcal{D}A_\varepsilon\right]_{\otimes}\mathbf{F}(\mathbf{e}_{u,k}^{[\iota]})\right\}}_{\mathcal{U}_{4,k}} \\
&\quad \underbrace{+\alpha\mathbb{E}\sum_{\iota=1}^{\ell-1} sym\left\{\mathbf{e}_{v,k}^{[\iota]T}\left[e^{-D_\circ h}Q\mathcal{D}\Gamma\right]_{\otimes B}\mathbf{e}_{v,k}^{[\iota]}\right\}}_{\mathcal{U}_{5,k}} \\
&\quad \underbrace{+\mathbb{E}\sum_{\iota=1}^{\ell-1} \Delta_{\hbar}^{2}\mathbf{e}_{u,k}^{[\iota-1]T}\left[M_\varepsilon^T\mathcal{D}Q\mathcal{D}M_\varepsilon\right]_{\otimes}\Delta_{\hbar}^{2}\mathbf{e}_{u,k}^{[\iota-1]}}_{\mathcal{U}_{6,k}} \\
&\quad \underbrace{+\mathbb{E}\sum_{\iota=1}^{\ell-1} sym\left\{\Delta_{\hbar}^{2}\mathbf{e}_{u,k}^{[\iota-1]T}\left[M_\varepsilon^T\mathcal{D}Q\mathcal{D}C_\varepsilon\right]_{\otimes}\mathbf{e}_{u,k}^{[\iota]}\right\}}_{\mathcal{U}_{7,k}} \\
&\quad \underbrace{+\mathbb{E}\sum_{\iota=1}^{\ell-1} sym\left\{\Delta_{\hbar}^{2}\mathbf{e}_{u,k}^{[\iota-1]T}\left[M_\varepsilon^T\mathcal{D}Q\mathcal{D}A_\varepsilon\right]_{\otimes}\mathbf{F}(\mathbf{e}_{u,k}^{[\iota]})\right\}}_{\mathcal{U}_{8,k}} \\
&\quad \underbrace{+\alpha\mathbb{E}\sum_{\iota=1}^{\ell-1} sym\left\{\Delta_{\hbar}^{2}\mathbf{e}_{u,k}^{[\iota-1]T}\left[M_\varepsilon^T\mathcal{D}Q\mathcal{D}\Gamma\right]_{\otimes B}\mathbf{e}_{v,k}^{[\iota]}\right\}}_{\mathcal{U}_{9,k}} \\
&\quad \underbrace{+\mathbb{E}\sum_{\iota=1}^{\ell-1} \mathbf{e}_{u,k}^{[\iota]T}\left[C_\varepsilon\mathcal{D}Q\mathcal{D}C_\varepsilon\right]_{\otimes}\mathbf{e}_{u,k}^{[\iota]}}_{\mathcal{U}_{10,k}} \\
&\quad \underbrace{+\mathbb{E}\sum_{\iota=1}^{\ell-1} sym\left\{\mathbf{e}_{u,k}^{[\iota]T}\left[C_\varepsilon\mathcal{D}Q\mathcal{D}A_\varepsilon\right]_{\otimes}\mathbf{F}(\mathbf{e}_{u,k}^{[\iota]})\right\}}_{\mathcal{U}_{11,k}} \\
&\quad \underbrace{+\alpha\mathbb{E}\sum_{\iota=1}^{\ell-1} sym\left\{\mathbf{e}_{u,k}^{[\iota]T}\left[C_\varepsilon\mathcal{D}Q\mathcal{D}\Gamma\right]_{\otimes B}\mathbf{e}_{v,k}^{[\iota]}\right\}}_{\mathcal{U}_{12,k}} \\
&\quad \underbrace{+\mathbb{E}\sum_{\iota=1}^{\ell-1} \mathbf{F}^T(\mathbf{e}_{u,k}^{[\iota]})\left[A_\varepsilon^T\mathcal{D}Q\mathcal{D}A_\varepsilon\right]_{\otimes}\mathbf{F}(\mathbf{e}_{u,k}^{[\iota]})}_{\mathcal{U}_{13,k}}
\end{aligned}
$$

$$
\begin{aligned}
&+\underbrace{\alpha\mathbb{E}\sum_{\iota=1}^{\ell-1} sym\left\{\mathbf{F}^T(\mathbf{e}_{u,k}^{[\iota]})\left[A_\varepsilon^T\mathcal{D}Q\mathcal{D}\Gamma\right]_{\otimes B}\mathbf{e}_{v,k}^{[\iota]}\right\}}_{\mathcal{U}_{14,k}} \\
&+\underbrace{\alpha^2\mathbb{E}\sum_{\iota=1}^{\ell-1}\mathbf{e}_{v,k}^{[\iota]T}\left[\Gamma^T\mathcal{D}Q\mathcal{D}\Gamma\right]_{\otimes_{B^TB}}\mathbf{e}_{v,k}^{[\iota]}}_{\mathcal{U}_{15,k}} \\
&+\underbrace{\mathbb{E}\sum_{\iota=1}^{\ell-1}\mathbf{G}^T(\mathbf{e}_{u,k}^{[\iota]})\left[\Xi_\varepsilon^T\mathcal{D}Q\mathcal{D}\Xi_\varepsilon\right]_{\otimes_{w_k^2}}\mathbf{G}(\mathbf{e}_{u,k}^{[\iota]})}_{\mathcal{U}_{16,k}}, \qquad (17)
\end{aligned}
$$

where $k \in \mathbf{Z}_0$.

According to Lemmas 1–3 and boundary conditions in Equation (11), we calculate

$$
\begin{aligned}
\mathcal{U}_{2,k} &\leq \mathbb{E}\sum_{\iota=1}^{\ell-1}\mathbf{e}_{v,k}^{[\iota]T}\left[e^{-D_\circ h}Qe^{-D_\circ h}\right]_\otimes\mathbf{e}_{v,k}^{[\iota]} + \mathbb{E}\sum_{\iota=1}^{\ell-1}\Delta_\hbar^2\mathbf{e}_{u,k}^{[\iota-1]T}\left[M_\varepsilon^T\mathcal{D}Q\mathcal{D}M_\varepsilon\right]_\otimes\Delta_\hbar^2\mathbf{e}_{u,k}^{[\iota-1]} \\
&\leq \mathbb{E}\sum_{\iota=1}^{\ell-1}\mathbf{e}_{v,k}^{[\iota]T}\left[e^{-D_\circ h}Qe^{-D_\circ h}\right]_\otimes\mathbf{e}_{v,k}^{[\iota]} + \frac{\mu_{\ell-1}}{\hbar^2}\mathbb{E}\sum_{\iota=1}^{\ell-1}\Delta_\hbar\mathbf{e}_{u,k}^{[\iota]T}\left[M_\varepsilon^T\mathcal{D}Q\mathcal{D}M_\varepsilon\right]_\otimes\Delta_\hbar\mathbf{e}_{u,k}^{[\iota]}, \qquad (18)
\end{aligned}
$$

$$
\begin{aligned}
\mathcal{U}_{6,k} &= \mathbb{E}\sum_{\iota=0}^{\ell-2}\Delta_\hbar^2\mathbf{e}_z^T(x_\iota,t_k)\left[M_\varepsilon^T\mathcal{D}Q\mathcal{D}M_\varepsilon\right]_\otimes\Delta_\hbar^2\mathbf{e}_{u,k}^{[\iota]} \\
&\leq \frac{\mu_{\ell-1}}{\hbar^2}\mathbb{E}\sum_{\iota=1}^{\ell-1}\Delta_\hbar\mathbf{e}_{u,k}^{[\iota]T}\left[M_\varepsilon^T\mathcal{D}Q\mathcal{D}M_\varepsilon\right]_\otimes\Delta_\hbar\mathbf{e}_{u,k}^{[\iota]}, \qquad (19)
\end{aligned}
$$

$$
\begin{aligned}
\mathcal{U}_{7,k} &= \frac{1}{\hbar}\mathbb{E}sym\left\{\mathbf{e}_{u,k}^{[\iota]T}\left[C_\varepsilon\mathcal{D}Q\mathcal{D}M_\varepsilon\right]_\otimes\Delta_\hbar\mathbf{e}_{u,k}^{[\iota-1]}\right\}\Big|_1^\ell - \mathbb{E}\sum_{\iota=1}^{\ell-1}sym\left\{\Delta_\hbar\mathbf{e}_{u,k}^{[\iota]T}\left[C_\varepsilon\mathcal{D}Q\mathcal{D}M_\varepsilon\right]_\otimes\Delta_\hbar\mathbf{e}_{u,k}^{[\iota]}\right\} \\
&= \frac{1}{\hbar}\mathbb{E}sym\left\{\mathbf{e}_{u,k}^{[\ell]T}\left[C_\varepsilon\mathcal{D}Q\mathcal{D}M_\varepsilon\right]_\otimes\rho_k\right\} - \mathbb{E}\sum_{\iota=1}^{\ell-1}\Delta_\hbar\mathbf{e}_{u,k}^{[\iota]T}sym\left[C_\varepsilon\mathcal{D}Q\mathcal{D}M_\varepsilon\right]_\otimes\Delta_\hbar\mathbf{e}_{u,k}^{[\iota]}, \qquad (20)
\end{aligned}
$$

$$
\begin{aligned}
\mathcal{U}_{8,k} &\leq \mathbb{E}\sum_{\iota=1}^{\ell-1}\Delta_\hbar^2\mathbf{e}_{u,k}^{[\iota-1]T}\left[M_\varepsilon^T\mathcal{D}Q\mathcal{D}M_\varepsilon\right]_\otimes\Delta_\hbar^2\mathbf{e}_{u,k}^{[\iota-1]} + \mathbb{E}\sum_{\iota=1}^{\ell-1}\mathbf{F}^T(\mathbf{e}_{u,k}^{[\iota]})\left[A_\varepsilon^T\mathcal{D}Q\mathcal{D}A_\varepsilon\right]_\otimes\mathbf{F}(\mathbf{e}_{u,k}^{[\iota]}) \\
&\leq \frac{\mu_{\ell-1}}{\hbar^2}\mathbb{E}\sum_{\iota=1}^{\ell-1}\Delta_\hbar\mathbf{e}_{u,k}^{[\iota]T}\left[M_\varepsilon^T\mathcal{D}Q\mathcal{D}M_\varepsilon\right]_\otimes\Delta_\hbar\mathbf{e}_{u,k}^{[\iota]} + \mathbb{E}\sum_{\iota=1}^{\ell-1}\mathbf{F}^T(\mathbf{e}_{u,k}^{[\iota]})\left[A_\varepsilon^T\mathcal{D}Q\mathcal{D}A_\varepsilon\right]_\otimes\mathbf{F}(\mathbf{e}_{u,k}^{[\iota]}), \qquad (21)
\end{aligned}
$$

$$
\begin{aligned}
\mathcal{U}_{9,k} &\leq \alpha^2\mathbb{E}\sum_{\iota=1}^{\ell-1}\mathbf{e}_{v,k}^{[\iota]T}\left[\Gamma^T\mathcal{D}Q\mathcal{D}\Gamma\right]_{\otimes_{B^TB}}\mathbf{e}_{v,k}^{[\iota]} + \mathbb{E}\sum_{\iota=1}^{\ell-1}\Delta_\hbar^2\mathbf{e}_{u,k}^{[\iota-1]T}\left[M_\varepsilon^T\mathcal{D}Q\mathcal{D}M_\varepsilon\right]_\otimes\Delta_\hbar^2\mathbf{e}_{u,k}^{[\iota-1]} \\
&\leq \alpha^2\mathbb{E}\sum_{\iota=1}^{\ell-1}\mathbf{e}_{v,k}^{[\iota]T}\left[\Gamma^T\mathcal{D}Q\mathcal{D}\Gamma\right]_{\otimes_{B^TB}}\mathbf{e}_{v,k}^{[\iota]} + \frac{\mu_{\ell-1}}{\hbar^2}\mathbb{E}\sum_{\iota=1}^{\ell-1}\Delta_\hbar\mathbf{e}_{u,k}^{[\iota]T}\left[M_\varepsilon^T\mathcal{D}Q\mathcal{D}M_\varepsilon\right]_\otimes\Delta_\hbar\mathbf{e}_{u,k}^{[\iota]}, \qquad (22)
\end{aligned}
$$

$$
\mathcal{U}_{16,k} = \mathbb{E}\sum_{\iota=1}^{\ell-1}\mathbf{G}^T(\mathbf{e}_{u,k}^{[\iota]})\left[\Xi_\varepsilon^T\mathcal{D}Q\mathcal{D}\Xi_\varepsilon\right]_\otimes\mathbf{G}(\mathbf{e}_{u,k}^{[\iota]}), \quad \forall k \in \mathbf{Z}_0. \qquad (23)
$$

With the help of **(F)**, we have

$$\sum_{\iota=1}^{\ell-1}\mathbf{F}^T(\mathbf{e}_{u,k}^{[\iota]})\mathbf{F}(\mathbf{e}_{u,k}^{[\iota]}) \leq \sum_{\iota=1}^{\ell-1}\mathbf{e}_{u,k}^{[\iota]T}(L_f)_{\otimes}\mathbf{e}_{u,k}^{[\iota]}, \quad \sum_{\iota=1}^{\ell-1}\mathbf{G}^T(\mathbf{e}_{u,k}^{[\iota]})\mathbf{G}(\mathbf{e}_{u,k}^{[\iota]}) \leq \sum_{\iota=1}^{\ell-1}\mathbf{e}_{u,k}^{[\iota]T}(L_g)_{\otimes}\mathbf{e}_{u,k}^{[\iota]}, \tag{24}$$

and by using $\hat{\mathbf{e}}_{u,\cdot}^{[\cdot]} := \mathbf{e}_{u,\cdot}^{[\ell]} - \mathbf{e}_{u,\cdot}^{[\cdot]}$ and Lemma 4, it gets

$$\begin{aligned}
\sum_{\iota=1}^{\ell}\hat{\mathbf{e}}_{u,k}^{[\iota]T}H_{\otimes}\hat{\mathbf{e}}_{u,k}^{[\iota]} &\leq \frac{\hbar^2}{\kappa_\ell}\sum_{\iota=1}^{\ell-1}\Delta_\hbar\hat{\mathbf{e}}_{u,k}^{[\iota]T}H_{\otimes}\Delta_\hbar\hat{\mathbf{e}}_{u,k}^{[\iota]} + \frac{1}{\kappa_\ell}\left[\mathbf{e}_{u,k}^{[\ell]} - \mathbf{e}_{u,k}^{[1]}\right]^T H_{\otimes}\left[\mathbf{e}_{u,k}^{[\ell]} - \mathbf{e}_{u,k}^{[1]}\right] \\
&= \frac{\hbar^2}{\kappa_\ell}\sum_{\iota=1}^{\ell-1}\Delta_\hbar\hat{\mathbf{e}}_{u,k}^{[\iota]T}H_{\otimes}\Delta_\hbar\hat{\mathbf{e}}_{u,k}^{[\iota]} + \frac{\hbar^2}{\kappa_\ell}\left[\sum_{\iota=1}^{\ell-1}\Delta_\hbar\hat{\mathbf{e}}_{u,k}^{[\iota]}\right]^T H_{\otimes}\left[\sum_{\iota=1}^{\ell-1}\Delta_\hbar\hat{\mathbf{e}}_{u,k}^{[\iota]}\right] \\
&\leq \frac{\hbar^2\ell}{\kappa_\ell}\sum_{\iota=1}^{\ell-1}\Delta_\hbar\mathbf{e}_{u,k}^{[\iota]T}H_{\otimes}\Delta_\hbar\hat{\mathbf{e}}_{u,k}^{[\iota]}, \quad \forall k \in \mathbf{Z}_0.
\end{aligned} \tag{25}$$

Considering Equation (20), we have

$$\begin{aligned}
\varrho_k &:= \frac{1}{\hbar}sym\left\{\mathbf{e}_{u,k}^{[\ell]T}\left[C_\varepsilon\mathcal{D}Q\mathcal{D}M_\varepsilon\right]_{\otimes}\rho_k\right\} \\
&\leq -\frac{1}{\hbar}\sum_{\iota=1}^{\ell-1}sym\left\{\mathbf{e}_{u,k}^{[\ell]T}\left[C_\varepsilon\mathcal{D}Q\mathcal{D}M_\varepsilon\Theta\right]_{\otimes}\mathbf{e}_{u,k}^{[\iota]}\right\} \\
&= -\frac{1}{\hbar}\sum_{\iota=1}^{\ell-1}sym\left\{\hat{\mathbf{e}}_{u,k}^{[\iota]T}\left[C_\varepsilon\mathcal{D}Q\mathcal{D}M_\varepsilon\Theta\right]_{\otimes}\mathbf{e}_{u,k}^{[\iota]}\right\} \\
&\quad -\frac{1}{\hbar}\sum_{\iota=1}^{\ell-1}sym\left\{\mathbf{e}_{u,k}^{[\iota]T}\left[C_\varepsilon\mathcal{D}Q\mathcal{D}M_\varepsilon\Theta\right]_{\otimes}\mathbf{e}_{u,k}^{[\iota]}\right\},
\end{aligned} \tag{26}$$

for all $k \in \mathbf{Z}_0$.

Taking into account Equations (16)–(26), we obtain

$$\mathbb{E}[\Delta V_k] = \mathbb{E}[\Delta V_{1,k}] + \mathbb{E}[\Delta V_{2,k}] \leq \mathbb{E}\sum_{\iota=1}^{\ell-1}\xi_k^{[\iota]T}\mathbb{O}\xi_k^{[\iota]}, \quad \forall k \in \mathbf{Z}_0, \tag{27}$$

where $\xi_k^{[\iota]} := \left(\mathbf{e}_{u,k}^{[\iota]}, \mathbf{e}_{v,k}^{[\iota]}, \hat{\mathbf{e}}_{u,k}^{[\iota]}, \Delta_\hbar\mathbf{e}_{u,k}^{[\iota]}, \mathbf{F}(\mathbf{e}_{u,k}^{[\iota]}), \mathbf{G}(\mathbf{e}_{u,k}^{[\iota]})\right)^T$ for $k \in \mathbf{Z}_0$, $\iota = 1, 2, \ldots, \ell$.

Based on Equation (27), we get

$$\mathbb{E}[\Delta V_k] \leq \lambda_{\max}(\mathbb{O})\sum_{\iota=1}^{\ell-1}\left[\mathbb{E}\left\|\mathbf{e}_{u,k}^{[\iota]}\right\|^2 + \mathbb{E}\left\|\mathbf{e}_{v,k}^{[\iota]}\right\|^2\right], \quad \forall k \in \mathbf{Z}_0. \tag{28}$$

With the help of Equation (13), we get

$$\mathbb{E}V_0 \leq \max\left\{\lambda_{\max}(P_{\otimes}), \lambda_{\max}(Q_{\otimes})\right\}\mathbb{E}\sum_{\iota=1}^{\ell-1}\left[\left\|\mathbf{e}_{u,0}^{\langle\iota\rangle}\right\|^2 + \left\|\mathbf{e}_{v,0}^{\langle\iota\rangle}\right\|^2\right] < \infty. \tag{29}$$

Noting that $\lambda_{\max}(\mathbb{O}) < 0$ owing to the assumption $\mathbb{O} < 0$ in Theorem 1, we can use Equations (28) and (29) to arrive at

$$\lambda_{\max}(\mathbb{O})\sum_{k=1}^{k'-1}\sum_{\iota=1}^{\ell-1}\left[\mathbb{E}\left\|\mathbf{e}_{u,k}^{[\iota]}\right\|^2 + \mathbb{E}\left\|\mathbf{e}_{v,k}^{[\iota]}\right\|^2\right] \geq \mathbb{E}V_{k'} - \mathbb{E}V_0 \geq -\mathbb{E}V_0,$$

which is equal to

$$\sum_{k=1}^{k'-1}\sum_{\iota=1}^{\ell-1}\left[\mathbb{E}\left\|\mathbf{e}_{u,k}^{[\iota]}\right\|^2+\mathbb{E}\left\|\mathbf{e}_{v,k}^{[\iota]}\right\|^2\right] \leq -\frac{\mathbb{E}V_0}{\lambda_{\max}(\mathbb{O})}<\infty$$
$$\xRightarrow{k'\to\infty} \sum_{k=1}^{\infty}\sum_{\iota=1}^{\ell-1}\left[\mathbb{E}\left\|\mathbf{e}_{u,k}^{[\iota]}\right\|^2+\mathbb{E}\left\|\mathbf{e}_{v,k}^{[\iota]}\right\|^2\right]<\infty. \quad (30)$$

Then,

$$\lim_{k\to\infty}\sum_{\iota=1}^{\ell-1}\mathbb{E}\left\|\mathbf{e}_{u,k}^{[\iota]}\right\|^2=0=\lim_{k\to\infty}\sum_{\iota=1}^{\ell-1}\mathbb{E}\left\|\mathbf{e}_{v,k}^{[\iota]}\right\|^2,$$

which implies that model Equation (11) achieves global mean-squared asymptotic stability. This completes the proof. □

From Lemma 4, the following inequality is valid:

$$\frac{\mu_{\ell-1}}{\hbar^2}\mathbb{E}\sum_{\iota=1}^{\ell-1}\Delta_\hbar\mathbf{e}_{u,k}^{[\iota]T}\left[M_\varepsilon^T\mathcal{D}Q\mathcal{D}M_\varepsilon\right]_\otimes\Delta_\hbar\mathbf{e}_{u,k}^{[\iota]}\leq\frac{4-\kappa_\ell}{\hbar^2}\frac{\mu_{\ell-1}}{\hbar^2}\mathbb{E}\sum_{\iota=1}^{\ell-1}\hat{\mathbf{e}}_{u,k}^{[\iota]T}\left[M_\varepsilon^T\mathcal{D}Q\mathcal{D}M_\varepsilon\right]_\otimes\hat{\mathbf{e}}_{u,k}^{[\iota]},$$

where $k\in\mathbf{Z}_0$. Further,

$$\mathbb{E}[\Delta V_k]\leq\mathbb{E}\sum_{\iota=1}^{\ell-1}\xi_k^{[\iota]T}\tilde{\mathbb{O}}\xi_k^{[\iota]},\quad\forall k\in\mathbf{Z}_0, \quad (31)$$

here $\tilde{\mathbb{O}}=(\tilde{\mathbb{O}}_{ij})_{1\leq i,j\leq 6}$ is defined as $\mathbb{O}$ defined in Theorem 1, except that

$$\tilde{\mathbb{O}}_{33}=-H_\otimes+\frac{4(1-\beta)(4-\kappa_\ell)\mu_{\ell-1}}{\hbar^4}\left[M_\varepsilon^T\mathcal{D}Q\mathcal{D}M_\varepsilon\right]_\otimes,$$

$$\tilde{\mathbb{O}}_{44}=-sym\left[C_\varepsilon\mathcal{D}Q\mathcal{D}M_\varepsilon\right]_\otimes+\frac{4\mu_{\ell-1}\beta}{\hbar^2}\left[M_\varepsilon^T\mathcal{D}Q\mathcal{D}M_\varepsilon\right]_\otimes+\frac{\hbar^2\ell}{\kappa_\ell}H_\otimes.$$

So, we have the following:

Corollary 1. *Assuming that* **(F)** *is valid, we pre-give values of $\varepsilon>0$ and $\beta\in[0,1]$. Additionally, we assume that $\mathcal{D}$ and M_ε are nonsingular, and we define Θ as indicated in Theorem 1. Under these conditions, the slave INNs Equation (1) stochastically synchronize with the master INNs Equation (5), meaning that the model Equation (11) achieves global mean-squared asymptotic stability. This holds true if the model has positive constants λ_f,λ_g, and positive definite n-order matrices P, Q, H, and K such that the $\tilde{\mathbb{O}}$ matrix defined in Equation (31) is negative definite.*

Remark 1. *Reports [22,24] addressed the issues of synchronization for inertial neural networks with reaction-diffusion terms. However, the networks in reports [22,24] were involved in the Dirichlet boundary condition and the controller is embedded in the model of the networks. In this article, the controller does not exist in the model of the networks, but it is designed in the boundary.*

3.2. Passivity-Based Control

The error vector networks described by Equation (11) with respect to a supply rate can be represented as

$$\varpi(\mathcal{Y},\gamma):=\sum_{\iota=1}^{\ell-1}\mathcal{Y}_{\cdot}^{[\iota]T}\gamma_{\cdot}^{[\iota]}\text{ for some }\mathcal{Y}\in\mathbb{R}^{Nn}. \quad (32)$$

This system is stochastically passive if there exists a nonnegative mapping θ that satisfies

$$\mathbb{E}\sum_{k=s_1}^{s_2-1}\sum_{\iota=1}^{\ell-1}\mathcal{Y}_k^{[\iota]T}\gamma_k^{[\iota]} \geq \theta(s_2)-\theta(s_1), \quad \forall s_1 < s_2, s_1, s_2 \in \mathbf{Z}_0.$$

Theorem 2. *Let Hypothesis* **(F)** *be satisfied, $\varepsilon > 0$ be given, and $\mathcal{D}$, M_ε be nonsingular. Additionally, let the controller gain Θ be as provided in Theorem 1. The error networks Equation (11) are stochastically passive if there exist positive constants λ_f, λ_g and n-order positive definite matrices P, Q, H, K, $\Re_1$, $\Re_2$, $\Re_3$ such that*

$$\mathcal{O} := \begin{bmatrix} \mathcal{O}_{11} & \mathcal{O}_{12} & \mathcal{O}_{13} & \mathcal{O}_{14} & \mathcal{O}_{15} & \mathcal{O}_{16} & \mathcal{O}_{17} \\ * & \mathcal{O}_{22} & \mathcal{O}_{23} & \mathcal{O}_{24} & \mathcal{O}_{25} & \mathcal{O}_{26} & \mathcal{O}_{27} \\ * & * & \mathcal{O}_{33} & \mathcal{O}_{34} & \mathcal{O}_{35} & \mathcal{O}_{36} & \mathcal{O}_{37} \\ * & * & * & \mathcal{O}_{44} & \mathcal{O}_{45} & \mathcal{O}_{46} & \mathcal{O}_{47} \\ * & * & * & * & \mathcal{O}_{55} & \mathcal{O}_{56} & \mathcal{O}_{57} \\ * & * & * & * & * & \mathcal{O}_{66} & \mathcal{O}_{67} \\ * & * & * & * & * & * & \mathcal{O}_{77} \end{bmatrix} < 0,$$

where

$$\mathcal{O}_{44} = \mathbb{O}_{44} + \frac{\mu_{\ell-1}}{\hbar^2}\left[M_\varepsilon^T\mathcal{D}Q\mathcal{D}M_\varepsilon\right]_\otimes, \quad \mathcal{O}_{17} = -(\Re_1)_\otimes + \left[C_\varepsilon\mathcal{D}Q\mathcal{D}\Lambda_\varepsilon\right]_\otimes,$$

$$\mathcal{O}_{27} = -(\Re_2)_\otimes + \left[e^{-D_\circ h}Q\mathcal{D}\Lambda_\varepsilon\right]_\otimes + \alpha\left[\Gamma^T\mathcal{D}Q\mathcal{D}\Lambda_\varepsilon\right]_{\otimes B^T}, \quad \mathcal{O}_{57} = \left[A_\varepsilon^T\mathcal{D}Q\mathcal{D}\Lambda_\varepsilon\right]_\otimes,$$

$$\mathcal{O}_{77} = -2(\Re_3)_\otimes + 2\left[\Lambda_\varepsilon^T\mathcal{D}Q\mathcal{D}\Lambda_\varepsilon\right]_\otimes, \quad \mathcal{O}_{37} = \mathcal{O}_{47} = \mathcal{O}_{67} = 0,$$

and the other unmentioned block matrices $\mathcal{O}_{ij}$ in $\mathcal{O}$ are equal to $\mathbb{O}_{ij}$ in $\mathbb{O}$ for $i, j = 1, 2, \ldots, 6$.

Proof. Define the Lyapunov-Krasovskii function V for the error vector networks Equation (11), following the approach described in Section 3.1. Additionally, introduce an output vector $\mathcal{Y} \in \mathbb{R}^{Nn}$ to the error vector networks Equation (11) using the expression

$$\mathcal{Y} = (I_N \otimes \Re_1)\mathbf{e}_u + (I_N \otimes \Re_2)\mathbf{e}_v + (I_N \otimes \Re_3)\gamma.$$

Similar to the argument in Equation (17), we get

$$\begin{aligned}\mathbb{E}[V_{2,k+1}] = & \sum_{i=1}^{16}\mathcal{U}_{i,k} + \underbrace{\mathbb{E}\sum_{\iota=1}^{\ell-1} sym\left\{\mathbf{e}_{v,k}^{[\iota]T}\left[e^{-D_\circ h}Q\mathcal{D}\Lambda_\varepsilon\right]_\otimes\gamma_k^{[\iota]}\right\}}_{\mathcal{U}_{17,k}} \\ & + \underbrace{\mathbb{E}\sum_{\iota=1}^{\ell-1} sym\left\{\Delta_\hbar^2\mathbf{e}_{u,k}^{[\iota-1]T}\left[M_\varepsilon^T\mathcal{D}Q\mathcal{D}\Lambda_\varepsilon\right]_\otimes\gamma_k^{[\iota]}\right\}}_{\mathcal{U}_{18,k}} \\ & + \underbrace{\mathbb{E}\sum_{\iota=1}^{\ell-1} sym\left\{\mathbf{e}_{u,k}^{[\iota]T}\left[C_\varepsilon\mathcal{D}Q\mathcal{D}\Lambda_\varepsilon\right]_\otimes\gamma_k^{[\iota]}\right\}}_{\mathcal{U}_{19,k}}\end{aligned}$$

$$+\underbrace{\mathbb{E}\sum_{\iota=1}^{\ell-1} sym\left\{\mathbf{F}^T(\mathbf{e}_{u,k}^{[\iota]})\left[A_\varepsilon^T\mathcal{D}Q\mathcal{D}\Lambda_\varepsilon\right]_\otimes \gamma_k^{[\iota]}\right\}}_{\mathcal{U}_{20,k}}$$

$$+\underbrace{\alpha\mathbb{E}\sum_{\iota=1}^{\ell-1} sym\left\{\mathbf{e}_{v,k}^{[\iota]T}\left[\Gamma^T\mathcal{D}Q\mathcal{D}\Lambda_\varepsilon\right]_{\otimes B^T} \gamma_k^{[\iota]}\right\}}_{\mathcal{U}_{21,k}}$$

$$+\underbrace{\mathbb{E}\sum_{\iota=1}^{\ell-1} \gamma_k^{[\iota]T}\left[\Lambda_\varepsilon^T\mathcal{D}Q\mathcal{D}\Lambda_\varepsilon\right]_\otimes \gamma_k^{[\iota]}}_{\mathcal{U}_{22,k}}, \quad \forall k \in \mathbf{Z}_0. \tag{33}$$

Meanwhile, similar to the estimates in inequalities Equations (18)–(23), we obtain from Equation (33) the following:

$$\begin{aligned}
\mathcal{U}_{18,k} &\leq \mathbb{E}\sum_{\iota=1}^{\ell-1} \Delta_\hbar^2\mathbf{e}_{u,k}^{[\iota-1]T}\left[M_\varepsilon^T\mathcal{D}Q\mathcal{D}M_\varepsilon\right]_\otimes \Delta_\hbar^2\mathbf{e}_{u,k}^{[\iota-1]} + \mathbb{E}\sum_{\iota=1}^{\ell-1} \gamma_k^{[\iota]T}\left[\Lambda_\varepsilon^T\mathcal{D}Q\mathcal{D}\Lambda_\varepsilon\right]_\otimes \gamma_k^{[\iota]} \\
&\leq \frac{\mu_{\ell-1}}{\hbar^2}\mathbb{E}\sum_{\iota=1}^{\ell-1} \Delta_\hbar\mathbf{e}_{u,k}^{[\iota]T}\left[M_\varepsilon^T\mathcal{D}Q\mathcal{D}M_\varepsilon\right]_\otimes \Delta_\hbar\mathbf{e}_{u,k}^{[\iota]} + \mathbb{E}\sum_{\iota=1}^{\ell-1} \gamma_k^{[\iota]T}\left[\Lambda_\varepsilon^T\mathcal{D}Q\mathcal{D}\Lambda_\varepsilon\right]_\otimes \gamma_k^{[\iota]}, \quad (34)
\end{aligned}$$

$\forall k \in \mathbf{Z}_0$.

By employing Equations (16)–(26) and (33) and (34), we can compute

$$\mathbb{E}[\Delta V_k] - 2\mathbb{E}\sum_{\iota=1}^{\ell-1} \mathcal{Y}_k^{[\iota]T}\gamma_k^{[\iota]} \leq \mathbb{E}\sum_{\iota=1}^{\ell-1} \eta_k^{[\iota]T}\mathcal{O}\eta_k^{[\iota]}, \quad \forall k \in \mathbf{Z}_0, \tag{35}$$

where $\eta_k^{[\iota]} := \left[\mathbf{e}_{u,k}^{[\iota]}, \mathbf{e}_{v,k}^{[\iota]}, \hat{\mathbf{e}}_{u,k}^{[\iota]}, \Delta_\hbar\mathbf{e}_{u,k}^{[\iota]}, \mathbf{F}(\mathbf{e}_{u,k}^{[\iota]}), \mathbf{G}(\mathbf{e}_{u,k}^{[\iota]}), \gamma_k^{[\iota]}\right]^T$ for $k \in \mathbf{Z}_0$, $\iota = 1, 2, \ldots, \ell$.

In accordance with Equation (35), we get

$$2\mathbb{E}\sum_{\iota=1}^{\ell-1} \mathcal{Y}_k^{[\iota]T}\gamma_k^{[\iota]} \geq \mathbb{E}[\Delta V_k],$$

which is equal to

$$2\mathbb{E}\sum_{k=s_1}^{s_2-1}\sum_{\iota=1}^{\ell-1} \mathcal{Y}_k^{[\iota]T}\gamma_k^{[\iota]} \geq \mathbb{E}V_{s_2} - \mathbb{E}V_{s_1}, \quad \forall s_1 < s_2, s_1, s_2 \in \mathbf{Z}_0.$$

Accordingly, INNs Equation (11) is stochastic passive. This completes the proof. □

So, we have the following:

Corollary 2. *Assuming that* **(F)** *is satisfied,* $\varepsilon > 0$ *and* $\beta \in [0,1]$ *are pre-given,* $\mathcal{D}$ *and* M_ε *are nonsingular, and the controller gain* Θ *is provided in Theorem 1, the error network Equation (11) is stochastically passive if there exist positive constants* λ_f, λ_g, *and n-order positive definite matrices* P, Q, H, K, $\Re_1$, $\Re_2$, *and* $\Re_3$ *such that* $\tilde{\mathcal{O}} < 0$. *Here,* $\tilde{\mathcal{O}} = (\tilde{\mathcal{O}}ij)1 \leq i,j \leq 7$ *is defined as* $\mathcal{O}$ *in Theorem 2 except for the following modifications:*

$$\tilde{\mathcal{O}}_{33} = -H_\otimes + \frac{5(1-\beta)(4-\kappa_\ell)\mu_{\ell-1}}{\hbar^4}\left[M_\varepsilon^T\mathcal{D}Q\mathcal{D}M_\varepsilon\right]_\otimes,$$

$$\tilde{\mathcal{O}}_{44} = -sym\left[C_\varepsilon\mathcal{D}Q\mathcal{D}M_\varepsilon\right]_\otimes + \frac{5\mu_{\ell-1}\beta}{\hbar^2}\left[M_\varepsilon^T\mathcal{D}Q\mathcal{D}M_\varepsilon\right]_\otimes + \frac{\hbar^2\ell}{\kappa_\ell}H_\otimes.$$

According to Theorems 1 and 2, a realizable algorithm for stochastic synchronization or passivity of INNs Equations (1) and (5) is designed as Algorithm 1, and its O-chart is described in Figure 1.

Algorithm 1 Stochastic synchronization or passivity of INNs Equations (1) and (5)

(1) Initialize the values of the coefficient matrices in INNs Equations (1) and (5)
(2) Compute LMIs in Theorems 1 or 2. When they are unviable, modify the values of coefficient matrices in INNs Equation (1); otherwise, switch to next step.
(3) Receive the values of matrices P, Q, K, etc. Calculate the controller gain $\Theta = \left[\mathcal{D}Q\mathcal{D}M_{\varepsilon}\right]^{-1} K$.
(4) Write iterative program based on INNs Equations (1) and (5) and plot the response trajectories.

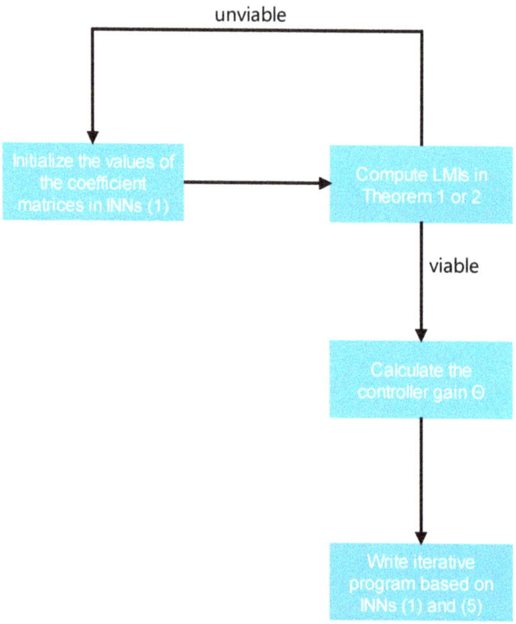

Figure 1. O-chart of Algorithm 1.

Remark 2. *Papers [44,45] investigated the passivity of inertial neural networks without reaction-diffusion terms. This paper considers the effects of the reaction diffusions, which complements the works in the literature [44,45].*

4. Numerical Example

In view of INNs Equation (1), we take $\alpha = 0.1$, $J = (10, 12)^T$,

$$D = 50\begin{bmatrix} 2 & 0 \\ 0 & 1 \end{bmatrix}, \quad C = 45\begin{bmatrix} 2 & 0 \\ 0 & 1 \end{bmatrix}, \quad M = 0.1\begin{bmatrix} 1 & 1 \\ 0 & 2 \end{bmatrix}, \quad A = 0.1\begin{bmatrix} 2 & -1 \\ 0 & 2 \end{bmatrix},$$

$$B = 0.1\begin{bmatrix} -2 & 2 \\ 1 & -1 \end{bmatrix}, \quad \Gamma = 0.01\begin{bmatrix} 2 & 0 \\ 0 & 3 \end{bmatrix}, \quad \Xi = 0.01\begin{bmatrix} 2 & 0 \\ 0 & 1 \end{bmatrix}.$$

Taking $\varepsilon = 0.1$, $h = 0.01$, $\hbar = 0.2$, $\ell = 25$, $f(x) = (f_1(x), f_2(x))^T = 0.1(\sin x_1, |x_2|)^T = (g_1(x), g_2(x))^T = g(x)$ for any $x = (x_1, x_2)^T \in \mathbb{R}^2$. From Theorem 1, we can determine that $\lambda_f = 32693$, $\lambda_g = 32686$,

$$P = \begin{bmatrix} 1.2059 & -0.0142 \\ -0.0142 & 1.6238 \end{bmatrix} \times 10^5, \quad Q = \begin{bmatrix} 2.5836 & -0.0082 \\ -0.0082 & 1.5422 \end{bmatrix} \times 10^4,$$

$$H = \begin{bmatrix} 6.9393 & 3.4242 \\ 3.4242 & 5.5926 \end{bmatrix}, \quad K = \begin{bmatrix} 0.0197 & 0.0049 \\ 0.0049 & 0.0042 \end{bmatrix}.$$

In addition,

$$\Theta = \begin{bmatrix} 0.0164 & 0.0026 \\ 0.0026 & 0.0022 \end{bmatrix}.$$

By Theorem 1, INNs Equations (1) and (5) realize stochastic synchronization, see Figures 2–5.

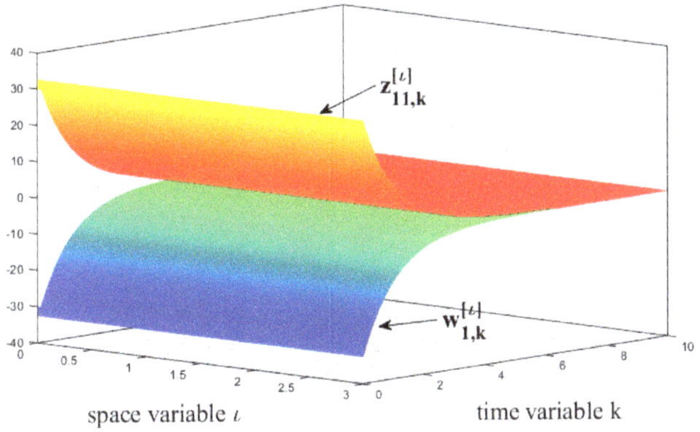

Figure 2. Stochastic synchronization to INNs Equations (1) and (5).

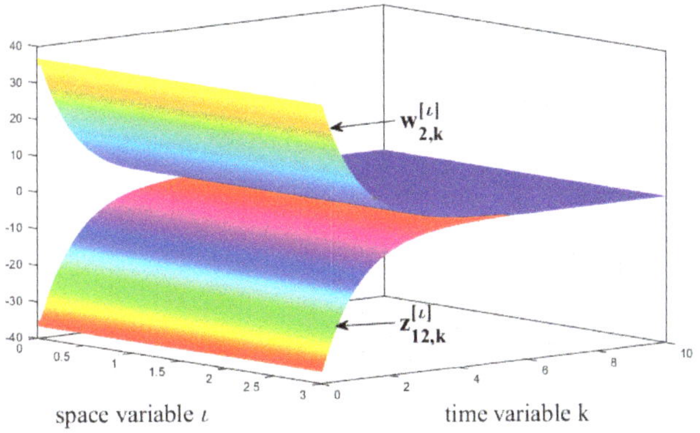

Figure 3. Stochastic synchronization to INNs Equations (1) and (5).

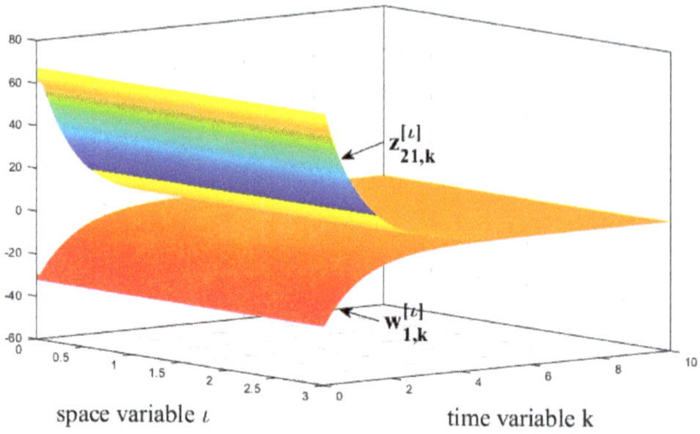

Figure 4. Stochastic synchronization to INNs Equations (1) and (5).

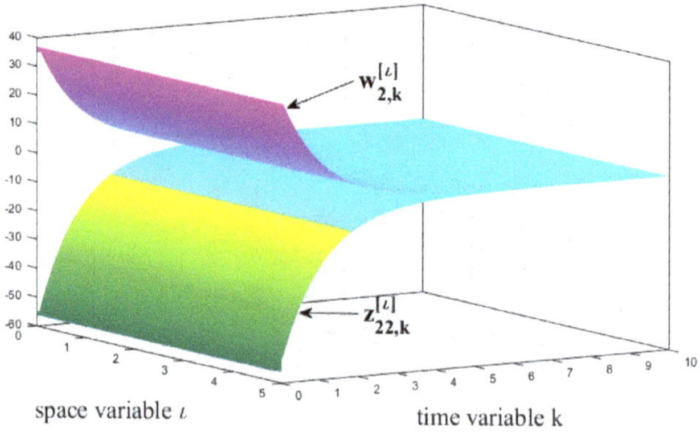

Figure 5. Stochastic synchronization to INNs Equations (1) and (5).

Furthermore, taking $\Lambda = 0.1\begin{bmatrix} 1 & 0 \\ 0 & 3 \end{bmatrix}$, $\gamma^{[\iota]}_{1,k} = (10+\sin(\iota+k), 8+\cos(\iota+k))^T$, $\gamma^{[\iota]}_{2,k} = (10+\sin(2\iota+k), 8+\cos(2\iota+k))^T$, $\forall k \in \mathbf{Z}_0$, $\iota = 1,2,\ldots,\ell$. The output vector $\mathcal{Y} \in \mathbb{R}^4$ for the network is defined as in Equation (32) with the following matrices:

$$\Re_1 = \begin{bmatrix} 183.9618 & -0.2256 \\ -0.2256 & 173.1908 \end{bmatrix}, \Re_2 = \begin{bmatrix} 376.9862 & 0.1127 \\ 0.1127 & 167.3857 \end{bmatrix}, \Re_3 = \begin{bmatrix} 1617.7 & -0.1 \\ -0.1 & 1721 \end{bmatrix}.$$

By Theorem 2, we have $\lambda_f = 1825.8$, $\lambda_g = 1825.7$,

$$P = \begin{bmatrix} 8041.2 & 71.1 \\ 71.1 & 8871.3 \end{bmatrix}, \quad Q = \begin{bmatrix} 1374.2 & 8.6 \\ 8.6 & 635.3 \end{bmatrix},$$

$$H = \begin{bmatrix} 0.4183 & 0.1974 \\ 0.1974 & 0.2709 \end{bmatrix}, \quad K = \begin{bmatrix} 0.0011 & 0.0005 \\ 0.0005 & 0.0011 \end{bmatrix}.$$

Now, the controller gain of the boundary controller is given by

$$\Theta = \begin{bmatrix} 0.0147 & -0.0058 \\ 0.0059 & 0.0142 \end{bmatrix}.$$

According to Theorem 2, INNs Equations (1) and (5) achieve stochastic passivity, as in Figures 6–11.

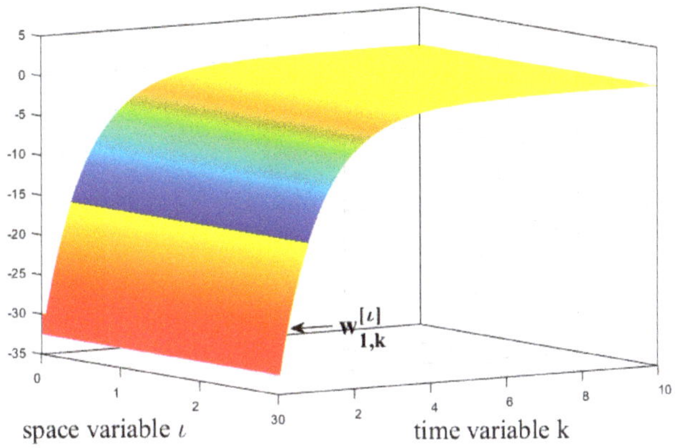

Figure 6. Trajectory of state variable $\mathbf{w}_1$ to INNs Equation (5).

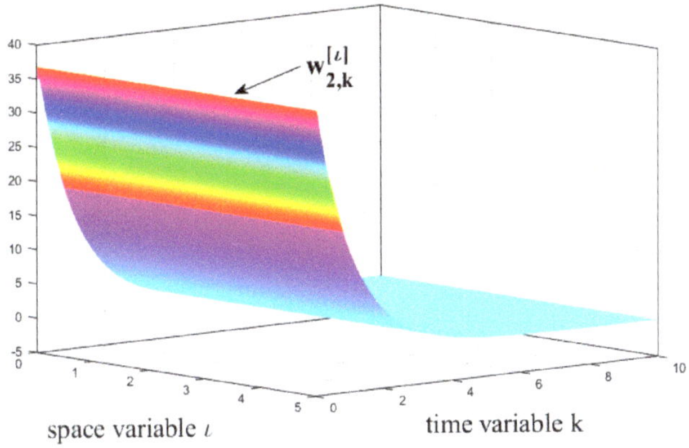

Figure 7. Trajectory of state variable $\mathbf{w}_2$ to INNs Equation (5).

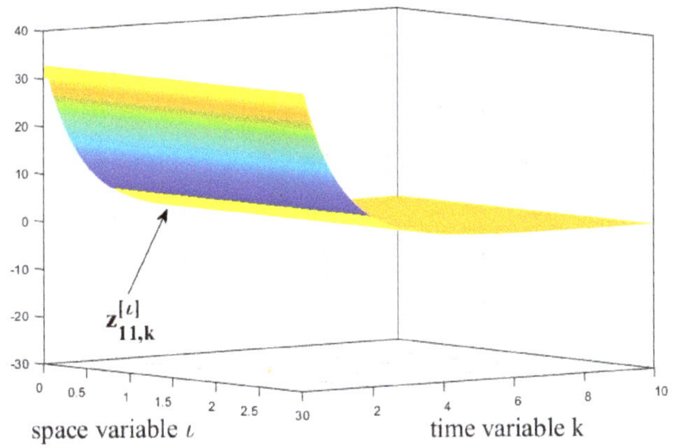

Figure 8. Trajectory of state variable $\mathbf{z}_{11}$ to INNs Equation (1).

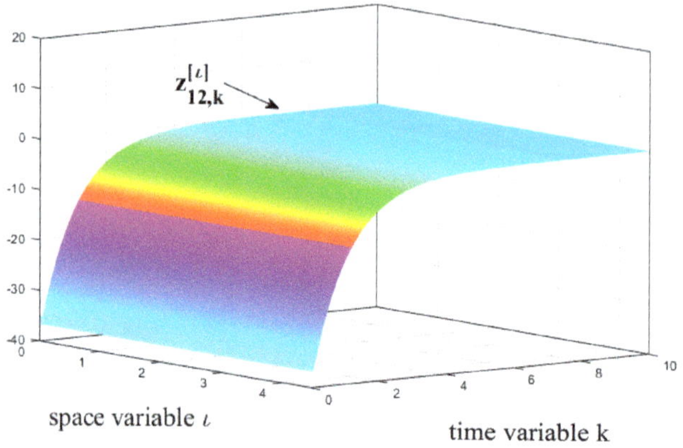

Figure 9. Trajectory of state variable $\mathbf{z}_{12}$ to INNs Equation (1).

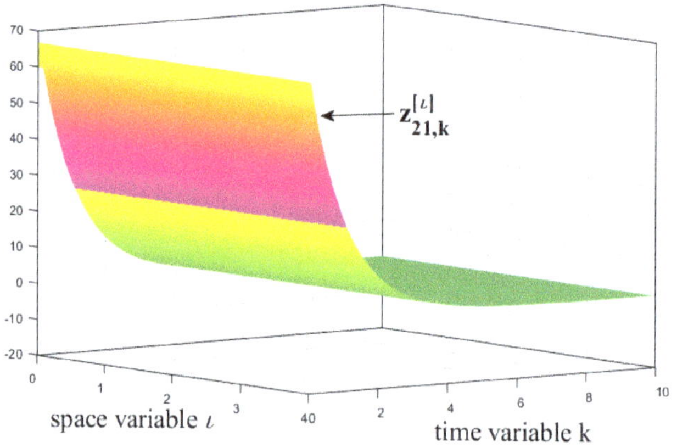

Figure 10. Trajectory of state variable $\mathbf{z}_{21}$ to INNs Equation (1).

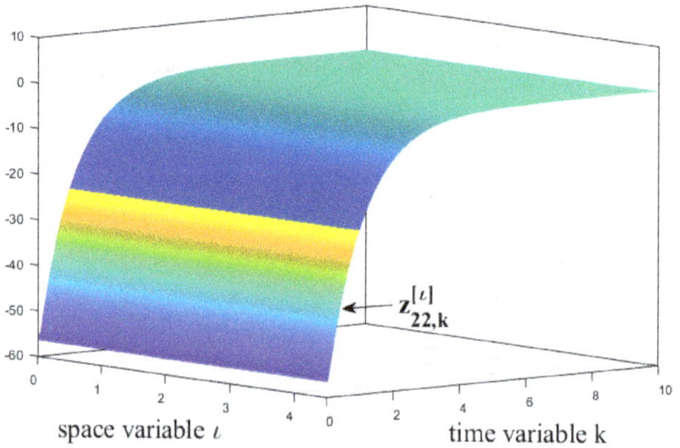

Figure 11. Trajectory of state variable $\mathbf{z}_{22}$ to INNs Equation (1).

Remark 3. *In the previous work in article [38], the authors discussed passivity of non-autonomous discrete-time inertial neural networks, overlooking discrete spatial diffusions. By contrast, the present literature addresses it, as can be seen in Figures 6–11.*

5. Conclusions and Future Works

For the first time, this discussion focuses on investigating discrete SINNs with the influence of spatial diffusions.

Firstly, we present the time and space difference model of SINNs with reaction diffusions using the time and space difference approaches, respectively.

Secondly, with the aid of a controller designed at the boundary, we address the issues of both stochastic synchronization and passivity-based control, employing the Lyapunov-Krasovskii function method.

As anticipated, we provide decision theorems for the aforementioned research topics concerning discrete SINNs. It is important to note that the method employed in this article predominantly considers homogeneous networks described by INNs Equations (1) and (5), making the study of heterogeneous networks challenging (see ref. [46]).

Moving forward, several aspects merit consideration in future work:

- Fractional dynamics has become a research hotspot in recent years, which could be discussed in the SINNs of this article.
- This paper only considers 1-dimensional space variables, which could be extended to higher dimensions.
- Exploration of alternative control techniques, such as impulsive controls and adaptive controls, holds promise for further investigation.

Author Contributions: Conceptualization, Y.Y. and T.Z.; Methodology, Y.Y. and T.Z.; Investigation, Y.Y., T.Z. and Z.L.; Writing-original draft, Y.Y., T.Z. and Z.L.; Writing-review and editing, Y.Y., T.Z. and Z.L. All authors have read and agreed to the published version of the manuscript.

Funding: This work was supported by the Key Scientific Research Projects of Colleges and Universities of Henan Province under Grant No. 21A110002.

Data Availability Statement: Not applicable.

Conflicts of Interest: The authors declare no conflict of interest.

References

1. Ganesan, B.; Mani, P.; Shanmugam, L.; Annamalai, M. Synchronization of stochastic neural networks using looped-Lyapunov functional and its application to secure communication. *IEEE Trans. Neural Netw. Learn. Syst.* 2022, *in press*. [CrossRef]
2. Alsaedi, A.; Cao, J.D.; Ahmad, B.; Alshehri, A.; Tan, X. Synchronization of master-slave memristive neural networks via fuzzy output-based adaptive strategy. *Chaos Soliton Fractal* **2022**, *158*, 112095. [CrossRef]
3. Liu, F.; Meng, W.; Lu, R.Q. Anti-synchronization of discrete-time fuzzy memristive neural networks via impulse sampled-data communication. *IEEE Trans. Cybern.* 2022, *in press*. [CrossRef]
4. Zhou, C.; Wang, C.; Sun, Y.; Yao, W.; Lin, H. Cluster output synchronization for memristive neural networks. *Inf. Sci.* **2022**, *589*, 459–477. [CrossRef]
5. Li, H.Y.; Fang, J.A.; Li, X.F.; Rutkowski, L.; Huang, T.W. Event-triggered synchronization of multiple discrete-time Markovian jump memristor-based neural networks with mixed mode-dependent delays. *IEEE Trans. Circuits Syst. I-Regul. Pap.* **2022**, *69*, 2095–2107. [CrossRef]
6. Boonsatit, N.; Rajendran, S.; Lim, C.P.; Jirawattanapanit, A.; Mohandas, P. New adaptive finite-time cluster synchronization of neutral-type complex-valued coupled neural networks with mixed time delays. *Fractal Fract.* **2022**, *6*, 6090515. [CrossRef]
7. Zaferani, E.J.; Teshnehlab, M.; Khodadadian, A.; Heitzinger, C.; Vali, M.; Noii, N.; Wick, T. Hyper-parameter optimization of stacked asymmetric auto-encoders for automatic personality traits perception. *Sensors* **2022**, *22*, 6206. [CrossRef]
8. Alimi, A.M.; Aouiti, C.; Assali, E.A. Finite-time and fixed-time synchronization of a class of inertial neural networks with multiproportional delays and its application to secure communication. *Neurocomputing* **2019**, *332*, 29–43. [CrossRef]
9. Song, X.N.; Man, J.; Park, J.H.; Song, S. Finite-time synchronization of reaction-diffusion inertial memristive neural networks via gain-scheduled pinning control. *IEEE Trans. Neural Netw. Learn. Syst.* **2022**, *33*, 5045–5056. [PubMed] [CrossRef]

10. Shen, H.; Huang, Z.; Wu, Z.; Cao, J.D.; Park, J.H. Nonfragile H_∞ synchronization of BAM inertial neural networks subject to persistent dwell-time switching regularity. *IEEE Trans. Cybern.* **2022**, *52*, 6591–6602. [CrossRef]
11. Shanmugasundaram, S.; Udhayakumar, K.; Gunasekaran, D.; Rakkiyappan, R. Event-triggered impulsive control design for synchronization of inertial neural networks with time delays. *Neurocomputing* **2022**, *483*, 322–332. [CrossRef]
12. Liu, J.; Shu, L.; Chen, Q.; Zhong, S. Fixed-time synchronization criteria of fuzzy inertial neural networks via Lyapunov functions with indefinite derivatives and its application to image encryption. *Fuzzy Sets Syst.* 2022, *in press*. [CrossRef]
13. Peng, Q.; Jian, J. Synchronization analysis of fractional-order inertial-type neural networks with time delays. *Math. Comput. Simul.* **2023**, *205*, 62–77. [CrossRef]
14. Zhou, W.J.; Long, M.; Liu, X.Z.; Wu, K.N. Passivity-based boundary control for stochastic delay reaction-diffusion systems. *Int. J. Syst. Sci.* 2022, *in press*. [CrossRef]
15. Padmaja, N.; Balasubramaniam, P. Mixed H_∞/passivity based stability analysis of fractional-order gene regulatory networks with variable delays. *Math. And Computers Simul.* **2022**, *192*, 167–181. [CrossRef]
16. Shafiya, M.; Nagamani, G. New finite-time passivity criteria for delayed fractional-order neural networks based on Lyapunov function approach, Chaos. *Solitons Fractals* **2022**, *158*, 112005. [CrossRef]
17. Wang, J.; Jiang, H.; Hu, C.; Ma, T. Exponential passivity of discrete-time switched neural networks with transmission delays via an event-triggered sliding mode control. *Neural Netw.* **2021**, *143*, 271–282. [CrossRef]
18. Huang, Y.; Wu, F. Finite-time passivity and synchronization of coupled complex-valued memristive neural networks. *Inf. Sci.* **2021**, *580*, 775–800. [CrossRef]
19. Han, X.X.; Wu, K.N.; Niu, Y. Asynchronous boundary control of Markov jump neural networks with diffusion terms. *IEEE Trans. Cybern.* 2022, *in press*. [CrossRef]
20. Liu, X.Z.; Wu, K.N.; Ding, X.; Zhang, W. Boundary stabilization of stochastic delayed Cohen-Grossberg neural networks with diffusion terms. *IEEE Trans. Neural Netw. Learn. Syst.* **2022**, *33*, 3227–3237. [CrossRef]
21. Wang, L.M.; He, H.B.; Zeng, Z.G. Intermittent stabilization of fuzzy competitive neural networks with reaction diffusions. *IEEE Trans. Fuzzy Syst.* **2021**, *29*, 2361–2372. [CrossRef]
22. Song, X.N.; Man, J.T.; Ahn, C.K.; Song, S. Finite-time dissipative synchronization for markovian jump generalized inertial neural networks with reaction-diffusion terms. *IEEE Trans. Syst. Man Cybern. Syst.* **2021**, *51*, 3650–3661. [CrossRef]
23. Sun, L.; Su, L.; Wang, J. Non-fragile dissipative state estimation for semi-Markov jump inertial neural networks with reaction-diffusion. *Appl. Math. Comput.* **2021**, *411*, 126404. [CrossRef]
24. Song, X.N.; Man, J.T.; Song, S.; Wang, Z. An improved result on synchronization control for memristive neural networks with inertial terms and reaction-diffusion items. *ISA Trans.* **2020**, *99*, 74–83. [PubMed] [CrossRef]
25. Chandrasekar, A.; Radhika, T.; Zhu, Q.X. Further results on input-to-state stability of stochastic Cohen-Grossberg BAM neural networks with probabilistic time-varying delays. *Neural Process. Lett.* **2022**, *54*, 613–635. [CrossRef]
26. Sriraman, R.; Cao, Y.; Samidurai, R. Global asymptotic stability of stochastic complex-valued neural networks with probabilistic time-varying delays. *Math. Comput. Simul.* **2020**, *171*, 103–118. [CrossRef]
27. Zhang, T.W.; Qu, H.Z.; Liu, Y.T.; Zhou, J.W. Weighted pseudo θ-almost periodic sequence solution and guaranteed cost control for discrete-time and discrete-space stochastic inertial neural networks. *Chaos Solitons Fractals* **2023**, *173*, 113658. [CrossRef]
28. Zhang, T.W.; Li, Z.H. Switching clusters' synchronization for discrete space-time complex dynamical networks via boundary feedback controls. *Pattern Recognit.* **2023**, *143*, 109763. [CrossRef]
29. Zhang, T.W.; Liu, Y.T.; Qu, H.Z. Global mean-square exponential stability and random periodicity of discrete-time stochastic inertial neural networks with discrete spatial diffusions and Dirichlet boundary condition. *Comput. Math. Appl.* **2023**, *141*, 116–128. [CrossRef]
30. Zhang, T.W.; Xiong, L.L. Periodic motion for impulsive fractional functional differential equations with piecewise Caputo derivative. *Appl. Math. Lett.* **2020**, *101*, 106072. [CrossRef]
31. Adhira, B.; Nagamani, G.; Dafik, D. Non-fragile extended dissipative synchronization control of delayed uncertain discrete-time neural networks. *Commun. Nonlinear Sci. Numer. Simul.* **2023**, *116*, 106820. [CrossRef]
32. Zhang, T.W.; Li, Y.K. Global exponential stability of discrete-time almost automorphic Caputo-Fabrizio BAM fuzzy neural networks via exponential Euler technique. *Knowl.-Based Syst.* **2022**, *246*, 108675. [CrossRef]
33. Huang, Z.K.; Mohamad, S.; Gao, F. Multi-almost periodicity in semi-discretizations of a general class of neural networks. *Math. Comput. Simul.* **2014**, *101*, 43–60. [CrossRef]
34. Zhang, T.W.; Han, S.F.; Zhou, J.W. Dynamic behaviours for semi-discrete stochastic Cohen-Grossberg neural networks with time delays. *J. Frankl. Inst.* **2020**, *357*, 13006–13040. [CrossRef]
35. Xiao, Q.; Huang, T.W.; Zeng, Z.G. On exponential stability of delayed discrete-time complex-valued inertial neural networks. *IEEE Trans. Cybern.* **2022**, *52*, 3483–3494. [PubMed] [CrossRef]
36. Xiao, Q.; Huang, T.W. Quasisynchronization of discrete-time inertial neural networks with parameter mismatches and delays. *IEEE Trans. Cybern.* **2021**, *51*, 2290–2295. [CrossRef] [PubMed]
37. Chen, X.; Lin, D.; Lan, W. Global dissipativity of delayed discrete-time inertial neural networks. *Neurocomputing* **2020**, *390*, 131–138. [CrossRef]

38. Chen, X.; Lin, D. Passivity analysis of non-autonomous discrete-time inertial neural networks with time-varying delays. *Neural Process. Lett.* **2020**, *51*, 2929–2944. [CrossRef]
39. Zhou, W.N.; Yang, J.; Zhou, L.W.; Tong, D.B. *Stability and Synchronization Control of Stochastic Neural Networks*; Springer: Berlin/Heidelberg, Germany, 2016.
40. Agarwal, R.P. *Difference Equations and Inequalities*; Marcel Dekker: New York, NY, USA, 2000.
41. Seuret, A.; Fridman, E. Wirtinger-like Lyapunov-Krasovskii functionals for discrete-time delay systems. *IMA J. Math. Control. Inf.* **2018**, *35*, 861–876. [CrossRef]
42. Milovanović, G.V.; Milovanović, I.Ž. On discrete inequalities of Wirtinger's type. *J. Math. Anal. Appl.* **1982**, *88*, 378–387. [CrossRef]
43. Mollaiyan, K. Generalization of Discrete-Time Wirtinger Inequalities and a Preliminary Study of Their Application to SNR Analysis of Sinusoids Buried in Noise. Master's Thesis, Concordia University, Montreal, QC, Canada, 2008.
44. Zhong, X.; Ren, J.; Gao, Y. Passivity-based bipartite synchronization of coupled delayed inertial neural networks via non-reduced order method. *Neural Process. Lett.* **2022**, *54*, 4869–4892. [CrossRef]
45. Fang, T.; Jiao, S.; Fu, D.; Su, L. Passivity-based synchronization for Markov switched neural networks with time delays and the inertial term. *Appl. Math. Comput.* **2021**, *394*, 125786. [CrossRef]
46. Chen, W.; Ren, G.; Yu, Y.; Yuan, X. Quasi-synchronization of heterogeneous stochastic coupled reaction-diffusion neural networks with mixed time-varying delays via boundary control. *J. Frankl. Inst.* **2023**, *360*, 10080–10099. [CrossRef]

axioms

MDPI

Article

Global Dynamics of an Age-Structured Tuberculosis Model with Vaccine Failure and Nonlinear Infection Force

Zhongkai Guo [1,*] and Liang Zhang [2,*]

[1] School of Traffic and Transportation, Lanzhou Jiaotong University, Lanzhou 730070, China
[2] College of Science, Northwest A&F University, Yangling 712100, China
* Correspondence: guozhonkai@lzjtu.edu.cn (Z.G.); zhanglsd@126.com (L.Z.)

Abstract: China bears a heavy burden due to tuberculosis (TB) with hundreds of thousands of people falling ill with the disease every year. Therefore, it is necessary to understand the effectiveness of current control measures in China. In this paper, we first present a TB model that incorporates both vaccination and treatment. Additionally, the model considers TB transmission characteristics such as relapse and variable latency. We then define the basic reproduction number $\mathcal{R}_0$ of the proposed model and indicate that the disease-free equilibrium state is globally asymptotically stable if $\mathcal{R}_0 < 1$, and the endemic equilibrium state is globally asymptotically stable if $\mathcal{R}_0 > 1$. We then apply the Grey Wolf Optimizer algorithm to obtain the parameters and initial values of the model by combining TB data collected in China from 2007 to 2020. Through the partial rank correlation coefficient method, we identify the parameters that are most sensitive to $\mathcal{R}_0$. Based on the analysis results of the model, we propose some suggestions for TB control measures in the conclusion section.

Keywords: tuberculosis; age structure; global stability; sensitivity analysis

MSC: 35B35; 35B40

check for updates

Citation: Guo, Z.; Zhang, L. Global Dynamics of an Age-Structured Tuberculosis Model with Vaccine Failure and Nonlinear Infection Force. *Axioms* **2023**, *12*, 805. https://doi.org/10.3390/axioms12090805

Academic Editor: Tianwei Zhang

Received: 10 July 2023
Revised: 31 July 2023
Accepted: 17 August 2023
Published: 22 August 2023

1. Introduction

Tuberculosis (TB) is a formidable infectious disease that kills millions of people every year. China has the third-highest TB burden worldwide, and in 2021, there were an estimated 780,000 new TB cases and 32,000 TB-related deaths. In 2014 and 2015, all member states of the World Health Organization (WHO) committed to ending the TB epidemic and adopted the WHO End TB Strategy. However, the reduction in the TB incidence rate (new cases per 100,000 population per year) from 2015 to 2021 only reached halfway towards the first milestone of the End TB Strategy, with a decrease of only 10%. The WHO believes that the main reason for this was the COVID-19 pandemic. The WHO's report on TB in 2022 pointed out that the COVID-19 pandemic has had a damaging impact on the prevention and control of TB. The WHO estimates that approximately 10.6 million people worldwide fell ill with TB in 2021, representing an increase of 4.5% from 10.1 million in 2020. Therefore, gaining a more comprehensive understanding of effective ways to control the TB epidemic is crucial for achieving the End TB Strategy [1].

The theoretical analysis and simulation of TB models that are in accordance with the transmission mechanism of TB provide a means to identify how to control the TB epidemic [2–9]. Therefore, we need to understand the transmission mechanism of TB and the main control measures that are currently in place. TB is caused by a bacillus called *Mycobacterium tuberculosis* (MTB). People can transmit the bacillus through the air. It is estimated that approximately one-fourth of the global population is infected with MTB, but only 5–10% of them will develop TB disease and potentially spread MTB to others. As a result, individuals infected with MTB can be categorized into two groups: those with a latent TB infection (who cannot spread MTB to others) and those with TB disease [10]. Some people who have a latent TB infection will clear the infection and recover. Recovered patients may develop TB disease due to endogenous reactivation (or relapse) [11]. Currently, the main ways to reduce the global burden of TB are vaccination against TB and treatment for TB disease [12–14]. The Bacille Calmette–Guérin (BCG) vaccine is the only licensed vaccine for preventing TB disease, and more than 100 million newborn babies receive it annually. Martinez et al. [13] found that BCG vaccination at birth is effective for preventing TB in young children but is ineffective in adolescents and adults, and the effectiveness of BCG vaccination against TB was shown to be 59% among tuberculin-skin-test-negative infants vaccinated at birth. Setiabudiawan et al. [14] suggested that the efficacy of BCG in preventing TB disease decreases over time. These findings suggest that the vaccine is not always effective against TB. Both latent TB infection and TB disease are treatable [15,16]. Kerantzas et al. [15] pointed out that "directly observed treatment, short-course", or DOTS, has been shown in some regions to be able to cure as many as 98% of drug-susceptible cases. Preventive treatment for TB can reduce the risk of latent TB infection progressing to TB disease. The WHO recommends TB preventive treatment for people infected with MTB who have a weak immune system. Without treatment, the death rate from TB disease is about 50%, but with currently recommended treatments, the success rate is at least 85%. Isoniazid and rifampicin are the two most effective first-line drugs. Resistance to both drugs is defined as multidrug-resistant TB (MDR-TB). Both MDR-TB and rifampicin-resistant TB (RR-TB) require treatment with second-line drugs. Treatment success rates for MDR/RR-TB are typically in the range of 50–75% [1]. The reasons why MDR/RR-TB continues to emerge and spread are the mismanagement of TB treatment and person-to-person transmission. It is necessary to test for drug resistance to ensure that the most effective treatment regimen can be selected as early as possible [17]. The factors mentioned above that impact the spread of TB will form the basis of our modeling.

Many TB models have been developed to better understand the control and transmission of TB. Li et al. [18] proposed a TB model that considers vaccination, treatment, relapse, and the variable latent period. Through a theoretical analysis and computer simulations, they suggested that education, treatment, and enhanced efficacy could reduce the TB incidence rate in the United States. Since the latent period of TB ranges from weeks to several years, many authors [19–21] have suggested the use of an age-structured equation to characterize the latent compartment in TB models. This approach can effectively capture the heterogeneity of the latent period. The incidence rate is a crucial indicator of the speed at which an infectious disease spreads. Mathematically, the commonly used incidence rates are bilinear and standard [22–24], but other nonlinear incidence rates have been proposed to describe the transmission of infectious diseases [25–28]. Sigdel et al. [26] proposed the nonlinear incidence rate $f(I)S$, where $f(I)$ represents the positive, increasing, and concave down nonlinear forces of infection. Many studies have demonstrated that models with a nonlinear force of infection exhibit complicated dynamics [25–28].

Through an analysis of the above two paragraphs, in this paper, we investigate the impacts of vaccine failure and treatment on the dynamics of a TB model that includes an age-structured latent period, endogenous relapse, and a nonlinear force of infection. The vaccine failure here includes the fact that it may not provide protection after vaccination, and even if protection is provided, it may not be long-lasting. The treatment here includes TB preventive treatment and TB disease treatment. Our goal is to use a theoretical analysis and numerical simulation to identify measures for controlling the spread of TB and to provide guidance to public health authorities on how to effectively allocate limited resources to mitigate the spread of TB. The rest of the paper is organized in the following manner: In the next section, we propose a TB model and discuss the fundamental properties of its solution. In Sections 3 and 4, we study, respectively, the existence and global stability of steady states. In Section 5, we present numerical simulations and a sensitivity analysis to identify the significant parameters related to the basic reproductive number. A brief conclusion is provided in the last section.

2. The TB Model and Its Fundamental Properties

2.1. The TB Model

At time t, the population is divided into five distinct subclasses: the susceptible subclass ($S(t)$), the vaccinated subclass ($V(t)$), the latent subclass ($e(t,a)$), the infectious subclass ($I(t)$), and the recovered subclass ($R(t)$). In $e(t,a)$, a represents the latent age of the exposed individuals. $e(t,a)$ represents the density of the latent class at time t with latent age a. Then, the total number of latent individuals at time t is $\int_0^{+\infty} e(t,a)da$. Figure 1 below illustrates the inter-relationships among these subclasses.

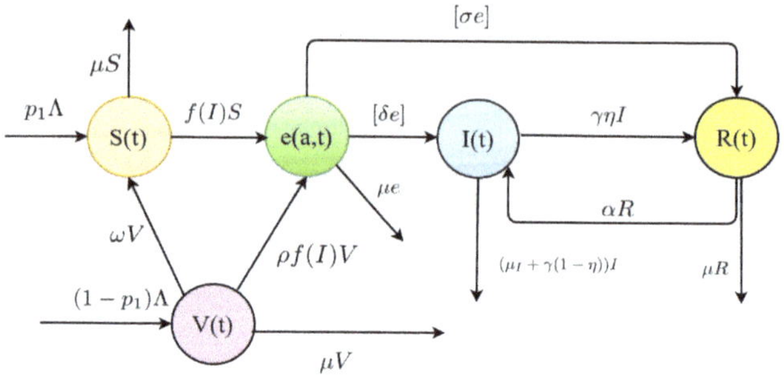

Figure 1. Flowchart of the transmission of TB.

Based on the flowchart shown in Figure 1, we construct the following model for TB transmission:

$$\begin{cases} \dfrac{dS(t)}{dt} = p_1\Lambda - f(I)S - \mu S + \omega V, \\ \dfrac{dV(t)}{dt} = (1-p_1)\Lambda - \rho f(I)V - (\mu+\omega)V, \\ \dfrac{\partial e(t,a)}{\partial t} + \dfrac{\partial e(t,a)}{\partial a} = -(\mu+\delta(a)+\sigma(a))e(t,a), \\ \dfrac{dI(t)}{dt} = \displaystyle\int_0^{+\infty} \delta(a)e(t,a)da + \alpha R - (\mu_I+\gamma)I, \\ \dfrac{dR(t)}{dt} = \gamma\eta I + \displaystyle\int_0^{+\infty} \sigma(a)e(t,a)da - (\mu+\alpha)R, \\ e(t,0) = f(I)(S+\rho V), \\ e(0,a) = e_0(a),\ S(0) = s_0, V(0) = v_0,\ I(0) = i_0,\ R(0) = r_0, \end{cases} \tag{1}$$

where $e_0(a) \in L^1_+(0,+\infty)$ and $s_0, v_0, i_0, r_0 \in \mathbb{R}_+$. We list the parameters used in model (1) in Table 1.

In order to facilitate the theoretical analysis of the model, certain assumptions and notations are presented:

(1) $\mu, \alpha, \eta, \gamma, \rho, \mu_I, \omega, \Lambda > 0$;

(2) $\delta(a), \sigma(a) \in L^\infty_+(0,+\infty)$. Their essential upper bounds are $\bar{\delta} > 0$ and $\bar{\sigma} > 0$, respectively;

(3) $f(I)$ is a twice differentiable function that satisfies (i) $f(0) = 0, f(I) > 0$ for $I > 0$; (ii) $f'(I) > 0, f''(I) \le 0$ for $I \ge 0$.

For $a \ge 0$, we let

$$k(a) = e^{-\int_0^a(\mu+\delta(s)+\sigma(s))ds}, \quad \mathscr{K}_1 = \int_0^{+\infty} \delta(a)k(a)da, \quad \mathscr{K}_2 = \int_0^{+\infty} \sigma(a)k(a)da,$$

$\mathscr{X} = \mathbb{R}_+^2 \times L_+^1(0, +\infty) \times \mathbb{R}_+^2$, and its norm is

$$\| (x_1, x_2, x_3, x_4, x_5) \|_{\mathscr{X}} = \sum_{i=1,2,4,5} | x_i | + \int_0^{+\infty} | x_3(s) | ds.$$

Table 1. The parameters' meanings in the model (1).

Notations	Definitions
Λ	the rate of recruitment of susceptible individuals
μ	the constant natural death rate of individuals in every compartment
$1 - p_1$	the coverage rate of the BCG vaccine
ω	the rate of vaccine-induced protection wanes
ρ	the reduction coefficient of the contagion rate
$\delta(a)$	the rate distribution of latent individuals entering the infectious subclass
$\sigma(a)$	the rate distribution of latent individuals entering the recovered subclass
γ	the rate of treatment
μ_I	the death rate of the infectious individuals
η	the proportion of effective treatment
α	the relapse rate

2.2. Well-Posedness

By applying a similar analysis to that presented in Section 2.2 of [2], we can show that the system (1) has a unique non-negative solution, which leads to the proposition below.

Proposition 1. *For $x_0 \in \mathscr{X}$, the system (1) has a unique continuous semi-flow $\Psi(t, x_0) : \mathbb{R}_+ \times \mathscr{X} \to \mathscr{X}$, and $\Psi(0, x_0) = x_0$. Moreover, the set* Y *that follows is positively invariant under system (1):*

$$\mathrm{Y} = \{x = (S(t), V(t), e(t,a), I(t), R(t)) \in \mathscr{X} : \| x \|_{\mathscr{X}} \leq \frac{\Lambda}{\mu}\},$$

where x_0 is the initial value of the semi-flow $\Psi(t, x_0)$, and Y *represents a set such that if the initial value is $x_0 \in \mathrm{Y}$, then $\Psi(t, x_0) \in \mathrm{Y}$ for $t \geq 0$.*

Proposition 2. *(1) For system (1), the semi-flow $\Psi(t, \cdot)$ is point dissipative, and* Y *can attract all points in the set $\mathscr{X}$;*

(2) If $C \subset \mathscr{X}$ is bounded, then $\Psi(t, C)$ is also bounded;

(3) For $x_0 \in \mathscr{X}$ with $\| x_0 \|_{\mathscr{X}} \leq r$, $S(t)$, $V(t)$, $\| e(t, \cdot) \|_{L_+^1}$, $I(t)$, $R(t), \leq \max\{r, \frac{\Lambda}{\mu}\}$.

Proof. $\| \Psi(t, x_0) \|_{\mathscr{Y}} = S(t) + V(t) + I(t) + R(t) + \int_0^{+\infty} e(t,a)da$, the time derivative of $\| \Psi(t, x_0) \|_{\mathscr{X}}$ satisfies the following differential inequality:

$$\frac{d}{dt} \| \Psi(t, x_0) \|_{\mathscr{X}} \leq \Lambda - \mu \| \Phi(t, x_0) \|_{\mathscr{X}} .$$

It follows from the comparison principle that

$$\| \Psi(t, x_0) \|_{\mathscr{X}} \leq \frac{\Lambda}{\mu} - e^{-\mu t}(\frac{\Lambda}{\mu} - \| x_0 \|_{\mathscr{X}}), \tag{2}$$

namely,

$$\| \Psi(t, x_0) \|_{\mathscr{X}} \leq \max\{\frac{\Lambda}{\mu}, \| x_0 \|_{\mathscr{X}}\}. \tag{3}$$

From inequality (2), we can conclude that both the first and second conclusions of Proposition 2 hold, while inequality (3) implies that its third conclusion holds. □

2.3. Asymptotic Smoothness

By integrating the third equation of system (1) along the characteristic line $t - a =$ const., we can derive

$$e(t,a) = \begin{cases} e_0(a-t)\dfrac{k(a)}{k(a-t)}, & 0 \le t < a, \\ e(t-a,0)k(a), & 0 \le a \le t. \end{cases} \tag{4}$$

The following lemmas [29] are utilized to demonstrate the asymptotic smoothness of the semi-flow $\{\Psi(t,\cdot)\}_{t\ge 0}$.

Lemma 1. *For any bounded closed set $\mathscr{B} \subset \mathscr{X}$ that satisfies $\Psi(t,\mathscr{B}) \subset \mathscr{B}$, when the following two conditions hold, the semi-flow $\Psi(t,x) = K_1(t,x) + K_2(t,x) : \mathbb{R}_+ \times \mathscr{X} \to \mathscr{X}$ is asymptotically smooth.*

(1) $\lim\limits_{t\to+\infty} diam K_2(t,\mathscr{B}) = 0$;

(2) *for some $t_{\mathscr{B}} \ge 0$, $K_1(t,\mathscr{B})$ has compact closure for each $t \ge t_{\mathscr{B}}$.*

For the space $L^1_+(0,+\infty)$, boundedness alone is insufficient to guarantee precompactness. Therefore, we need to employ the following lemma in order to deduce its precompactness.

Lemma 2. *If a bounded set $\mathscr{A} \subset L^1_+(0,+\infty)$ satisfies the following four conditions, then $\mathscr{A}$ is the compact closure.*

(1) $\sup\limits_{g\in\mathscr{A}} \int_0^{+\infty} \mid g(s) \mid ds < +\infty$;

(2) $\lim\limits_{\theta\to+\infty} \int_\theta^{+\infty} \mid g(s) \mid ds = 0$ *uniformly in* $g \in \mathscr{A}$;

(3) $\lim\limits_{\theta\to 0^+} \int_0^{+\infty} \mid g(s+\theta) - g(s) \mid ds = 0$ *uniformly in* $g \in \mathscr{A}$;

(4) $\lim\limits_{\theta\to 0^+} \int_0^{\theta} \mid g(s) \mid ds = 0$ *uniformly in* $g \in \mathscr{A}$.

According to the two lemmas mentioned above, we can deduce the following theorem:

Theorem 1. *The continuous semi-flow $\{\Psi(t,\cdot)\}_{t\ge 0}$ generated by model (1) is asymptotically smooth.*

Proof. Define the following two semi-flows:

$$K_1(t,x) = (S(t), V(t), \tilde{e}(t,\cdot), I(t), R(t)), \quad K_2(t,x) = (0, 0, \phi_e(t,\cdot), 0, 0),$$

where

$$\phi_e(t,a) = \begin{cases} e_0(a-t)\dfrac{k(a)}{k(a-t)}, & 0 \le t < a, \\ 0, & 0 \le a \le t, \end{cases} \qquad \tilde{e}(t,a) = \begin{cases} 0, & 0 \le t < a, \\ e(t-a,0)k(a), & 0 \le a \le t, \end{cases}$$

for $x = (S(0), V(0), e_0(a), I(0), R(0)) \in \mathscr{X}$, we can state $\Psi(t,x) = K_1(t,x) + K_2(t,x)$.

Let $\mathscr{B} \subset \mathscr{X}$ be bounded; that is, a positive number $c \ge \frac{\Lambda}{\mu}$ exists, such that $\| x \|_{\mathscr{X}} \le c$ for each $x \in \mathscr{B}$. Then, we have

$$\begin{aligned} \| K_2(t,x) \|_{\mathscr{X}} &= \int_t^{+\infty} e_0(\theta - t)\frac{k(\theta)}{k(\theta - t)} d\theta \\ &= \int_0^{+\infty} e_0(u)\frac{k(u+t)}{k(u)} du \\ &= \int_0^{+\infty} e_0(u) e^{-\int_u^{u+t}(\mu+\delta(l)+\sigma(l))dl} du \\ &\le e^{-\mu t} \| x \|_{\mathscr{X}} \le c e^{-\mu t}. \end{aligned}$$

Thus, $\lim\limits_{t\to+\infty} diam\ K_2(t,\mathscr{B}) = 0$. Next, we show that $K_1(t,\mathscr{B})$ has compact closure for each $t \geq 0$.

It follows from Proposition 2 that $S(t), V(t), I(t), andR(t)$ remain in the compact set $[0,c]$ for each $t \geq 0$. In the following part, we try to prove that $\widetilde{e}(t,a)$ remains in a precompact subset of $L^1_+(0,+\infty)$ which is not dependent on x. It follows from

$$0 \leq \widetilde{e}(t,a) = \begin{cases} 0, & 0 \leq t < a, \\ e(t-a,0)k(a), & 0 \leq a \leq t, \end{cases}$$

and system (1) that

$$0 \leq \widetilde{e}(t,a) \leq f'(0)(1+\rho)c^2 e^{-\mu a}.$$

Therefore, conditions (1), (2), and (4) of Lemma 2 hold. Our next task is to demonstrate

$$\lim_{\theta\to 0^+} \int_0^{+\infty} \mid \widetilde{e}(t,a+\theta) - \widetilde{e}(t,a) \mid da = 0.$$

$$\begin{aligned}
&\int_0^{+\infty} \mid \widetilde{e}(t,a+\theta) - \widetilde{e}(t,a) \mid da \\
&= \int_0^{t-\theta} \mid \widetilde{e}(t,a+\theta) - \widetilde{e}(t,a) \mid da + \int_{t-\theta}^{t} \mid \widetilde{e}(t,a) \mid da \\
&= \int_0^{t-\theta} \mid e(t-a-\theta,0)k(a+\theta) - e(t-a,0)k(a) \mid da + \int_{t-\theta}^{t} \mid e(t-a,0)k(a) \mid da \\
&\leq \int_0^{t-\theta} \mid e(t-a-\theta,0) \mid\mid k(a+\theta) - k(a) \mid + \mid e(t-a-\theta,0) - e(t-a,0) \mid\mid k(a) \mid da \\
&\quad + f'(0)(1+\rho)c^2\theta,
\end{aligned}$$

where

$$\begin{aligned}
&\int_0^{t-\theta} \mid e(t-a-\theta,0) \mid\mid k(a+\theta) - k(a) \mid da \\
&\leq f'(0)(1+\rho)c^2\left(\int_0^{t-\theta} k(a)da - \int_0^{t-\theta} k(a+\theta)da\right) \\
&= f'(0)(1+\rho)c^2\left(\int_0^{t-\theta} k(a)da - \int_\theta^{t} k(s)ds\right) \\
&= f'(0)(1+\rho)c^2\left(\int_0^{\theta} k(a)da - \int_{t-\theta}^{t} k(s)ds\right) \\
&\leq f'(0)(1+\rho)c^2\theta.
\end{aligned}$$

It should be noted that

$$\mid \frac{dS(t)}{dt} \mid \leq p_1\Lambda + f'(0)c^2 + (\mu+\omega)c,$$

$$\mid \frac{dV(t)}{dt} \mid \leq (1-p_1)\Lambda + (\omega+\mu)c + \rho f'(0)c^2,$$

$$\mid \frac{dI(t)}{dt} \mid \leq (\bar{\delta} + \mu_I + \alpha + \gamma)c,$$

then

$$
\begin{aligned}
&| e(t-a-\theta,0) - e(t-a,0) | \\
\leq & | S(t-a-\theta)f(I(t-a-\theta)) - S(t-a)f(I(t-a)) | \\
&+ \rho | V(t-a-\theta)f(I(t-a-\theta)) - V(t-a)f(I(t-a)) | \\
= & (| S(t-a-\theta) || f(I(t-a-\theta)) - f(I(t-a)) | + | f(I(t-a)) || S(t-a-\theta) - S(t-a) |) \\
&+ \rho(| V(t-a-\theta) || f(I(t-a-\theta)) - f(I(t-a)) | \\
&+ | f(I(t-a)) || V(t-a-\theta) - V(t-a) |) \\
\leq & f'(0)\Xi\theta,
\end{aligned}
$$

where

$$
\begin{aligned}
\Xi = & (1+\rho)c(\bar{\delta}+\mu_I+\alpha+\gamma)c + c(p_1\Lambda + f'(0)c^2 + (\mu+\omega)c) \\
&+ \rho f'(0)c((1-p_1)\Lambda + (\omega+\mu)c + \rho f'(0)c^2).
\end{aligned}
$$

Then,

$$
\int_0^{t-\theta} | e(t-a-\theta,0) - e(t-a,0) || k(a) | da \leq f'(0)\Xi\theta \int_0^{t-\theta} e^{-\mu s} ds \leq \frac{f'(0)\Xi}{\mu}\theta.
$$

Hence,

$$
\int_0^{+\infty} | \tilde{e}(t,a+\theta) - \tilde{e}(t,a) | da \leq (2f'(0)(1+\rho)c^2 + \frac{f'(0)\Xi}{\mu})\theta,
$$

which means that condition (3) of Lemma 2 holds. Then, we can conclude that $\tilde{e}(t,a)$ satisfies all conditions of Lemma 2. As a result, we know that $K_1(t,\mathscr{B})$ has compact closure for all $t \geq 0$. It follows from Lemma 1 that the continuous semi-flow $\{\Psi(t,\cdot)\}_{t\geq 0}$ is asymptotically smooth. □

By utilizing Proposition 2.2, Theorem 1, and Theorem 2.6 from [30], we can derive the following theorem.

Theorem 2. *A global attractor $\mathcal{B}$ exists in $\mathscr{X}$ for the continuous semi-flow $\{\Psi(t,\cdot)\}_{t\geq 0}$, which can attract any bounded set in $\mathscr{X}$.*

3. Existence of Equilibrium States

The dynamic system characterized by (1) has a disease-free equilibrium state $E_0 = (S_0, V_0, 0_{L^1(0,+\infty)}, 0, 0)$, where $V_0 = \frac{(1-p_1)\Lambda}{\mu+\omega}, S_0 = \frac{p_1\Lambda}{\mu} + \frac{\omega V^0}{\mu}$. Define the mathematical expression for the basic reproduction number by

$$
\mathscr{R}_0 = \frac{\gamma\eta\alpha + f'(0)(S_0+\rho V_0)(\mathscr{K}_1(\mu+\alpha) + \mathscr{K}_2\alpha)}{(\mu_I+\gamma)(\mu+\alpha)}. \tag{5}
$$

$\mathscr{R}_0$ measures the expected number of secondary infectious individuals that a primary infectious individual may infect during the entire infection period in a completely susceptible population. Ref. [22] provides a detailed derivation of $\mathscr{R}_0$.

The endemic equilibrium state $(S^*, V^*, e^*(a), I^*, R^*)$ of system (1) satisfies the following equations:

$$\begin{cases} p_1\Lambda - S^* f(I^*) - \mu S^* + \omega V^* = 0, \\ (1-p_1)\Lambda - \rho V^* f(I^*) - (\mu+\omega)V^* = 0, \\ \dfrac{de^*(a)}{da} = -(\mu + \delta(a) + \sigma(a))e^*(a), \\ e^*(0) = (S^* + \rho V^*) f(I^*), \\ e^*(0)\mathscr{K}_1 - \mu_I I^* - \gamma I^* + \alpha R^* = 0, \\ \gamma\eta I^* + e^*(0)\mathscr{K}_2 - (\mu+\alpha)R^* = 0. \end{cases} \tag{6}$$

By performing a simple calculation, we can determine that I^* is the root of the following equation:

$$g(x) = 1, \text{where } g(x) = \frac{\gamma\eta\alpha + \frac{f(x)}{x}(\mathscr{S}(x) + \rho\mathscr{V}(x))(\mathscr{K}_1(\mu+\alpha) + \mathscr{K}_2\alpha)}{(\mu_I + \gamma)(\mu+\alpha)}, x > 0.$$

In this equation, $\mathscr{V}(x) = \frac{(1-p_1)\Lambda}{\rho f(x)+\mu+\omega}$, $\mathscr{S}(x) = \frac{p_1\Lambda + \omega V(x)}{f(x)+\mu}$. Clearly, we have $\lim_{x\to 0^+} g(x) = \mathscr{R}_0$. From the properties of $f(x)$, we know that $\lim_{x\to+\infty} f(x) = const.$ or $\lim_{x\to+\infty} f(x) = +\infty$. If $\lim_{x\to+\infty} f(x) = const.$, we have $\lim_{x\to+\infty} g(x) = \frac{\gamma\eta\alpha}{(\mu_I+\gamma)(\mu+\alpha)}$. If $\lim_{x\to+\infty} f(x) = +\infty$, It is not difficult to find that $\lim_{x\to+\infty} g(x) = \frac{\gamma\eta\alpha}{(\mu_I+\gamma)(\mu+\alpha)}$. Thus, $\lim_{x\to+\infty} g(x) = \frac{\gamma\eta\alpha}{(\mu_I+\gamma)(\mu+\alpha)} < 1$. Now, we demonstrate that $g'(x)$ is negative. We have

$$g'(x) = \frac{(\mathscr{K}_1(\mu+\alpha) + \mathscr{K}_2\alpha)}{(\mu_I+\gamma)(\mu+\alpha)}\left(\frac{f'(x)x - f(x)}{x^2}(\mathscr{S}(x) + \rho\mathscr{V}(x)) + \frac{f(x)}{x}\frac{d(\mathscr{S}(x) + \rho\mathscr{V}(x))}{dx}\right),$$

where

$$\begin{aligned} &\frac{d(\mathscr{S}(x) + \rho\mathscr{V}(x))}{dx} \\ &= -f'(x)\Lambda\left(\frac{\rho(1-p_1)(\rho(\mu+f(x)) + \omega)}{(\mu+\omega+\rho f(x))^2(\mu+f(x))} + \frac{p_1(\mu+\omega+\rho f(x)) + \omega(1-p_1)}{(\mu+f(x))^2(\mu+\omega+\rho f(x))}\right). \end{aligned}$$

Based on the properties of $f(x)$, we can infer that $g'(x)$ is negative when x is greater than 0. Hence, $g(x) = 1$ has only a positive and real root if $\mathscr{R}_0 > 1$; namely, if $\mathscr{R}_0 > 1$, system (1) has only a endemic equilibrium state: $E^* = (S^*, V^*, e^*(a), I^*, R^*)$. For system (1), we arrive at the following result.

Theorem 3. *The disease-free equilibrium state E_0 is always feasible in system (1), while the endemic equilibrium state E^* is also feasible if $\mathscr{R}_0 > 1$.*

4. Uniform Persistence and Global Stability

4.1. Uniform Persistence

In this section of the paper, we analyze the uniform persistence of the system (1). Let us define

$$\Gamma = \{(x_1, x_2, x_3, x_4, x_5) \in \mathscr{X} \,|\, \exists\, t_1, t_2 \in \mathbb{R}_+ : \int_0^{+\infty} \delta(a+t_1)x_3(a)da + \int_0^{+\infty} \sigma(a+t_2)x_3(a)da$$
$$+x_4 + x_5 > 0\},$$

and $\partial\Gamma = \mathscr{X} \setminus \Gamma$. We know that $\mathscr{X} = \Gamma \cup \partial\Gamma$.

Theorem 4. *For the semi-flow $\Psi(t,\cdot)$, both Γ and $\partial\Gamma$ are positively invariant sets. Moreover, in set $\partial\Gamma$, the equilibrium state E_0 is globally asymptotically stable.*

Proof. Let $\Psi(0, x_0) \in \Gamma$. If $I(0) > 0$ or $R(0) > 0$, based on system (1), it is easy to verify that $I(t) > I(0)e^{-(\gamma+\mu_I)t} > 0$ or $R(t) > R(0)e^{-(\alpha+\mu)t} > 0$. Then, Γ is a positively invariant set of the semi-flow $\Psi(t, \cdot)$. If $I(0) = 0$ and $R(0) = 0$, without a loss of generality, we assume that $\exists\, t_1 \in \mathbb{R}_+$, such that $\int_0^{+\infty} \delta(a + t_1)e(0, a)da > 0$. Then, $\forall t \in [0, t_1]$, $s = t_1 - t \geq 0$, such that

$$\begin{aligned}\int_0^{+\infty} \delta(a+s)e(t,a)da &\geq \int_t^{+\infty} \delta(a+s)e(t,a)da \\ &= \int_0^{+\infty} \delta(a+t+s)e(t,a+t)da \\ &= \int_0^{+\infty} \delta(a+t_1)e(0,a)\tfrac{k(a+t)}{k(a)}da \\ &\geq e^{-(\mu+\bar{\delta}+\bar{\sigma})t}\int_0^{+\infty} \delta(a+t_1)e(0,a)da > 0.\end{aligned} \tag{7}$$

If $\exists\, t_2 \in (0, t_1]$, such that $I(t_2) > 0$, then $I(t) > 0$ for $\forall t > t_2$. Otherwise, according to (7), we have

$$\frac{dI(t_1)}{dt} \geq \int_0^{+\infty} \delta(a)e(t_1, a)da > 0.$$

Then, $I(t) > 0$ for $\forall t > t_1$. This means that $\Psi(t, \Gamma) \subset \Gamma$ for all $t \geq 0$. That is to say, Γ is a positively invariant set of the semi-flow $\Psi(t, \cdot)$.

Let $\Psi(0, x_0) \in \partial\Gamma$. We construct the following model

$$\begin{cases} \dfrac{\partial e(t,a)}{\partial t} + \dfrac{\partial e(t,a)}{\partial a} = -(\mu + \delta(a) + \sigma(a))e(t,a), \\ \dfrac{dI(t)}{dt} = \displaystyle\int_0^{+\infty} \delta(a)e(t,a)da + \alpha R - (\gamma + \mu_I)I(t), \\ \dfrac{dR(t)}{dt} = \displaystyle\int_0^{+\infty} \sigma(a)e(t,a)da + \gamma\eta I(t) - (\mu + \alpha)R(t), \\ e(t,0) = Sf(I) + \rho V f(I), \\ e(0,a) = e_0(a),\ I(0) = 0,\ R(0) = 0. \end{cases} \tag{8}$$

Since $S(t), V(t) \leq C$, where $C = max\{\| x_0 \|_{\mathscr{X}}, \dfrac{\Lambda}{\mu}\}$, it is easy to verify that

$$I(t) \leq \hat{I}(t),\ \ R(t) \leq \hat{T}(t), \| e(t,s) \|_{L^1_+} \leq \| \hat{e}(t,s) \|_{L^1_+}, \tag{9}$$

where

$$\begin{cases} \dfrac{\partial \hat{e}(t,a)}{\partial t} + \dfrac{\partial \hat{e}(t,a)}{\partial a} = -(\mu + \delta(a) + \delta(a))\hat{e}(t,a), \\ \dfrac{d\hat{I}(t)}{dt} = \displaystyle\int_0^{+\infty} \delta(a)\hat{e}(t,a)da + \alpha\hat{R} - (\gamma + \mu_I)\hat{I}(t), \\ \dfrac{d\hat{R}(t)}{dt} = \displaystyle\int_0^{+\infty} \sigma(a)\hat{e}(t,a)da + \gamma\eta\hat{I}(t) - (\mu + \alpha)\hat{R}(t), \\ \hat{e}(t,0) = Cf(\hat{I})(1+\rho), \\ \hat{e}(0,a) = e_0(a),\ \hat{I}(0) = 0,\ \hat{R}(0) = 0. \end{cases} \tag{10}$$

Similar to the formulation (4), we derive

$$\hat{e}(t,a) = \begin{cases} e_0(a-t)\dfrac{k(a)}{k(a-t)}, & 0 \leq t < a, \\ \hat{e}(t-a,0)k(a), & 0 \leq a \leq t. \end{cases} \tag{11}$$

By substituting Equation (11) into the second and third equations of (10), we can obtain the following equations

$$\begin{cases} \dfrac{d\hat{I}(t)}{dt} = \int_0^t \delta(a)\hat{e}(t-a,0)k(a)da + G_1(t) + \alpha\hat{R} - (\gamma+\mu_I)\hat{I}(t), \\ \dfrac{d\hat{R}(t)}{dt} = \gamma\eta\hat{I}(t) + \int_0^t \sigma(a)\hat{e}(t-a,0)k(a)da + G_2(t) - (\mu+\alpha)\hat{R}(t), \\ \hat{I}(0) = 0, \ \hat{R}(0) = 0. \end{cases} \tag{12}$$

where

$$G_1(t) = \int_t^{+\infty} \delta(a)e_0(a-t)\frac{k(a)}{k(a-t)}da, \ G_2(t) = \int_t^{+\infty} \sigma(a)e_0(a-t)\frac{k(a)}{k(a-t)}da$$

since

$$G_1(t) \le \int_t^{+\infty} \delta(a)e_0(a-t)da = \int_0^{+\infty} \delta(a+t)e_0(a)da,$$

$$G_2(t) \le \int_t^{+\infty} \sigma(a)e_0(a-t)da = \int_0^{+\infty} \sigma(a+t)e_0(a)da.$$

Based on $\Psi(0,x_0) \in \partial\Gamma$, we know $G_1(t), G_2(t) \equiv 0$ for $t \ge 0$. Then, the system (12) can be rewritten in the following equations:

$$\begin{cases} \dfrac{d\hat{I}(t)}{dt} = \int_0^t \delta(a)k(a)C(1+\rho)f(\hat{I}(t-a))da + \alpha\hat{R} - (\gamma+\mu_I)\hat{I}(t), \\ \dfrac{d\hat{R}(t)}{dt} = \gamma\eta\hat{I}(t) + \int_0^t \sigma(a)k(a)C(1+\rho)f(\hat{I}(t-a))da - (\mu+\alpha)\hat{R}(t), \\ \hat{I}(0) = 0, \ \hat{R}(0) = 0. \end{cases}$$

It is easy to conclude that system (12) has a unique solution: $\hat{I}(t) \equiv 0, \hat{R}(t) \equiv 0$ for $t \ge 0$. Depending on (10) and (11), we know that $\hat{e}(t,s) = 0$ for $0 \le s \le t$. Thus,

$$\| \delta(a+u)\hat{e}(t,a) \|_{L_+^1} = \int_t^{+\infty} \delta(a+u)e_0(a-t)\frac{k(a)}{k(a-t)}da \le \| \delta(t+u+s)e_0(s) \|_{L_+^1} = 0,$$

$$\| \sigma(a+u)\hat{e}(t,a) \|_{L_+^1} = \int_t^{+\infty} \sigma(a+u)e_0(a-t)\frac{k(a)}{k(a-t)}da \le \| \sigma(t+u+s)e_0(s) \|_{L_+^1} = 0.$$

According to (9), we can conclude that

$$I(t) = 0, \ R(t) = 0, \| \delta(a+t_1)e(t,a) \|_{L_+^1} = 0, \| \sigma(a+t_2)e(t,a) \|_{L_+^1} = 0, for\ all\ t, t_1, t_2 \ge 0.$$

Thus, $\partial\Gamma$ is a positively invariant set of the semi-flow $\Psi(t,\cdot)$.

In the set $\partial\Gamma$, system (1) reduces to the following system:

$$\begin{cases} \dfrac{dS(t)}{dt} = p_1\Lambda - \mu S(t) + \omega V, \\ \dfrac{dV(t)}{dt} = (1-p_1)\Lambda - (\mu+\omega)V(t). \end{cases} \tag{13}$$

We can easily find that $\lim\limits_{t\to+\infty} V(t) = \frac{(1-p_1)\Lambda}{\mu+\omega}$ and $\lim\limits_{t\to+\infty} (S(t)+V(t)) = \frac{\Lambda}{\mu}$. Hence, $\lim\limits_{t\to+\infty} S(t) = \frac{\Lambda}{\mu} - \frac{(1-p_1)\Lambda}{\mu+\omega}$. In other words, in the set $\partial\Gamma$, the equilibrium state E_0 is globally asymptotically stable. □

Theorem 5. *The semi-flow $\{\Psi(t,\cdot)\}_{t\ge0}$ is uniformly persistent with respect to $(\Gamma, \partial\Gamma)$ when $\mathscr{R}_0 > 1$. Apart from this, there is a global attractor $\mathcal{B}_0 \subset \Gamma$ for $\{\Psi(t,\cdot)\}_{t\ge0}$.*

Proof. Theorem 4 proves the global stability of E_0 for the set $\partial\Gamma$. According to Theorem 4.2 in [31], we only need to verify

$$\omega_s(E_0) \cap \Gamma = \emptyset,$$

where $\omega_s(E_0) = \{x \in \mathscr{X} \mid \lim_{t\to+\infty} \Psi(t,x) = E_0\}$. Assume that there is a $x_0 = (s_0, v_0, e_0(a), i_0, r_0) \in \Gamma \cap \omega_s(E_0)$. Then the sequence $\{x_n\} \subset \Gamma$ exists, such that

$$\| \Psi(t,x_n) - E_0 \|_{\mathscr{X}} < \frac{1}{n}, t \geq 0.$$

Let us define $\Psi(t,x_n) = (S_n(t), V_n(t), e_n(t,\cdot), I_n(t), R_n(t))$. Then,

$$S_0 - \frac{1}{n} < S_n(t) < S_0 + \frac{1}{n}, \quad V_0 - \frac{1}{n} < V_n(t) < V_0 + \frac{1}{n}, \quad 0 \leq I_n(t) < \frac{1}{n}$$

and $\Psi(t,x_n) \subset \Gamma$, for all $t \geq 0$.

Similar to the analysis that Γ is a positively invariant set in Theorem 4, we know that $t_0 \geq 0$ exists, such that $I(t) > 0$ or $R(t) > 0$ for all $t \geq t_0$. We may as well let $t_0 = 0$ and $I_n(0) > 0$. If n is sufficiently large, we can assume that $S_0 > \frac{1}{n}$, $V_0 > \frac{1}{n}$ and

$$M(n) = \frac{\gamma\eta\alpha + f'(\frac{1}{n})((S^0 - \frac{1}{n}) + \rho(V^0 - \frac{1}{n}))(\mathscr{K}_1(\mu+\alpha) + \mathscr{K}_2\alpha)}{(\mu_I + \gamma)(\mu+\alpha)} > 1, \tag{14}$$

when $\mathcal{R}_0 > 1$. From the properties of $f(x)$, we know that $f(\hat{I}) \geq f'(\frac{1}{n})\hat{I}$ if $\hat{I} \leq \frac{1}{n}$. Next, we build the following system:

$$\begin{cases} \dfrac{\partial \hat{e}(t,a)}{\partial t} + \dfrac{\partial \hat{e}(t,a)}{\partial a} = -(\mu + \delta(a) + \sigma(a))\hat{e}(t,a), \\ \dfrac{d\hat{I}(t)}{dt} = \displaystyle\int_0^{+\infty} \delta(a)\hat{e}(t,a)da + \alpha\hat{R} - (\gamma + \mu_I)\hat{I}(t), \\ \dfrac{d\hat{R}(t)}{dt} = \displaystyle\int_0^{+\infty} \sigma(a)\hat{e}(t,a)da + \gamma\eta\hat{I}(t) - (\mu+\alpha)\hat{R}(t), \\ \hat{e}(t,0) = (S_0 - \dfrac{1}{n}) + \rho(V_0 - \dfrac{1}{n}))f'(\dfrac{1}{n})\hat{I}, \\ \hat{e}(0,a) = e_n(0,a), \ \hat{I}(0) = I_n(0), \ \hat{R}(0) = R_n(0). \end{cases} \tag{15}$$

Similar to the analysis presented in Section 2.2, we can conclude that a unique non-negative solution exists for system (15). It follows from the comparison principle that

$$I_n(t) \geq \hat{I}(t), \ R_n(t) \geq \hat{R}(t), e_n(t,s) \geq \hat{e}(t,s), \text{for t} \geq 0. \tag{16}$$

Similar to the formulation (4), we can obtain

$$\hat{e}(t,a) = \begin{cases} e_0(a-t)\dfrac{k(a)}{k(a-t)}, & 0 \leq t < a, \\ \hat{e}(t-a,0)k(a), & 0 \leq a \leq t. \end{cases} \tag{17}$$

We substitute (17) into the second and third equations of (15) and obtain the following inequations:

$$\begin{cases} \dfrac{d\hat{I}(t)}{dt} \geq \displaystyle\int_0^t \delta(a)k(a)((S_0 - \frac{1}{n}) + \rho(V_0 - \frac{1}{n}))f'(\frac{1}{n})\hat{I}(t-a)da - (\mu_I+\gamma)\hat{I}(t) + \alpha\hat{R}(t), \\ \dfrac{d\hat{R}(t)}{dt} \geq \gamma\eta\hat{I}(t) + \displaystyle\int_0^t \sigma(a)k(a)((S_0 - \frac{1}{n}) + \rho(V_0 - \frac{1}{n}))f'(\frac{1}{n})\hat{I}(t-a)da - (\mu+\alpha)\hat{R}(t), \\ \hat{I}(0) = I_n(0), \ \hat{R}(0) = R_n(0). \end{cases} \tag{18}$$

If $\hat{I}(t)$ and $\hat{R}(t)$ are bounded, we take the Laplace transform of both sides of (18) and obtain the following inequations:

$$\begin{cases} -\hat{I}(0)+\lambda\mathcal{L}[\hat{I}](\lambda) \geq \mathcal{L}[u_1](\lambda)\mathcal{L}[\hat{I}](\lambda)-(\gamma+\mu_I)\mathcal{L}[\hat{I}](\lambda)+\alpha\mathcal{L}[\hat{R}](\lambda), \\ -\hat{R}(0)+\lambda\mathcal{L}[\hat{R}](\lambda) \geq \gamma\eta\mathcal{L}[\hat{I}](\lambda)+\mathcal{L}[u_2](\lambda)\mathcal{L}[\hat{I}](\lambda)-(\mu+\alpha)\mathcal{L}[\hat{R}](\lambda), \end{cases} \tag{19}$$

where

$$\mathcal{L}[\hat{I}](\lambda)=\int_0^{+\infty}e^{-\lambda t}\hat{I}(t)dt,\quad \mathcal{L}[\hat{R}](\lambda)=\int_0^{+\infty}e^{-\lambda t}\hat{R}(t)dt,$$

$$\mathcal{L}[u_1](\lambda)=\int_0^{\infty}\delta(a)k(a)f'(\frac{1}{n})((S_0-\frac{1}{n})+\rho(V_0-\frac{1}{n}))e^{-\lambda a}da,$$

$$\mathcal{L}[u_2](\lambda)=\int_0^{\infty}\sigma(a)k(a)f'(\frac{1}{n})((S_0-\frac{1}{n})+\rho(V_0-\frac{1}{n}))e^{-\lambda a}da.$$

From inequations (19), we can derive

$$\begin{aligned} &\frac{(\lambda+\mu+\alpha)(\lambda+\mu_I+\gamma)}{\alpha}[1-\frac{\alpha\gamma\eta+\alpha\mathcal{L}[u_2](\lambda)+\mathcal{L}[u_1](\lambda)(\lambda+\mu+\alpha)}{(\lambda+\mu+\alpha)(\lambda+\mu_I+\gamma)}]\mathcal{L}[\hat{I}](\lambda) \\ &\geq \hat{R}(0)+\frac{\lambda+\mu+\alpha}{\alpha}\hat{I}(0)>0. \end{aligned} \tag{20}$$

By applying the Dominated Convergence Theorem, we know that $\mathcal{L}[u_i](\lambda)\to\mathcal{L}[u_i](0)$, $(i=1,2)$ as $\lambda\to 0$, since

$$\begin{aligned} &\frac{(\lambda+\mu+\alpha)(\lambda+\mu_I+\gamma)}{\alpha}[1-\frac{\alpha\gamma\eta+\alpha\mathcal{L}[u_2](\lambda)+\mathcal{L}[u_1](\lambda)(\lambda+\mu+\alpha)}{(\lambda+\mu+\alpha)(\lambda+\mu_I+\gamma)}]\,|_{\lambda=0} \\ &=\frac{(\mu+\alpha)(\mu_I+\gamma)}{\alpha}(1-M(n))<0, \end{aligned}$$

which means that a positive number ε exists, such that

$$\frac{(\lambda+\mu+\alpha)(\lambda+\mu_I+\gamma)}{\alpha}[1-\frac{\alpha\gamma\eta+\alpha\mathcal{L}[u_2](\lambda)+\mathcal{L}[u_1](\lambda)(\lambda+\mu+\alpha)}{(\lambda+\mu+\alpha)(\lambda+\mu_I+\gamma)}]<0,$$

for each $\lambda\in[0,\varepsilon)$. It follows from (20) that $\mathcal{L}[\hat{I}](\lambda)<0$ for each $\lambda\in(0,\varepsilon)$. But, there is a contradiction with the non-negative of $\hat{I}(t)(t\geq 0)$. That is to say, $\hat{I}(t)$ and $\hat{R}(t)$ cannot both be bounded. It can be inferred from the inequalities $I_n(t)\geq\hat{I}(t)$ and $R_n(t)\geq\hat{R}(t)$ that both $I_n(t)$ and $R_n(t)$ cannot be bounded. This contradicts Proposition 2. Thus, $\omega_s(E_0)\cap\Gamma=\emptyset$ holds. By using Theorem 4.2 [31], it is easy to show that the semi-flow $\{\Psi(t,\cdot)\}_{t\geq 0}$ of system (1) is uniformly persistent. By using Theorem 3.7 [30], we know that there is a global attractor $\mathcal{B}_0\subset\Gamma$ for $\{\Psi(t,\cdot)\}_{t\geq 0}$. □

4.2. Global Stability

Theorem 6. *The disease-free equilibrium state E_0 is locally asymptotically stable (unstable) for $\mathscr{R}_0<1$ (for $\mathscr{R}_0>1$).*

Proof. At E_0, the linearized system of system (1) can be expressed as the following equations:

$$\begin{cases} \dfrac{ds(t)}{dt} = -f'(0)S_0 i(t) - \mu s(t) + \omega v(t), \\ \dfrac{dv(t)}{dt} = -\omega v(t) - f'(0)\rho V_0 i(t) - \mu v(t), \\ \dfrac{\partial \mathbf{e}(t,a)}{\partial t} + \dfrac{\partial \mathbf{e}(t,a)}{\partial a} = -(\mu + \delta(a) + \sigma(a))\mathbf{e}(t,a), \\ \dfrac{di(t)}{dt} = \displaystyle\int_0^{+\infty} \delta(a)\mathbf{e}(t,a)da - (\mu_I + \gamma)i(t) + \alpha r(t), \\ \dfrac{dr(t)}{dt} = \gamma\eta i(t) + \displaystyle\int_0^{+\infty} \sigma(a)\mathbf{e}(t,a)da - (\mu + \alpha)r(t), \\ \mathbf{e}(t,0) = f'(0)S_0 i(t) + f'(0)\rho V_0 i(t), \end{cases} \tag{21}$$

where $s(t) = S(t) - S_0,\ v = V(t) - V_0,\ \mathbf{e}(t,a) = e(t,a),\ i(t) = I(t),\ and r(t) = R(t)$.

Let

$$k_1(\lambda) = \int_0^{+\infty} \alpha(a) e^{-\int_0^a (\lambda+\mu+\sigma(s)+\delta(s))ds} da,\ k_2(\lambda) = \int_0^{+\infty} \delta(a) e^{-\int_0^a (\lambda+\mu+\sigma(s)+\delta(s))ds} da.$$

In system (21), we set $s(t) = S^0 e^{\lambda t},\ v(t) = V^0 e^{\lambda t},\ \mathbf{e}(t,a) = e^0(a)e^{\lambda t},\ i(t) = I^0 e^{\lambda t}, and$ $r(t) = R^0 e^{\lambda t}$ and derive the following equations:

$$\begin{cases} \lambda S^0 = -f'(0)S_0 I^0 - \mu S^0 + \omega V^0, \\ \lambda V^0 = -\omega V^0 - f'(0)\rho V_0 I^0 - \mu V^0, \\ \dot{e}^0(a) = -(\lambda + \mu + \delta(a) + \sigma(a))e^0(a), \\ (\lambda + \mu_I + \gamma)I^0 = \displaystyle\int_0^{+\infty} \delta(a)e^0(a)da + \alpha R^0, \\ (\lambda + \mu + \alpha)R^0 = \gamma\eta I^0 + \displaystyle\int_0^{+\infty} \sigma(a)e^0(a)da, \\ e^0(0) = f'(0)S_0 I^0 + f'(0)\rho V_0 I^0. \end{cases} \tag{22}$$

By solving the system (22), we have

$$S^0 = \frac{\omega V^0 - f'(0)S_0 I^0}{\lambda + \mu},\ V^0 = \frac{-\rho f'(0)V_0 I^0}{\lambda + \mu + \omega},\ R^0 = \frac{\gamma\eta I^0 + e^0(0)k_2(\lambda)}{\lambda + \mu + \alpha},$$

$$e^0(0) = \frac{\lambda + \mu_I + \gamma - \frac{\alpha\gamma\eta}{\lambda+\mu+\alpha}}{k_1(\lambda) + \frac{\alpha k_2(\lambda)}{\lambda+\mu+\alpha}} I^0.$$

By combining the above expressions with the last equation of system (22), we obtain the following equation:

$$f'(0)(S_0 + \rho V_0)I^0 = \frac{(\lambda + \mu_I + \gamma) - \frac{\alpha\gamma\eta}{\lambda+\mu+\alpha}}{k_1(\lambda) + \frac{\alpha k_2(\lambda)}{\lambda+\mu+\alpha}} I^0.$$

This indicates that the characteristic equation of system (21) can be expressed in the following form at the equilibrium state E_0:

$$F(\lambda) = \frac{f'(0)(\rho V_0 + S_0)[(\lambda + \mu + \alpha)k_1(\lambda) + \alpha k_2(\lambda)] + \alpha\gamma\eta}{(\lambda + \mu + \alpha)(\lambda + \mu_I + \gamma)}.$$

It is easy to find $F'(\lambda) < 0$, $F(0) = \mathscr{R}_0$ and $\lim_{\lambda \to +\infty} F(\lambda) = 0$. Hence, when $\mathscr{R}_0 > 1$, a positive real root exists for the equation $F(\lambda) = 1$, indicating that the equilibrium state E_0 is unstable. For $\mathscr{R}_0 < 1$, if $\lambda_0 = a_0 + ib_0$ is a root of $F(\lambda) = 1$ with $a_0 \geq 0$. However,

$$| F(a_0 + ib_0) | \leq \mathscr{R}_0 < 1.$$

As a consequence, for $\mathscr{R}_0 < 1$, all eigenvalues of $F(\lambda) = 1$ have negative real parts, indicating that E_0 is locally asymptotically stable. □

Theorem 7. *For system (1), if $\mathcal{R}_0 < 1$, the disease-free equilibrium state E_0 is globally asymptotically stable.*

Proof. Let us define $h(x) = x - \ln x - 1$. It is easy to conclude that $h(x)$ achieves a global minimum at $x = 1$ and $h(1) = 0$. Thus, $h(x) > 0$ for all $x > 0$ and $x \neq 1$. By following the same reasoning as Lemma 4.2 [32], we can verify that any solution to system (1) on $\mathcal{B}$ is satisfied, such that $S(t), V(t) > 0$ for any $t \in \mathbb{R}$. Next, we define the Lyapunov function $W = W_1 + W_2 + W_3 + W_4 + W_5$ on $\mathcal{B}$. It follows from the compactness of $\mathcal{B}$ that W is bounded on $\mathcal{B}$, where

$$W_1 = (\mathscr{K}_1 + \frac{\alpha}{\mu+\alpha}\mathscr{K}_2)S_0 h(\frac{S}{S_0}),\ W_2 = (\mathscr{K}_1 + \frac{\alpha}{\mu+\alpha}\mathscr{K}_2)V_0 h(\frac{V}{V_0}),\ W_4 = I,\ W_5 = \frac{\alpha}{\mu+\alpha}R,$$

$$W_3 = \int_0^{+\infty} H(a)e(t,a)da,\ H(a) = \int_a^{+\infty} (\delta(u) + \frac{\alpha}{\mu+\alpha}\sigma(u))e^{-\int_a^u (\mu+\delta(s)+\sigma(s))ds}du.$$

Now, we calculate the derivatives of W_1, W_2, W_3, W_4, and W_5 along the solutions of (1). Since $\mu = p_1\Lambda\frac{1}{S_0} + \omega\frac{V_0}{S_0}$, we have

$$\dot{W}_1 = (\mathscr{K}_1 + \frac{\alpha}{\mu+\alpha}\mathscr{K}_2)(-p_1\Lambda\frac{(S-S_0)^2}{SS_0} - f(I)(S-S_0) + \omega V_0(\frac{V}{V_0} - \frac{S}{S_0} - \frac{S_0 V}{SV_0} + 1)),$$

Since $(1-p_1)\Lambda = (\mu+\omega)V_0$, we have

$$\dot{W}_2 = (\mathscr{K}_1 + \frac{\alpha}{\mu+\alpha}\mathscr{K}_2)(-(\mu+\omega)\frac{(V-V_0)^2}{V} - \rho f(I)(V-V_0)),$$

Further, we have

$$\begin{aligned}
\dot{W}_3 &= -\textstyle\int_0^{+\infty} H(a)((\mu+\delta(a)+\sigma(a))e(t,a) + \frac{\partial e}{\partial a})da \\
&= H(0)e(t,0) - \textstyle\int_0^{+\infty} (\delta(a) + \frac{\alpha}{\mu+\alpha}\sigma(a))e(t,a)da \\
&= (\mathscr{K}_1 + \frac{\alpha}{\mu+\alpha}\mathscr{K}_2)(S+\rho V)f(I) - \textstyle\int_0^{+\infty} (\delta(a) + \frac{\alpha}{\mu+\alpha}\sigma(a))e(t,a)da, \\
\dot{W}_4 &= \textstyle\int_0^{+\infty} \delta(a)e(t,a)da - (\gamma+\mu_I)I + \alpha R, \\
\dot{W}_5 &= \frac{\alpha}{\mu+\alpha}(\textstyle\int_0^{+\infty} \sigma(a)e(t,a)da + \gamma\eta I - (\mu+\alpha)R).
\end{aligned}$$

Thus, we can obtain

$$\begin{aligned}
\frac{dW}{dt} = &(\mathscr{K}_1 + \frac{\alpha}{\mu+\alpha}\mathscr{K}_2)(S_0+\rho V_0)f(I) - (\mu_I+\gamma)I + \frac{\alpha}{\mu+\alpha}\gamma\eta I \\
&+(\mathscr{K}_1 + \frac{\alpha}{\mu+\alpha}\mathscr{K}_2)\omega V_0(-\frac{S}{S_0} - \frac{S_0 V}{SV_0} - \frac{V_0}{V} + 3) \\
&-(\mathscr{K}_1 + \frac{\alpha}{\mu+\alpha}\mathscr{K}_2)(p_1\Lambda\frac{(S-S_0)^2}{SS_0} + \mu\frac{(V-V_0)^2}{V}).
\end{aligned}$$

Notice that $-\frac{S}{S_0}-\frac{S_0V}{SV_0}-\frac{V_0}{V}+3\leq 0, f(I)\leq f'(0)I$. Thus, we have

$$\frac{dW}{dt}\leq(\gamma+\mu_I)I(\mathcal{R}_0-1)-(\mathscr{K}_1+\frac{\alpha}{\mu+\alpha}\mathscr{K}_2)(p_1\Lambda\frac{(S-S_0)^2}{SS_0}+\mu\frac{(V-V_0)^2}{V}).$$

As a consequence, if $\mathcal{R}_0<1$, then $\frac{dW}{dt}\leq 0$ holds. Let T be the largest invariant subset of $\{\frac{dW}{dt}|_{(1)}=0\}$. The equality holds only if $S(t)=S^0, I=0, V=V^0$. In T, $S(t)=S^0, I=0$, and $V=V^0$ for all $t\in\mathbb{R}$. Then, we have $e(t,a)=0$. By combining this with system (1), it follows that $R(t)=0$ for all $t\in\mathbb{R}$. Hence, $T=\{E_0\}$. It follows from the LaSalle invariance principle [33] and Theorem 6 that E_0 is globally asymptotically stable. □

When $\mathcal{R}_0>1$, the system (1) has a global attractor $\mathcal{B}_0\subset\Gamma$. Let $x\in\mathcal{B}_0$. Then, a total trajectory $\{\Psi(t,x)\}_{t\in\mathbb{R}}$ exists in $\mathcal{B}_0$. By following the same reasoning as that presented in Section 3.2 in [32], the system (1) reduces to the following total trajectory system:

$$\begin{cases}\frac{dS(t)}{dt}=p_1\Lambda-Sf(I)-\mu S+\omega V,\\ \frac{dV(t)}{dt}=(1-p_1)\Lambda-\rho Vf(I)-(\mu+\omega)V,\\ e(t,a)=k(a)(S(t-a)f(I(t-a))+\rho V(t-a)f(I(t-a))),\\ \frac{dI(t)}{dt}=\int_0^{+\infty}\delta(a)e(t,a)da+\alpha R-(\gamma+\mu_I)I(t),\\ \frac{dR(t)}{dt}=\gamma\eta I(t)+\int_0^{+\infty}\sigma(a)e(t,a)da-(\mu+\alpha)R(t),\\ (S(0),\ V(0),\ e(0,a),\ I(0),\ R(0))\in\mathcal{B}_0.\end{cases}\tag{23}$$

To prove that E^* is globally stable, it is mandatory to prove that $S(t),\ V(t),\ e(t,a),\ I(t),\ R(t)>0$.

Lemma 3. *All solutions to systems (1) or (23) on $\mathcal{B}_0$ satisfy the following inequalities:*

$$\epsilon\leq S(t),\ V(t),\ I(t),\ R(t)\leq M,\ f(\epsilon)(1+\rho)\epsilon k(a)\leq e(t,a)\leq f(M)(1+\rho)Mk(a),$$

for all $t\in\mathbb{R}$, $a\in\mathbb{R}_+$, where ϵ and M are positive constants.

Proof. Let $\Psi(t,x)=(S(t),V(t),e(t,a),I(t),R(t))\subset\mathcal{B}_0$.

Now, we are going to prove that $S(t)>0$ for all $t\in\mathbb{R}$. We assume that $S(t_0)=0$ for some $t_0\in\mathbb{R}$. Clearly, $\frac{dS(t_0)}{dt}\geq p_1\Lambda>0$. We can know from here that $S(t_0-\eta_0)<0$ for some $\eta_0>0$. This is a contradiction to $\mathcal{B}_0\subset\Gamma$. Hence, $S(t)>0$ for all $t\in\mathbb{R}$. Similarly, we can also derive $V(t)>0$ for any $t\in\mathbb{R}$.

Next, we are going to prove that $I(t)>0,\ R(t)>0$ for any $t\in\mathbb{R}$. We assume that $I(t_0)=0$ and $R(t_0)=0$ for some $t_0\in\mathbb{R}$. From (23), it is easy to derive that $I(t)=0,\ R(t)=0$ when $t\leq t_0$. Furthermore, we have $\int_0^{+\infty}e(t,a)da=0$ for all $t\leq t_0$. This is a contradiction to $\Psi(t,x)\subset\mathcal{B}_0$. Further, we assume that $I(t_0)=0,\ R(t_0)>0$ for some $t_0\in\mathbb{R}$. It follows from (23) that $\frac{dI(t_0)}{dt}\geq\alpha R(t_0)>0$. From here, we know that $I(t_0-\eta_1)<0$ for some $\eta_1>0$. This is a contradiction to $\mathcal{B}_0\subset\Gamma$. Similarly, the assumption that $I(t_0)>0,\ R(t_0)=0$ for some $t_0\in\mathbb{R}$ is not true. Hence, $I(t)>0,\ R(t)>0$ for any $t\in\mathbb{R}$. Furthermore, it follows from (23) that $e(t,a)>0$ for any $(t,a)\in(\mathbb{R},\ \mathbb{R}_+)$. Then, it follows from the compactness of $\mathcal{B}_0$ that the conclusions of Lemma 3 hold. □

Theorem 8. *For systems (1) or (23) in Γ, if $\mathcal{R}_0 > 1$, the equilibrium state E^* is globally asymptotically stable.*

Proof. Let us define the Lyapunov function $G(t) = G_1 + G_2 + G_3 + G_4 + G_5$ on $\mathcal{B}_0$. It follows from Lemma 3 that $G(t)$ is bounded, where

$$G_1 = (\mathscr{K}_1 + \frac{\alpha}{\mu+\alpha}\mathscr{K}_2)S^* h(\frac{S}{S^*}),\ G_2 = (\mathscr{K}_1 + \frac{\alpha}{\mu+\alpha}\mathscr{K}_2)V^* h(\frac{V}{V^*}),$$

$$G_3 = \int_0^{+\infty} H(a)e^*(a)h(\frac{e(t,a)}{e^*(a)})da,\ G_4 = I^* h(\frac{I}{I^*}),\ G_5 = \frac{\alpha}{\mu+\alpha}R^* h(\frac{R}{R^*}),$$

and

$$h(x) = x - lnx - 1,\ \ H(a) = \int_a^{+\infty} (\delta(u) + \frac{\alpha}{\mu+\alpha}\sigma(u))e^{-\int_a^u (\mu+\delta(s)+\sigma(s))ds}du.$$

Along with any solution to $\mathcal{B}_0$, we take the derivative versus time of G. Since $p_1\Lambda = \mu S^* + f(I^*)S^* - \omega V^*$, we have

$$\begin{aligned}
\dot{G}_1 = &\ (\mathscr{K}_1 + \frac{\alpha}{\mu+\alpha}\mathscr{K}_2)(1-\frac{S^*}{S})[\mu(S^*-S) + \omega(V-V^*) + (f(I^*)S^* - f(I)S)] \\
= &\ (\mathscr{K}_1 + \frac{\alpha}{\mu+\alpha}\mathscr{K}_2)[\mu S^*(-h(\frac{S}{S^*}) - h(\frac{S^*}{S})) + \omega V^*(h(\frac{V}{V^*}) - h(\frac{S^*V}{SV^*}) + h(\frac{S^*}{S})) \\
&+ S^* f(I^*)(h(\frac{f(I)}{f(I^*)}) - h(\frac{S^*}{S}) - h(\frac{Sf(I)}{S^*f(I^*)}))].
\end{aligned}$$

Since $(1-p_1)\Lambda = \mu V^* + \rho f(I^*)V^* + \omega V^*$, we have

$$\begin{aligned}
\dot{G}_2 = &\ (\mathscr{K}_1 + \tfrac{\alpha}{\mu+\alpha}\mathscr{K}_2)(1-\frac{V^*}{V})[-(\mu+\omega)(V-V^*) - \rho(f(I)V - f(I^*)V^*)] \\
= &\ (\mathscr{K}_1 + \frac{\alpha}{\mu+\alpha}\mathscr{K}_2)[(\mu+\omega)V^*(-h(\frac{V}{V^*}) - h(\frac{V^*}{V})) \\
&+ \rho V^* f(I^*)(h(\frac{f(I)}{f(I^*)}) - h(\frac{V^*}{V}) - h(\frac{Vf(I)}{V^*f(I^*)}))].
\end{aligned}$$

Further, we have

$$\begin{aligned}
\dot{G}_3 = &\ \int_0^{+\infty} H(a)(1-\frac{e^*(a)}{e(t,a)})\tfrac{\partial e}{\partial t}da = -\int_0^{+\infty} H(a)e^*(a)\frac{\partial}{\partial a}h(\frac{e(t,a)}{e^*(a)})da \\
= &\ H(0)e^*(0)h(\frac{e(t,0)}{e^*(0)}) - \int_0^{+\infty}(\delta(a) + \tfrac{\alpha}{\mu+\alpha}\sigma(a))e^*(a)h(\frac{e(t,a)}{e^*(a)})da \\
= &\ H(0)f(I^*)S^*(h(\frac{f(I)S}{f(I^*)S^*}) - h(\frac{e^*(0)f(I)S}{e(t,0)f(I^*)S^*})) \\
&- \int_0^{+\infty}(\delta(a) + \tfrac{\alpha}{\mu+\alpha}\sigma(a))e^*(a)h(\frac{e(t,a)}{e^*(a)})da \\
&+ H(0)\rho f(I^*)V^*(h(\frac{f(I)V}{f(I^*)V^*}) - h(\frac{e^*(0)f(I)V}{e(t,0)f(I^*)V^*})).
\end{aligned}$$

Since $\gamma + \mu_I = \frac{1}{I^*}(\int_0^{+\infty}\delta(a)e^*(a)da + \alpha R^*)$, we have

$$\begin{aligned}
\dot{G}_4 = &\ \int_0^{+\infty}\delta(a)e^*(a)(\frac{e(t,a)}{e^*(a)} - \frac{I}{I^*} - \frac{e(t,a)I^*}{e^*(a)I} + 1)da + \alpha R^*(\frac{R}{R^*} - \frac{I}{I^*} - \frac{I^*R}{IR^*} + 1) \\
= &\ \int_0^{+\infty}\delta(a)e^*(a)(h(\frac{e(t,a)}{e^*(a)}) - h(\frac{I}{I^*}) - h(\frac{e(t,a)I^*}{e^*(a)I}))da + \alpha R^*(h(\frac{R}{R^*}) - h(\frac{I}{I^*}) - h(\frac{I^*R}{R^*I})).
\end{aligned}$$

Since $\mu+\alpha=\frac{1}{R^*}(\int_0^{+\infty}\sigma(a)e^*(a)da+\gamma\eta I^*)$, we have

$$\begin{aligned}
\dot{G}_5 = &\frac{\alpha}{\mu+\alpha}\int_0^{+\infty}\sigma(a)e^*(a)(\frac{e(t,a)}{e^*(a)}-\frac{R}{R^*}-\frac{e(t,a)R^*}{e^*(a)R}+1)da \\
&+\frac{\alpha}{\mu+\alpha}\gamma\eta I^*(\frac{I}{I^*}-\frac{R}{R^*}-\frac{R^*I}{RI^*}+1) \\
= &\frac{\alpha}{\mu+\alpha}\int_0^{+\infty}\sigma(a)e^*(a)(h(\frac{e(t,a)}{e^*(a)})-h(\frac{R}{R^*})-h(\frac{e(t,a)R^*}{e^*(a)R}))da \\
&+\frac{\alpha}{\mu+\alpha}\gamma\eta I^*(h(\frac{I}{I^*})-h(\frac{R}{R^*})-h(\frac{IR^*}{I^*R})).
\end{aligned}$$

Thus, we can obtain

$$\begin{aligned}
\dot{G} = &-(\mathscr{K}_1+\frac{\alpha}{\mu+\alpha}\mathscr{K}_2)p_1\Lambda h(\frac{S^*}{S})-(\mathscr{K}_1+\frac{\alpha}{\mu+\alpha}\mathscr{K}_2)\mu S^*h(\frac{S}{S^*}) \\
&-(\mathscr{K}_1+\frac{\alpha}{\mu+\alpha}\mathscr{K}_2)\omega V^*h(\frac{S^*V}{SV^*}) \\
&-(\mathscr{K}_1+\frac{\alpha}{\mu+\alpha}\mathscr{K}_2)\mu V^*h(\frac{V}{V^*})-(\mathscr{K}_1+\frac{\alpha}{\mu+\alpha}\mathscr{K}_2)((\mu+\omega)V^*+\rho f(I^*)V^*)h(\frac{V^*}{V}) \\
&-H(0)S^*f(I^*)h(\frac{e^*(0)Sf(I)}{e(t,0)S^*f(I^*)})-H(0)\rho V^*f(I^*)h(\frac{e^*(0)Vf(I)}{e(t,0)V^*f(I^*)}) \\
&-\int_0^{+\infty}\delta(a)e^*(a)h(\frac{e(t,a)I^*}{e^*(a)I})da-\alpha R^*h(\frac{I^*R}{R^*I})-\frac{\alpha}{\mu+\alpha}\int_0^{+\infty}\sigma(a)e^*(a)h(\frac{e(t,a)R^*}{e^*(a)R})da \\
&-\frac{\alpha}{\mu+\alpha}\gamma\eta I^*h(\frac{IR^*}{I^*R})+(\mathscr{K}_1+\frac{\alpha}{\mu+\alpha}\mathscr{K}_2)e^*(0)(h(\frac{f(I)}{f(I^*)})-h(\frac{I}{I^*})).
\end{aligned}$$

From Proposition A.1 in [26], we know that $h(\frac{f(I)}{f(I^*)})-h(\frac{I}{I^*})\leq 0$. Then, $\frac{dG}{dt}\leq 0$ holds. It follows from the analysis of Theorem 5.6 [27] that $\mathcal{B}_0=\{E^*\}$. Therefore, the global asymptotic stability of E^* is derived. □

5. Parameter Estimation and Sensitivity Analysis

5.1. Parameter Estimation

In this section, we estimate the parameters of system (1) using annual tuberculosis patient data from China collected between 2007 and 2020. After being infected with TB, some individuals may exhibit symptoms of the disease within a few weeks due to their lack of immunity to the bacillus. As time passes, their immune system gradually fights off the bacillus, reducing the likelihood of displaying symptoms and increasing the chances of recovery [34,35]. In the numerical simulation, we use years as the unit with a few weeks being negligible in terms of the time length. Consequently, we establish two monotonic functions to represent $\delta(a)$ and $\sigma(a)$, respectively.

$$\delta(a)=\delta_1e^{-\delta_2a},\quad \sigma(a)=\sigma_1(1-e^{-\sigma_2a}).$$

We also assume that $e_0(a)=e(0)\mu e^{-\mu a}$. Since $f(I)$ in (1) is monotonically increasing and concave down, we choose the following function to represent $f(I)$:

$$f(I)=I(\beta-\frac{\beta_1I}{m_1+I}),\quad \textit{where } \beta>\beta_1.$$

Next, we set the values or intervals of all parameters and initial values:

(1) Based on the National Bureau of the Statistics of China (NBSC) data [36], the average newborn population in China was 16,289,670 persons per year during this period with an average life expectancy was 76.34 years old. Thus, we take $\Lambda=16{,}289{,}670$ and $\mu=1/76.34$. The World Health Organization estimates that approximately one-quarter of the world's population has been infected with TB and about 85 % of people who

develop TB disease can be successfully treated with a 6-month drug regimen. Thus, we take $S(0) = 0.75 * 1{,}314{,}480{,}000$ persons, $\int_0^{+\infty} e(0,a)da = 0.25 * 1{,}314{,}480{,}000$ persons, $\eta = 0.85$. Trollfors et al. [12] suggested that the BCG vaccine exhibits a significant effect on latent tuberculosis infection (LTBI) with an efficacy rate of 59%. Thus, we take $\rho = 0.41$. Guo et al. [2] suggested that the death rate due to TB is 0.0056 per year. Thus, $\mu_I = \mu + 0.0056$ per year. The initial infectious population is $I(0) = 5011912$ persons, and the initial recovered population is $R(0) = 7493719$ persons. Xue et al. [37] suggested that $1 - p_1 = 0.99$ in China.

(2) In [2], The authors adopted the bilinear incidence rate βSI and estimated the coefficient value to be $\beta = 1.15 \times 10^{-10}$. Thus, we take the range of β as $[1 \times 10^{-11}, 1 \times 10^{-10}]$. In order to ensure the non-negativity of $f(I)$, we take the range of β_1 as $[1 \times 10^{-12}, 1 \times 10^{-11}]$. Assuming m_1 is on the same order of magnitude as $I(0)$, we take the range of m_1 as [1,000,000, 2,000,000].

(3) As found by Martinez et al. [13], BCG vaccination at birth only provides significant protection against TB for children under 5 years of age and has little effect on adolescents and adults. In [38], Huang et al. found that the BCG is effective against LTBI for adults of at least 18 years of age (adulthood) when given at birth. We assume that $\omega \in [1/20, 1/5]$.

(4) There is no evidence to show the range of the parameters $\delta_1, \delta_2, \sigma_1$, and σ_2. We assume that the range of these parameters is $[1 \times 10^{-6}, 1]$.

(5) TB treatment generally needs to take 4 to 9 months [10]. But, multidrug-resistant TB treatment takes much longer. Thus, we take the range of γ as [0.2, 2]. In [37], the authors suggested that the range of the relapse rate α is [0.005, 0.025].

(6) Based on the newborn population per year and the protection period of the vaccine, we assume that the range is $V(0) = [1 \times 10^8, 2 \times 10^8]$.

The data on annual tuberculosis patients (Table 2) were obtained from the Chinese Center for Disease Control and Prevention [39].

Table 2. The data of TB cases in China (persons).

Year	2007	2008	2009	2010	2011	2012	2013
Cases	1,163,959	1,169,540	1,076,938	991,350	953,275	951,508	904,434
Year	2014	2015	2016	2017	2018	2019	2020
Cases	889,381	864,015	836,236	835,193	823,342	775,764	670,538

Next, we simulate the following parameters and the initial conditions of system (1)

$$\hat{\Theta} = (\delta_1, \delta_2, \sigma_1, \sigma_2, \omega, \beta, \beta_1, m_1, \alpha, \gamma, V(0)).$$

We represent the number of new tuberculosis patients in the tth year as $P(t, \hat{\Theta})$, which can be expressed as follows:

$$P(t, \hat{\Theta}) = X(t) - X(t-1),$$

where $X(t)$ denotes the cumulative number of patients with TB disease by the tth year. We can derive the expression for $X(t)$ as:

$$\frac{dX(t)}{dt} = \int_0^{+\infty} \delta(a)e(t,a)da + \alpha R(t).$$

Next, we utilize $P(t, \hat{\Theta})$ to simulate China's annual tuberculosis patient data. We use MATLAB 2018b software to estimate $\hat{\Theta}$. Using the Grey Wolf Optimizer (GWO) algorithm, we can estimate the unknown parameters and initial values for model (1), as shown in Table 3. The results of the simulation are presented in Figure 2.

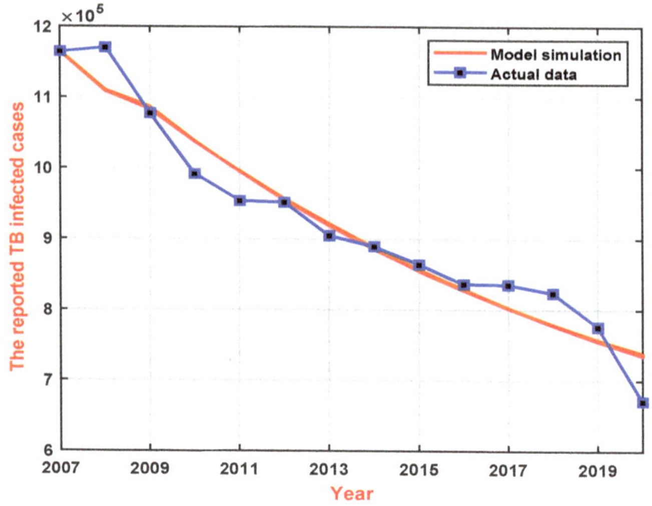

Figure 2. The comparison between the simulation results of the GWO algorithm and the actual data.

Table 3. Unknown parameters and initial values estimated by the GWO algorithm.

Parameters	Value	Source	Parameters	Value	Source
δ_1	0.01518682	Fitting	β_1	$2.8311140 \times 10^{-12}$	Fitting
δ_2	0.047465098	Fitting	m_1	1,805,707	Fitting
σ_1	0.086799875	Fitting	α	0.010890517	Fitting
σ_2	0.000960051	Fitting	γ	0.200034765	Fitting
ω	0.090614519	Fitting	$V(0)$	129,832,691	Fitting
β	4.887090×10^{-11}				

5.2. Sensitivity Analysis

The output of the model (1) is determined by its initial values and parameters. The GWO algorithm is used to estimate some parameters and initial values, which may introduce uncertainty into their selection. Therefore, we need to conduct an uncertainty analysis (UA) in order to determine the reliability of parameter estimates. To ensure the reliability of the estimates through the GWO, we employ the Markov Chain Monte Carlo (MCMC) method with the Delayed Rejection and Adaptive Metropolis (DRAM) algorithm [40]. We estimate the convergence of the Markov chain by using Geweke's Z-scores [41]. The expectations, standard deviations, and confidence intervals of the parameters and initial values are listed in Table 4.

Table 4. The parameters and initial values of the model (1).

Parameters	Mean	Std	95% CI	Gewekes Z-Score
δ_1	0.015224	0.0017461	[0.01521682, 0.015232125]	0.99492
δ_2	0.047357	0.0054654	[0.047333118, 0.047381024]	0.9904
σ_1	0.08693	0.010083	[0.0868855, 0.086973908]	0.98351
σ_2	0.00095903	0.00011069	[0.000958544, 0.000959514]	0.99975
ω	0.090725	0.010535	[0.090678698, 0.09077104]	0.99583
β	4.8889×10^{-11}	5.6062×10^{-12}	$[4.88647 \times 10^{-11}, 4.891385 \times 10^{-11}]$	0.99636
β_1	2.824×10^{-12}	3.2717×10^{-13}	$[2.82254 \times 10^{-12}, 2.825412 \times 10^{-12}]$	0.98896
m_1	1,801,600	209,190	[1,800,674, 1,802,508]	0.99182
α	0.010882	0.0012476	[0.010876, 0.010887]	0.98807
γ	0.19972	0.023108	[0.1996197, 0.199822]	0.9752
$V(0)$	13,038,000	1.5×10^7	[130,309,596, 130,441,079]	0.99426

In this paper, a sensitivity analysis (SA) is used to identify the parameter that has the greatest impact on $\mathcal{R}_0$. We use the partial rank correlation coefficient (PRCC) to analyze the sensitivity, which is based on Latin hypercube sampling (LHS). For the parameters presented in Table 4, we let m_1, $V(0)$ take the expected value, and we assume that other parameters follow normal distributions with the expectations and standard deviations shown in Table 4. Because the parameters are sampled normally, we can observe that the distribution of $\mathcal{R}_0$ is also normal in Figure 3. Figure 3 shows that the average of $\mathcal{R}_0 < 1$. It follows from Theorem 7 that the model 1 is globally asymptotically stable to the disease-free equilibrium state, which suggests that TB transmission will eventually disappear. However, this does not mean that China will achieve the End TB Strategy of the WHO (reducing the incidence of TB by 90 % by 2035 compared to 2015) [1,2]. Thus, China should find the most effective measures to achieve the goal of the WHO. Figure 4 shows the values of PRCC for $\mathcal{R}_0$. It follows from the values of PRCC that $\delta(a)$, β, α, and γ have significant influences on $\mathcal{R}_0$.

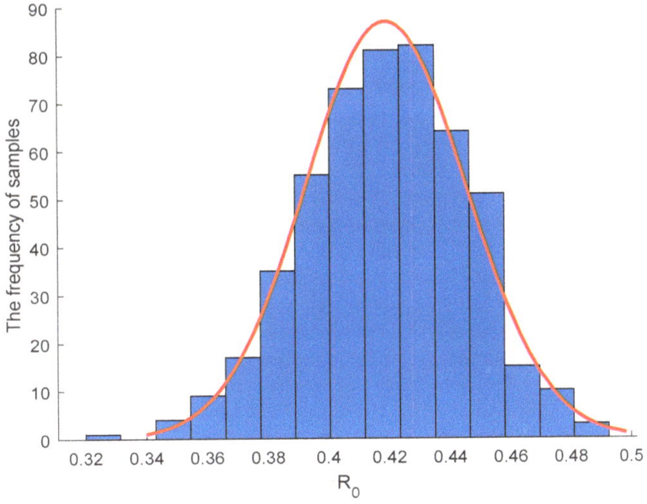

Figure 3. The distribution histogram of $\mathcal{R}_0$.

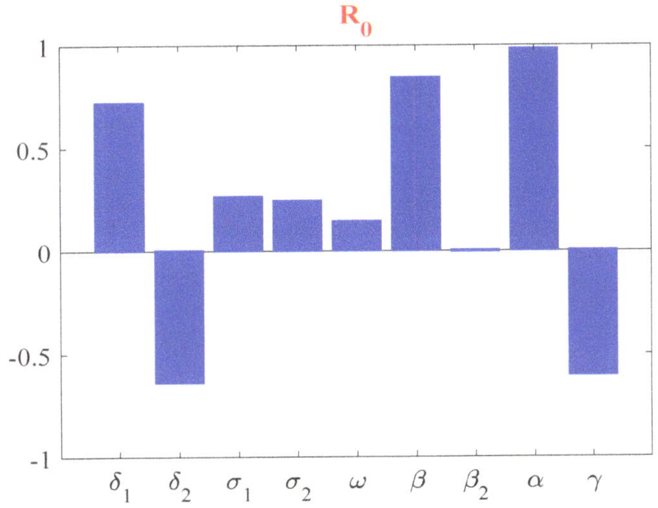

Figure 4. The PRCC values.

6. Discussion and Conclusions

The rate $\delta(a)$ at which latent individuals enter the infectious class has a significant influence on $\mathcal{R}_0$. But, we think it is difficult to implement control measures on the parameter in China's public health at present. The parameter α represents the relapse rate. If the relapse rate α is reduced, we can see a significant reduction in $\mathcal{R}_0$, which will lead to a significant reduction in the number of new cases. Therefore, gaining a better understanding of the causes and risk factors associated with TB relapse is crucial for controlling the spread of TB in China. The TB transmission coefficient β has a significant impact on $\mathcal{R}_0$. To decrease β, effort is needed to prevent susceptible populations from becoming TB latent populations. This includes paying attention to personal protection, accepting TB treatment and prevention education, avoiding unhealthy living habits, and more. The treatment rate γ exerts a significant influence on $\mathcal{R}_0$. To increase γ, efforts are needed to expand the coverage of TB treatment and improve treatment success rates for patients with TB disease. Therefore, implementing these measures could effectively reduce the TB incidence rate in China. However, we also found that the waning rate ω of vaccine-induced protection has no significant effect on $\mathcal{R}_0$. We suggest that this does not necessarily mean that the BCG vaccine has no effect on preventing and controlling TB. The possible reason for this is that we assumed a fixed efficacy rate for the vaccine in the simulation. If the vaccine's effectiveness were improved, it would be possible to significantly reduce the number of new TB cases. Therefore, the development of novel vaccines is also a focal point for the goal of TB control.

In this paper, we present an age-structured mathematical model for TB infection based on the characteristics of TB transmission in order to gain a better understanding of the spread of TB in China. The aim of our research was to propose control strategies to mitigate the risk of TB spread. We defined the basic reproduction number $\mathcal{R}_0$ and demonstrated that it is the key determinant of the global dynamics in our proposed model. Based on annual data on TB in China collected from 2007 to 2020, we estimated the model parameters and calculated the PRCC between these parameters and the basic reproduction number $\mathcal{R}_0$. From the PRCC values, we can see that $\delta(a)$, β, α, and γ have the most important influences on $\mathcal{R}_0$. In light of the actual controllability, we proposed some measures to control the spread of TB in China. There are still some deficiencies in our study. Firstly, we did not take into account the time lag caused by treatment in our modeling, which may pose great difficulties for the dynamic analysis of the model. Secondly, we did not consider drug resistance, as the treatment success rate for patients with drug resistance is significantly lower. Thirdly, the distributions of $\delta(a)$ and $\sigma(a)$ are based on our hypothesis and will be studied further when relevant data become publicly available.

Author Contributions: Z.G. carried out the methodology, investigation, and writing of the draft. L.Z. supervised the research and reviewed the final draft. All authors have read and agreed to the published version of the manuscript.

Funding: This research was supported by Natural Science Foundation of Gansu of China (Grant No. 22JR5RA350, No. 22JR5RA337).

Institutional Review Board Statement: Not applicable.

Informed Consent Statement: Not applicable.

Data Availability Statement: Not applicable.

Acknowledgments: We wish to thank the reviewers, whose careful reading and comments greatly improved the paper.

Conflicts of Interest: The authors declare no conflict of interest.

References

1. WHO. Global Tuberculosis Report 2022. Available online: https://www.who.int/publications/i/item/9789240061729 (accessed on 5 April 2023).
2. Guo, Z.K.; Xiang, H.; Huo, H.F. Analysis of an age-structured tuberculosis model with treatment and relapse. *J. Math. Biol.* **2021**, *82*, 45. [CrossRef] [PubMed]
3. Das, D.K.; Khajanchi, S.; Kar, T. Transmission dynamics of tuberculosis with multiple re-infections. *Chaos Solitons Fractals* **2020**, *130*, 109450. [CrossRef]
4. Choi, S.; Jung, E.; Lee, S.M. Optimal intervention strategy for prevention tuberculosis using a smoking-tuberculosis model. *J. Theor. Biol.* **2015**, *380*, 256–270. [CrossRef] [PubMed]
5. Liu, Q.; Jiang, D. The dynamics of a stochastic vaccinated tuberculosis model with treatment. *Phys. A Stat. Mech. Appl.* **2019**, *527*, 121274. [CrossRef]
6. Ozcaglar, C.; Shabbeer, A.; Vandenberg, S.L.; Yener, B.; Bennett, K.P. Epidemiological models of *Mycobacterium tuberculosis* complex infections. *Math. Biosci.* **2012**, *236*, 77–96. [CrossRef] [PubMed]
7. Choi, S.; Jung, E. Optimal Tuberculosis Prevention and Control Strategy from a Mathematical Model Based on Real Data. *Bull. Math. Biol.* **2014**, *76*, 1566–1589. [CrossRef] [PubMed]
8. Huo, H.F.; Zou, M.X. Modelling effects of treatment at home on tuberculosis transmission dynamics. *Appl. Math. Model.* **2016**, *40*, 9474–9484. [CrossRef]
9. Zhang, W. Analysis of an in-host tuberculosis model for disease control. *Appl. Math. Lett.* **2020**, *99*, 105983. [CrossRef]
10. CDC. Basic TB Facts. Available online: https://www.cdc.gov/tb/topic/basics/default.htm (accessed on 5 April 2023).
11. Burman, W.J.; Bliven, E.E.; Cowan, L.; Bozeman, L.; Nahid, P.; Diem, L.; Vernon, A. Relapse associated with active disease caused by Beijing strain of Mycobacterium tuberculosis. *Emerg. Infect. Dis.* **2009**, *15*, 1061–1067. [CrossRef]
12. Trollfors, B.; Sigurdsson, V.; Dahlgren-Aronsson, A. Prevalence of Latent TB and Effectiveness of BCG Vaccination Against Latent Tuberculosis: An Observational Study. *Int. J. Infect. Dis.* **2021**, *109*, 279–282. [CrossRef]
13. Martinez, L.; Cords, O.; Liu, Q.; Acuna-Villaorduna, C.; Bonnet, M.; Fox, G.J.; Carvalho, A.C.C.; Chan, P.C.; Croda, J.; Hill, P.C.; et al. Infant BCG vaccination and risk of pulmonary and extrapulmonary tuberculosis throughout the life course: A systematic review and individual participant data meta-analysis. *Lancet Glob. Health* **2022**, *10*, e1307–e1316. [CrossRef] [PubMed]
14. Setiabudiawan, T.P.; Reurink, R.K.; Hill, P.C.; Netea, M.G.; van Crevel, R.; Koeken, V.A. Protection against tuberculosis by Bacillus Calmette-Guérin (BCG) vaccination: A historical perspective. *Med* **2022**, *3*, 6–24. [CrossRef] [PubMed]
15. Kerantzas, C.A.; Jacobs, W.R. Origins of Combination Therapy for Tuberculosis: Lessons for Future Antimicrobial Development and Application. *mBio* **2017**, *8*. [CrossRef] [PubMed]
16. Hosseiniporgham, S.; Sechi, L.A. A Review on Mycobacteriophages: From Classification to Applications. *Pathogens* **2022**, *11*, 777. [CrossRef] [PubMed]
17. WHO. Tuberculosis: Multidrug-Resistant Tuberculosis (MDR-TB). Available online: https://www.who.int/news-room/questions-and-answers/item/tuberculosis-multidrug-resistant-tuberculosis-(mdr-tb) (accessed on 29 July 2023).
18. Li, Y.; Liu, X.; Yuan, Y.; Li, J.; Wang, L. Global analysis of tuberculosis dynamical model and optimal control strategies based on case data in the United States. *Appl. Math. Comput.* **2022**, *422*, 126983. [CrossRef]
19. Ren, S. Global stability in a tuberculosis model of imperfect treatment with age-dependent latency and relapse. *Math. Biosci. Eng.* **2017**, *14*, 1337–1360. [CrossRef]
20. Iannelli, M.; Milner, F. *The Basic Approach to Age-Structured Population Dynamics*; Springer Nature: Dordrecht, The Netherlands, 2017.
21. Guo, Z.K.; Huo, H.F.; Xiang, H. Analysis of an age-structured model for HIV-TB co-infection. *Discret. Contin. Dyn. Syst.* **2022**, *27*, 199–228. [CrossRef]
22. Guo, Z.K.; Huo, H.F.; Xiang, H. Global dynamics of an age-structured malaria model with prevention. *Math. Biosci. Eng.* **2019**, *16*, 1625–1653. [CrossRef]
23. Inaba, H.; Sekine, H. A mathematical model for Chagas disease with infection-age-dependent infectivity. *Math. Biosci.* **2004**, *190*, 39–69. [CrossRef]
24. Ghosh, I.; Tiwari, P.K.; Samanta, S.; Elmojtaba, I.M.; Al-Salti, N.; Chattopadhyay, J. A simple SI-type model for HIV/AIDS with media and self-imposed psychological fear. *Math. Biosci.* **2018**, *306*, 160–169. [CrossRef]
25. Li, T.; Zhang, F.; Liu, H.; Chen, Y. Threshold dynamics of an SIRS model with nonlinear incidence rate and transfer from infectious to susceptible. *Appl. Math. Lett.* **2017**, *70*, 52–57. [CrossRef]
26. Sigdel, R.P.; McCluskey, C.C. Global stability for an SEI model of infectious disease with immigration. *Appl. Math. Comput.* **2014**, *243*, 684–689. [CrossRef]
27. Wang, L.; Liu, Z.; Zhang, X. Global dynamics for an age-structured epidemic model with media impact and incomplete vaccination. *Nonlinear Anal. Real World Appl.* **2016**, *32*, 136–158. [CrossRef]
28. Chen, Y.; Zou, S.; Yang, J. Global analysis of an SIR epidemic model with infection age and saturated incidence. *Nonlinear Anal. Real World Appl.* **2016**, *30*, 16–31. [CrossRef]
29. Smith, H.L.; Thieme, H.R. *Dynamical Systems and Population Persistence*; American Mathematical Society: Providence, RI, USA, 2011.

30. Magal, P.; Zhao, X.Q. Global Attractors and Steady States for Uniformly Persistent Dynamical Systems. *SIAM J. Math. Anal.* **2005**, *37*, 251–275. [CrossRef]
31. Hale, J.K.; Waltman, P. Persistence in Infinite-Dimensional Systems. *SIAM J. Math. Anal.* **1989**, *20*, 388–395. [CrossRef]
32. Browne, C.J.; Pilyugin, S.S. Global analysis of age-structured within-host virus model. *Discret. Contin. Dyn. Syst. Ser. B* **2013**, *18*, 1999–2017. [CrossRef]
33. Lasalle, J.P. Some Extensions of Liapunov's Second Method. *Ire Trans. Circuit Theory* **1960**, *7*, 520–527. [CrossRef]
34. World Health Organization. Available online: https://www.who.int/health-topics/tuberculosis#tab=tab_1 (accessed on 18 August 2023).
35. Centers for Disease Control and Prevention. Available online: https://www.cdc.gov/tb/ (accessed on 18 August 2023).
36. National Bureau of Statistics of China. Available online: http://www.stats.gov.cn/ (accessed on 18 August 2023).
37. Xue, L.; Jing, S.; Wang, H. Evaluating Strategies For Tuberculosis to Achieve the Goals of WHO in China: A Seasonal Age-Structured Model Study. *Bull. Math. Biol.* **2022**, *84*, 1–50. [CrossRef]
38. Huang, W.; Fang, Z.; Luo, S.; Lin, S.; Xu, L.; Yan, B.; Liu, X.; Xia, L.; Fan, X.; Lu, S. The effect of BCG vaccination and risk factors for latent tuberculosis infection among college freshmen in China. *Int. J. Infect. Dis.* **2022**, *122*, 321–326. [CrossRef]
39. Chinese Center for Disease Control and Prevention. Available online: http://www.chinacdc.cn/ (accessed on 18 August 2023).
40. Haario, H.; Laine, M.; Mira, A.; Saksman, E. DRAM: Efficient adaptive MCMC. *Stat. Comput.* **2006**, *16*, 339–354. [CrossRef]
41. MCMC Toolbox for Matlab. Available online: https://mjlaine.github.io/mcmcstat/index.html#org0701d35 (accessed on 18 August 2023).

axioms

MDPI

Article

A Proof of Chaos for a Seasonally Perturbed Version of Goodwin Growth Cycle Model: Linear and Nonlinear Formulations

Marina Pireddu

Department of Mathematics and Its Applications, University of Milano—Bicocca, U5 Building, Via R. Cozzi 55, 20125 Milano, Italy; marina.pireddu@unimib.it

Abstract: We show the existence of complex dynamics for a seasonally perturbed version of the Goodwin growth cycle model, both in its original formulation and for a modified formulation, encompassing nonlinear expressions of the real wage bargaining function and of the investment function. The need to deal with a modified formulation of the Goodwin model is connected with the economically sensible position of orbits, which have to lie in the unit square, in contrast to what occurs in the model's original formulation. In proving the existence of chaos, we follow the seminal idea by Goodwin of studying forced models in economics. Namely, the original and the modified formulations of Goodwin model are described by Hamiltonian systems, characterized by the presence of a nonisochronous center, and the seasonal variation of the parameter, representing the ratio between capital and output, which is common to both frameworks, is empirically grounded. Hence, exploiting the periodic dependence on time of that model parameter we enter the framework of Linked Twist Maps. The topological results valid in this context allow us to prove that the Poincaré map, associated with the considered systems, is chaotic, focusing on sets that lie in the unit square, and also when dealing with the original version of the Goodwin model. Accordingly, the trademark features of chaos follow, such as sensitive dependence on initial conditions and positive topological entropy.

Keywords: Goodwin growth cycle model; nonisochronous center; parameter seasonal perturbation; linked twist maps; chaotic dynamics

MSC: 34C28; 91B55

Citation: Pireddu, M. A Proof of Chaos for a Seasonally Perturbed Version of Goodwin Growth Cycle Model: Linear and Nonlinear Formulations. *Axioms* **2023**, *12*, 344. https://doi.org/10.3390/axioms12040344

Academic Editor: Tianwei Zhang

Received: 16 December 2022
Revised: 20 March 2023
Accepted: 23 March 2023
Published: 31 March 2023

1. Introduction

In the last years of his research activity, Goodwin in [1] studied, by means of numerical experiments, what can be obtained by the superimposition of exogenous cycles to cycles endogenously generated by a model, focusing, in particular, on the one by Rössler [2], and concluding that, "*At this point it becomes appropriate to consider the relevance, if any, that these forced models have to economics. The answer is not difficult to find: the economy consists of a very large number of separate and distinct parts, with the result that these parts are subject to continual exogenous forces. To begin with there are the individual national economies increasingly acted on by the movements of the world economy. Then within the economy there are various markets with dynamics particular to them. There is the annual solar cycle with its influence on various markets, for example the agricultural, the touristic, the fuel, and any number of others*" ([1], pp. 121–123).

Taking inspiration from such considerations, we investigate the effect produced on the dynamics of both the original version and a modified formulation of his celebrated growth cycle model (see [3,4]) (The interested reader can find in [5] a survey on the vast literature about the Goodwin model, concerning possible extensions or modifications of the original setting, in [3,4]), by the exogenous periodic variation in one of the model parameters, the seasonal oscillation of which is empirically grounded.

We recall that the Goodwin model represents, in Goodwin's own words, a *"starkly schematized"*, yet incisive, manner, the relationships between capitalists and workers. The need to deal with a modified formulation of the growth cycle model comes from the fact that the original formulation, proposed in [3,4], is not coherent. Indeed, despite the linearity of the real wage bargaining function and of the investment function, the original Goodwin model consists of two nonlinear differential equations of the Lotka–Volterra type, the variables of which are wage share in national income and proportion of labor force employed, which, by definition, cannot exceed unit. On the other hand, orbits of the Goodwin model can lie everywhere in the first quadrant, possibly outside the unit square (Goodwin was aware of this fact and, indeed, in ([3], p. 57), he wrote *"Both u* [wage share in national income] *and v* [employment proportion] *must be positive and v must, by definition, be less than unity; u normally will be also but may, exceptionally, be greater than unity (wages and consumption greater than total product by virtue of losses and disinvestment)"*). Some contributions, such as those by Desai et al. [6] and Harvie et al. [7], were devoted to fixing such an issue in an economically sensible manner. Nonetheless, as shown by Madotto et al. in [8], those works do not solve the problem with the orbit position, since the assumptions made in those two papers are not sufficient to guarantee that orbits lie inside the unit square. Hence, keeping the settings in [6,7] as a starting point, but taking into consideration the results obtained in [8], we deal here with a different reformulation of the Goodwin growth cycle model, which, in its outcomes, is consistent with the meanings of the variables and, in particular, with their admissible ranges. In more detail, in our revisitation of the model, in regard to the real wage bargaining function, we opt for the nonlinear formulation of the Phillips curve proposed by Phillips in [9], and considered, for example, in [6]. For the investment function, we deal with a similar nonlinear formulation, used in the simulative analysis performed in [8], and satisfying the conditions found in that work, so as to ensure that orbits lie in the feasible region. We stress that a nonlinear investment function is also grounded from an economic viewpoint, since, according to [10], followed by [11], it is suitable to encompass the description of a more flexible savings behavior with respect to its linear counterpart. Moreover, the nonlinear version of the Phillips curve [9] was initially considered by Goodwin, too, who then linearized that expression in its well-known model so as to obtain an approximation for it, *"in the interest of lucidity and ease of analysis"* ([3], p. 55) (see also [6], p. 2666). Still, the economic interpretation requires the real wage bargaining function to be increasing in the proportion of labor force employed, while the investment function has to be decreasing in wage share in the national income.

Since the modified formulation of the Goodwin model that we are going to analyze fulfills the conditions in [8], we know that, like the original framework in [3,4], it is still a Hamiltonian system, characterized by the presence of a global, nonisochronous center. Hence, in order to analytically show the dynamic consequences produced on its periodic orbits by the exogenous periodic variation in one of the model parameters, we use the Linked Twist Maps (LTMs, hereinafter) method, recently employed, for instance, in [12] to show the existence of complex dynamics in two evolutionary game theoretical contexts. In particular, we assume that the chosen parameter alternates in a periodic fashion between two different values, e.g., due to a seasonal effect, and this allows us to prove the existence of chaotic dynamics. In order to make our choice empirically grounded, we focus on the parameter that describes the ratio between capital and output, since, keeping the capital level constant, production is no doubt influenced by phenomena that are periodic in nature. We can, for instance, take into consideration the oscillatory behavior during the solar year of the energy price in electricity markets in consequence of the varying demand over the months, as investigated, for example, in [13,14], or the different supply in the agricultural commodity markets in various seasons. We stress, however, that the same assumption about a periodic variation between two different values made on any other model parameter would produce analogous results in terms of generated dynamics, since all parameters influence the center position (We remark that this is a sufficient, albeit not necessary, condition in order to apply the LTMs method whenever we deal with a nonisochronous center, as long as the switching times between the regimes described by the two different parameter values are large enough. As shown, for example, in [12,15], the LTMs technique can be used even when, in consequence of the periodic perturbation of one of the model parameters, the center position does not vary, but the shape of the orbits is modified in a suitable manner).

In order to explain the LTMs technique we need to recall, on the one hand, the original setting of linked twist maps, as studied, for instance, in [16–18], with the corresponding assumptions of smoothness, preservation of Lebesgue measure and monotonicity of the angular speed with respect to the radial coordinate, and, on the other hand, the Stretching Along the Paths (henceforth, SAP) method, developed in the planar case in [19,20] and extended to higher dimensional frameworks in [21]. The SAP method is a topological technique that allows the existence of fixed points, periodic points and chaotic dynamics for continuous maps that expand the arcs along one direction and that are defined on sets homeomorphic to the unit cube in Euclidean spaces. The context of LTMs represents a geometrical framework in which it is possible to employ the SAP method in view of proving, as done, for example, in [22,23], the presence of the trademark features of chaos, such as sensitive dependence on initial conditions and positive topological entropy. In more detail, by a Linked Twist Map we mean the composition of two twist maps, each acting on an annulus, with the two annuli linked together, i.e., crossing in the two-dimensional case along two (or more) planar sets homeomorphic to the unit square, that we call generalized rectangles. Since our approach is purely topological, different from that in [16–18], we just need a twist condition on the boundary of the two linked annuli, similar to what is required in the Poincaré-Birkhoff fixed point theorem.

As explained above, in the present paper, we are going to apply the LTMs method to the original and to the modified formulations of the Goodwin model, that, according to the findings in [8], are Hamiltonian systems with nonisochronous centers, the position of the center varying when the value of one of the model parameters changes. In particular, in both frameworks we act on the ratio between capital and output, since it is sensible to assume that it alternates, due to a seasonal effect, in a periodic fashion between two different levels, one of which may be seen as a perturbation of the other. In this manner, starting either from the original or the modified formulation of the Goodwin model, we obtain two conservative systems, the unperturbed and the perturbed ones, and for each system we can consider an annulus made of energy level lines. Under suitable conditions, the orbits the two annuli are linked together, crossing in two disjoint generalized rectangles. In our settings, the LTMs technique consists of finding two such linked annuli, having intersections containing chaotic sets. Their existence is established by applying the SAP method to the Poincaré map obtained as composition of the Poincaré maps associated with the unperturbed system and the perturbed one. This leads us to work with discrete-time dynamical systems. Like what has happened in other contexts in which the LTMs method was used (see e.g., [12,23]), our results about the existence of complex dynamics are robust with respect to small changes, in L^1 norm, in the coefficients of the considered settings.

We stress that the nonisochronicity of the center plays a crucial role in applying the SAP method, because it implies that the Poincaré maps produce a twist effect on the linked annuli, since the orbits composing them are run with a different speed. In this manner, the generalized rectangles, where the annuli meet, are increasingly deformed with the passing of time. Hence, if the regimes governed by the unperturbed system and by the perturbed one are sufficiently long-lasting, the Poincaré maps transform the generalized rectangles into spiral-like sets, that intersect the same generalized rectangles many times, so that the stretching property required by the SAP method, in order to guarantee the existence of chaotic sets inside the generalized rectangles, is fulfilled.

Regarding the nonisochronicity of the center in the settings that we analyze in this manuscript, for the original formulation proposed in [3,4], we rely on the classical results in [24,25] about the monotonicity of the period of orbits for the Lotka–Volterra predator–prey model with respect to the energy level, since the Goodwin growth cycle model is a special case of that more general framework. For the modified formulation of the Goodwin model that we take into account we instead make reference to the findings obtained in [8] about the period of small and large cycles for a wide class of Hamiltonian systems encompassing the one here considered. More precisely, although an exhaustive analysis of the period of the orbits does not seem to be easy to perform, as discussed in [8], due to the presence of singularities in the model, Madotto et al. proved, on the one hand, that the approximation of the period length of small cycles by means of the period of the linearized system is valid near the equilibrium point and, on the other hand, that the period length of large cycles, approaching the boundary of the feasible set, i.e., the unit square in our context, is arbitrarily high. In view of illustrating, by means of a concrete example, our main result about the existence of complex dynamics for the modified formulation of the Goodwin model, we numerically checked that the periods of the orbits coinciding with the inner and the outer boundaries of the linked annuli, considered in our example, did not coincide, finding, in particular, that the period of the orbits increased with the energy level, in analogy with the classical results in [24,25] for the original formulation of the Goodwin model. This is in agreement with the simulative experiments performed in [8] for the same setting that we investigate. Indeed, using a different notation, the framework that we study has been essentially proposed in (Section 5.3 in [8]) to illustrate the difficulties which arise when trying to prove that the period map connected with the general class of Hamiltonian systems analyzed in that paper is increasing, even if the detailed numerical simulations performed in [8] suggest that the period monotonicity holds true for the system that we consider.

Hence, our contribution is strongly based, on the one hand, on the results contained in [8] about the period of cycles of a suitable class of Hamiltonian systems. On the other hand, our work belongs to the research strand which, starting from [22,23], shows how to use the LTMs method to prove the existence of complex dynamics in various continuous-time settings (see e.g., [26–28]). In more detail, the paper that is closest to ours is [23], where the LTMs method was applied to investigate the dynamical effects produced by a periodic harvesting in the predator–prey model. Namely, the original formulation of the Goodwin growth cycle model is a special case of the Lotka–Volterra predator–prey model. However, our analysis does not coincide with that performed in [23], since, led by the economic argument about the ratio between capital and output explained above, we perturb in a periodic fashion a different parameter with respect to [23], and this produces a dissimilar effect on the center position. Moreover, orbits were run counterclockwise in [23], while they are run clockwise in the present framework, and this aspect also affects the proof of our result about LTMs, in which we need to count the laps completed by suitable paths around the centers.

In addition to the fact that the LTMs method has not been applied to the Goodwin model yet, two further reasons led us to deal with its original formulation in our investigation.

The first one is to provide robustness to the results that we obtain for the model modified formulation, which, indeed, in their general conclusions do not depend on the particular expression of the equations involved, as long as we enter the class of Hamiltonian systems considered in [8]. Only the kind of geometrical configuration for orbits in the phase plane, and, thus, the way to use the LTMs method, could vary according to the formulation of the model equations and on the basis of how they depend on the parameter that is periodically perturbed. We remark that different nonlinear expressions for the real wage bargaining function, and for the investment function, could be sensible, as well. Nonetheless, we chose two formulations that, in addition to having already been considered in the existing literature, satisfy the conditions found in [8], ensuring that the center is nonisochronous and that orbits lie in the feasible region, i.e., the unit square, since the state variables, being wage share in national income and proportion of labor force employed, can neither be negative, nor exceed unity.

The second reason for considering the Goodwin original formulation of the growth cycle model lies in the possibility of showing how to use the LTMs method to prove the existence of chaotic sets lying inside the unit square, despite the previously mentioned issue with the orbit position in the original Goodwin setting. Namely, the chaotic sets are contained in the detected pair of linked annuli, that jointly constitute an invariant set under the action of the Poincaré map obtained as composition of the Poincaré maps associated with the unperturbed system and the perturbed one, since each annulus, being made of periodic orbits, is invariant under the action of the Poincaré map describing the corresponding regime. Choosing linked together annuli contained in the unit square solves the problem. As our illustrative examples show, this can be done even when dealing with parameter configurations analogous to those considered in [6,7]. We stress that the issue with the orbit position did not occur in [23], since the variables in the original Lotka–Volterra model, describing the size of prey and predator populations, are not confined to lying in the unit square.

The remainder of the paper is organized as follows. In Section 2, we recall the original formulation of the Goodwin growth cycle model and we explain how to apply the LTMs method in such a context, highlighting the differences with [23]. In Section 3, we introduce the modified formulation of the Goodwin model, for which we check the existence of chaotic dynamics by means of the LTMs technique. In Section 4, we recall the definitions and the results connected with the LTMs method used in the preceding sections. In Section 5, we conclude. Appendix A contains the mathematical proof of our results, as well as some related comments.

2. The LTMs Method for the Goodwin Model Original Formulation

Following Goodwin's seminal idea in [1], of studying forced models in economics, we apply the Linked Twist Maps (henceforth, LTMs) method, the main features of which are described in Section 4, to his celebrated growth cycle model, in order to show the effects produced on its dynamics by the exogenous periodic variation in one of the model parameters, the seasonal oscillation of which is empirically grounded.

We start by briefly recalling the model's original formulation proposed in [3,4].

Denoting by $u(t) \in [0,1]$ the wage share in national income and by $v(t) \in [0,1]$ the employment proportion, the Goodwin model reads as

$$\begin{cases} u' = u(-(\alpha + \chi) + \rho v) \\ v' = v\left(-(\alpha + \beta) + \frac{1-u}{\sigma}\right) \end{cases} \tag{1}$$

where all parameters are positive and, in particular, α is the exogenous labor productivity growth rate, β is the exogenous labor force growth rate, σ is the capital–output ratio, while χ and ρ characterize the real wage growth rate, which is of the form $-\chi + \rho v$., We stress that, rather than χ, the symbol γ is generally used in the Goodwin model. However, we preferred to save γ to denote paths (see e.g., Definition 2) in agreement with the existing literature on the SAP method. The first equation in (1) derives from Goodwin's linearized version of the Phillips curve [9] in real wages (see the first equation in (9) for its nonlinear formulation). We refer the interested reader to [6] for the derivation of the second equation, based on the assumptions that capitalists reinvest all profits and workers consume all wages, and to [6,7] for further details on the model.

Although state variables, due to their meanings, can neither be negative nor exceed unity, the latter condition is not guaranteed by (1). Namely, those equations describe a conservative system with closed orbits lying everywhere in the first quadrant of $\mathbb{R}^2$ and surrounding the center

$$P = \left(1 - \sigma(\alpha + \beta), \frac{\alpha + \chi}{\rho}\right).$$

We stress that P lies in the unit square when

$$\sigma < \frac{1}{\alpha+\beta}, \qquad \alpha+\chi<\rho. \tag{2}$$

The origin $O = (0,0)$ is an equilibrium, being a saddle. As it is immediate to check, System (1) is a special case of the Lotka–Volterra predator–prey model (see e.g., [29])

$$\begin{cases} x' = x(a-by) \\ y' = y(-c+dx) \end{cases} \tag{3}$$

where $u(t)$ corresponds to $y(t)$ and $v(t)$ corresponds to $x(t)$, even if $x(t)$ and $y(t)$ are not confined to lie in $[0,1]$, since they are non-negative variables describing the size of the prey and of the predator populations, respectively. In particular, as in [23], we focused only on $x(t) > 0$ and $y(t) > 0$, being therein interested in dynamic outcomes characterized by the coexistence between prey and predator. In what follows we confine our analysis to positive values of $u(t)$ and $v(t)$. Specifically, System (3) describes the twofold, at one time beneficial and detrimental, nature of the interactions between predators and preys. Similarly, the Goodwin model schematically represents the involved relationship between capitalists and workers, with the wage share in national income being the predator variable and the employment proportion being the prey.

Both (1) and (3) describe Hamiltonian systems. In the former case, orbit equations are given by

$$E(u,v) = \frac{u}{\sigma} - \left(\frac{1}{\sigma} - \alpha - \beta\right)\log(u) + \rho v - (\alpha+\chi)\log(v) = \ell,$$

for some $\ell \geq \ell_0$, where ℓ_0 is the minimum energy level attained by $E(u,v)$ on the open unit square $(0,1)^2$, i.e., $\ell_0 = E(P)$. Notice that, under (2), the minimum level attained by $E(u,v)$ on $(0,1)^2$ coincides with the minimum level attained on $(0,+\infty)^2$, since we assume that $P \in (0,1)^2$. Moreover, the period of the orbits of System (1) increases with the energy level, due to the possibility of relying on the classical results in [24,25] on the monotonicity of the period of the orbits for the Lotka–Volterra predator–prey model in (3). On the other hand, contrary to what happens with System (3), orbits for System (1) are run clockwise, as the analysis of the phase portrait shows. This is due to the fact that, as observed above, comparing Systems (1) and (3), $u(t)$ corresponds to $y(t)$ and $v(t)$ corresponds to $x(t)$.

While Goodwin investigated, by means of numerical experiments in [1], the dynamic outcomes that can be obtained by superimposing exogenous cycles to cycles endogenously generated by a model, we analytically show the effect produced on the periodic orbits of System (1) by the exogenous periodic variation in one of the model parameters. In view of making our choice empirically grounded, we focus on σ, i.e., the capital–output ratio, since, keeping the capital level constant, production is certainly influenced by phenomena that are periodic in nature. We can, for example, consider the oscillatory behavior during the solar year of the energy price in electricity markets in consequence of the varying demand over the months, or the different supply in the agricultural commodity markets in the various seasons. To fix ideas, we concentrate on the second phenomenon, since it is clear that north of the equator, for instance, in Europe and in the United States, supply in the agricultural commodity markets is larger from April to October than during the remaining part of the year. Hence, for the capital–output ratio σ we can assume a periodic alternation between a higher value, that we call $\sigma^{(I)}$, referring to fall and winter, and a lower value, which may be seen as a perturbation of the former, that we call $\sigma^{(II)}$, referring to spring and summer (In regard to seasonal variations in demand and energy price in electricity markets, according to [14], which refers to [13], "*Cycles and seasonality have for a long time been observed in electricity markets. There are hourly, daily, weekly, and seasonal fluctuations in prices and demand*". See also [30] for a seasonal electricity demand and pricing analysis). We stress, however, that a similar assumption about a periodic variation made on any other model parameter would produce analogous results in terms of generated dynamics, since all parameters affect, in some way, the center position.

Supposing then that the capital–output ratio alternates between $\sigma^{(I)}$, for $t \in [0, T^{(I)})$, and $\sigma^{(II)}$, for $t \in [T^{(I)}, T^{(I)} + T^{(II)})$, with $\sigma^{(I)} > \sigma^{(II)}$, and that the same alternation between the two regimes recurs with T-periodicity, where $T = T^{(I)} + T^{(II)}$, we can assume that we are dealing with a system with periodic coefficients of the form

$$\begin{cases} u' = u(-(\alpha(t) + \chi(t)) + \rho(t)v) \\ v' = v\Big(-(\alpha(t) + \beta(t)) + \frac{1-u}{\sigma(t)}\Big) \end{cases} \tag{4}$$

where

$$k(t) \equiv k, \text{ for } k \in \{\alpha, \beta, \chi, \rho\}, \text{ and } \sigma(t) = \begin{cases} \sigma^{(I)} & \text{for } t \in [0, T^{(I)}) \\ \sigma^{(II)} & \text{for } t \in [T^{(I)}, T) \end{cases} \tag{5}$$

with

$$0 < \sigma^{(II)} < \sigma^{(I)} < \frac{1}{\alpha + \beta}, \qquad \alpha + \chi < \rho \tag{6}$$

as a consequence of (2). The function $\sigma(t)$ is supposed to be extended to the whole real line by T-periodicity.

When the capital–output ratio takes value $\sigma^{(i)}$, and, thus, we are in the regime having dynamics governed by the system that we call (i), the center coincides with $P^{(i)} = \Big(1 - \sigma^{(i)}(\alpha + \beta), \frac{\alpha+\chi}{\rho}\Big)$, for $i \in \{I, II\}$. Notice that, passing from $P^{(I)}$ to $P^{(II)}$, the ordinate of the center does not change, while its abscissa rises. In regard to orbits, they are closed for both Systems (I) and (II), surrounding $P^{(I)}$ and $P^{(II)}$, respectively, and they are run clockwise. In the former case, orbits have equation

$$E^{(I)}(u, v) = \frac{u}{\sigma^{(I)}} - \left(\frac{1}{\sigma^{(I)}} - \alpha - \beta\right)\log(u) + \rho v - (\alpha + \chi)\log(v) = \ell, \tag{7}$$

for some $\ell \geq \ell_0^{(I)}$, while, in the latter case, orbits have equation

$$E^{(II)}(u, v) = \frac{u}{\sigma^{(II)}} - \left(\frac{1}{\sigma^{(II)}} - \alpha - \beta\right)\log(u) + \rho v - (\alpha + \chi)\log(v) = h, \tag{8}$$

for some $h \geq h_0^{(II)}$, where $\ell_0^{(I)}$ and $h_0^{(II)}$ are the minimum energy levels attained by $E^{(I)}(u, v)$ and $E^{(II)}(u, v)$ on $(0, 1)^2$, respectively, i.e., $\ell_0^{(I)} = E^{(I)}(P^{(I)})$ and $h_0^{(II)} = E^{(II)}(P^{(II)})$.

The sets $\Gamma^{(I)}(\ell) = \{(u, v) \in (0, +\infty)^2 : E^{(I)}(u, v) = \ell\}$, for $\ell > \ell_0^{(I)}$, are simple closed curves surrounding $P^{(I)}$, while $\Gamma^{(II)}(h) = \{(u, v) \in (0, +\infty)^2 : E^{(II)}(u, v) = h\}$, for $h > h_0^{(II)}$, are simple closed curves surrounding $P^{(II)}$. We call an *annulus around* $P^{(I)}$ *System* (I) any set $\mathcal{C}^{(I)}(\ell_1, \ell_2) = \{(u, v) \in (0, +\infty)^2 : \ell_1 \leq E^{(I)}(u, v) \leq \ell_2\}$ with $\ell_0^{(I)} < \ell_1 < \ell_2$, having an inner boundary coinciding with $\Gamma^{(I)}(\ell_1)$, and an outer boundary coinciding with $\Gamma^{(I)}(\ell_2)$. Similarly, we call an *annulus around* $P^{(II)}$ *System* (II) any set $\mathcal{C}^{(II)}(h_1, h_2) = \{(u, v) \in (0, +\infty)^2 : h_1 \leq E^{(II)}(u, v) \leq h_2\}$ with $h_0^{(II)} < h_1 < h_2$, having an inner boundary coinciding with $\Gamma^{(II)}(h_1)$ and an outer boundary coinciding with $\Gamma^{(II)}(h_2)$. In particular, we are interested in annuli for Systems (I) and (II) contained in $(0, 1)^2$, due to the meaning of variables u and v. This configuration is achieved by choosing annuli whose outer (and consequently, inner) boundary set lies sufficiently close to the corresponding center, i.e., for low enough values of the energy levels $\ell_2 > \ell_0^{(I)}$ and $h_2 > h_0^{(II)}$ (see, e.g., Figure 1).

In view of providing conditions of the energy levels that ensure that two annuli are linked together, thus, crossing in two disjoint generalized rectangles (see Section 4 for the corresponding definition), let us consider the straight line r joining $P^{(I)}$ and $P^{(II)}$, having equation $v = (\alpha + \chi)/\rho$, the ordering inherited from the horizontal axis, so that, given the points $R = (u_R, v^*)$ and $S = (u_S, v^*)$ belonging to r, and hence with $v^* = (\alpha + \chi)/\rho$, it holds that $R \lhd S$ (resp. $R \unlhd S$) if and only if $u_R < u_S$ (resp. $u_R \leq u_S$). We are now in a position to introduce the following:

Definition 1. *Given the annulus $\mathcal{C}^{(I)}(\ell_1, \ell_2)$ around $P^{(I)}$ and the annulus $\mathcal{C}^{(II)}(h_1, h_2)$ around $P^{(II)}$, we say that they are linked together if*

$$P_{2,-}^{(I)} \lhd P_{1,-}^{(I)} \unlhd P_{2,-}^{(II)} \lhd P_{1,-}^{(II)} \unlhd P_{1,+}^{(I)} \lhd P_{2,+}^{(I)} \unlhd P_{1,+}^{(II)} \lhd P_{2,+}^{(II)}$$

where, for $j \in \{1, 2\}$, $P_{j,-}^{(I)}$ and $P_{j,+}^{(I)}$ denote the intersection points between $\Gamma^{(I)}(\ell_j)$ and the straight line r, with $P_{j,-}^{(I)} \lhd P^{(I)} \lhd P_{j,+}^{(I)}$, and, similarly, $P_{j,-}^{(II)}$ and $P_{j,+}^{(II)}$ denote the intersection points between $\Gamma^{(II)}(h_j)$ and r, with $P_{j,-}^{(II)} \lhd P^{(II)} \lhd P_{j,+}^{(II)}$.

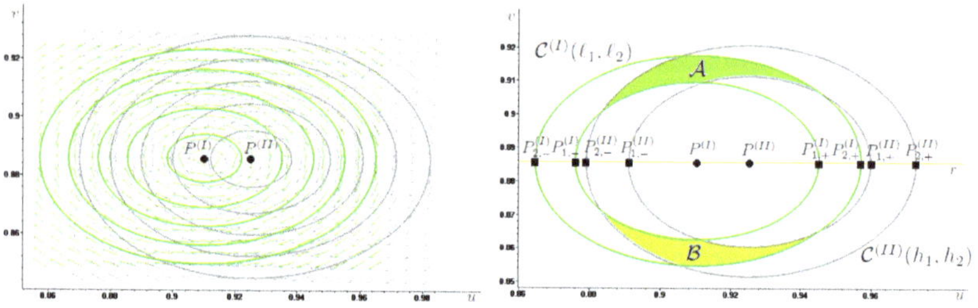

(A) (B)

Figure 1. In (**A**) we draw in green some energy level lines associated with System (I), surrounding $P^{(I)}$, and in gray some energy level lines associated with System (II), surrounding $P^{(II)}$, together with the corresponding phase portrait. In (**B**), we illustrate Definition 1, showing how to obtain two linked together annuli by suitably choosing two level lines for each system. In particular, we call $\mathcal{C}^{(I)}(\ell_1, \ell_2)$, $\mathcal{C}^{(II)}(h_1, h_2)$ the two linked annuli, and $\mathcal{A}$ (colored in dark green), $\mathcal{B}$ (colored in light green) the two disjoint generalized rectangles obtained as the intersection between the two annuli.

We stress that, for $\ell_j > \ell_0^{(I)}$ and $h_j > h_0^{(II)}$, $j \in \{1, 2\}$, the boundary sets $\Gamma^{(I)}(\ell_j)$ and $\Gamma^{(II)}(h_j)$ intersect the straight line r in exactly two points, because $\{(u, v) \in (0, +\infty)^2 : E^{(I)}(u, v) \leq \ell\}$ and $\{(u, v) \in (0, +\infty)^2 : E^{(II)}(u, v) \leq h\}$, coinciding with the lower contour sets of the convex functions $E^{(I)}$ in (7) and $E^{(II)}$ in (8), are star-shaped for all $\ell > \ell_0^{(I)}$ and for every $h > h_0^{(II)}$, respectively. We refer the reader to Figure 1B for a graphical illustration of Definition 1.

We recall that a geometrical configuration analogous to that depicted in Figure 1B, except for the need for orbits to lie in the unit square, was found in [28] (cf. Figure 2 therein), where the LTMs method was applied to a periodically forced asymmetric second order ODE. However, in that case, the abscissa of the center decreased passing from the unperturbed regime to the perturbed one and the centers of the systems corresponding to the two regimes were located on the horizontal axis. Although both dissimilarities would not require the introduction of relevant differences in the statement and proof of the main result in [28] (cf. Theorem 1.2 therein), in adapting them to our framework, we provide a slightly more general (In (Theorem 1.2 in [28]) the special case of Proposition 1 with $m^{(I)} = m \geq 2$ and $m^{(II)} = 1$ considered) version of (Theorem 1.2 in [28]) in Proposition 1, together with a complete proof (contained in the Appendix A) for the reader's convenience.

To achieve such an aim, in addition to exploiting the tools recalled in Section 4 and, in particular, the stretching relation in (16), we need to introduce the Poincaré map Ψ of System (4), which associates with any initial condition (u_0, v_0) belonging to $(0, +\infty)^2$

the position at time T of the solution $\varsigma(\cdot,(u_0,v_0)) = (u(\cdot,(u_0,v_0)), v(\cdot,(u_0,v_0)))$ to (4) starting at time $t = 0$ from (u_0, v_0). In symbols, $\Psi : (0,+\infty)^2 \to (0,+\infty)^2$, $(u_0,v_0) \mapsto \varsigma(T,(u_0,v_0))$. The paper's solutions are meant to be considered in the Carathéodory sense, being absolutely continuous and satisfying the corresponding system for almost every $t \in \mathbb{R}$. We recall that a classical method to show the existence of periodic solutions for systems of first order ODEs with periodic coefficients is based on the search of the periodic points for the associated Poincaré map, under the assumption of uniqueness of the solutions for the Cauchy problems (cf. [31]). Notice that Ψ is a homeomorphism on $(0,+\infty)^2$ and that it may be decomposed as $\Psi = \Psi^{(II)} \circ \Psi^{(I)}$, where $\Psi^{(I)}$ is the Poincaré map associated with System (I) for $t \in [0, T^{(I)}]$ and $\Psi^{(II)}$ is the Poincaré map associated with System (II) for $t \in [0, T^{(II)}]$. Moreover, since every annulus $\mathcal{C}^{(I)}(\ell_1,\ell_2)$ around $P^{(I)}$ is invariant under the action of the map $\Psi^{(I)}$, being composed of the invariant orbits $\Gamma^{(I)}(\ell)$, for $\ell \in [\ell_1,\ell_2]$, and, similarly, since every annulus $\mathcal{C}^{(II)}(h_1,h_2)$ around $P^{(II)}$ is invariant under the action of the map $\Psi^{(II)}$, it holds that every pair of linked together annuli is invariant under the action of the composite map Ψ. In Proposition 1 we denote $\tau^{(I)}(\ell)$, for all $\ell > \ell_0^{(I)}$, the period of $\Gamma^{(I)}(\ell)$, i.e., the time needed by the solution $\varsigma^{(I)}(\cdot,(u_0,v_0))$ to System (I), starting from any $(u_0,v_0) \in \Gamma^{(I)}(\ell)$, to complete one turn around $P^{(I)}$ moving along $\Gamma^{(I)}(\ell)$, and by $\tau^{(II)}(h)$, for all $h > h_0^{(II)}$, the period of $\Gamma^{(II)}(h)$, i.e., the time needed by the solution $\varsigma^{(II)}(\cdot,(u_0,v_0))$ to System (II), starting from any $(u_0,v_0) \in \Gamma^{(II)}(h)$, to complete one turn around $P^{(II)}$ moving along $\Gamma^{(II)}(h)$. Orbits surrounding either $P^{(I)}$ or $P^{(II)}$ are run clockwise and $\tau^{(I)}(\cdot)$ and $\tau^{(II)}(\cdot)$ are monotonically increasing with the energy levels, since both features are fulfilled for System (1), as remarked above. Hence, for any annulus $\mathcal{C}^{(I)}(\ell_1,\ell_2)$ around $P^{(I)}$ it holds that $\tau^{(I)}(\ell_1) < \tau^{(I)}(\ell_2)$, as well as for each annulus $\mathcal{C}^{(II)}(h_1,h_2)$ around $P^{(II)}$ it holds that $\tau^{(II)}(h_1) < \tau^{(II)}(h_2)$.

Our result in regard to System (4) reads as follows:

Proposition 1. *For any choice of the positive parameters α, β, χ, ρ, $\sigma^{(I)}$, $\sigma^{(II)}$ satisfying* (6)*, given the annulus $\mathcal{C}^{(I)}(\ell_1,\ell_2)$ around $P^{(I)}$, for some $\ell_0^{(I)} < \ell_1 < \ell_2$, and the annulus $\mathcal{C}^{(II)}(h_1,h_2)$ around $P^{(II)}$, for some $h_0^{(II)} < h_1 < h_2$, assume that they are linked together, calling $\mathcal{A}$ and $\mathcal{B}$ the connected components of $\mathcal{C}^{(I)}(\ell_1,\ell_2) \cap \mathcal{C}^{(II)}(h_1,h_2)$. Then, for every $m^{(I)} \geq 1$ and $m^{(II)} \geq 1$ with $m = m^{(I)}m^{(II)} \geq 2$ there exist two positive constants $t^{(I)} = t^{(I)}(m^{(I)},\tau^{(I)}(\ell_1),\tau^{(I)}(\ell_2))$ and $t^{(II)} = t^{(II)}(m^{(II)},\tau^{(II)}(h_1),\tau^{(II)}(h_2))$ such that if $T^{(i)} > t^{(i)}$, for $i \in \{I, II\}$, the Poincaré map $\Psi = \Psi^{(II)} \circ \Psi^{(I)}$ of System* (4) *induces chaotic dynamics on m symbols in $\mathcal{A}$ and in $\mathcal{B}$, and all the properties listed in Theorem 1 are fulfilled for Ψ.*

According to Proposition 1, whenever we have two linked together annuli related to Systems (I) and (II), if the switching times between the regimes described by those two systems are large enough, then the Poincaré map $\Psi = \Psi^{(II)} \circ \Psi^{(I)}$ induces chaotic dynamics on $m \geq 2$ symbols in the sets in which the two annuli intersect. As is clear from the proof of Proposition 1 (see the Appendix A), chaotic behavior is generated by the twist effect produced on the linked annuli by the different speeds with which their inner and outer boundary sets are run. Namely, after a long enough time, this twist effect suffices to make the image through $\Psi^{(I)}$ and $\Psi^{(II)}$ of the paths joining the inner and the outer boundary sets of the annuli spiral inside them and cross many times the intersection sets $\mathcal{A}$ and $\mathcal{B}$ between the linked annuli. In this manner, Ψ satisfies the stretching relation described in Theorem 1 and, thus, all properties listed therein hold true for the composite Poincaré map.

We further notice that, under the assumptions in (6), which ensure that the centers of Systems (I) and (II) belong to the open unit square, when applying Proposition 1 to linked annuli, having inner and outer boundary sets lying sufficiently close to the centers, i.e., for low enough values of the energy levels $\ell_2 > \ell_1 > \ell_0^{(I)}$ and $h_2 > h_1 > h_0^{(II)}$, the chaotic invariant sets contained in $\mathcal{A}$ and in $\mathcal{B}$ lie in the open unit square, too. The same is true not only for the chaotic sets, but for a whole pair of linked annuli when the outer boundary sets $\Gamma^{(I)}(\ell_2)$ and $\Gamma^{(II)}(h_2)$ are contained in $(0,1)^2$. Figure 1A shows this happening, where the parameter values are $\alpha = 0.03$, $\beta = 0.01$, $\chi = 0.63$, $\rho = 0.7$, $\sigma = 3$. We stress that such parameter configuration is analogous to that considered in ([7], p. 77). The parameters in Figure 1A are similar to the those in ([6], p. 2668), where the authors set $\alpha = 0.001$, $\beta = 0.001$, $\chi = 0.95$, $\rho = 1$, $\sigma = 3$. In the works mentioned, the symbol γ was used instead of χ. $\alpha = 0.02$, $\beta = 0.01$, $\chi = 0.6$, $\rho = 0.7$, $\sigma^{(I)} = 3$, $\sigma^{(II)} = 2.5$, so that $P^{(I)} = (0.910, 0.886)$ and $P^{(II)} = (0.925, 0.886)$. In particular, as shown in Figure 1B, we obtain two linked together annuli $\mathcal{C}^{(I)}(\ell_1,\ell_2)$ and $\mathcal{C}^{(II)}(h_1,h_2)$, contained in $(0,1)^2$ and crossing in the two disjoint generalized rectangles denoted by $\mathcal{A}$ and $\mathcal{B}$, e.g., for $\ell_1 = 1.0274$, $\ell_2 = 1.0276$, $h_1 = 1.0943$, $h_2 = 1.0946$.

Indeed, despite the previously recalled issue (see (2) and the lines above it) with the orbit position for the original formulation of the Goodwin model in (1), every annulus around $P^{(i)}$ for System (i), with $i \in \{I, II\}$, being made of periodic orbits, is invariant under the action of the Poincaré map $\Psi^{(i)}$. Consequently, each pair of linked annuli jointly constitutes an invariant set under the action of the composite Poincaré map $\Psi = \Psi^{(II)} \circ \Psi^{(I)}$, so that, even for System (1), the LTMs method allows the detection of complex dynamics that are consistent from an economic viewpoint.

Nonetheless, in Section 3 we introduce and analyze a modified formulation of the Goodwin growth cycle model (cf. (9)), whose orbits are all contained in the unit square, since the necessary and sufficient conditions found in [8] are fulfilled.

Before turning to that new framework, we stress that, like (Theorem 1.2 in [28]), Proposition 1 is also robust with respect to small changes, in L^1 norm, in the coefficients of System (4). Namely, from the proof of Proposition 1 it follows that, if $T^{(I)}$ and $T^{(II)}$ satisfy the conditions described in its statement, then, recalling System (4) and the definition of its coefficients in (5), there exists a positive constant ε, such that the same conclusions of Proposition 1 hold true for the system

$$\begin{cases} u' = u(-(\check{\alpha}(t) + \check{\chi}(t)) + \check{\rho}(t)v) \\ v' = v\Big(-(\check{\alpha}(t) + \check{\beta}(t)) + \frac{1-u}{\check{\sigma}(t)}\Big) \end{cases}$$

with $\check{\alpha}$, $\check{\beta}$, $\check{\chi}$, $\check{\rho}$, $\check{\sigma} : \mathbb{R} \to \mathbb{R}$ being T-periodic functions with $T = T^{(I)} + T^{(II)}$, as long as

$$\int_0^T \big|\check{k}(t) - k\big|\, dt < \varepsilon, \quad \text{for } k \in \{\alpha, \beta, \chi, \rho\},$$

and

$$\int_0^T \big|\check{\sigma}(t) - \sigma(t)\big|\, dt = \int_0^{T^{(I)}} \big|\check{\sigma}(t) - \sigma^{(I)}\big|\, dt + \int_{T^{(I)}}^T \big|\check{\sigma}(t) - \sigma^{(II)}\big|\, dt < \varepsilon.$$

Due to the similar arguments that are needed in its proof, Proposition 2, i.e., the main result that we present in Section 3 about the Goodwin model modified formulation, is also robust with respect to small changes in the coefficients of System (13), in L^1 norm.

We conclude the present section by recalling that, in [23], the LTMs method was applied to the Lotka–Volterra System (3) under the assumption of a periodic harvesting, that perturbed the center position, causing an alternation for it between two points. However, since in [23] it was supposed that not only prey, but also predators decrease in number during the harvesting season, then both coordinates of the center change in that framework. Furthermore, orbits of System (3) are run counter-clockwise, rather than clockwise, like happens with the orbits of System (1), and, thus, the definition of the rotation number used in [23] does not coincide with that employed in the proof of Proposition 1 (cf. (A3) and (A4)). Those two differences between [23] and the above described context pushed us to provide a specific, complete presentation in the here analyzed setting of the LTMs method, and in its application to (1) in Proposition 1. Indeed, as recently shown in [12], the way in which the LTMs method can be used depends on the meaning attached to the variables and parameters of the considered model. Moreover, the detailed presentation of the LTMs method provided above is useful in view of Section 3, too, where it suffices for us to focus on the main steps, highlighting the dissimilarities with what we have already explained.

3. The Goodwin Model Modified Formulation

Rather than dealing with the linear expressions for the real wage bargaining function and for the investment function seen in Section 2, we now consider a modified formulation of such a setting, motivated by the issue with the orbit position in the original Goodwin model [3].

In regard to the real wage bargaining function, the most natural choice is given by the Phillips nonlinear specification in [9], even for real, rather than money, wages (cf. the first equation in System (9)). This was indeed what Goodwin initially assumed, before linearizing the Phillips curve so as to obtain the first equation in (1) as an approximation (see [3], p. 55). We recall that the nonlinear formulation of the Phillips curve in [9] was considered by, for example, by Desai et al., in [6], in their attempt to guarantee that the orbits of the growth cycle model lay inside the unit square. On the other hand, as shown by Madotto et al. in [8], the attempt by Desai et al. in [6] was not successful in fixing the problem with the orbit position because of their choice of the investment function (cf. Equation (10) in [6], page 2667), that describes a framework in which capitalists, depending on profitability, do not necessarily invest all profits. We stress that in [8] it is proven that even the modified version of the Goodwin model proposed by Harvie et al. in [7], does not ensure that orbits lie inside the unit square. In order to avoid similar issues, for the investment function we considered a nonlinear formulation (see the second equation in System (9)) satisfying the conditions found in [8], and that are recalled below, so as to guarantee that orbits lay in the feasible region. In more detail, for the investment function we dealt with the formulation used in the simulative analysis performed in (Section 5.3 in [8]). We underline that a nonlinear investment function is grounded also from an economic viewpoint, since, according to [10], followed by [11], it is suitable to describe more flexible savings behavior. Still, the economic interpretation requires the real wage bargaining function to increase in proportion to the labor force employed, while the investment function has decrease in the wage share in national income.

Since the modified formulation of the Goodwin model in (9), that we analyze satisfies the conditions in [8], we know that, like the original framework in [3,4], it is still a Hamiltonian system characterized by the presence of a global, nonisochronous center. Hence, in order to analytically show what the dynamic consequences produced on its periodic orbits by an exogenous periodic variation in one of the model parameters are, we to use the LTMs method. In particular, in view of making our parameter choice empirically grounded, due to the same argument explained in Section 2, we focus on the parameter that describes the ratio between capital and output, assuming that it alternates in a periodic fashion between two different values, due, for example, to a seasonal effect. This allows us to prove the existence of chaotic dynamics for System (13), i.e., the analog of System (4) obtained from (9). Nonetheless, as explained in Section 2, assuming a periodic variation on any other model parameter would lead to analogous conclusions about the system's dynamic behavior, since the center position is influenced by all parameters.

In symbols, $u(t) \in [0,1]$ still denotes the wage share in national income and $v(t) \in [0,1]$ the employment proportion, our modified formulation of the Goodwin model reads as

$$\begin{cases} u' = u\Big(-(\chi+\alpha) + \frac{\rho}{(1-v)^{\delta}}\Big) \\ v' = v\Big(-(\alpha+\beta) + \frac{1}{\sigma}\Big(c - \frac{\eta}{(1-u)^{\mu}}\Big)\Big) \end{cases} \tag{9}$$

where all parameters are positive and, in addition to α, β and σ, that still describe the exogenous labor productivity growth rate, the exogenous labor force growth rate and the capital–output ratio, respectively, we have χ, ρ and δ characterizing the real wage growth rate, which, in agreement with [9], is now in the form $-\chi + \frac{\rho}{(1-v)^{\delta}}$, while c, η and μ, together with σ, characterize the output growth rate, now formulated as $\frac{1}{\sigma}\left(c - \frac{\eta}{(1-u)^{\mu}}\right)$. In particular, as in the model's original version in [3,4], it is assumed that capitalists reinvest all profits and workers consume all wages.

In addition to the origin $O = (0,0)$, which is still a saddle, the other equilibrium for System (9) is given by

$$\widehat{P} = \left(1 - \left(\frac{\eta}{c - \sigma(\alpha+\beta)}\right)^{\frac{1}{\mu}}, 1 - \left(\frac{\rho}{\chi+\alpha}\right)^{\frac{1}{\delta}}\right),$$

that belongs to the open unit square $(0,1)^2$ when

$$\sigma < \frac{c-\eta}{\alpha+\beta}, \quad \rho < \chi+\alpha, \quad \delta \geq 1, \quad \mu \geq 1. \tag{10}$$

In order to ensure that $\widehat{P}$ is a global center for System (9), whose orbits lie in the square $(0,1)^2$, which is again the feasible region, due to the meaning of u and v, and in view of applying someof the results obtained in [8] on the period of orbits, we need to check the conditions described on p. 778 therein for the general system

$$\begin{cases} u' = u\,f(u)\,\psi(v) \\ v' = -v\,g(v)\,\varphi(u) \end{cases} \tag{11}$$

are fulfilled with the considered formulations of the real wage bargaining function and of the investment function, under the parameter assumptions in (10). When adapted to our framework, the conditions in [8] require that $f, g : (0,1) \to (0,+\infty)$ are continuous functions and that $\varphi, \psi : (0,1) \to \mathbb{R}$ are C^1 maps with positive derivative on $(0,1)$, satisfying $\lim_{u\to 0^+} \varphi(u) \in (-\infty,0)$, $\lim_{v\to 0^+} \psi(v) \in (-\infty,0)$, $\lim_{u\to 1^-} \varphi(u) > 0$, $\lim_{v\to 1^-} \psi(v) > 0$. All this is true in our context, since, setting $f(u) = 1$, $\psi(v) = -(\chi+\alpha) + \frac{\rho}{(1-v)^{\delta}}$, $g(v) = 1$, $\varphi(u) = (\alpha+\beta) - \frac{1}{\sigma}\left(c - \frac{\eta}{(1-u)^{\mu}}\right)$, holds that f, g are continuous maps taking positive values only and φ, ψ are C^1 increasing maps in $(0,1)$, satisfying

$$\begin{aligned} &\lim_{u\to 0^+} \varphi(u) = \alpha + \beta - \tfrac{1}{\sigma}(c-\eta) \in (-\infty,0), \\ &\lim_{v\to 0^+} \psi(v) = -(\chi+\alpha) + \rho \in (-\infty,0), \\ &\lim_{u\to 1^-} \varphi(u) = +\infty, \quad \lim_{v\to 1^-} \psi(v) = +\infty \end{aligned}$$

under (10). Moreover, setting

$$A(u) = \int \frac{\varphi(u)}{u f(u)}\,du = \int \frac{1}{u}\left((\alpha+\beta) - \frac{1}{\sigma}\left(c - \frac{\eta}{(1-u)^{\mu}}\right)\right)du$$

and

$$B(v) = \int \frac{\psi(v)}{v g(v)}\,dv = \int \frac{1}{v}\left(-(\chi+\alpha) + \frac{\rho}{(1-v)^{\delta}}\right)dv, \tag{12}$$

it holds that

$$\lim_{u\to 0^+} A(u) = \lim_{u\to 1^-} A(u) = \lim_{v\to 0^+} B(v) = \lim_{v\to 1^-} B(v) = +\infty,$$

as required in [8], too. Hence, System (9) admits $\widehat{E}(u,v) = A(u) + B(v)$ as first integral, having $\widehat{P}$ as minimum point and, according to Theorem 3.1 in [8], its solutions are periodic and describe closed orbits, contained in the unit square, around $\widehat{P}$, that is a global center. In symbols, the orbit equations are then given by $\widehat{E}(u,v) = \ell$ for some $\ell \geq \widehat{\ell}_0$, where $\widehat{\ell}_0 = \widehat{E}(\widehat{P})$. Although an exhaustive analysis of the period of the orbits of System (9) seems not to be easy to perform, as discussed in [8], due to the presence of singularities in the model at $u = v = 1$, Madotto et al. prove useful results about the period of small and large orbits for System (11).

On the one hand, they show that the approximation of the period length of small cycles by means of the period of the linearized system is valid near the equilibrium point (cf. Corollary 5.2 in [8]) and, on the other hand, they prove that the period length of large cycles, approaching the boundary of the feasible set, is arbitrarily high, in the case when f and g are, for instance, $\mathcal{C}^1$ functions on the open interval $(0,1)$, that are continuous in 0, too (cf. Theorem 5.3 in [8]), as happens in our framework. As previously mentioned, in view of its applying to System (9), or more precisely to (13) below, the method of the LTMs in some concrete scenarios (cf. Example 1) is used. Firstly, we perturb the center position by supposing that σ alternates in a periodic fashion between two different levels, due to a seasonal effect, so as to obtain two conservative systems, for which we can find two linked together annuli and suitably choose an annulus made of energy level lines for each system. Then, we numerically check that the periods of the orbits coinciding with the inner and the outer boundaries of the considered linked annuli do not coincide. Actually, all the numerical simulations that we performed suggest the increasing monotonicity of the period of the orbits for System (9) with respect to the energy level, in analogy with the classical results in [24,25] for the original formulation of the Goodwin model, and in agreement with the numerical simulations reported in [8], even if, to the best of our knowledge, a rigorous proof of the period monotonicity for System (9) is not available in the literature. In fact, using a different, more abstract, notation, such a system was, essentially, proposed in (Section 5.3 in [8]) to illustrate the difficulties which arise when trying to prove that the period map connected with the general framework analyzed in that paper, described by (11), was increasing. The detailed numerical investigations performed in [8] suggest that the desired result holds true for the setting we dealt with, even if the period map had a different behavior in the four regions, called quadrants in [8], in which the feasible set $(0,1)^2$ is split by the horizontal and vertical lines passing through the center $\widehat{P}$. In more detail, Figures 3–7 in (Section 5.3 in [8]) show that the period is very long and increases with the energy level in the third quadrant, where both u and v assume low values, while it decreases in the first quadrant, and is not monotone in the second and fourth quadrants.

Let us assume that the capital–output ratio alternates in a T-periodic fashion between the same two positive values considered in Section 2, i.e., $\sigma^{(I)} > \sigma^{(II)}$, for the time intervals $t \in [0, T^{(I)})$ and $t \in [T^{(I)}, T^{(I)} + T^{(II)})$, respectively (Indeed, the values of $\sigma^{(i)}$ and $T^{(i)}$, for $i \in \{I, II\}$, are determined by the economic features of the capital–output ratio, rather than by the model formulation. Nonetheless, considering different values for $\sigma^{(i)}$ and $T^{(i)}$ with respect to Section 2 would not affect the way in which the LTMs can be applied and the conclusions that can be drawn, as long as $0 < \sigma^{(II)} < \sigma^{(I)}$ and $T^{(I)}$, $T^{(II)}$ are large enough) with $T = T^{(I)} + T^{(II)}$, where $\sigma^{(II)}$ may be seen as a perturbation of $\sigma^{(I)}$. We can then suppose that we are dealing with the following system with periodic coefficients

$$\begin{cases} u' = u\Big(-(\chi(t) + \alpha(t)) + \frac{\rho(t)}{(1-v)^{\delta(t)}}\Big) \\ v' = v\Big(-(\alpha(t) + \beta(t)) + \frac{1}{\sigma(t)}\Big(c(t) - \frac{\eta(t)}{(1-u)^{\mu(t)}}\Big)\Big) \end{cases} \tag{13}$$

in which $\kappa(t)$ coincides with κ, for $\kappa \in \{\alpha, \beta, \chi, c, \delta, \eta, \mu, \rho\}$, $\sigma(t)$ is as in (5), assuming that it is extended to the whole real line by T-periodicity, and

$$0 < \sigma^{(II)} < \sigma^{(I)} < \frac{c - \eta}{\alpha + \beta}, \quad \rho < \chi + \alpha, \quad \delta \geq 1, \quad \mu \geq 1 \tag{14}$$

as a consequence of (10).

Calling (Mi), where M stands for "Modified (version of the Goodwin model)", the system that we obtain when the capital–output ratio takes value $\sigma^{(i)}$, for $i \in \{I, II\}$, it is conservative, with the center coinciding with

$$\widehat{P}^{(i)} = \left(1 - \left(\frac{\eta}{c - \sigma^{(i)}(\alpha+\beta)}\right)^{\frac{1}{\mu}}, 1 - \left(\frac{\rho}{\chi+\alpha}\right)^{\frac{1}{\delta}}\right). \tag{15}$$

Similar to what happened in Section 2, passing from $\widehat{P}^{(I)}$ to $\widehat{P}^{(II)}$, the abscissa of the center rises, while its ordinate does not change. The orbits of Systems (MI) and (MII) are closed, surrounding the corresponding center, and a straightforward analysis of the phase portrait shows that they run clockwise (cf. Figure 2A). Setting $A^{(i)}(u) = \int \frac{1}{u}\left((\alpha+\beta) - \frac{1}{\sigma^{(i)}}\left(c - \frac{\eta}{(1-u)^{\mu}}\right)\right)du$, for $i \in \{I, II\}$, and, recalling the definition of $B(v)$ in (12), the orbits of Systems (MI) and (MII) have, respectively, equation $\widehat{E}^{(I)}(u,v) = A^{(I)}(u) + B(v) = \ell$ for some $\ell \geq \widehat{\ell}_0^{(I)} = \widehat{E}^{(I)}(\widehat{P}^{(I)})$ and $\widehat{E}^{(II)}(u,v) = A^{(II)}(u) + B(v) = h$ for some $h \geq \widehat{h}_0^{(II)} = \widehat{E}^{(II)}(\widehat{P}^{(II)})$. The sets $\widehat{\Gamma}^{(I)}(\ell)$ and $\widehat{\Gamma}^{(II)}(h)$ can then be defined like in Section 2 for $\ell > \widehat{\ell}_0^{(I)}$ and $h > \widehat{h}_0^{(II)}$, just replacing $E^{(i)}$ with $\widehat{E}^{(i)}$ for $i \in \{I, II\}$, and they are still simple closed curves surrounding $\widehat{P}^{(I)}$ and $\widehat{P}^{(II)}$, respectively. We can proceed analogously to Section 2 in defining the annuli $\widehat{\mathcal{C}}^{(I)}(\ell_1, \ell_2)$ around $\widehat{P}^{(I)}$, with $\widehat{\ell}_0^{(I)} < \ell_1 < \ell_2$, for System (MI) and $\widehat{\mathcal{C}}^{(II)}(h_1, h_2)$ around $\widehat{P}^{(II)}$, with $\widehat{h}_0^{(II)} < h_1 < h_2$, for System (MII), too. Notice, however, that, differing from Section 2, we do not need to consider energy levels close to $\widehat{\ell}_0^{(I)}$ and $\widehat{h}_0^{(II)}$ to have annuli for Systems (MI) and (MII) contained in $(0,1)^2$, thanks to the above recalled results obtained in [8] (cf. in particular Theorem 3.1 therein). Due to the similar effect produced by a variation in σ on the center position for Systems (1) and (9), the definition of linked together annuli in the new context is analogous to that introduced in Definition 1 as well, being based on the same ordering relation $\lhd$, this time on the straight line $\widehat{r}$ joining $\widehat{P}^{(I)}$ and $\widehat{P}^{(II)}$, which has equation $v = 1 - \left(\frac{\rho}{\chi+\alpha}\right)^{\frac{1}{\delta}}$. See Figure 2B for a graphical illustration of two linked annuli $\widehat{\mathcal{C}}^{(I)}(\ell_1, \ell_2)$ and $\widehat{\mathcal{C}}^{(II)}(h_1, h_2)$ for System (13). We stress that in the present framework their boundary sets $\widehat{\Gamma}^{(I)}(\ell_j)$ and $\widehat{\Gamma}^{(II)}(h_j)$, with $j \in \{1, 2\}$, also intersect the straight line $\widehat{r}$ in exactly two points because the functions $\widehat{E}^{(I)}$ and $\widehat{E}^{(II)}$ are convex. Namely, their second derivative is non-negative under (14) because $(1-z)^{\nu} > (1 - z(\nu+1))$, $\forall z \in [0,1]$, $\forall \nu > 0$, where, in our case, $z \in \{u, v\}$ and $\nu \in \{\mu+1, \delta+1\}$, respectively.

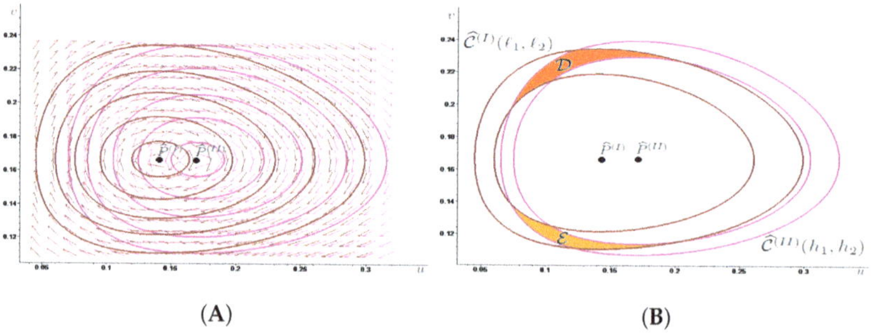

(A) **(B)**

Figure 2. In (**A**) we draw in brown some energy level lines associated with System (MI), around $\widehat{P}^{(I)}$, and in magenta some energy level lines associated with System (MII), around $\widehat{P}^{(II)}$, also showing the corresponding phase portrait. In (**B**), we illustrate two linked together annuli, that we call $\widehat{\mathcal{C}}^{(I)}(\ell_1, \ell_2)$ and $\widehat{\mathcal{C}}^{(II)}(h_1, h_2)$, obtained by suitably choosing two level lines for each system, as well as the two disjoint generalized rectangles $\mathcal{D}$ (colored in dark orange) and $\mathcal{E}$ (colored in light orange) where the annuli meet.

In view of stating our result about System (13) (cf. Proposition 2 below), for which we do not provide a proof, due to its similarity with the verification of Proposition 1, we introduce the Poincaré map $\widehat{\Psi}$ associated with System (13), that can be decomposed as $\widehat{\Psi} = \widehat{\Psi}^{(II)} \circ \widehat{\Psi}^{(I)}$, where $\widehat{\Psi}^{(I)}$ is the Poincaré map associated with System (MI) for $t \in [0, T^{(I)}]$ and $\widehat{\Psi}^{(II)}$ is the Poincaré map associated with System (MII) for $t \in [0, T^{(II)}]$. Notice that every pair of linked together annuli for System (13), being made of energy level lines of Systems (Mi), $i \in \{I, II\}$, are invariant under the action of $\widehat{\Psi}$. We denote by $\widehat{\tau}^{(I)}(\ell)$, for all $\ell > \widehat{\ell}_0^{(I)}$, the period of $\widehat{\Gamma}^{(I)}(\ell)$, and by $\widehat{\tau}^{(II)}(h)$, for all $h > \widehat{h}_0^{(II)}$, the period of $\widehat{\Gamma}^{(II)}(h)$, recalling that the period of an orbit is the time needed by the solution to the considered system, starting from a certain point of the orbit, to complete one turn around the corresponding center, moving around the orbit itself. As discussed above, the increasing monotonicity of $\widehat{\tau}^{(I)}(\,\cdot\,)$ and $\widehat{\tau}^{(II)}(\,\cdot\,)$ with the energy levels is suggested by the many simulative experiments that we performed and by the accurate numerical analysis in (Section 5.3 in [8]), but, to the best of our knowledge, a rigorous proof is not available in the literature. In the absence of a result showing that the period of orbits of Systems (MI) and (MII) always increases with energy levels, in Proposition 2 we assume that, given two linked together annuli for System (13), the period of the orbits composing their inner boundary is smaller than the period of the orbits composing their outer boundary. The main difference between Propositions 1 and 2 lies, indeed, in the necessity to exclude in the latter the fact that the period remains unchanged between the inner and outer boundaries of the linked annuli, since a variation in the periods is required for the Poincaré map to produce a twist effect on the annuli, which in turn allows the LTMs method to be applied. We recall that for System (4) such a variation was granted by the results in [24,25] on the monotonicity of the period of orbits for the Lotka–Volterra predator–prey model.

Proposition 2. *For any choice of the positive parameters $\alpha, \beta, \chi, c, \delta, \eta, \mu, \rho, \widehat{\sigma}^{(I)}, \widehat{\sigma}^{(II)}$ satisfying* (14)*, given the annulus $\widehat{\mathcal{C}}^{(I)}(\ell_1, \ell_2)$ around $\widehat{P}^{(I)}$, for some $\widehat{\ell}_0^{(I)} < \ell_1 < \ell_2$, and the annulus $\widehat{\mathcal{C}}^{(II)}(h_1, h_2)$ around $\widehat{P}^{(II)}$, for some $\widehat{h}_0^{(II)} < h_1 < h_2$, assume that they are linked together, calling $\mathcal{D}$ and $\mathcal{E}$ the connected components of $\widehat{\mathcal{C}}^{(I)}(\ell_1, \ell_2) \cap \widehat{\mathcal{C}}^{(II)}(h_1, h_2)$. Then, if $\widehat{\tau}^{(I)}(\ell_1) < \widehat{\tau}^{(I)}(\ell_2)$, $\widehat{\tau}^{(II)}(h_1) < \widehat{\tau}^{(II)}(h_2)$, it holds that for every $\widehat{m}^{(I)} \geq 1$ and $\widehat{m}^{(II)} \geq 1$ with $\widehat{m} = \widehat{m}^{(I)}\widehat{m}^{(II)} \geq 2$ there exist two positive constants $\widehat{t}^{(I)} = \widehat{t}^{(I)}(\widehat{m}^{(I)}, \widehat{\tau}^{(I)}(\ell_1), \widehat{\tau}^{(I)}(\ell_2))$ and $\widehat{t}^{(II)} = \widehat{t}^{(II)}(\widehat{m}^{(II)}, \widehat{\tau}^{(II)}(h_1), \widehat{\tau}^{(II)}(h_2))$ such that if $T^{(i)} > \widehat{t}^{(i)}$, for $i \in \{I, II\}$, the Poincaré map $\widehat{\Psi} = \widehat{\Psi}^{(II)} \circ \widehat{\Psi}^{(I)}$ of System* (13) *induces chaotic dynamics on $\widehat{m}$ symbols in $\mathcal{D}$ and in $\mathcal{E}$, and all the properties listed in Theorem 1 are fulfilled for $\widehat{\Psi}$.*

We remark that the same conclusions in Proposition 2 would also hold true if the period of the inner boundary were larger (rather than smaller) with respect to the period of the outer boundary for at least one of the linked together annuli (Notice that, in those cases, the position of the boundary periods should be exchanged on the denominator of the fractions defining $\widehat{t}^{(I)}$ and/or $\widehat{t}^{(II)}$, which, respectively, coincide with those for $t^{(I)}$ and $t^{(II)}$ in the proof of Proposition 1 (see Appendix A), when replacing $\tau^{(i)}$ with $\widehat{\tau}^{(i)}$, for $i \in \{I, II\}$.) In Proposition 2 we chose to focus on the framework in which the period of the inner boundary is smaller than the period of the outer boundary for both the linked together annuli, because this is the scenario observed in the numerical experiments in (Section 5.3 in [8]), as well as in all the simulations that we performed. We find the same framework in Example 1, that concludes the present investigation of the modified version of the Goodwin model by illustrating a numerical context, in which Proposition 2 can be applied to show the existence of chaotic dynamics.

Notice that the parameter configuration considered in Example 1, and in its illustration in Figure 2, coincides with that used to draw Figure 1 in Section 2, as well as Figures A1 and A2 in Appendix A, except for the parameters c, δ, η and μ, which were not present in the model's original formulation in (1), and parameters χ and ρ, whose values have now been interchanged, in order to satisfy the second condition in (14), i.e., $\rho < \alpha + \chi$, guarantees that the ordinate of the centers for System (13) lies in the interval $(0, 1)$. Such an hypothesis is incompatible with the last condition in (6), which played the same role in regard to the ordinate of the centers for System (4). Hence, some differences in the parameter values for the original and the modified versions of the Goodwin model need to be introduced, but we avoid adding unnecessary ones. In regard to the new parameters δ and μ, we deal with the same values, i.e., $\delta = 1$ and $\mu = 1.2$, used in the numerical simulations performed in (Section 5.3 in [8]) where, as already mentioned, the authors illustrate the issues which arise when trying to prove that the period map connected with System (9) is increasing, even if numerical evidence of such a conjecture for the above values of δ and μ. is found. We stress that the case $\delta = 1$ was also considered in [6] (cf. p. 2668 therein), although in that framework the parameter μ was not present.

Example 1. *We take* $\alpha = 0.02$, $\beta = 0.01$, $\chi = 0.7$, $\rho = 0.6$, $\sigma^{(I)} = 3$, $\sigma^{(II)} = 2.5$, $c = 0.45$, $\eta = 0.3$, $\delta = 1$, $\mu = 1.2$ *and recall* (15), *System* (MI) *has a center in* $\widehat{P}^{(I)} = (0.141, 0.167)$ *while System* (MII) *has a center in* $\widehat{P}^{(II)} = (0.170, 0.167)$.

As shown in Figure 2B, two linked together annuli $\widehat{\mathcal{C}}^{(I)}(e_1, e_2)$ *and* $\widehat{\mathcal{C}}^{(II)}(h_1, h_2)$ *can be obtained for* $e_1 = 0.8657$, $e_2 = 0.8696$, $h_1 = 0.9865$, $h_2 = 0.9892$, *intersecting in the two disjoint generalized rectangles denoted by* $\mathcal{D}$ *and* $\mathcal{E}$. *Software-assisted computations show that* $\widehat{\tau}^{(I)}(e_1) \approx 111 < \widehat{\tau}^{(I)}(e_2) \approx 114$ *and* $\widehat{\tau}^{(II)}(h_1) \approx 89 < \widehat{\tau}^{(II)}(h_2) \approx 90$. *Hence, Proposition 2 guarantees the existence of chaotic dynamics for the Poincaré map* $\widehat{\Psi} = \widehat{\Psi}^{(II)} \circ \widehat{\Psi}^{(I)}$ *associated with System* (13) *provided that the switching times* $\widehat{T}^{(I)}$ *and* $\widehat{T}^{(II)}$ *are large enough.*

4. Recalling the Linked Twist Maps Method

In the present section we briefly recall the planar results of the Linked Twist Maps (LTMs) method that we used in Sections 2 and 3, referring the interested reader to [22,23] for further details and to [32] for a three-dimensional version.

Although in the literature different assumptions, connected, for example, with measure theory and differential calculus, have been made on linked twist maps (see, e.g., [16–18]), we rely only on topological hypotheses. Indeed, given two annuli crossing along two (or more) planar sets homeomorphic to the unit square, by means of a linked twist map we mean the composition of two twist maps, each acting on one of the two annuli, which are homeomorphisms and that, similar to what is required in the Poincaré-Birkhoff fixed point theorem, produce a twist effect on the boundary sets of the two annuli, leaving them invariant. In the applications of LTMs illustrated in the present paper, we analyze Hamiltonian systems with a nonisochronous center, the position of which varies when modifying a parameter for which it is sensible to assume, due to a seasonal effect, a periodic alternation between two different values, one of which may be seen as a perturbation of the other. Thanks to this alternation, we obtain two conservative systems with a nonisochronous center and for each of them we can consider an annulus composed of energy level lines. Under certain conditions on the orbits, the two annuli cross in two generalized rectangles. The LTMs method consists in proving the presence of chaotic dynamics for the Poincaré map obtained as a composition of the Poincaré maps associated with the unperturbed system and with the perturbed one, which are homeomorphisms, by checking that they satisfy suitable stretching relations (cf. conditions (C_F) and (C_G) in Theorem 1, as well as (16)). We stress that the nonisochronicity of the centers is crucial in the above described procedure, because it implies that the orbits composing the linked annuli run with a different speed, so that the Poincaré maps produce a twist effect on the linked annuli, despite the invariance of closed orbits under the action of the Poincaré maps.

The stretching relation in (16) is the kernel of the Stretching Along the Paths (henceforth, SAP) method, i.e., the topological technique developed in the planar case in [19,20] and extended to the N-dimensional framework in [21], that allows the existence of fixed points, periodic points and chaotic dynamics for continuous maps that expand the arcs along one direction and that are defined on sets homeomorphic to the unit square. We start by introducing its main aspects, in order to be able to state Theorem 1, so that we can then more precisely describe what we mean by chaos.

We call *path* in $\mathbb{R}^2$ any continuous function $\gamma : [0,1] \to \mathbb{R}^2$ and we set $\overline{\gamma} := \gamma([0,1])$. By a *generalized rectangle* we mean a subset $\mathcal{R}$ of $\mathbb{R}^2$ homeomorphic to the unit square $[0,1]^2$, through a homeomorphism $H : \mathbb{R}^2 \supseteq [0,1]^2 \to \mathcal{R} \subseteq \mathbb{R}^2$. We also introduce the *left* and the *right sides* of $\mathcal{R}$, defined respectively as $\mathcal{R}_l^- := H(\{0\} \times [0,1])$ and $\mathcal{R}_r^- := H(\{1\} \times [0,1])$. We call the pair

$$\widetilde{\mathcal{R}} := (\mathcal{R}, \mathcal{R}^-)$$

an *oriented rectangle of* $\mathbb{R}^2$, where $\mathcal{R}^- := \mathcal{R}_l^- \cup \mathcal{R}_r^-$.

The *stretching along the paths* relation for maps between oriented rectangles can then be defined as follows:

Definition 2. *Given $\widetilde{\mathcal{N}} := (\mathcal{N}, \mathcal{N}^-)$ and $\widetilde{\mathcal{O}} := (\mathcal{O}, \mathcal{O}^-)$ oriented rectangles of $\mathbb{R}^2$, let $F : \mathcal{N} \to \mathbb{R}^2$ be a function and $\mathcal{H} \subseteq \mathcal{N}$ be a compact set. We say that $(\mathcal{H}, F)$ stretches $\widetilde{\mathcal{N}}$ to $\widetilde{\mathcal{O}}$ along the paths, and write*

$$(\mathcal{H}, F) : \widetilde{\mathcal{N}} \Longleftrightarrow \widetilde{\mathcal{O}}, \tag{16}$$

if

- *F is continuous on $\mathcal{H}$;*
- *for every path $\gamma : [0,1] \to \mathcal{N}$ with $\gamma(0) \in \mathcal{N}_l^-$ and $\gamma(1) \in \mathcal{N}_r^-$ or with $\gamma(0) \in \mathcal{N}_r^-$ and $\gamma(1) \in \mathcal{N}_l^-$ there exists $[t', t''] \subseteq [0,1]$ such that $\gamma([t', t'']) \subseteq \mathcal{H}$, $F \circ \gamma([t', t'']) \subseteq \mathcal{O}$, with $F(\gamma(t')) \in \mathcal{O}_l^-$ and $F(\gamma(t'')) \in \mathcal{O}_r^-$ or with $F(\gamma(t')) \in \mathcal{O}_r^-$ and $F(\gamma(t'')) \in \mathcal{O}_l^-$.*

We stress that to check the stretching relation in (16) we may need to consider paths $\gamma : [0,1] \to \mathcal{N}$ with $\gamma(0) \in \mathcal{N}_r^-$ and $\gamma(1) \in \mathcal{N}_l^-$; for example, when dealing with the composition of two functions (like in (17) where $\Phi := G \circ F$), since the image through the first map of paths joining the opposite sides of a certain oriented rectangle $\widetilde{\mathcal{M}}$ from left to right can connect the sides of $\mathcal{N}^-$ from right to left through a path that is the starting point of the second function. Nonetheless in the proof of Proposition 1, contained in Appendix A, it suffices for us to focus on paths joining the left and the right sides of the generalized rectangles where the functions start from, since we are not directly dealing with composite mappings. Namely, thanks to Theorem 1 (cf. in particular (C_F) and (C_G) therein), in order to check the existence of chaotic dynamics for the Poincaré map obtained as a composition of the Poincaré maps associated with the unperturbed Hamiltonian system and with the perturbed one, we can deal with the two Poincaré maps separately.

Theorem 1. *Let $F : \mathbb{R}^2 \supseteq D_F \to \mathbb{R}^2$ and $G : \mathbb{R}^2 \supseteq D_G \to \mathbb{R}^2$ be continuous maps defined on the sets D_F and D_G, respectively. Let also $\widetilde{\mathcal{N}} := (\mathcal{N}, \mathcal{N}^-)$ and $\widetilde{\mathcal{O}} := (\mathcal{O}, \mathcal{O}^-)$ be oriented rectangles of $\mathbb{R}^2$. Suppose that the following conditions are satisfied:*

(C_F) there are $\hat{m} \geq 1$ pairwise disjoint compact sets $\mathcal{H}_0, \dots, \mathcal{H}_{\hat{m}-1} \subseteq \mathcal{N} \cap D_F$ such that $(\mathcal{H}_i, F) : \widetilde{\mathcal{N}} \Longleftrightarrow \widetilde{\mathcal{O}}$, for $i = 0, \dots, \hat{m} - 1$;

(C_G) there are $\check{m} \geq 1$ pairwise disjoint compact sets $\mathcal{K}_0, \dots, \mathcal{K}_{\check{m}-1} \subseteq \mathcal{O} \cap D_G$ such that $(\mathcal{K}_j, G) : \widetilde{\mathcal{O}} \Longleftrightarrow \widetilde{\mathcal{N}}$, for $j = 0, \dots, \check{m} - 1$;

(C_m) $m := \hat{m} \cdot \check{m} \geq 2$;

(C_Φ) the composite map $\Phi := G \circ F$ is injective on

$$\mathcal{H}^* := \bigcup_{\substack{i = 0, \dots, \hat{m}-1 \\ j = 0, \dots, \check{m}-1}} \mathcal{H}'_{i,j}, \quad \text{with } \mathcal{H}'_{i,j} := \mathcal{H}_i \cap F^{-1}(\mathcal{K}_j).$$

Then, setting

$$X_\infty := \bigcap_{n=-\infty}^{\infty} \Phi^{-n}(\mathcal{H}^*),$$

there exists a nonempty compact set

$$X \subseteq X_\infty \subseteq \mathcal{H}^*$$

in which the following properties are fulfilled:

(*i*) *X is invariant for Φ (that is, $\Phi(X) = X$);*

(*ii*) *$\Phi \restriction_X$ is semi-conjugate to the two-sided Bernoulli shift on m symbols, i.e., there exists a continuous map π from X onto $\Sigma_m := \{0, \dots, m-1\}^{\mathbb{Z}}$, endowed with the distance*

$$d(\mathbf{s}', \mathbf{s}'') := \sum_{i \in \mathbb{Z}} \frac{|s'_i - s''_i|}{m^{|i|+1}},$$

for $\mathbf{s}' = (s'_i)_{i\in\mathbb{Z}}$ and $\mathbf{s}'' = (s''_i)_{i\in\mathbb{Z}} \in \Sigma_m$, such that the diagram

$$\begin{array}{ccc} X & \xrightarrow{\Phi} & X \\ {\scriptstyle \pi}\downarrow & & \downarrow{\scriptstyle \pi} \\ \Sigma_m & \xrightarrow[\sigma]{} & \Sigma_m \end{array}$$

commutes, i.e., $\pi \circ \Phi = \sigma \circ \pi$, where $\sigma : \Sigma_m \to \Sigma_m$ is the Bernoulli shift defined by $\sigma((s_i)_i) := (s_{i+1})_i$, $\forall i \in \mathbb{Z}$;

(*iii*) *the set $\mathcal{P}$ of the periodic points of $\Phi \restriction_{X_\infty}$ is dense in X and the preimage $\pi^{-1}(\mathbf{s}) \subseteq X$ of every k-periodic sequence $\mathbf{s} = (s_i)_{i\in\mathbb{Z}} \in \Sigma_m$ contains at least one k-periodic point.*

Furthermore, from conclusion (ii) it follows that:

(*iv*)

$$h_{\text{top}}(\Phi) \geq h_{\text{top}}(\Phi \restriction_X) \geq h_{\text{top}}(\sigma) = \log(m),$$

where h_{top} is the topological entropy;

(*v*) *there exists a compact invariant set $\Lambda \subseteq X$, such that $\Phi|_\Lambda$ is semi-conjugate to the two-sided Bernoulli shift on m symbols, topologically transitive and displaying sensitive dependence on initial conditions.*

Proof. The crucial step consists in showing that

$$(\mathcal{H}'_{i,j}, \Phi) : \widetilde{\mathcal{N}} \Longleftrightarrow\!\!\!\!\!\!\rightarrow \widetilde{\mathcal{N}}, \; i = 0, \dots, \widehat{m}-1, \; j = 0, \dots, \check{m}-1. \tag{17}$$

See Theorem 3.1 in [33] for a verification of this property in more general spaces for the case $\widehat{m} = m \geq 2$, $\check{m} = 1$. The condition in (17) is then easy to check (cf. Theorem 3.2 in [33] for a result analogous to ours, which follows as a corollary from Theorem 3.1 therein).

Recalling Definition 2.3 in [33], as a consequence of (17) it holds that Φ *induces chaotic dynamics on m symbols* in the set $\mathcal{N}$. Conclusions (i)–(v) then follow by Theorem 2.2 and by Footnote 4 in [34], where however, the case $m = 2$ is considered. □

In the proof of Theorem 1, we mentioned the concept of a map inducing chaotic dynamics on $m \geq 2$ symbols on a set according to Definition 2.3 in [33]. For brevity's sake, we do not go into detail, but stress that such a notion of chaos for the case $m = 2$ bears a deep resemblance to the concept of chaos in the coin-tossing sense, discussed in [35]; however, being stronger than it. Namely, in addition to the requirement in [35] that every two-sided sequence of two symbols is realized through the iterates of the map, jumping between two disjoint compact subsets, Definition 2.3 in [33] also requires periodic sequences of symbols to be reproduced by periodic orbits of the map. We refer the interested reader to [34] for a comparison with other notions of chaos widely considered in the literature.

Notice that, in light of Definition 2.3 in [33], we can rephrase the statement of Theorem 1 above by saying that, when conditions (C_F), (C_G), (C_m) and (C_Φ) therein are satisfied, the composite map $\Phi = G \circ F$ induces chaotic dynamics on $m \geq 2$ symbols in $\mathcal{N}$, knowing that from this fact all the properties listed in Theorem 1 hold true for $G \circ F$, in regard to the existence of periodic points, too. We indeed used such reformulation of Theorem 1 in Sections 2 and 3 (see, for instance, the statement of Propositions 1 and 2) when dealing with the composition of the Poincaré maps associated with unperturbed and with perturbed Hamiltonian systems.

5. Concluding Remarks

In the present work, following the seminal idea by Goodwin, in [1], that studying forced models in economics, obtained superimposing exogenous cycles to cycles endogenously generated by a model, we showed the existence of complex dynamics in both the original version of his celebrated growth cycle model (see [3,4]), and in a modified formulation of it, encompassing nonlinear expressions of the real wage bargaining function and of the investment function, already considered in the literature. In particular, in regard to the real wage bargaining function we dealt with the formulation proposed by Phillips in [9], while for the investment function we used an expression employed in [8]. The need to consider a modified formulation of the Goodwin model was motivated by the observation that its original version does not guarantee that orbits lie in the unit square, as they should, since the state variables are wage share in national income and proportion of labor force employed, which can neither be negative, nor exceed unity. We, however, underline that a nonlinear investment function is also grounded from an economic viewpoint, since it encompasses a description of more flexible savings behavior (cf. [10,11]). Goodwin initially considered the nonlinear version of the Phillips curve in [9], then linearized it so as to obtain an approximation *"in the interest of lucidity and ease of analysis"* ([3], p. 55).

Exploiting, in both the original and the modified settings, the periodic dependence on time of one of the model parameters and the Hamiltonian structure, characterized by the presence of a global nonisochronous center, we proved the presence of chaos for the Poincaré map associated with the considered systems by means of the Linked Twist Maps (LTMs) method, used, for example, in [22,23]. This led us to work with discrete-time dynamical systems. We stress that the obtained results, in their general conclusions, do not depend on the particular expression of the equations involved, as long as the class of Hamiltonian systems, considered in [8], is entered, for which it is therein proven that the center is nonisochronous and that orbits lie in the unit square. Concerning the necessary economic assumptions, we recall that the real wage bargaining function has to increase in proportion to the labor force employed, while the investment function has to decrease in wage share in national income.

Despite the issue with the orbit position in the original Goodwin model, even for that formulation we were able to prove the existence of chaotic sets lying in the unit square, thanks to the features of the LTMs method. Namely, the chaotic sets are located inside the generalized rectangular regions obtained as an intersection of the detected pair of linked annuli, that jointly constitute an invariant set under the action of the composite Poincaré map. Indeed each annulus, being made of periodic orbits, is invariant under the action of the Poincaré map describing the corresponding regime. Choosing linked together annuli contained in the unit square solves the problem. As our illustrative examples showed, this can be done even when dealing with parameter configurations analogous to those considered in [6,7].

The seminal idea by Goodwin in [1] of studying forced models in economics has been recently applied to a three-dimensional setting in [36], where the authors investigated the implications of describing exports as a function of the capital stock in the framework introduced in [37], which extended the original Goodwin model in [3] to an open economy setting that included the balance-of-payments constraint (BoPC) on growth. In more detail, in agreement with Goodwin's insight, in [38], that Schumpeterian innovations requiring investment occur periodically, the authors in [36] added a nonlinear forcing term in the capital accumulation function and, referring to their Figure 5 on p. 266, say that *"In this way, we obtain a scenario in which a non-linear system with a "natural" oscillation frequency interacts with an external "force" resulting in a chaotic attractor, as shown in Figure 5. The interplay between two or more independent frequencies characterizing the dynamics of the system is a well-known route to more complex behaviour"*. It would then be interesting to check whether the LTMs method, or, more generally, the SAP (Stretching Along the Paths) technique, on which the LTMs method is based, could be employed in that setting, too, in order to rigorously prove the existence of complex dynamics.

In regard to three-dimensional applications of the LTMs technique, we recall [32] where, dealing with linked together cylindrical sets, the focus was on a 3D non-Hamiltonian system describing a predator–prey model with a Beddington–DeAngelis functional response in a periodically varying environment. Related to this, we also mention the 3D continuous-time non-Hamiltonian framework representing the Lotka–Volterra model with two predators and one prey in a periodic environment, considered in [39], for which the presence of chaos was shown by means of the SAP technique, without relying on LTMs geometry. Despite such dissimilarity in the employed method, the common starting point in the proofs of chaos for the frameworks analyzed in [32,39] is given by a study of the properties of the classical planar Lotka–Volterra system. Since, as we have seen, the Goodwin growth cycle model in [3,4] is a special case of the predator–prey setting, in view of proving the existence of chaotic phenomena for its 3D extension, proposed in [36], we could try to apply similar arguments to those used in [32,39]. We will investigate this possibility in a future work.

Funding: This research received no external funding.

Data Availability Statement: Data sharing is not applicable to this article. No new data were created or analyzed in this study.

Acknowledgments: Many thanks to Ahmad Naimzada for helpful conversations about the Goodwin model and to Fabio Zanolin for interesting discussions about the state-of-the art in applications of the Linked Twist Maps method.

Conflicts of Interest: The author declares no conflict of interest.

Appendix A. Proof of Proposition 1

Proof of Proposition 1. Given the linked together annuli $\mathcal{C}^{(I)}(\ell_1,\ell_2)$ and $\mathcal{C}^{(II)}(h_1,h_2)$, we call $\mathcal{C}_t^{(I)}(\ell_1,\ell_2)$ (resp. $\mathcal{C}_b^{(I)}(\ell_1,\ell_2)$) the subset of $\mathcal{C}^{(I)}(\ell_1,\ell_2)$ which lies above (resp. below) (Namely, t stands for "top" and b stands for "bottom") the horizontal line r, joining $P^{(I)}$ and $P^{(II)}$; analogously, $\mathcal{C}_t^{(II)}(h_1,h_2)$ (resp. $\mathcal{C}_b^{(II)}(h_1,h_2)$) is the subset of $\mathcal{C}^{(II)}(h_1,h_2)$ which lies above (resp. below) r. In this manner it holds that $\mathcal{C}^{(I)}(\ell_1,\ell_2)=\mathcal{C}_t^{(I)}(\ell_1,\ell_2)\cup\mathcal{C}_b^{(I)}(\ell_1,\ell_2)$ and $\mathcal{C}^{(II)}(h_1,h_2)=\mathcal{C}_t^{(II)}(h_1,h_2)\cup\mathcal{C}_b^{(II)}(h_1,h_2)$. Moreover, we introduce the generalized rectangles $\mathcal{A}:=\mathcal{C}_t^{(I)}(\ell_1,\ell_2)\cap\mathcal{C}_t^{(II)}(h_1,h_2)$ and $\mathcal{B}:=\mathcal{C}_b^{(I)}(\ell_1,\ell_2)\cap\mathcal{C}_b^{(II)}(h_1,h_2)$. Let us fix $m^{(I)}\geq 1$ and $m^{(II)}\geq 1$ such that $m=m^{(I)}m^{(II)}\geq 2$. We are going to show that, if we orientate $\mathcal{A}$ and $\mathcal{B}$ e.g., by setting $\mathcal{A}^-=\mathcal{A}_l^-\cup\mathcal{A}_r^-$ and $\mathcal{B}^-=\mathcal{B}_l^-\cup\mathcal{B}_r^-$, with $\mathcal{A}_l^-:=\mathcal{A}\cap\Gamma^{(I)}(\ell_1)$, $\mathcal{A}_r^-:=\mathcal{A}\cap\Gamma^{(I)}(\ell_2)$, $\mathcal{B}_l^-:=\mathcal{B}\cap\Gamma^{(II)}(h_2)$, $\mathcal{B}_r^-:=\mathcal{B}\cap\Gamma^{(II)}(h_1)$, then there exist $m^{(I)}\geq 1$ pairwise disjoint compact subsets $\mathcal{H}_0,\ldots,\mathcal{H}_{m^{(I)}-1}$ of $\mathcal{A}$ such that

$$(\mathcal{H}_i,\Psi^{(I)}):\widetilde{\mathcal{A}}\Leftrightarrow\!\!\!\!\to\widetilde{\mathcal{B}},\quad i=0,\ldots,m^{(I)}-1 \tag{A1}$$

(cf. Figure A1A for a graphical illustration with $m^{(I)}=1$), as well as $m^{(II)}\geq 1$ pairwise disjoint compact subsets $\mathcal{K}_0,\ldots,\mathcal{K}_{m^{(II)}-1}$ of $\mathcal{B}$ such that

$$(\mathcal{K}_j,\Psi^{(II)}):\widetilde{\mathcal{B}}\Leftrightarrow\!\!\!\!\to\widetilde{\mathcal{A}},\quad j=0,\ldots,m^{(II)}-1 \tag{A2}$$

(see Figure A1B for an illustration with $m^{(II)}=2$). If this is the case, (C_F) and (C_G) in Theorem 1 are fulfilled for the oriented rectangles $\widetilde{\mathcal{A}}:=(\mathcal{A},\mathcal{A}^-)$ and $\widetilde{\mathcal{B}}:=(\mathcal{B},\mathcal{B}^-)$, with $F=\Psi^{(I)}$ and $G=\Psi^{(II)}$. Since $m=m^{(I)}m^{(II)}\geq 2$, and (C_m) in Theorem 1 holds true, too, the Poincaré map $\Psi=\Psi^{(II)}\circ\Psi^{(I)}$ of System (4) induces chaotic dynamics on m symbols in $\mathcal{A}$. Recalling that the Poincaré map Ψ is a homeomorphism on $(0,+\infty)^2$, and, thus, injective and continuous, in particular. on the set $\mathcal{H}^* := \bigcup_{\substack{i=0,\dots,m^{(I)}-1 \\ j=0,\dots,m^{(II)}-1}} \mathcal{H}_i \cap \left(\Psi^{(I)}\right)^{-1}(\mathcal{K}_j)$, also condition (C_Φ) in Theorem 1 is satisfied for $\Phi = \Psi$ and it is then possible to apply Theorem 1 to conclude that all the properties listed therein are fulfilled for Ψ.

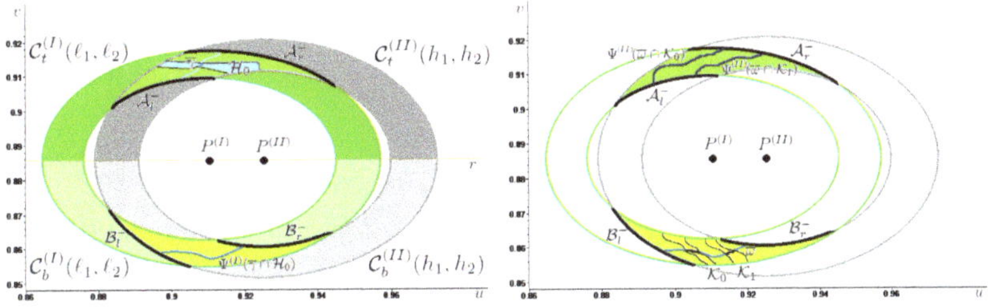

(A) **(B)**

Figure A1. In (**A**), given the linked together annuli $\mathcal{C}^{(I)}(\ell_1,\ell_2)$ and $\mathcal{C}^{(II)}(h_1,h_2)$, we draw in orange the straight line r joining the centers $P^{(I)}$, $P^{(II)}$ and separating the top sets $\mathcal{C}_t^{(I)}(\ell_1,\ell_2)$, $\mathcal{C}_t^{(II)}(h_1,h_2)$, colored, respectively, in green and gray, from the bottom sets $\mathcal{C}_b^{(I)}(\ell_1,\ell_2)$, $\mathcal{C}_b^{(II)}(h_1,h_2)$, colored respectively in light green and light gray. For $\mathcal{A} := \mathcal{C}_t^{(I)}(\ell_1,\ell_2) \cap \mathcal{C}_t^{(II)}(h_1,h_2)$ and $\mathcal{B} := \mathcal{C}_b^{(I)}(\ell_1,\ell_2) \cap \mathcal{C}_b^{(II)}(h_1,h_2)$, suitably oriented by the choice of their left and right sides, we illustrate in (A) the condition (A1) with $m^{(I)} = 1$ and in (**B**) the condition (A2) with $m^{(II)} = 2$.

In view of checking (A1), we introduce a system of polar coordinates $(\rho^{(I)}, \theta^{(I)})$ centered at $P^{(I)}$, so that the solution $\varsigma^{(I)}(t,(u_0,v_0)) = (u(t,(u_0,v_0)), v(t,(u_0,v_0)))$ to System (I) with initial point in $(u_0,v_0) \in (0,+\infty)^2$ can be expressed as $\varsigma^{(I)}(t,(u_0,v_0)) = \|\varsigma^{(I)}(t,(u_0,v_0)) - P^{(I)}\| \,(\cos(\theta^{(I)}(t,(u_0,v_0))), \sin(\theta^{(I)}(t,(u_0,v_0))))$. Moreover, we define the rotation number, describing the normalized angular displacement during the time interval $[0,t] \subseteq [0,T^{(I)}]$ of the solution $\varsigma^{(I)}(t,(u_0,v_0))$ as

$$\mathrm{rot}^{(I)}(t,(u_0,v_0)) := \frac{\theta^{(I)}(0,(u_0,v_0)) - \theta^{(I)}(t,(u_0,v_0))}{2\pi} \tag{A3}$$

in order to count positive the turns around $P^{(I)}$ in the clockwise sense, since orbits for System (I) are run clockwise. Recalling the definition of $\tau^{(I)}(\ell)$, for $\ell > \ell_0^{(I)}$, as a consequence of the star-shape with respect to $P^{(I)}$ of the lower contour sets $\{(u,v) \in (0,+\infty)^2 : E^{(I)} \leq \ell\}$, with $E^{(I)}$ as in (7), we find that the following properties hold true for every $(u_0,v_0) \in \Gamma^{(I)}(\ell)$, $t \in [0,T^{(I)}]$ and $n \geq 1$. Hence, we have $\mathrm{rot}^{(I)}(t,(u_0,v_0)) \in (n,n+1) \iff t \in (n\,\tau^{(I)}(\ell),(n+1)\,\tau^{(I)}(\ell))$.

$$\begin{aligned}
\mathrm{rot}^{(I)}(t,(u_0,v_0)) < n &\iff t < n\,\tau^{(I)}(\ell) \\
\mathrm{rot}^{(I)}(t,(u_0,v_0)) = n &\iff t = n\,\tau^{(I)}(\ell) \\
\mathrm{rot}^{(I)}(t,(u_0,v_0)) > n &\iff t > n\,\tau^{(I)}(\ell)
\end{aligned}$$

To check (A1), let $\gamma : [0,1] \to \mathcal{A}$ be a generic path with $\gamma(0) \in \mathcal{A}_l^-$, $\gamma(1) \in \mathcal{A}_r^-$. For every $\lambda \in [0,1]$, we consider $\Psi^{(I)}(\gamma(\lambda))$, i.e., the position at time $T^{(I)}$ of the solution $\varsigma^{(I)}(t,\gamma(\lambda))$ to System (I) starting at $t = 0$ from $\gamma(\lambda) \in \mathcal{A}$, together with the corresponding angular coordinate $\theta^{(I)}(T^{(I)},\gamma(\lambda))$. We stress that, due to the continuity of γ and by the continuous dependence of the solutions from the initial data, the function $\lambda \mapsto \theta^{(I)}(T^{(I)},\gamma(\lambda))$ is continuous, too. Moreover, recalling that $\tau^{(I)}(\ell_1) < \tau^{(I)}(\ell_2)$ and $\mathcal{A}_l^- \subset \Gamma^{(I)}(\ell_1)$, $\mathcal{A}_r^- \subset \Gamma^{(I)}(\ell_2)$, we show that if $T^{(I)} > t^{(I)} := \left(m^{(I)} + \frac{7}{2}\right) \frac{\tau^{(I)}(\ell_1)\tau^{(I)}(\ell_2)}{(\tau^{(I)}(\ell_2) - \tau^{(I)}(\ell_1))}$ then $\theta^{(I)}(T^{(I)},\gamma(1)) - \theta^{(I)}(T^{(I)},\gamma(0)) > \left(2m^{(I)} + 1\right)\pi$.

If this is true, there exists $n^* \in \mathbb{N}$ such that $[-2(n^*+i)\pi - \pi, -2(n^*+i)\pi]$ is contained in the interval $\{\theta^{(I)}(T^{(I)}, \gamma(\lambda)) : \lambda \in [0,1]\}$ for $i \in \{0, \dots, m^{(I)} - 1\}$. Thus, by means of the Bolzano theorem, there are $m^{(I)}$pairwise disjoint maximal intervals $[\lambda_i', \lambda_i'']$ of $[0,1]$ such that for $i \in \{0, \dots, m^{(I)} - 1\}$ it holds that $\{\theta^{(I)}(T^{(I)}, \gamma(\lambda)) : \lambda \in [\lambda_i', \lambda_i'']\} \subseteq [-2(n^* + i)\pi - \pi, -2(n^*+i)\pi]$, with $\theta^{(I)}(T^{(I)}, \gamma(\lambda_i')) = -2(n^*+i)\pi - \pi$ and $\theta^{(I)}(T^{(I)}, \gamma(\lambda_i'')) = -2(n^*+i)\pi$. In order to have the stretching relation (A1) satisfied, we then set $\mathcal{H}_i := \{(u_0, v_0) \in \mathcal{A} : \theta^{(I)}(T^{(I)}, (u_0, v_0)) \in [-2(n^*+i)\pi - \pi, -2(n^*+i)\pi]\}$ for $i \in \{0, \dots, m^{(I)} - 1\}$. Indeed, for $i \in \{0, \dots, m^{(I)} - 1\}$, $\mathcal{H}_i$ is a compact set containing $\{\gamma(\lambda)) : \lambda \in [\lambda_i', \lambda_i'']\}$. Moreover, for $i \in \{0, \dots, m^{(I)} - 1\}$ and $\lambda \in [\lambda_i', \lambda_i'']$, it holds that $\gamma(\lambda) \in \mathcal{H}_i$, $\Psi^{(I)}(\gamma(\lambda)) \in \mathcal{C}_b^{(I)}(\ell_1, \ell_2)$ and $E^{(II)}(\Psi^{(II)}(\gamma(\lambda_i'))) \geq h_2$, $E^{(II)}(\Psi^{(II)}(\gamma(\lambda_i''))) \leq h_1$. Hence, there exists an interval $[\lambda_i^*, \lambda_i^{**}] \subseteq [\lambda_i', \lambda_i'']$ such that $\Psi^{(I)}(\gamma(\lambda)) \in \mathcal{B}$ for every $\lambda \in [\lambda_i^*, \lambda_i^{**}]$, and $E^{(II)}(\Psi^{(I)}(\gamma(\lambda_i^*))) = h_2$, $E^{(II)}(\Psi^{(I)}(\gamma(\lambda_i^{**}))) = h_1$. Since $\mathcal{B}_l^- = \mathcal{B} \cap \Gamma^{(II)}(h_2)$, $\mathcal{B}_r^- = \mathcal{B} \cap \Gamma^{(II)}(h_1)$, this means that $\Psi^{(I)}(\gamma(\lambda_i^*)) \in \mathcal{B}_l^-$ and $\Psi^{(I)}(\gamma(\lambda_i^{**})) \in \mathcal{B}_r^-$, concluding the verification of (A1).

We then have to check that, for any path, $\gamma : [0,1] \to \mathcal{A}$ with $\gamma(0) \in \mathcal{A}_l^- = \mathcal{A} \cap \Gamma^{(I)}(\ell_1)$ and $\gamma(1) \in \mathcal{A}_r^- = \mathcal{A} \cap \Gamma^{(I)}(\ell_2)$, it holds that $T^{(I)} > t^{(I)}$ then $\theta^{(I)}(T^{(I)}, \gamma(1)) - \theta^{(I)}(T^{(I)}, \gamma(0)) > \left(2m^{(I)} + 1\right)\pi$. Since $\mathrm{rot}^{(I)}(t, \gamma(0)) \geq \lfloor t/\tau^{(I)}(\ell_1) \rfloor$ and $\mathrm{rot}^{(I)}(t, \gamma(1)) \leq \lceil t/\tau^{(I)}(\ell_2) \rceil$ for every $t > 0$, it follows that $\mathrm{rot}^{(I)}(t, \gamma(0)) - \mathrm{rot}^{(I)}(t, \gamma(1)) \geq \lfloor t/\tau^{(I)}(\ell_1) \rfloor - \lceil t/\tau^{(I)}(\ell_2) \rceil > t \, \frac{\tau^{(I)}(\ell_2) - \tau^{(I)}(\ell_1)}{\tau^{(I)}(\ell_1)\, \tau^{(I)}(\ell_2)} - 2$ for every $t > 0$. Hence, for $T^{(I)} > t^{(I)}$ it holds that

$$
\begin{aligned}
\mathrm{rot}^{(I)}(T^{(I)}, \gamma(0)) - \mathrm{rot}^{(I)}(T^{(I)}, \gamma(1)) &> T^{(I)} \, \frac{\tau^{(I)}(\ell_2) - \tau^{(I)}(\ell_1)}{\tau^{(I)}(\ell_1)\, \tau^{(I)}(\ell_2)} - 2 \\
&> m^{(I)} + \tfrac{7}{2} - 2 = m^{(I)} + \tfrac{3}{2} > m^{(I)} + 1.
\end{aligned}
$$

As a consequence, recalling the definition of $\mathrm{rot}^{(I)}$ given in (A3), we have $\theta^{(I)}(T^{(I)}, \gamma(1)) - \theta^{(I)}(T^{(I)}, \gamma(0)) > 2(m^{(I)} + 1)\pi + \theta^{(I)}(0, \gamma(1)) - \theta^{(I)}(0, \gamma(0))$. Since $\gamma([0,1]) \subset \mathcal{A} := \mathcal{C}_t^{(I)}(\ell_1, \ell_2) \cap \mathcal{C}_t^{(II)}(h_1, h_2)$, it holds that both $\theta^{(I)}(0, \gamma(0))$ and $\theta^{(I)}(0, \gamma(1))$ belong to $[0, \pi]$, and are, thus, $\theta^{(I)}(0, \gamma(1)) - \theta^{(I)}(0, \gamma(0)) > -\pi$. It follows that $\theta^{(I)}(T^{(I)}, \gamma(1)) - \theta^{(I)}(T^{(I)}, \gamma(0)) > (2m^{(I)} + 1)\pi$, as needed.

Let us now turn to the proof of the stretching relation in (A2). Due to its similarity with the verification of (A1), we sketch just the main steps. In this case we consider the image through $\Psi^{(II)}$ of any path $\omega : [0,1] \to \mathcal{B}$ joining $\mathcal{B}_l^-$ with $\mathcal{B}_r^-$ and check that it completely crosses $\mathcal{A}$, from $\mathcal{A}_l^-$ to $\mathcal{A}_r^-$, at least $m^{(II)}$ times when $T^{(II)} > t^{(II)} := \left(m^{(II)} + \frac{7}{2}\right) \frac{\tau^{(II)}(h_1)\tau^{(II)}(h_2)}{(\tau^{(II)}(h_2) - \tau^{(II)}(h_1))}$, recalling that also orbits for System (II) are run clockwise and that $\tau^{(II)}(h_1) < \tau^{(II)}(h_2)$ (see Figure A1B for the case $m^{(II)} = 2$). Introducing a system of polar coordinates $(\rho^{(II)}, \theta^{(II)})$ centered at $P^{(II)}$, we can define the rotation number as

$$
\mathrm{rot}^{(II)}(t, (u_0, v_0)) := \frac{\theta^{(II)}(0, (u_0, v_0)) - \theta^{(II)}(t, (u_0, v_0))}{2\pi} \tag{A4}
$$

describing the normalized angular displacement during the time interval $[0, t] \subseteq [0, T^{(II)}]$ of the solution $\varsigma^{(II)}(t, (u_0, v_0))$ to System (II) with initial point in $(u_0, v_0) \in (0, +\infty)^2$. As happened with the proof of (A1), the key step in the verification of (A2) consists in showing that if $T^{(II)} > t^{(II)}$ then $\theta^{(II)}(T^{(II)}, \omega(1)) - \theta^{(II)}(T^{(II)}, \omega(0)) > \left(2m^{(II)} + 1\right)\pi$. Indeed, using the Bolzano Theorem, we can conclude that there are $m^{(II)} \geq 1$ pairwise disjoint compact subsets $\mathcal{K}_0, \dots, \mathcal{K}_{m^{(II)}-1}$ of $\mathcal{B}$ which satisfy (A2).

Once the validity of (A1) and (A2) is verified, it follows that $\Psi = \Psi^{(II)} \circ \Psi^{(I)}$ induces chaotic dynamics in m symbols in $\mathcal{A}$ by Theorem 1, together with all the properties listed therein.

This concludes the first half of our proof, that is complete when we show that Ψ induces chaotic dynamics on $m = m^{(I)}m^{(II)} \geq 2$ symbols in $\mathcal{B}$, as well. With this aim in mind, we can, for example, orientate $\mathcal{A}$ by setting $\mathcal{A}^{--} = \mathcal{A}_l^{--} \cup \mathcal{A}_r^{--}$, with $\mathcal{A}_l^{--} := \mathcal{A} \cap \Gamma^{(II)}(h_1)$, $\mathcal{A}_r^{--} := \mathcal{A} \cap \Gamma^{(II)}(h_2)$, and $\mathcal{B}$ by setting $\mathcal{B}^{--} = \mathcal{B}_l^{--} \cup \mathcal{B}_r^{--}$, with $\mathcal{B}_l^{--} := \mathcal{B} \cap \Gamma^{(I)}(\ell_1)$, $\mathcal{B}_r^{--} := \mathcal{B} \cap \Gamma^{(I)}(\ell_2)$, and we verify that the image through $\Psi^{(I)}$ of any path joining in $\mathcal{B}$ the sides $\mathcal{B}_l^{--}$ and $\mathcal{B}_r^{--}$ crosses $\mathcal{A}$, from $\mathcal{A}_l^{--}$ to $\mathcal{A}_r^{--}$, at least $m^{(I)}$ times when $T^{(I)} > t^{(I)}$, and then check that the image through $\Psi^{(II)}$ of any path in $\mathcal{A}$ joining $\mathcal{A}_l^{--}$ with $\mathcal{A}_r^{--}$ crosses $\mathcal{B}$, from $\mathcal{B}_l^{--}$ to $\mathcal{B}_r^{--}$, at least $m^{(II)}$ times when $T^{(II)} > t^{(II)}$. Namely, this amounts to show that there exist $m^{(I)} \geq 1$ pairwise disjoint compact subsets $\mathcal{H}'_0, \ldots, \mathcal{H}'_{m^{(I)}-1}$ of $\mathcal{B}$ such that

$$(\mathcal{H}'_i, \Psi^{(I)}) : \widetilde{\widetilde{\mathcal{B}}} \Leftrightarrow\!\!\!\!\rightarrow \widetilde{\widetilde{\mathcal{A}}}, \quad i = 0, \ldots, m^{(I)} - 1, \tag{A5}$$

as well as $m^{(II)} \geq 1$ pairwise disjoint compact subsets $\mathcal{K}'_0, \ldots, \mathcal{K}'_{m^{(II)}-1}$ of $\mathcal{A}$ such that

$$(\mathcal{K}'_j, \Psi^{(II)}) : \widetilde{\widetilde{\mathcal{A}}} \Leftrightarrow\!\!\!\!\rightarrow \widetilde{\widetilde{\mathcal{B}}}, \quad j = 0, \ldots, m^{(II)} - 1, \tag{A6}$$

where we set $\widetilde{\widetilde{\mathcal{B}}} := (\mathcal{B}, \mathcal{B}^{--})$ and $\widetilde{\widetilde{\mathcal{A}}} := (\mathcal{A}, \mathcal{A}^{--})$ (see Figure A2). In such a case, (C_F) and (C_G) in Theorem 1 are fulfilled for the newly introduced oriented rectangles $\widetilde{\widetilde{\mathcal{B}}} := (\mathcal{B}, \mathcal{B}^{--})$, $\widetilde{\widetilde{\mathcal{A}}} := (\mathcal{A}, \mathcal{A}^{--})$ and with $F = \Psi^{(I)}$, $G = \Psi^{(II)}$. Since $m = m^{(I)}m^{(II)} \geq 2$, it is then possible to apply Theorem 1 to conclude that the Poincaré map $\Psi = \Psi^{(II)} \circ \Psi^{(I)}$ of System (4) induces chaotic dynamics on m symbols in $\mathcal{B}$, as well. Moreover, Ψ has all the features listed in Theorem 1, because (C_Φ) therein holds true, as $\Phi = \Psi$ is injective and continuous, in particular on the set $\mathcal{H}'^* := \bigcup_{\substack{i = 0, \ldots, m^{(I)} - 1 \\ j = 0, \ldots, m^{(II)} - 1}} \mathcal{H}'_i \cap \left(\Psi^{(I)}\right)^{-1}(\mathcal{K}'_j)$.

Due to their resemblance to (A1) and (A2), we leave the details in the verification of (A5) and (A6), that allow completion of the proof, to the reader. □

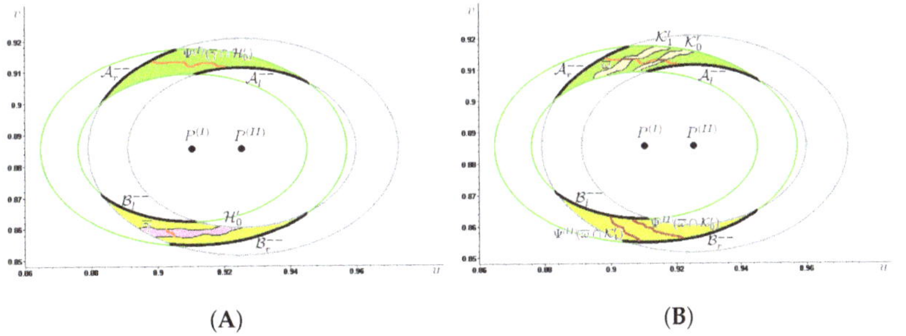

Figure A2. For the sets $\mathcal{A}$ and $\mathcal{B}$, introduced in Figure A1, we now orientate them in a different manner by suitably choosing the left and the right sides, we illustrate in (**A**) the stretching relation (A5) with $m^{(I)} = 1$ and in (**B**) the condition (A6) with $m^{(II)} = 2$.

Focusing on the first half of the proof of Proposition 1, in which we show that Ψ induces chaotic dynamics in $\mathcal{A}$, in Figure A1A we provide a qualitative representation of what happens when the stretching relation in (A1) is fulfilled with $m^{(I)} = 1$, and, in Figure A1B, we illustrate the condition (A2) with $m^{(II)} = 2$. For (A1) to be satisfied with $m^{(I)} = 1$ we need to verify that the image through $\Psi^{(I)}$ of any path γ (in cyan) joining in $\mathcal{A}$ its left and right sides crosses $\mathcal{B}$ once from left to right when $T^{(I)}$ is sufficiently large. This is true in Figure A1A since, calling $\mathcal{H}_0$ the compact subset of $\mathcal{A}$ in pale blue and setting $\overline{\gamma} := \gamma([0,1])$, it holds that $\overline{\gamma} \cap \mathcal{H}_0$ (in blue) is transformed by $\Psi^{(I)}$ into a path (in blue) connecting $\mathcal{B}_l^-$ and $\mathcal{B}_r^-$ in $\mathcal{B}$. To check (A2) with $m^{(II)} = 2$ we need to verify that the image through $\Psi^{(II)}$ of any path ω (in blue) joining in $\mathcal{B}$ its left and right sides crosses $\mathcal{A}$ twice from left to right when $T^{(II)}$ is large enough. This is true in Figure A1B, due to the existence of the pairwise disjoint compact subsets $\mathcal{K}_0, \mathcal{K}_1$ of $\mathcal{B}$ (in yellow) with the property that $\Psi^{(II)}(\overline{\omega} \cap \mathcal{K}_i)$ (in dark blue) connects $\mathcal{A}_l^-$ and $\mathcal{A}_r^-$ in $\mathcal{A}$, for $i \in \{1,2\}$.

Similarly, in regard to the second half of the proof of Proposition 1, in which we show that Ψ induces chaotic dynamics in $\mathcal{B}$, we illustrate, in Figure A2A, condition (A5) with $m^{(I)} = 1$ and, in Figure A2B, condition (A6) with $m^{(II)} = 2$. Notice that $\mathcal{A}$ and $\mathcal{B}$ now need to be oriented in a different manner with respect to Figure A1 to have the stretching relations in (A5) and (A6) satisfied. Indeed, in Figure A2A we draw (in lilac) the compact subset $\mathcal{H}_0'$ of $\mathcal{B}$ with the property that the restriction to it (represented in orange) of any path γ (in light orange) joining $\mathcal{B}_l^{--}$ and $\mathcal{B}_r^{--}$ in $\mathcal{B}$ is transformed by $\Psi^{(I)}$ into a path (in orange) connecting $\mathcal{A}_l^{--}$ and $\mathcal{A}_r^{--}$ in $\mathcal{A}$. In (B) we draw (in beige) the two disjoint compact subsets $\mathcal{K}_0'$, $\mathcal{K}_1'$ of $\mathcal{A}$ such that the restriction to them (represented in dark orange) of any path ω (in orange) joining $\mathcal{A}_l^{--}$ and $\mathcal{A}_r^{--}$ in $\mathcal{A}$ is transformed by $\Psi^{(II)}$ into paths (in dark orange) connecting $\mathcal{B}_l^{--}$ and $\mathcal{B}_r^{--}$ in $\mathcal{B}$.

References

1. Goodwin, R.M. *Chaotic Economic Dynamics*; Oxford University Press: Oxford, UK, 1990.
2. Rössler, O.E. An equation for continuous chaos. *Phys. Lett.* **1976**, *57A*, 397–398. [CrossRef]
3. Goodwin, R.M. A growth cycle. In *Socialism, Capitalism and Economic Growth*; Feinstein, C.H., Ed.; Cambridge University Press: Cambridge, UK, 1967; pp. 54–58.
4. Goodwin, R.M. A growth cycle. In *A Critique of Economic Theory*; Hunt, E.K., Schwartz, J.G., Eds.; Penguin: Harmondsworth, UK, 1972; pp. 442–449.
5. Veneziani, R.; Mohun, S. Structural stability and Goodwin's growth cycle. *Struct. Chang. Econ. Dynam.* **2006**, *17*, 437–451. [CrossRef]
6. Desai, M.; Henry, B.; Mosley, A.; Pemberton, M. A clarification of the Goodwin model of the growth cycle. *J. Econ. Dyn. Control* **2006**, *30*, 2661–2670. [CrossRef]
7. Harvie, D.; Kelmanson, M.A.; Knapp, D.G. A dynamical model of business-cycle asymmetries: Extending Goodwin. *Econ. Issues* **2007**, *12*, 53–92.
8. Madotto, M.; Gaudenzi, M.; Zanolin, F. A generalized approach for the modeling of Goodwin-type cycles. *Adv. Nonlinear Stud.* **2016**, *16*, 775–793. [CrossRef]
9. Phillips, A.W.H. The relationship between unemployment and the rate of change of money wage rates in the United Kingdom, 1861–1957. *Economica* **1958**, *25*, 283–299.
10. Flaschel, P. Some stability properties of Goodwin's growth cycle. A critical elaboration. *Z. Nationalökon.* **1984**, *44*, 63–69. [CrossRef]
11. Zhang, W. Cyclical economic growth—Re-examining the Goodwin model. *Acta Math. Appl. Sin.* **1991**, *7*, 114–120. [CrossRef]
12. Pireddu, M. Chaotic dynamics in the presence of medical malpractice litigation: A topological proof via linked twist maps for two evolutionary game theoretic contexts. *J. Math. Anal. Appl.* **2021**, *501*, 125224. [CrossRef]
13. Alvarez-Ramirez, J.; Escarela-Perez, R.; Espinosa-Perez, G.; Urrea, R. Dynamics of electricity market correlations. *Physica A* **2009**, *388*, 2173–2188. [CrossRef]
14. Arango, S.; Larsen, E. Cycles in deregulated electricity markets: Empirical evidence from two decades. *Energy Policy* **2011**, *39*, 2457–2466. [CrossRef]
15. Pascoletti, A.; Zanolin, F. From the Poincaré-Birkhoff fixed point theorem to linked twist maps: Some applications to planar Hamiltonian systems. In *Differential and Difference Equations with Applications*; Pinelas, S., Chipot, M., Dosla, Z., Eds.; Springer Proceedings in Mathematics & Statistics, 47; Springer: New York, NY, USA, 2013; pp. 197–213.
16. Przytycki, F. Ergodicity of toral linked twist mappings. *Ann. Sci. École Norm. Super.* **1983**, *16*, 345–354. [CrossRef]
17. Przytycki, F. Periodic points of linked twist mappings. *Stud. Math.* **1986**, *83*, 1–18. [CrossRef]
18. Burton, R.; Easton, R.W. Ergodicity of linked twist maps. In *Global Theory of Dynamical Systems, Proceedings of the International Conference Held at Northwestern University, Evanston, IL, USA, 18–22 June 1979*; Lecture Notes in Mathematics, 819; Springer: Berlin, Germany, 1980; pp. 35–49.
19. Papini, D.; Zanolin, F. On the periodic boundary value problem and chaotic-like dynamics for nonlinear Hill's equations. *Adv. Nonlinear Stud.* **2004**, *4*, 71–91. [CrossRef]
20. Papini, D.; Zanolin, F. Fixed points, periodic points, and coin-tossing sequences for mappings defined on two-dimensional cells. *Fixed Point Theory Appl.* **2004**, *2004*, 113–134. [CrossRef]
21. Pireddu, M.; Zanolin, F. Cutting surfaces and applications to periodic points and chaotic-like dynamics. *Topol. Methods Nonlinear Anal.* **2007**, *30*, 279–319; Erratum in *Topol. Methods Nonlinear Anal.* **2009**, *33*, 395.
22. Pascoletti, A.; Zanolin, F. Example of a suspension bridge ODE model exhibiting chaotic dynamics: A topological approach. *J. Math. Anal. Appl.* **2008**, *339*, 1179–1198. [CrossRef]

23. Pireddu, M.; Zanolin, F. Chaotic dynamics in the Volterra predator-prey model via linked twist maps. *Opusc. Math.* **2008**, *28/4*, 567–592.
24. Rothe, F. The periods of the Volterra-Lotka system. *J. Reine Angew. Math.* **1985**, *355*, 129–138.
25. Waldvogel, J. The period in the Lotka-Volterra system is monotonic. *J. Math. Anal. Appl.* **1986**, *114*, 178–184. [CrossRef]
26. Burra, L.; Zanolin, F. Chaotic dynamics in a vertically driven planar pendulum. *Nonlinear Anal.* **2010**, *72*, 1462–1476. [CrossRef]
27. Margheri, A.; Rebelo, C.; Zanolin, F. Chaos in periodically perturbed planar Hamiltonian systems using linked twist maps. *J. Differ. Equ.* **2010**, *249*, 3233–3257. [CrossRef]
28. Pascoletti, A.; Zanolin, F. Chaotic dynamics in periodically forced asymmetric ordinary differential equations. *J. Math. Anal. Appl.* **2009**, *352*, 890–906. [CrossRef]
29. Braun, M. *Differential Equations and Their Applications. An Introduction to Applied Mathematics*, 4th ed.; Texts in Applied Mathematics, 11; Springer: New York, NY, USA, 1993.
30. Lillard, L.A.; Acton, J.P. Seasonal electricity demand and pricing analysis with a variable response model. *Bell J. Econ.* **1981**, *12*, 71–92. [CrossRef]
31. Krasnosel'skiĭ, M.A. *The Operator of Translation along the Trajectories of Differential Equations*; Translations of Mathematical Monographs, 19; American Mathematical Society: Providence, RI, USA, 1968.
32. Ruiz-Herrera, A.; Zanolin, F. An example of chaotic dynamics in 3D systems via stretching along paths. *Ann. Mat. Pura Appl.* **2014**, *193*, 163–185. [CrossRef]
33. Pascoletti, A.; Pireddu, M.; Zanolin, F. Multiple periodic solutions and complex dynamics for second order ODEs via linked twist maps. *Electron. J. Qual. Theory Differ. Equ.* **2008**, *14*, 1–32.
34. Medio, A.; Pireddu, M.; Zanolin, F. Chaotic dynamics for maps in one and two dimensions: A geometrical method and applications to economics. *Int. J. Bifurc. Chaos Appl. Sci. Eng.* **2009**, *19*, 3283–3309. [CrossRef]
35. Kirchgraber, U.; Stoffer, D. On the definition of chaos. *Z. Angew. Math. Mech.* **1989**, *69*, 175–185. [CrossRef]
36. Dávila-Fernández, M.J.; Sordi, S. Path dependence, distributive cycles and export capacity in a BoPC growth model. *Struct. Chang. Econ. Dyn.* **2019**, *50*, 258–272. [CrossRef]
37. Dávila-Fernández, M.J.; Sordi, S. Distributive cycles and endogenous technical change in a BoPC growth model. *Econ. Model.* **2019**, *77*, 216–233. [CrossRef]
38. Goodwin, R. The nonlinear accelerator and the persistence of business cycles. *Econometrica* **1951**, *19*, 1–17. [CrossRef]
39. Ruiz-Herrera, A.; Zanolin, F. Horseshoes in 3D equations with applications to Lotka-Volterra systems. *NoDEA Nonlinear Differ. Equ. Appl.* **2015**, *22*, 877–897. [CrossRef]

axioms

MDPI

Article

Asynchronous Switching Control of Discrete Time Delay Linear Switched Systems Based on MDADT

Jimin Yu [1,2], Xiaoyu Qi [1,*] and Yabin Shao [1]

[1] School of Science, Chongqing University of Posts and Telecommunications, Chongqing 400065, China; yujm@cqupt.edu.cn (J.Y.); shaoyb@cqupt.edu.cn (Y.S.)
[2] College of Automation, Chongqing University of Posts and Telecommunications, Chongqing 400065, China
* Correspondence: s210603010@stu.cqupt.edu.cn

Abstract: Ideally, switching between subsystems and controllers occurs synchronously. In other words, whenever a subsystem requires switching, its corresponding sub-controller will be promptly activated. However, in reality, due to network delays, system detection, etc., the activation of candidate controllers frequently lags, which causes issues with asynchronous switching between controllers and subsystems. This asynchronous switching problem may affect system performance and even make the system unstable because the state between the subsystem and the controller may be inconsistent, resulting in the controller not being able to control the subsystem correctly. To keep the system stable while using asynchronous switching, this work suggests an asynchronous control technique for a class of discrete linear switching systems with time delay based on the mode-dependent average dwell time (MDADT). First, we construct a state feedback controller and establish a closed-loop system. In the asynchronous and synchronous intervals of subsystems and controllers, different Lyapunov functions are selected, and sufficient conditions for exponential stability and the H_∞ performance of the closed-loop system under asynchronous switching are obtained. In addition, using the MDADT switching strategy, the relevant parameters of each subsystem are designed and the corresponding state–feedback controller gain matrix can be obtained. Finally, a switching system with three subsystems is shown. The approach is confirmed by simulating it using the average dwell time (ADT) switching strategy and the MDADT switching strategy separately.

Keywords: asynchronous control; average dwell time; exponential stability; mode dependent; time delay

MSC: 93B36; 93C05; 93C65; 93D23

Citation: Yu, J.; Qi, X.; Shao, Y. Asynchronous Switching Control of Discrete Time Delay Linear Switched Systems Based on MDADT. *Axioms* **2023**, *12*, 747. https://doi.org/10.3390/axioms12080747

Academic Editor: Martin Bohner and Tianwei Zhang

Received: 9 June 2023
Revised: 22 July 2023
Accepted: 26 July 2023
Published: 29 July 2023

1. Introduction

A discrete system refers to all systems that are not continuous in time and space. They are ubiquitous in practical problems. It is expected that when computers assist people in simulating, controlling, and analyzing systems, they usually need to discretize time. In addition, there are some discrete mathematical models in the fields of biology, industry, and economics. For example, research on image encryption [1], human infectious diseases [2], and changes in the market economy [3] all require the application of discrete systems. A discrete switching system is an important type of discrete system. It realizes different functions and behaviors through state switching, and it can also realize complex logic operations, control, and decision-making functions.

The benefits of switching systems in terms of model composition have garnered increased attention. Switched systems are not only widely studied in theory but also have extensive applications in many engineering fields, such as electronic equipment [4], aerospace technology [5], traffic management [6], environmental governance [7], and others. The switched system is often a dynamical system made up of switching signals and a finite number of continuous or discrete dynamic subsystems. A piecewise constant function that depends on state or time is the switching signal, which is also known as the switching rule, switching strategy, or switching law. The stability of the switching system is somewhat impacted by the choice of switching signal. When an inappropriate switching signal is selected, the trajectories of the switched system that may make all subsystems stable are divergent; similarly, when a suitable switching signal is selected, it is possible to stabilize a switched system with unstable subsystems.

Research on switching signals is mainly reflected in the design of its dwell time. At present, typical research on switching signals mainly includes arbitrary switching signals [8], dwell time switching signals (DT) [9], average dwell time switching signals (ADT) [10], mode-dependent average dwell time switching signals (MDADT) [11], and persistent dwell time switching signals (PDT) [12]. DT restricts the switching time of two consecutive subsystems to be no less than a constant τ. ADT requires a constant τ_a for the average running time of the subsystem in the limited switching interval. MDADT makes each subsystem have its own ADT, which reduces the conservativeness of research, so it has a broader range of applications compared with the former two. The PDT switching mechanism consists of fast switching and slow switching alternately: the τ part can represent slow switching and T part can represent fast switching. However, DT and ADT cannot represent fast switching because they have strict constraints on the number of switches in a given period. As this implies, PDT is more general than DT and ADT. The complexity of PDT is much higher than that of DT and ADT, so there are few related studies.

There have been abundant research achievements in switched systems on system stability analysis [13], tracking control problems [14], time delay problems [15], robust control [16], gain analysis [17], etc. In recent years, scholars have also paid more attention to asynchronous switching control [18–23]. Asynchronous switching refers to a situation where the subsystem does not match the controller; that is, the switching signals of the subsystem and the controller are inconsistent. Since the identification of subsystems and the matching of corresponding controllers takes a certain amount of time, asynchronous situations cannot be avoided. In [24], based on the asynchronous switching of subsystems and filters, the design of the filter for discrete switched T-S fuzzy systems was discussed. The challenge of designing a controller for time delay nonlinear switching systems with asynchronous switching was investigated in [25]. During this operation of the system, the system cannot always operate in an ideal state, and signal interference and fault phenomena are inevitable. If the cause and location of the fault cannot be found in time, certain losses will be caused. Therefore, introducing fault diagnosis and detection mechanisms is an essential means to ensure system security. Considering the filter and subsystem asynchrony, fault detection on switched systems is carried out in [26]. The time trigger control is frequently used in sampling control to sample periodically; however, because it samples in the form of cycles, wasting system resources, the proposed event trigger mechanism aims to overcome this problem by monitoring changes in system performance in real time by designing event triggers. Ref. [27] studies the multi-asynchronous switching issue in switching systems with event triggering. In contrast to the prior asynchrony, the system's stability and controller design are investigated, along with the many asynchronous challenges of subsystems, event triggers, and controllers. Due to the reasons of the system itself or the technical limitations of the measurement means, it is impossible to measure all of the system's status information. By constructing an observer and using the input or output information of the original system to construct a new system, studying the new system allows one to discover the pertinent characteristics of the previous system. In [28], the issue of observer design for nonlinear switching systems with asynchronous situations is covered. There are few studies on asynchronous control of discrete switched systems, and most of them are based on the ADT switching strategy. Thus, combining the MDADT approach with asynchronous switching is essential.

The asynchronous control problem of discrete time delay switched systems is investigated in this work using MDADT. The majority of research on switched systems up to now has centered on synchronous switching. The switched system finds it challenging to sustain synchronous switching in practical circumstances. Since each subsystem and sub-controller in the system operates at a different speed and responds to commands differently, the associated controller may still be working on the current task when the subsystem has begun to execute the next task. This affects the stability of the system by causing confusion over the order in which different subsystems and sub-controllers should be executed. The main problem with current asynchronous switching is how to ensure the stability of the whole system when the subsystem does not match the corresponding sub-controller. In this paper, we present a parameter associated with exponential decay that tackles this problem by restricting the proportion of matching and mismatching durations between the controller and its corresponding subsystem. The majority of earlier investigations used the ADT technique, which meant that the dwell time and other parameters for each subsystem were constant. However, these parameters are not optimal due to the differences in each subsystem. Relatively speaking, MDADT technology is more flexible. It allows each subsystem to choose the most-suitable parameters according to its own needs to determine its dwell time, and it can set the switching delay of each sub-controller so that they do not have to be all the same. The main motivation is to use this feature of MDADT to improve system performance, and this approach to system performance verification differs from earlier ones. The following are its primary contributions:

1. An innovative asynchronous control method is provided for discrete time delay switched systems.

2. Using the MDADT switching strategy, the switched system's exponential stability and the necessary conditions for H_∞ performance are discovered, and the gain matrix of the controller is also computed.

The sections of this essay are organized as follows. The problem and definitions that apply to it are presented in Section 2. In Section 3, adequate requirements for exponential stability of discrete time delay switched systems and H_∞ performance are laid out, and controllers are also built. To test the efficacy of the asynchronous control method, Section 4 presents a discrete time delay switching system with two subsystems. Simulations are run under the ADT switching signal and the MDADT switching signal. Section 5 presents the results of the simulations of the example and the definition proof.

Notations: R^n represents n-dimensional Euclidean vector space, $L_2[0,\infty]$ is square integrable function space, $\|\cdot\|$ stands for Euclidean norm, $X > 0$ and X^T are positive definite matrices and transpose matrices, $\lambda_{min}\{\cdots\}$ and $\lambda_{max}\{\cdots\}$ represent the minimum and maximum eigenvalues of the matrix, respectively, $col\{\cdots\}$ represents a column vector, and $*$ represents the symmetric block in the block matrix.

2. Problem Statement

This section presents the discussed system and the design of the controller.

2.1. System Description

Consider the following discrete time delay linear switched system:

$$\begin{aligned} x(\varsigma+1) &= A_{\sigma(\varsigma)}x(\varsigma) + B_{\sigma(\varsigma)}u(\varsigma) + A_{1\sigma(\varsigma)}x(\varsigma-d) + B_{1\sigma(\varsigma)}\varpi(\varsigma), \varsigma \geq 0 \\ z(\varsigma) &= C_{\sigma(\varsigma)}x(\varsigma) + D_{\sigma(\varsigma)}u(\varsigma), \varsigma \geq 0 \\ x(\varsigma) &= \varphi(\varsigma), \varsigma \in \{-d,\cdots,0\} \end{aligned} \tag{1}$$

where $x \in R^{n_x}$, $u \in R^{n_u}$, and $z \in R^{n_z}$ are the state vector, control input, and controlled output of the system, respectively; $\varpi \in R^{n_\varpi}$ represents the disturbance input and belongs to $L_2[0,\infty)$; $\varphi(\varsigma)$ represents the initial vector-valued function; and d represents a constant delay time. The symbol $\sigma(\varsigma) : N \to M = \{1,2,\cdots,m\}$, $m \in N^+$ stands for the switching signal; $\{(\varsigma_0,\sigma(\varsigma_0)),(\varsigma_1,\sigma(\varsigma_1)),\cdots,(\varsigma_l,\sigma(\varsigma_l)),\cdots,l = 0,1,2,3,\cdots\}$ represents the system's switching time sequence; ς_0 indicates the initial switching time; and ς_l indicates the

l-th switching time. If the l-th subsystem is turned on, $\varsigma \in [\varsigma_l, \varsigma_{l+1})$ results. $A_{\sigma(\varsigma)}$, $B_{\sigma(\varsigma)}$, $A_{1\sigma(\varsigma)}$, $B_{1\sigma(\varsigma)}$, $C_{\sigma(\varsigma)}$, and $D_{\sigma(\varsigma)}$ are constant matrices.

Definition 1 ([29]). *For any switching signal $\sigma(\varsigma)$, let $N_{\sigma,j}(\varsigma_0, \varsigma)$ and $T_j(\varsigma_0, \varsigma)$ denote the switching times and running times of the j-th subsystem activated on $[\varsigma_0, \varsigma)$, respectively. If $\exists N_{0j} > 0$, $\tau_{aj} > 0$, such that*

$$N_{\sigma,j}(\varsigma_0, \varsigma) \leq N_{0j}(\varsigma_0, \varsigma) + \frac{T_j(\varsigma_0, \varsigma)}{\tau_{aj}}, \forall \varsigma \geq \varsigma_0 \geq 0,$$

then τ_{aj} and N_{0j} are known as MDADT and the chatter bound, respectively.

Definition 2 ([30]). *The switched system is exponentially stable if there exist constants $c > 0$ and $0 < \zeta < 1$ such that the solution of the system satisfies:*

$$\|x(\varsigma)\|_2 < c\zeta^{(\varsigma - \varsigma_0)} \|x(\varsigma_0)\|_2, \forall \varsigma > \varsigma_0.$$

Definition 3 ([30]). *Given $\delta > 0$ and $c > 0$, if the switching system is exponentially stable and under zero initial conditions, for all nonzero ϖ, the following inequality holds:*

$$\sum_{s=k_0}^{\infty} e^{-cs} z^T(s) z(s) \leq \delta^2 \sum_{s=k_0}^{\infty} \varpi^T(s) \varpi(s).$$

Then the switched system is exponentially stable with an exponential H_∞ index δ.

Lemma 1 ([31]). *For symmetric matrices X and $W > 0$ of any appropriate dimension and for any constant ξ, the following inequalities hold:*

$$-XW^{-1}X \leq \xi^2 W - 2\xi X.$$

2.2. Controller

Establish a state–feedback controller in System (1):

$$u(\varsigma) = K_{\sigma'(\varsigma)} x(\varsigma),$$

where $\sigma'(\varsigma)$ and $K_{\sigma'(\varsigma)}$ represent the switching signal and control gain matrix of the controller, respectively. Let Δ_l be the switching delay time of the controller relative to the subsystem, and satisfy $\Delta_l < \varsigma_{l+1} - \varsigma_l$. Then $\{(\varsigma_0 + \Delta_0, \sigma'(\varsigma_0)), (\varsigma_1 + \Delta_1, \sigma'(\varsigma_1)), \cdots, (\varsigma_l + \Delta_l, \sigma'(\varsigma_l)), \cdots, l = 0, 1, 2, 3, \cdots\}$ is the controller's switching sequence.

2.3. Build a Closed-Loop System

Substituting the dynamic output feedback controller into the switching System (1), the following closed-loop switched system can be obtained:

$$\begin{aligned} x(\varsigma+1) &= (A_{\sigma(\varsigma)} + B_{\sigma(\varsigma)} K_{\sigma'(\varsigma)}) x(\varsigma) + A_{1\sigma(\varsigma)} x(\varsigma - d) + B_{1\sigma(\varsigma)} \varpi(\varsigma), \varsigma \geq 0 \\ z(\varsigma) &= (C_{\sigma(\varsigma)} + D_{\sigma(\varsigma)} K_{\sigma'(\varsigma)}) x(\varsigma), \varsigma \geq 0 \\ x(\varsigma) &= \varphi(\varsigma), \forall \varsigma \in \{-d, \cdots, 0\} \end{aligned} \tag{2}$$

If $\sigma(\varsigma_l) = i$, the i-th subsystem is activated at the moment of system switching ς_l; likewise, if $\sigma(\varsigma_{l-1}) = j$, the j-th subsystem is enabled at the time of system switching ς_{l-1}. $T^-(\varsigma_0, \varsigma)$ and $T^+(\varsigma_0, \varsigma)$ are utilized to indicate the matching and mismatching intervals between the subsystem and the controller while the system is running in $[\varsigma_0, \varsigma)$.$T^-(\varsigma - \varsigma_0)$, and $T^+(\varsigma - \varsigma_0)$ represent the interval lengths of $T^-(\varsigma_0, \varsigma)$ and $T^+(\varsigma_0, \varsigma)$.

In $[\varsigma_l, \varsigma_l + \Delta_l)$, the l-th subsystem has already started running, but due to factors such as controller model recognition, the controller at this time is from the $(l-1)$-th subsystem, which results in a mismatch between the subsystem and the controller. In $[\varsigma_l + \Delta_l, \varsigma_{l+1})$, the l-th controller is activated and the subsystem matches the controller. Thus, System (2) is expressed as follows:

$$\begin{cases} x(\varsigma+1) = \bar{A}_{ij}x(\varsigma) + A_{1i}x(\varsigma-d) + B_{1i}\varpi(\varsigma), \\ z(\varsigma) = \bar{C}_{ij}x(\varsigma), \qquad \varsigma \in [\varsigma_l, \varsigma_l + \Delta_l), \\ x(\varsigma) = \varphi(\varsigma), \end{cases} \tag{3a}$$

$$\begin{cases} x(\varsigma+1) = \bar{A}_{i}x(\varsigma) + A_{1i}x(\varsigma-d) + B_{1i}\varpi(\varsigma), \\ z(\varsigma) = \bar{C}_{i}x(\varsigma), \qquad \varsigma \in [\varsigma_l + \Delta_l, \varsigma_{l+1}), \\ x(\varsigma) = \varphi(\varsigma), \end{cases} \tag{3b}$$

where $\bar{A}_{ij} = A_i + B_iK_j$, $\bar{C}_{ij} = C_i + D_iK_j$, $\bar{A}_i = A_i + B_iK_i$, $\bar{C}_i = C_i + D_iK_i$.

When $\varpi = 0$, considering the stability of the system, System (3) becomes:

$$x(\varsigma+1) = \begin{cases} \bar{A}_{ij}x(\varsigma) + A_{1i}x(\varsigma-d), \varsigma \in [\varsigma_l, \varsigma_l + \Delta_l), \\ \bar{A}_{i}x(\varsigma) + A_{1i}x(\varsigma-d), \varsigma \in [\varsigma_l + \Delta_l, \varsigma_{l+1}), \end{cases} \tag{4}$$

where $\bar{A}_{ij} = A_i + B_iK_j$,$\bar{A}_i = A_i + B_iK_i$.

3. Main Results

For the above switched System (2), this section mainly discusses two issues:

(1) Solve the sufficient conditions for the time delay closed-loop switched System (2) to be exponentially stable and have the H_∞ performance index under asynchronous switching;

(2) Solve for the H_∞ controller gains based on the stability condition.

The following theorem gives sufficient conditions to ensure the exponential stability of System (4) by using multiple Lyapunov functions and the MDADT technique.

Theorem 1. *For System (4), given the parameters $\alpha_i > 0$, $\beta_i > 0$, $0 < \varepsilon_i^* < \beta_i$, and $\mu_i > 1$, if there exist matrices $P_i > 0$, $Q_i > 0$, and $R_i > 0$ satisfying*

$$\begin{bmatrix} -e^{\alpha_i}P_i + Q_i & 0 & (\bar{A}_{ij} - I)^T R_i & \bar{A}_{ij}^T P_i \\ * & -e^{d\alpha_i}Q_i & A_{1i}^T R_i & A_{1i}^T P_i \\ * & * & -d^{-1}R_i & 0 \\ * & * & * & -P_i \end{bmatrix} < 0, \tag{5}$$

$$\begin{bmatrix} -e^{-\beta_i}P_i + Q_i & 0 & (\bar{A}_{i} - I)^T R_i & \bar{A}_{i}^T P_i \\ * & -e^{-d\beta_i}Q_i & A_{1i}^T R_i & A_{1i}^T P_i \\ * & * & -d^{-1}R_i & 0 \\ * & * & * & -P_i \end{bmatrix} < 0, \tag{6}$$

$$P_i \le \mu_i P_j, Q_i \le \mu_i Q_j, R_i \le \mu_i R_j, \tag{7}$$

$$\inf_{\varsigma > \varsigma_0} \frac{T^-_{\sigma(\varsigma_f)}(\varsigma_{f+1} - \varsigma_f)}{T^+_{\sigma(\varsigma_f)}(\varsigma_{f+1} - \varsigma_f)} \ge \frac{\alpha_i + \varepsilon_i^*}{\beta_i - \varepsilon_i^*}, \tag{8}$$

where $f \in \psi(i) = \sigma(k_f) = i$, $i \in M$, then System (4) is exponentially stable, and any MDADT switching signal satisfies

$$\tau_{ai} > \frac{ln(\mu_i \theta_i)}{\varepsilon_i^*}. \tag{9}$$

Proof. When $\varsigma \in [\varsigma_l, \varsigma_l + \Delta_l)$, the subsystem does not match the controller at this time. Consider the following Lyapunov function:

$$V_\alpha(x_\varsigma,\varsigma)=x^T(\varsigma)P_ix(\varsigma)+\sum_{s=\varsigma-d}^{\varsigma-1}e^{\alpha_i(\varsigma-1-s)}x^T(s)Q_ix(s)+\sum_{r=1-d}^{0}\sum_{s=\varsigma+r-1}^{\varsigma-1}e^{\alpha_i(\varsigma-1-s)}h^T(s)R_ih(s), \tag{10}$$

where $h(s)=x(s+1)-x(s)$.

Denote $\Delta V_\alpha(x_\varsigma,\varsigma) = V_\alpha(x_{\varsigma+1},\varsigma+1)-e^{\alpha_i}V_\alpha(x_\varsigma,\varsigma)$ and $\xi(\varsigma) = col(x(\varsigma),x(\varsigma-d))$. Then

$$\begin{aligned}\Delta V_\alpha(x_\varsigma,\varsigma)&=V_\alpha(x_{\varsigma+1},\varsigma+1)-e^{\alpha_i}V_\alpha(x_\varsigma,\varsigma)\\&\le x^T(\varsigma+1)P_ix(\varsigma+1)-e^{\alpha_i}x^T(\varsigma)P_ix(\varsigma)+x^T(\varsigma)Q_ix(\varsigma)\\&-e^{d\alpha_i}x^T(\varsigma-d)Q_ix(\varsigma-d)+dh^T(\varsigma)R_ih(\varsigma)\end{aligned} \tag{11}$$

It follows from (4) that

$$x^T(\varsigma+1)P_ix(\varsigma+1)=\xi^T(\varsigma)\begin{bmatrix}\bar{A}_{ij} & A_{1i}\end{bmatrix}^TP_i\begin{bmatrix}\bar{A}_{ij} & A_{1i}\end{bmatrix}\xi(\varsigma), \tag{12}$$

and

$$\begin{aligned}dg^T(\varsigma)R_ig(\varsigma)&=d(x(\varsigma+1)-x(\varsigma))^TR_i(x(\varsigma+1)-x(\varsigma))\\&=d\xi^T(\varsigma)\begin{bmatrix}\bar{A}_{ij}-I & A_{1i}\end{bmatrix}^TR_i\begin{bmatrix}\bar{A}_{ij}-I & A_{1i}\end{bmatrix}\xi(\varsigma).\end{aligned} \tag{13}$$

From (11)–(13), we can obtain

$$\Delta V_\alpha(x_\varsigma,\varsigma)=V_\alpha(x_\varsigma,\varsigma)-e^{\alpha_i}V_\alpha(x_\varsigma,\varsigma)\le\xi^T(\varsigma)\Omega_{ij}\xi(\varsigma), \tag{14}$$

where

$$\begin{aligned}\Omega_{ij}=&\begin{bmatrix}\bar{A}_{ij} & A_{1i}\end{bmatrix}^TP_i\begin{bmatrix}\bar{A}_{ij} & A_{1i}\end{bmatrix}+diag(-e^{\alpha_i}P_i+Q_i,-e^{d\alpha_i}Q_i)\\&+d\begin{bmatrix}\bar{A}_{ij}-I & A_{1i}\end{bmatrix}^TR_i\begin{bmatrix}\bar{A}_{ij}-I & A_{1i}\end{bmatrix}.\end{aligned} \tag{15}$$

According to Schur's complement, Equations (5) and (15) are equivalent; we can obtain

$$\Delta V_\alpha(x_\varsigma,\varsigma)=V_\alpha(x_{\varsigma+1},\varsigma+1)-e^{\alpha_i}V_\alpha(x_\varsigma,\varsigma)\le 0. \tag{16}$$

This implies

$$V_{\alpha\sigma(\varsigma_l)}(x_\varsigma)\le e^{\alpha_{\sigma(\varsigma_l)}(\varsigma-\varsigma_l)}V_{\alpha\sigma(\varsigma_l)}(x_{\varsigma_l}). \tag{17}$$

When $\varsigma\in[\varsigma_l+\Delta_l,\varsigma_{l+1})$, the subsystem is matched with the controller at this time. Consider the following Lyapunov function:

$$V_\beta(x_\varsigma,\varsigma)=x^T(\varsigma)P_ix(\varsigma)+\sum_{s=\varsigma-d}^{\varsigma-1}e^{\beta_i(s-\varsigma+1)}x^T(s)Q_ix(s)+\sum_{r=1-d}^{0}\sum_{s=\varsigma+r-1}^{\varsigma-1}e^{\beta_i(s-\varsigma+1)}h^T(s)R_ih(s), \tag{18}$$

Denote $\Delta V_\beta(x_\varsigma,\varsigma)=V_\beta(x_{\varsigma+1},\varsigma+1)-e^{-\beta_i}V_\beta(x_\varsigma,\varsigma)$. Similarly, we have

$$\Delta V_\beta(x_\varsigma,\varsigma)=V_\beta(x_\varsigma,\varsigma)-e^{-\beta_i}V_\beta(x_\varsigma,\varsigma)\le\xi^T(\varsigma)\Omega_i\xi(\varsigma), \tag{19}$$

where

$$\begin{aligned}\Omega_i=&\begin{bmatrix}\bar{A}_i & A_{1i}\end{bmatrix}^TP_i\begin{bmatrix}\bar{A}_i & A_{1i}\end{bmatrix}+diag(-e^{-\beta_i}P_i+Q_i,-e^{-d\beta_i}Q_i)\\&+d\begin{bmatrix}\bar{A}_i-I & A_{1i}\end{bmatrix}^TR_i\begin{bmatrix}\bar{A}_i-I & A_{1i}\end{bmatrix}.\end{aligned} \tag{20}$$

According to Schur's complement, Equations (6) and (20) are equivalent; we can obtain

$$\Delta V_{\beta}(x_{\varsigma},\varsigma) = V_{\beta}(x_{\varsigma+1},\varsigma+1) - e^{-\beta_i}V_{\beta}(x_{\varsigma},\varsigma) \leq 0. \tag{21}$$

Thus,

$$V_{\beta\sigma(\varsigma_l)}(x_{\varsigma}) \leq e^{-\beta_{\sigma(\varsigma_l)}(\varsigma-\varsigma_l-\Delta_l)}V_{\beta\sigma(\varsigma_l)}(x_{\varsigma_l}+\Delta_l). \tag{22}$$

In the whole interval $[0,\varsigma]$, the Lyapunov function consists of (10) and (18):

$$V_{\sigma(\varsigma)}(\varsigma) = \begin{cases} V_{\alpha\sigma(\varsigma)}, \varsigma \in [\varsigma_l, \varsigma_l+\Delta_l), \\ V_{\beta\sigma(\varsigma)}, \varsigma \in [\varsigma_l+\Delta_l, \varsigma_{l+1}). \end{cases} \tag{23}$$

From (7), (10) and (18), we have

$$V_{\beta}(x_{\varsigma},\varsigma) \leq \mu_i V_{\alpha}(x_{\varsigma},\varsigma), V_{\alpha}(x_{\varsigma},\varsigma) \leq \theta_i V_{\beta}(x_{\varsigma},\varsigma), (\theta_i = \mu_i e^{(\alpha_i+\beta_i)d}). \tag{24}$$

When $\varsigma \in [\varsigma_l, \varsigma_{l+1})$, from (17), (22) and (24), we have

$$\begin{aligned}
V_{\sigma(\varsigma_l)}(x_{\varsigma}) &\leq e^{-\beta_{\sigma(\varsigma_l)}T^-(\varsigma_{l+1}-\varsigma_l)}V_{\beta\sigma(\varsigma_l)}(x_{\varsigma_l+\Delta_l}) \\
&\leq \mu_{\sigma(\varsigma_l)}e^{-\beta_{\sigma(\varsigma_l)}T^-(\varsigma_{l+1}-\varsigma_l)}V_{\alpha\sigma(\varsigma_l)}(x^-_{\varsigma_l+\Delta_l}) \\
&\leq \mu_{\sigma(\varsigma_l)}e^{-\beta_{\sigma(\varsigma_l)}T^-(\varsigma_{l+1}-\varsigma_l)}e^{\alpha_{\sigma(\varsigma_l)}T^+(\varsigma_{l+1}-\varsigma_l)}V_{\alpha\sigma(\varsigma_l)}(x_{\varsigma_l}) \\
&\leq \mu_{\sigma(\varsigma_l)}\theta_{\sigma(\varsigma_l)}e^{-\beta_{\sigma(\varsigma_l)}T^-(\varsigma_{l+1}-\varsigma_l)}e^{\alpha_{\sigma(\varsigma_l)}T^+(\varsigma_{l+1}-\varsigma_l)}V_{\beta\sigma(\varsigma_l)}(x^-_{\varsigma_l}) \\
&\leq \mu_{\sigma(\varsigma_l)}\theta_{\sigma(\varsigma_l)}e^{-\beta_{\sigma(\varsigma_l)}T^-(\varsigma_{l+1}-\varsigma_l)}e^{\alpha_{\sigma(\varsigma_l)}T^+(\varsigma_{l+1}-\varsigma_l)} \\
&\times \mu_{\sigma(\varsigma_{l-1})}\theta_{\sigma(\varsigma_{l-1})}e^{-\beta_{\sigma(\varsigma_{l-1})}T^-(\varsigma_l-\varsigma_{l-1})}e^{\alpha_{\sigma(\varsigma_{l-1})}T^+(\varsigma_l-\varsigma_{l-1})} \times V_{\beta\sigma(\varsigma_{l-1})}(x^-_{\varsigma_{l-1}}) \\
&\leq \cdots \leq \mu_{\sigma(\varsigma_l)}\theta_{\sigma(\varsigma_l)}\mu_{\sigma(\varsigma_{l-1})}\theta_{\sigma(\varsigma_{l-1})}\cdots\mu_{\sigma(\varsigma_1)}\theta_{\sigma(\varsigma_1)} \times e^{-\beta_{\sigma(\varsigma_l)}T^-(\varsigma_{l+1}-\varsigma_l)}e^{\alpha_{\sigma(\varsigma_l)}T^+(\varsigma_{l+1}-\varsigma_l)} \\
&\times e^{-\beta_{\sigma(\varsigma_{l-1})}T^-(\varsigma_l-\varsigma_{l-1})}e^{\alpha_{\sigma(\varsigma_{l-1})}T^+(\varsigma_l-\varsigma_{l-1})} \times \cdots \times e^{-\beta_{\sigma(\varsigma_0)}T^-(\varsigma_1-\varsigma_0)}e^{\alpha_{\sigma(\varsigma_0)}T^+(\varsigma_1-\varsigma_0)}V_{\sigma(\varsigma_0)} \\
&= \prod_{i\in M}(\mu_i\theta_i)^{N_{\sigma,i}} \times e^{\sum\limits_{i\in M, f\in\psi(i)} \alpha_i T^+(\varsigma_{f+1}-\varsigma_f)-\beta_i T^-(\varsigma_{f+1}-\varsigma_f)} \times V_{\sigma(\varsigma_0)}(x_{\varsigma_0}).
\end{aligned} \tag{25}$$

It follows from (8) that

$$\alpha_i T^+(\varsigma_{l+1}-\varsigma_l) - \beta_i T^-(\varsigma_{l+1}-\varsigma_l) \leq -\varepsilon_i^*(\varsigma_{l+1}-\varsigma_l). \tag{26}$$

From (25) and (26), we can obtain

$$\begin{aligned}
&V_{\sigma(\varsigma_l)}(x_{\varsigma}) \\
&\leq \prod_{i\in M}(\mu_i\theta_i)^{N_{\sigma,i}} \times e^{\sum\limits_{i\in M, f\in\psi(i)} \alpha_i T^+(\varsigma_{f+1}-\varsigma_f)-\beta_i T^-(\varsigma_{f+1}-\varsigma_f)} \times V_{\sigma(\varsigma_0)}(x_{\varsigma_0}) \\
&\leq \prod_{i\in M}(\mu_i\theta_i)^{N_{\sigma,i}} \times e^{\sum\limits_{i\in M, f\in\psi(i)} -\varepsilon_i^*(\varsigma_{f+1}-\varsigma_f)} V_{\sigma(\varsigma_0)}(x_{\varsigma_0}) \\
&\leq e^{\sum\limits_{i\in M} N_{0,i} ln(\mu_i\theta_i)} e^{\sum\limits_{i\in M, f\in\psi(i)} (\frac{ln(\mu_i\theta_i)}{\tau_{ai}}-\varepsilon_i^*)(\varsigma_{f+1}-\varsigma_f)} V_{\sigma(\varsigma_0)}(x_{\varsigma_0}).
\end{aligned} \tag{27}$$

Meanwhile, considering the Lyapunov function, there are positive numbers $\tilde{a}$ and $\tilde{b}$ satisfying

$$\tilde{a}\|x(\varsigma)\|^2 \leq V(x_{\varsigma}) \leq \tilde{b}\|x(\varsigma)\|^2, \tag{28}$$

where

$$\tilde{a} = \min_{i\in M}\{\lambda_{min}(P_i)\},$$
$$\tilde{b} = \max_{i\in M}\{\lambda_{max}(P_i)\} + d\max_{i\in M}\{e^{d\alpha_i}\lambda_{max}(Q_i)\} + \frac{d(d+1)}{2}\max_{i\in M}\{e^{d\alpha_i}\lambda_{max}(R_i)\}.$$

By Definition 2, $c = \sqrt{\frac{\tilde{b}}{\tilde{a}}}e^{\frac{1}{2}\max_{i\in M}\{N_{0,i}ln(\mu_i\theta_i)\}}$ is a constant, and $0 < \zeta = e^{\frac{1}{2}\max_{i\in M}\{\frac{ln(\mu_i\theta_i)}{\tau_{ai}}-\varepsilon_i^*\}} < 1$; we have

$$\|x(\varsigma)\| \le c\zeta^{(\varsigma-\varsigma_0)}\|x(\varsigma_0)\|. \tag{29}$$

Therefore, System (4) is exponentially stable . □

The following theorem provides sufficient conditions for resolving the controller gain of System (4) based on Theorem 1.

Theorem 2. *For System (4), given the parameters $\alpha_i > 0$, $\beta_i > 0$, $0 < \varepsilon_i^* < \beta_i$, and $\mu_i > 1$, if there exist matrices $X_i > 0$, $Q_i > 0$, $R_i > 0$, and $Y_i > 0$ satisfying*

$$\begin{bmatrix} \Theta_1 & 0 & \Theta_2 & \Theta_3 & X_j \\ * & \Theta_4 & X_iA_{1i}^T & X_iA_{1i}^T & 0 \\ * & * & -d^{-1}R_i' & 0 & 0 \\ * & * & * & -X_i & 0 \\ * & * & * & * & -Q_i' \end{bmatrix} < 0, \tag{30}$$

$$\begin{bmatrix} \Theta_1^1 & 0 & \Theta_2^1 & \Theta_3^1 & X_i \\ * & \Theta_4^1 & X_iA_{1i}^T & X_iA_{1i}^T & 0 \\ * & * & -d^{-1}R_i' & 0 & 0 \\ * & * & * & -X_i & 0 \\ * & * & * & * & -Q_i' \end{bmatrix} < 0, \tag{31}$$

$$\begin{bmatrix} -\mu_iX_j & X_j \\ * & -X_i \end{bmatrix} \le 0, \begin{bmatrix} -\mu_iQ_j' & Q_j' \\ * & -Q_i' \end{bmatrix} \le 0, \begin{bmatrix} -\mu_iR_j' & R_j' \\ * & -R_i' \end{bmatrix} \le 0, \tag{32}$$

where

$$\Theta_1 = e^{\alpha_i}(X_i - 2X_j), \Theta_2 = X_jA_i^T + Y_j^TB_i^T - X_j, \Theta_3 = X_jA_i^T + Y_j^TB_i^T, \Theta_4 = e^{d\alpha_i}(Q_i' - 2X_i),$$
$$\Theta_1^1 = -e^{-\beta_i}X_i, \Theta_2^1 = X_iA_i^T + Y_i^TB_i^T - X_i, \Theta_3^1 = X_iA_i^T + Y_i^TB_i^T, \Theta_4^1 = e^{-d\beta_i}(Q_i' - 2X_i).$$

Therefore, the corresponding state-feedback controller gain matrix $K_i = Y_iX_i^{-1}$ can be obtained.

Proof. Suppose the controller gain $K_i = Y_iP_i$; let $X_i = P_i^{-1}$, $R_i^{-1} = R_i'$ and $Q_i^{-1} = Q_i'$. Multiply both sides of (5) by $diag\{X_j, X_i, R_i', X_i\}$ at the same time, and multiply both sides of (6) by $diag\{X_i, X_i, R_i', X_i\}$ at the same time. Through Lemma 1, we can obtain

$$-X_jP_iX_j \le X_i - 2X_j, -X_iQ_iX_i \le Q_i' - 2X_i. \tag{33}$$

By Schur's complement and (33), Conditions (30) and (31) are obtained. In addition, Condition (32) is obtained by multiplying both sides of the inequality (7) by X_i, Q_i', and R_i', respectively.

According to Theorem 1, we establish the exponential stability of System (4) in the absence of perturbations and subsequently demonstrate that System (3) with perturbations satisfies the sufficient conditions for H_∞ performance. □

Theorem 3. *For System (3), given the parameters $\alpha_i > 0$, $\beta_i > 0$, $0 < \varepsilon_i^* < \beta_i$, $\mu_i > 1$, and $\gamma > 0$, if there exist matrices $P_i > 0$, $Q_i > 0$, and $R_i > 0$ satisfying*

$$\begin{bmatrix} -e^{\alpha_i}P_i+Q_i & 0 & 0 & (\bar{A}_{ij}-I)^T R_i & \bar{A}_{ij}^T P_i & \bar{C}_{ij}^T \\ * & -e^{d\alpha_i}Q_i & 0 & A_{1i}^T R_i & A_{1i}^T P_i & 0 \\ * & * & -\gamma I & B_{1i}^T R_i & B_{1i}^T P_i & 0 \\ * & * & * & -d^{-1}R_i & 0 & 0 \\ * & * & * & * & -P_i & 0 \\ * & * & * & * & * & -I \end{bmatrix} < 0, \tag{34}$$

$$\begin{bmatrix} -e^{-\beta_i}P_i+Q_i & 0 & 0 & (\bar{A}_{i}-I)^T R_i & \bar{A}_{i}^T P_i & \bar{C}_{i}^T \\ * & -e^{-d\beta_i}Q_i & 0 & A_{1i}^T R_i & A_{1i}^T P_i & 0 \\ * & * & -\gamma I & B_{1i}^T R_i & B_{1i}^T P_i & 0 \\ * & * & * & -d^{-1}R_i & 0 & 0 \\ * & * & * & * & -P_i & 0 \\ * & * & * & * & * & -I \end{bmatrix} < 0, \tag{35}$$

$$P_i \leq \mu_i P_j, Q_i \leq \mu_i Q_j, R_i \leq \mu_i R_j, \tag{36}$$

$$\inf_{\varsigma>\varsigma_0} \frac{T^-_{\sigma(\varsigma_f)}(\varsigma_{f+1}-\varsigma_f)}{T^+_{\sigma(\varsigma_f)}(\varsigma_{f+1}-\varsigma_f)} \geq \frac{\alpha_i+\varepsilon_i^*}{\beta_i-\varepsilon_i^*}, \tag{37}$$

where $f \in \psi(i) = \sigma(k_f) = i$, $i \in M$, then the switched System (3) is exponentially stable and has H_∞ performance index $\bar{\gamma} = \sqrt{\gamma}$. Meanwhile, any MDADT switching signal satisfies

$$\tau_{ai} > \frac{\ln(\mu_i\theta_i)}{\varepsilon_i^*}. \tag{38}$$

Proof. Consider System (3): denote $F(\varsigma) = z^T(\varsigma)z(\varsigma) - \gamma\varpi^T(\varsigma)\varpi(\varsigma)$.

When $\varsigma \in [\varsigma_l, \varsigma_l+\Delta_l)$, the subsystem does not match the controller at this time; we can obtain

$$V_{\alpha\sigma(\varsigma_l)}(x_\varsigma) \leq e^{\alpha_{\sigma(\varsigma_l)}}V_{\alpha\sigma(\varsigma_l)}(x_{\varsigma-1}) - F(\varsigma-1). \tag{39}$$

By iterating through the formula, we have

$$\begin{aligned} &V_{\alpha\sigma(\varsigma_l)}(x_\varsigma) \\ &\leq e^{\alpha_{\sigma(\varsigma_l)}}V_{\alpha\sigma(\varsigma_l)}(x_{\varsigma-1}) - F(\varsigma-1) \\ &\leq e^{\alpha_{\sigma(\varsigma_l)}}(e^{\alpha_{\sigma(\varsigma_l)}}V_{\alpha\sigma(\varsigma_l)}(x_{\varsigma-2}) - F(\varsigma-2)) - F(\varsigma-1) \\ &\cdots \\ &\leq e^{\alpha_{\sigma(\varsigma_l)}(\varsigma-\varsigma_l)}V_{\alpha\sigma(\varsigma_l)}(x_{\varsigma_l}) - \sum_{s=\varsigma_l}^{\varsigma_l+\Delta_l-1} e^{\alpha_{\sigma(\varsigma_l)}(\varsigma_l+\Delta_l-s-1)}F(s). \end{aligned} \tag{40}$$

When $\varsigma \in [\varsigma_l+\Delta_l, \varsigma_{l+1})$, the subsystem is matched with the controller at this time; we can obtain

$$V_{\beta\sigma(\varsigma_l)}(x_\varsigma) \leq e^{-\beta_i}V_{\beta\sigma(\varsigma_l)}(x_{\varsigma-1}) - F(\varsigma-1). \tag{41}$$

Similarly, we can obtain

$$\begin{aligned} &V_{\beta\sigma(\varsigma_l)}(x_\varsigma) \\ &\leq e^{-\beta_{\sigma(\varsigma_l)}}V_{\beta\sigma(\varsigma_l)}(x_{\varsigma-1}) - F(\varsigma-1) \\ &\leq e^{-\beta_{\sigma(\varsigma_l)}}(e^{-\beta_{\sigma(\varsigma_l)}}V_{\sigma(\varsigma_l)}(x_{\varsigma-2}) - F(\varsigma-2)) - F(\varsigma-1) \\ &\cdots \\ &\leq e^{-\beta_{\sigma(\varsigma_l)}(\varsigma-\varsigma_l-\Delta_l)}V_{\beta\sigma(\varsigma_l)}(x_{\varsigma_l+\Delta_l}) - \sum_{s=\varsigma_l+\Delta_l}^{\varsigma-1} e^{-\beta_{\sigma(\varsigma_l)}(\varsigma-s-1)}F(s). \end{aligned} \tag{42}$$

From (24), combined with equations (40) and (42), when $\varsigma \in [\varsigma_l, \varsigma_{l+1})$, it can be known that

$$
\begin{aligned}
&V_{\sigma(\varsigma_l)}(x_\varsigma) \\
&\le e^{-\beta_{\sigma(\varsigma_l)}(\varsigma-\varsigma_l-\Delta_l)} V_{\beta\sigma(\varsigma_l)}(x_{\varsigma_l+\Delta_l}) - \sum_{s=\varsigma_l+\Delta_l}^{\varsigma-1} e^{-\beta_{\sigma(\varsigma_l)}(\varsigma-s-1)} F(s) \\
&\le \mu_{\sigma(\varsigma_l)} e^{-\beta_{\sigma(\varsigma_l)}(\varsigma-\varsigma_l-\Delta_l)} V_{\alpha\sigma(\varsigma_l)}(x^-_{\varsigma_l+\Delta_l}) - \sum_{s=\varsigma_l+\Delta_l}^{\varsigma-1} e^{-\beta_{\sigma(\varsigma_l)}(\varsigma-s-1)} F(s) \\
&\le \mu_{\sigma(\varsigma_l)} e^{-\beta_{\sigma(\varsigma_l)}(\varsigma-\varsigma_l-\Delta_l)} (e^{\alpha_{\sigma(\varsigma_l)}\Delta_l} V_{\alpha\sigma(\varsigma_l)}(x_{\varsigma_l}) - \sum_{s=\varsigma_l}^{\varsigma_l+\Delta_l-1} e^{\alpha_{\sigma(\varsigma_l)}(\varsigma_l+\Delta_l-s-1)} F(s)) \\
&- \sum_{s=\varsigma_l+\Delta_l}^{\varsigma-1} e^{-\beta_{\sigma(\varsigma_l)}(\varsigma-s-1)} F(s) \\
&\le \mu_{\sigma(\varsigma_l)} e^{-\beta_{\sigma(\varsigma_l)}(\varsigma-\varsigma_l-\Delta_l)} (e^{\alpha_{\sigma(\varsigma_l)}\Delta_l} \theta_{\sigma(\varsigma_l)} V_{\beta\sigma(\varsigma_l)}(x^-_{\varsigma_l}) - \sum_{s=\varsigma_l}^{\varsigma_l+\Delta_l-1} e^{\alpha_{\sigma(\varsigma_l)}(\varsigma_l+\Delta_l-s-1)} F(s)) \\
&- \sum_{s=\varsigma_l+\Delta_l}^{\varsigma-1} e^{-\beta_{\sigma(\varsigma_l)}(\varsigma-s-1)} F(s) \\
&\le \mu_{\sigma(\varsigma_l)} e^{-\beta_{\sigma(\varsigma_l)}(\varsigma-\varsigma_l-\Delta_l)} (e^{\alpha_{\sigma(\varsigma_l)}\Delta_l} \theta_{\sigma(\varsigma_l)} (\mu_{\sigma(\varsigma_{l-1})} \times e^{-\beta_{\sigma(\varsigma_{l-1})}(\varsigma_l-\varsigma_{l-1}-\Delta_{l-1})} (e^{\alpha_{\sigma(\varsigma_{l-1})}\Delta_{l-1}} \theta_{\sigma(\varsigma_{l-1})} \\
&\times V_{\beta\sigma(\varsigma_{l-1})}(x^-_{\varsigma_{l-1}}) - \sum_{s=\varsigma_{l-1}}^{\varsigma_{l-1}+\Delta_{l-1}-1} e^{\alpha_{\sigma(\varsigma_{l-1})}(\varsigma_{l-1}+\Delta_{l-1}-s-1)} F(s)) - \sum_{s=\varsigma_{l-1}+\Delta_{l-1}}^{\varsigma_l-1} e^{-\beta_{\sigma(\varsigma_{l-1})}(\varsigma-s-1)} F(s)) \\
&- \sum_{s=\varsigma_l}^{\varsigma_l+\Delta_l-1} e^{\alpha_{\sigma(\varsigma_l)}(\varsigma_l+\Delta_l-s-1)} F(s)) - \sum_{s=\varsigma_l+\Delta_l}^{\varsigma-1} e^{-\beta_{\sigma(\varsigma_l)}(\varsigma-s-1)} F(s) \\
&\le \cdots \le e^{-\beta_{\sigma(\varsigma_l)}(\varsigma-\varsigma_l-\Delta_l)} \times (e^{\alpha_{\sigma(\varsigma_l)}\Delta_l} \mu_{\sigma(\varsigma_l)} \theta_{\sigma(\varsigma_l)} \times \cdots \times \mu_{\sigma(\varsigma_1)} \theta_{\sigma(\varsigma_1)} \times (e^{-\beta_{\sigma(\varsigma_0)}(\varsigma_1-\varsigma_0-\Delta_0)} \\
&\times (e^{\alpha_{\sigma(\varsigma_0)}\Delta_0} V_{\sigma(\varsigma_0)}(x_{\varsigma_0}) - \sum_{s=\varsigma_0}^{\varsigma_0+\Delta_0-1} e^{\alpha_{\sigma(\varsigma_0)}(\varsigma_0+\Delta_0-s-1)} F(s)) - \sum_{s=\varsigma_0+\Delta_0}^{\varsigma_1-1} e^{-\beta_{\sigma(\varsigma_0)}(\varsigma_1-s-1)} F(s)) \\
&- \cdots - \sum_{s=\varsigma_l}^{\varsigma_l+\Delta_l-1} e^{\alpha_{\sigma(\varsigma_l)}(\varsigma_l+\Delta_l-s-1)} F(s)) - \sum_{s=\varsigma_l+\Delta_l}^{\varsigma-1} e^{-\beta_{\sigma(\varsigma_l)}(\varsigma-s-1)} F(s)
\end{aligned}
\tag{43}
$$

Under zero initial conditions, i.e., $x(\varsigma_0) = 0$, from (37) and (43), we have

$$
\sum_{s=\varsigma_0}^{\varsigma-1} e^{\sum\limits_{i\in M, f\in\psi(i)} -\varepsilon_i^*(\varsigma_{f+1}-s-1)} z^T(s)z(s) \le \gamma \sum_{s=\varsigma_0}^{\varsigma-1} e^{\sum\limits_{i\in M, f\in\psi(i)} -\varepsilon_i^*(\varsigma_{f+1}-s-1)} \varpi^T(s)\varpi(s). \tag{44}
$$

Multiply both sides of (44) by $e^{\sum\limits_{i\in M, f\in\psi(i)} N_{\sigma,i}(s,\varsigma_{f+1}) ln(\mu_i\theta_i)}$; we have

$$
\begin{aligned}
&\sum_{s=\varsigma_0}^{\varsigma-1} e^{\sum\limits_{i\in M, f\in\psi(i)} -\varepsilon_i^*(\varsigma_{f+1}-s-1)+N_{\sigma,i}(s,\varsigma_{f+1}) ln(\mu_i\theta_i)} z^T(s)z(s) \\
&\quad \le \gamma \sum_{s=\varsigma_0}^{\varsigma-1} e^{\sum\limits_{i\in M, f\in\psi(i)} -\varepsilon_i^*(\varsigma_{f+1}-s-1)+N_{\sigma,i}(s,\varsigma_{f+1}) ln(\mu_i\theta_i)} \varpi^T(s)\varpi(s).
\end{aligned}
\tag{45}
$$

Multiply both sides of inequality (45) by $e^{\sum_{i\in M, f\in\psi(i)} -N_{\sigma,i}(\varsigma_f,\varsigma_{f+1}) ln(\mu_i\theta_i)}$; we have

$$\sum_{s=\varsigma_0}^{\varsigma-1} e^{\sum_{i\in M, f\in\psi(i)} -\varepsilon_i^*(\varsigma_{f+1}-s-1)-N_{\sigma,i}(\varsigma_f,s) ln(\mu_i\theta_i)} z^T(s)z(s) \leq \gamma \sum_{s=\varsigma_0}^{\varsigma-1} e^{\sum_{i\in M, f\in\psi(i)} -\varepsilon_i^*(\varsigma_{f+1}-s-1)-N_{\sigma,i}(\varsigma_f,s) ln(\mu_i\theta_i)} \varpi^T(s)\varpi(s). \tag{46}$$

Note $N_{\sigma,i}(\varsigma_f,s) < \frac{s-\varsigma_f}{\tau_{ai}}$. From (38), we have

$$N_{\sigma,i}(\varsigma_f,s) ln(\mu_i\theta_i) \leq \varepsilon_i^*(s-\varsigma_f). \tag{47}$$

It follows from (46) and (47) that

$$\sum_{s=\varsigma_0}^{\varsigma-1} e^{\sum_{i\in M, f\in\psi(i)} -\varepsilon_i^*(\varsigma_{f+1}-\varsigma_f-1)} z^T(s)z(s) \leq \gamma \sum_{s=\varsigma_0}^{\varsigma-1} e^{\sum_{i\in M, f\in\psi(i)} -\varepsilon_i^*(\varsigma_{f+1}-s-1)} \varpi^T(s)\varpi(s). \tag{48}$$

Thus,

$$\sum_{s=\varsigma_0}^{\varsigma-1} e^{\sum_{i\in M, f\in\psi(i)} -\varepsilon_i^*(s-\varsigma_f)} z^T(s)z(s) \leq \gamma \sum_{s=\varsigma_0}^{\varsigma-1} \varpi^T(s)\varpi(s). \tag{49}$$

This implies

$$\sum_{s=\varsigma_0}^{\infty} e^{\sum_{i\in M, f\in\psi(i)} -\varepsilon_i^*(s-\varsigma_f)} z^T(s)z(s) \leq \gamma \sum_{s=\varsigma_0}^{\infty} \varpi^T(s)\varpi(s). \tag{50}$$

According to Definition 3, System (3) is exponentially stable and has H_∞ performance index $\bar{\gamma} = \sqrt{\gamma}$.

The following theorem provides sufficient conditions for resolving the controller gain of System (3) based on Theorem 3. □

Theorem 4. *For System (3), given the parameters $\alpha_i > 0$, $\beta_i > 0$, $0 < \varepsilon_i^* < \beta_i$, $\mu_i > 1$, and $\gamma > 0$, if there exist matrices $X_i > 0$, $Q_i > 0$, $R_i > 0$, and $Y_i > 0$ satisfying*

$$\begin{bmatrix} \Sigma_1 & 0 & 0 & \Sigma_2 & \Sigma_3 & \Sigma_4 & X_j \\ * & \Sigma_5 & 0 & X_iA_{1i}^T & X_iA_{1i}^T & 0 & 0 \\ * & * & -\gamma I & B_{1i}^T & B_{1i}^T & 0 & 0 \\ * & * & * & -d^{-1}R_i' & 0 & 0 & 0 \\ * & * & * & * & -X_i & 0 & 0 \\ * & * & * & * & * & -I & 0 \\ * & * & * & * & * & * & -Q_i' \end{bmatrix} < 0, \tag{51}$$

$$\begin{bmatrix} \Sigma_1^1 & 0 & 0 & \Sigma_2^1 & \Sigma_3^1 & \Sigma_4^1 & X_i \\ * & \Sigma_5^1 & 0 & X_iA_{1i}^T & X_iA_{1i}^T & 0 & 0 \\ * & * & -\gamma I & B_{1i}^T & B_{1i}^T & 0 & 0 \\ * & * & * & -d^{-1}R_i' & 0 & 0 & 0 \\ * & * & * & * & -X_i & 0 & 0 \\ * & * & * & * & * & -I & 0 \\ * & * & * & * & * & * & -Q_i' \end{bmatrix} < 0, \tag{52}$$

$$\begin{bmatrix} -\mu_i X_j & X_j \\ * & -X_i \end{bmatrix} \leq 0, \begin{bmatrix} -\mu_i Q_j' & Q_j' \\ * & -Q_i' \end{bmatrix} \leq 0, \begin{bmatrix} -\mu_i R_j' & R_j' \\ * & -R_i' \end{bmatrix} \leq 0, \tag{53}$$

where

$$\Sigma_1 = e^{\alpha_i}(X_i - 2X_j), \Sigma_2 = X_jA_i^T + Y_j^TB_i^T - X_j, \Sigma_3 = X_jA_i^T + Y_j^TB_i^T, \Sigma_4 = X_jC_i^T + Y_j^TD_i^T,$$
$$\Sigma_5 = e^{d\alpha_i}(Q_i' - 2X_i), \Sigma_1^1 = e^{-\beta_i}X_i, \Sigma_2^1 = X_iA_i^T + Y_i^TB_i^T - X_i, \Sigma_3^1 = X_iA_i^T + Y_i^TB_i^T,$$
$$\Sigma_4^1 = X_iC_i^T + Y_i^TD_i^T, \Sigma_5^1 = e^{-d\beta_i}(Q_i' - 2X_i).$$

Therefore, the corresponding state–feedback controller gain matrix $K_i = Y_iX_i^{-1}$ can be obtained.

Proof. Multiply both sides of (34) by $diag\{X_j, X_i, I, R_i', X_i, I\}$ at the same time, and multiply both sides of (35) by $diag\{X_i, X_i, I, R_i', X_i, I\}$ at the same time. Similarly, by Schur's complement, conditions (51)–(53) can be obtained. □

4. Numerical Example

Consider the discrete time delay switching System (1) with three subsystems, whose parameters are set as follows:

$$A_1 = \begin{bmatrix} -0.1 & 0 \\ 0 & 0.2 \end{bmatrix}, B_1 = \begin{bmatrix} -0.4 & 0 \\ -1.8 & -0.6 \end{bmatrix}, A_{11} = \begin{bmatrix} -0.6 & 0 \\ 0.5 & 0.7 \end{bmatrix}, B_{11} = \begin{bmatrix} -0.07 & 0 \\ 0 & -0.2 \end{bmatrix},$$
$$C_1 = \begin{bmatrix} -0.6 & 0.8 \\ 1.7 & 0.5 \end{bmatrix}, D_1 = \begin{bmatrix} -1.9 & 1 \\ 0.8 & 1.2 \end{bmatrix}, A_2 = \begin{bmatrix} 0.01 & 0 \\ 0 & -0.08 \end{bmatrix}, B_2 = \begin{bmatrix} -1.1 & -0.07 \\ 1.6 & 0.5 \end{bmatrix},$$
$$A_{12} = \begin{bmatrix} 0.1 & 0 \\ 0 & -0.2 \end{bmatrix}, B_{12} = \begin{bmatrix} -0.3 & 0 \\ 0 & -0.4 \end{bmatrix}, C_2 = \begin{bmatrix} 0.3 & -1.4 \\ -0.8 & -1 \end{bmatrix}, D_2 = \begin{bmatrix} 1 & 0.1 \\ -0.3 & -1.5 \end{bmatrix},$$
$$A_3 = \begin{bmatrix} -0.1 & 0 \\ 0 & 0.1 \end{bmatrix}, B_3 = \begin{bmatrix} -0.8 & 0.6 \\ 1.6 & 0.5 \end{bmatrix}, A_{13} = \begin{bmatrix} 0.1 & -0.1 \\ 0 & -0.8 \end{bmatrix}, B_{13} = \begin{bmatrix} -0.008 & 0 \\ 0 & -0.1 \end{bmatrix},$$
$$C_3 = \begin{bmatrix} -0.3 & -1.6 \\ -1.5 & 1.1 \end{bmatrix}, D_3 = \begin{bmatrix} -0.4 & 0.7 \\ 0.2 & -1.2 \end{bmatrix}, \omega(\varsigma) = \begin{bmatrix} 2^{-\varsigma}sin(2\varsigma) & 2^{-\varsigma}cos(2\varsigma) \end{bmatrix}^T.$$

We compare this switched system under the MDADT switching strategy and the ADT switching strategy. A set of appropriate data is chosen by contrasting the impact of each parameter on the system, as illustrated in Table 1. The MDADT switching strategy makes each subsystem have its own ADT; that is, the parameters of each subsystem are different. Choose $\alpha_1 = 1.7$, $\beta_1 = 2.5$, $\mu_1 = 1.1$, and $\varepsilon_1^* = 1.7$; then obtain $\tau_{a1} > 9.99$ s by solving (9); similarly, choose $\alpha_2 = 1.2$, $\beta_2 = 2.1$, $\mu_2 = 2.2$, and $\varepsilon_2^* = 1.4$ and obtain $\tau_{a2} > 10.26$ s; choose $\alpha_3 = 1.8$, $\beta_3 = 2$, $\mu_3 = 2.3$, and $\varepsilon_3^* = 1.3$ and obtain $\tau_{a3} > 12.97$ s. By solving (51)–(53), we can get the gain matrix of the controller:

$$K_1 = \begin{bmatrix} 0.4062 & 0.7363 \\ -1.0538 & -1.1525 \end{bmatrix}, K_2 = \begin{bmatrix} -0.2024 & -0.2399 \\ -0.6497 & 0.1711 \end{bmatrix}, K_3 = \begin{bmatrix} 0.4055 & -0.1867 \\ -0.7019 & -0.0834 \end{bmatrix},$$

The running time of each subsystem is the same when using the ADT switching strategy, so choose $\alpha = 1.8$, $\beta = 2.5$, $\mu = 1.03$, and $\varepsilon^* = 1.7$, and obtain $\tau_a > 10.15$ s. By solving (51)–(53), we can get the gain matrix of the controller:

$$K_1 = \begin{bmatrix} 0.3793 & 1.0235 \\ -1.0086 & -1.2475 \end{bmatrix}, K_2 = \begin{bmatrix} -0.1863 & -0.2506 \\ -0.7474 & 0.2720 \end{bmatrix}, K_3 = \begin{bmatrix} 0.5937 & -0.3481 \\ -0.8036 & 0.0012 \end{bmatrix},$$

To eliminate the impact of other variables, the MDADT switching strategy is chosen with the values $\alpha_1 = \alpha_2 = \alpha_3 = 1.8$, $\beta_1 = \beta_2 = \beta_3 = 2.5$, $\mu_1 = \mu_2 = \mu_3 = 1.03$, $\varepsilon_1^* = \varepsilon_2^* = \varepsilon_3^* = 1.7$; however, two sets of distinct average dwell times $\tau_{a1} = 11$ s, $\tau_{a2} = 12$ s, $\tau_{a3} = 14$ s and $\tau_{a1} = 11$ s, $\tau_{a2} = 13$ s, $\tau_{a3} = 15$ s are selected. Because the parameters of these two groups are the same as those under the ADT switching strategy (but the dwell time of each subsystem is different), the controller gain matrices of these two groups are the same as those under the ADT switching strategy.

Table 1. The parameters and calculation results of the system under the ADT switching signal and the MDADT switching signal.

Switching Schemes	ADT	MDADT	MDADT	MDADT
Parameters	$\alpha = 1.8, \beta = 2.5,$ $\mu = 1.03, \varepsilon^* = 1.7,$ $d = 4$	$\alpha_1 = \alpha_2 = 1.8,$ $\alpha_3 = 1.8, \beta_1 = 2.5,$ $\beta_2 = \beta_3 = 2.5,$ $\mu_1 = \mu_2 = 1.03,$ $\mu_3 = 1.03, \varepsilon_1^* = 1.7,$ $\varepsilon_2^* = \varepsilon_3^* = 1.7,$ $d = 4$	$\alpha_1 = \alpha_2 = 1.8,$ $\alpha_3 = 1.8, \beta_1 = 2.5,$ $\beta_2 = \beta_3 = 2.5,$ $\mu_1 = \mu_2 = 1.03,$ $\mu_3 = 1.03, \varepsilon_1^* = 1.7,$ $\varepsilon_2^* = \varepsilon_3^* = 1.7,$ $d = 4$	$\alpha_1 = 1.7, \alpha_2 = 1.2,$ $\alpha_3 = 1.8, \beta_1 = 2.5,$ $\beta_2 = 2.1, \beta_3 = 2,$ $\mu_1 = 1.1, \mu_2 = 2.2,$ $\mu_3 = 2.3, \varepsilon_1^* = 1.7,$ $\varepsilon_2^* = 1.4, \varepsilon_3^* = 1.3,$ $d = 4$
Dwell time	$\tau_a = 11$	$\tau_{a1} = 11, \tau_{a2} = 12,$ $\tau_{a3} = 14$	$\tau_{a1} = 11, \tau_{a2} = 13,$ $\tau_{a3} = 15$	$\tau_{a1} = 11, \tau_{a2} = 12,$ $\tau_{a3} = 13$
H_∞ index	1.14	1.14	1.14	0.78

Figures 1–4 describe the switching signals of the subsystem and controller. When $\varpi = 0$, let $x(0) = [0.3, -2.3]^T$. The motion trajectories of the system under the switching strategy of ADT and MDADT are illustrated in Figures 5–8, respectively. According to the graph, under the ADT switching strategy, the system gradually tends to be stable at 30 s, but it is still accompanied by fluctuations until it stabilizes at 60 s. The highest amplitude of the system is about 7.5, and the fluctuation is large before the system is stable. However, under the MDADT switching strategy, we can see that the system has stabilized around 30 s. Figure 6 has obvious fluctuations around 60 s and 96 s, Figure 7 also has obvious fluctuations around 62 s, and Figure 8 almost stabilizes after 30 s. Prior to achieving stability, it is noticeable that the vibration amplitude in Figure 5 is considerably greater than that in Figures 6–8 and exhibits a clear and dramatic variation. On the other hand, the paths of the systems depicted in Figures 6–8 exhibit comparatively smaller fluctuations within a specific range. Hence, we can observe that if the residence time of each subsystem is changed, the motion path of the system will be changed accordingly. In line with the MDADT switching strategy, we have the flexibility to select distinct parameters for each subsystem in order to modify its residence time, thereby facilitating rapid stabilization of the system.

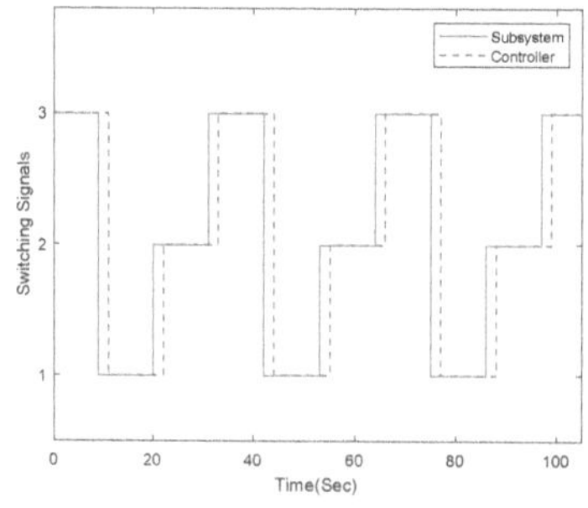

Figure 1. ADT switching signal.

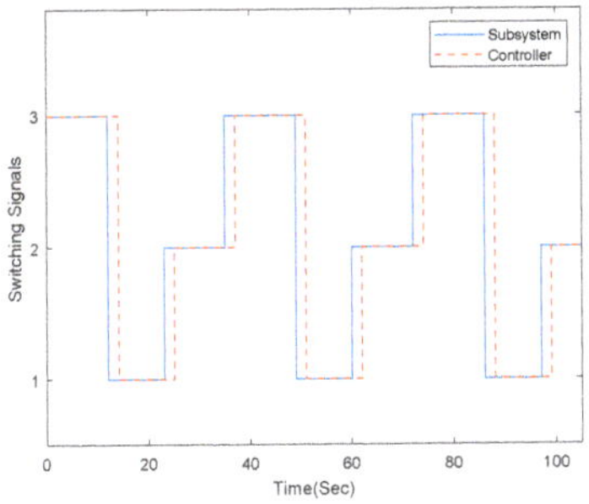

Figure 2. MDADT switching signal with $\tau_{a1} = 11$, $\tau_{a2} = 12$, and $\tau_{a3} = 14$.

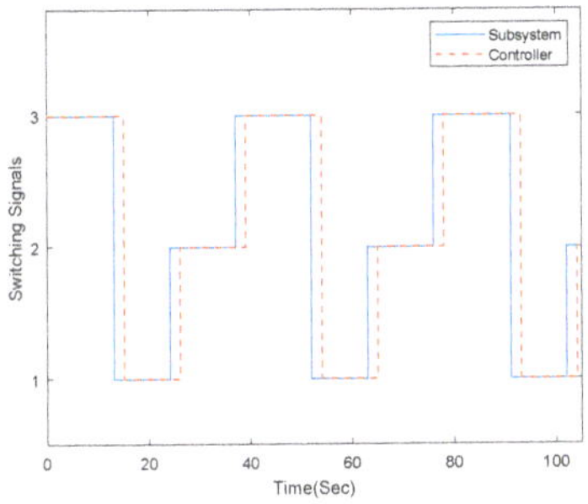

Figure 3. MDADT switching signal with $\tau_{a1} = 11$, $\tau_{a2} = 13$, and $\tau_{a3} = 15$.

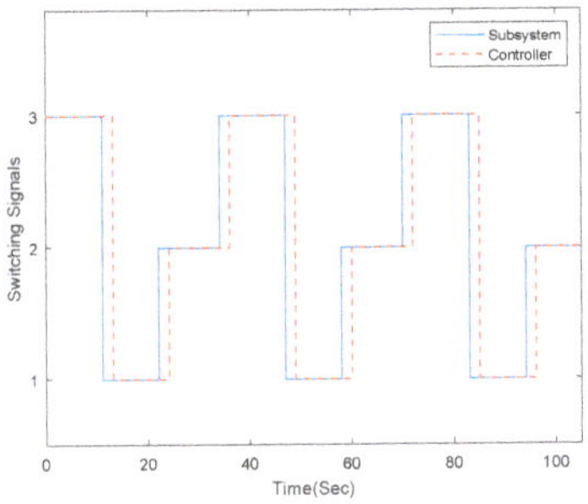

Figure 4. MDADT switching signal with $\tau_{a1} = 11$, $\tau_{a2} = 12$, and $\tau_{a3} = 13$.

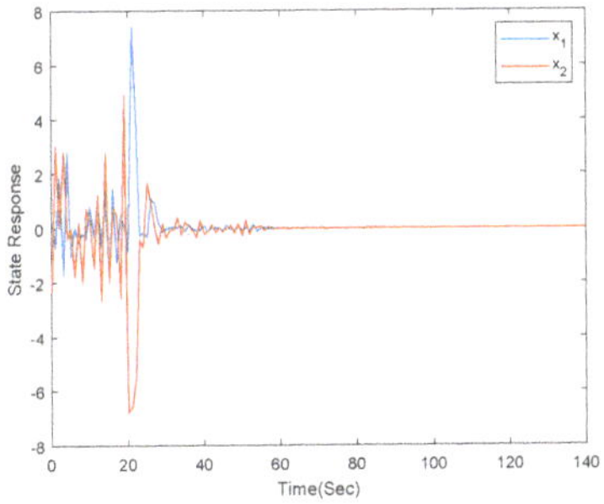

Figure 5. State response of System (4) under ADT switching signal.

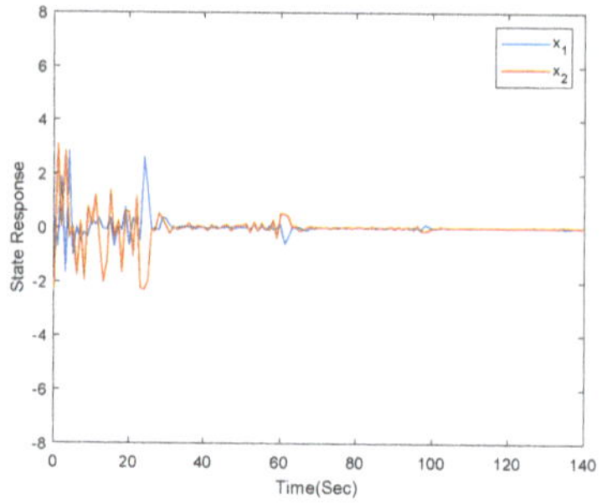

Figure 6. State response of System (4) under MDADT switching signal with $\tau_{a1} = 11$, $\tau_{a2} = 12$, $\tau_{a3} = 14$.

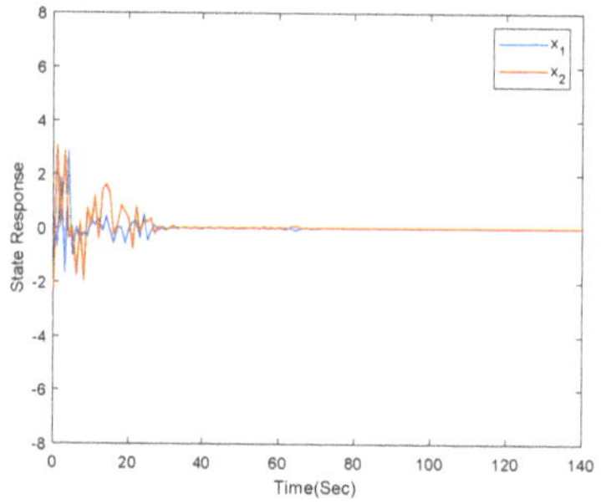

Figure 7. State response of System (4) under MDADT switching signal with $\tau_{a1} = 11$, $\tau_{a2} = 13$, and $\tau_{a3} = 15$.

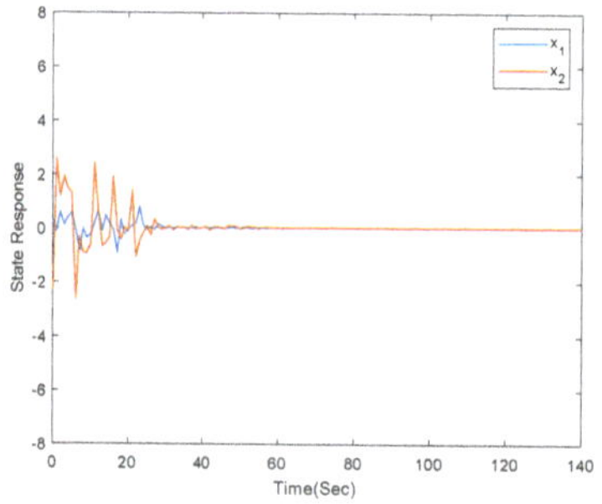

Figure 8. State response of System (4) under MDADT switching signal with $\tau_{a1} = 11$, $\tau_{a2} = 12$, and $\tau_{a3} = 13$.

Let $x(0) = [0,0]^T$ when there is a disturbance. Figures 9–12 depict the switching system's movement trajectory under asynchronous switching based on the ADT switching strategy and the MDADT switching strategy. The figure shows that when using the ADT switching strategy, the system in Figure 9 experienced obvious drastic changes before it was stable, and it began to stabilize at about 30 s, but it was still accompanied by obvious fluctuations, and it was not completely stable until 57 s, with the largest amplitude being 0.038. In contrast, under the MDADT switching strategy, the system in Figure 10 tends to be stable at about 30 s, but there are still obvious fluctuations around 59 s and 97 s. The system in Figure 11 is generally stable around 33 s and has minimal fluctuations. The system in Figure 12 is nearly stable around 25 s, has significantly reduced fluctuation compared to Figure 9, and has a maximum amplitude of 0.021.

Therefore, under the MDADT switching strategy, we can set the dwell time for each subsystem so that the system can reach a stable state faster. However, the ADT switching strategy limits the dwell time for each subsystem, resulting in equal dwell times for each subsystem, which has certain limitations. Clearly, compared to the ADT switching strategy, the MDADT switching strategy can better maintain the robust performance of the system.

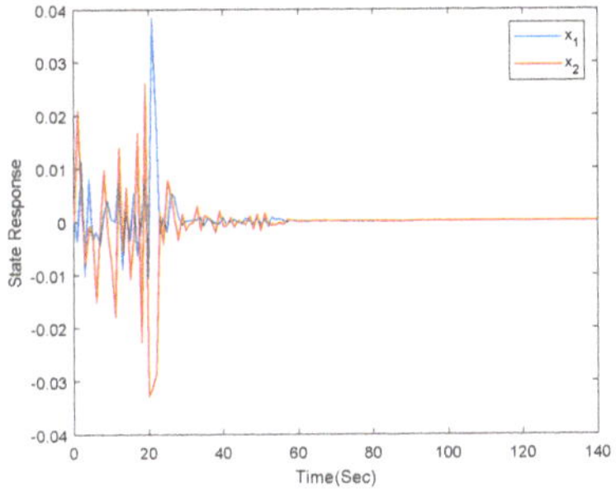

Figure 9. State response of System (3) under ADT switching signal.

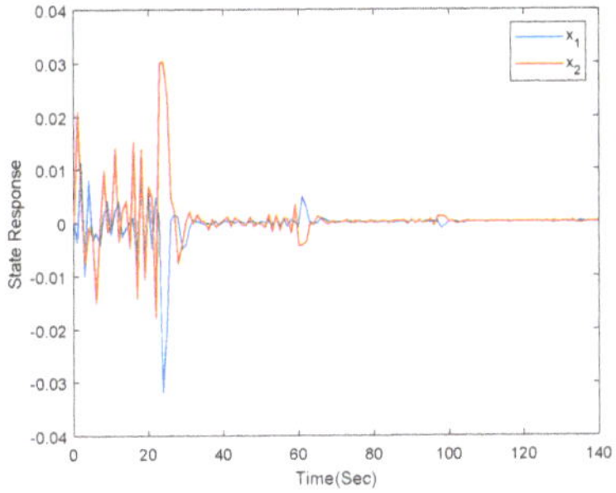

Figure 10. State response of system (3) under MDADT switching signal with $\tau_{a1} = 11$, $\tau_{a2} = 12$, and $\tau_{a3} = 14$.

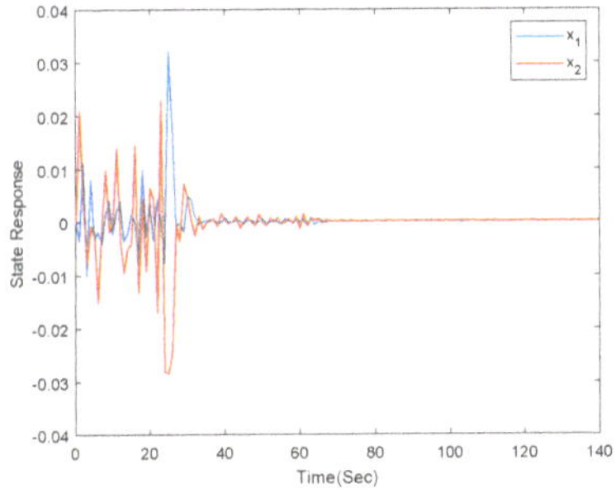

Figure 11. State response of System (3) under MDADT switching signal with $\tau_{a1} = 11$, $\tau_{a2} = 13$, and $\tau_{a3} = 15$.

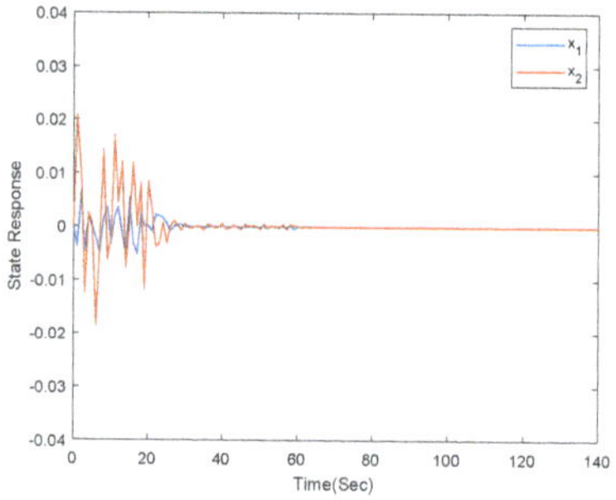

Figure 12. State response of System (3) under MDADT switching signal with $\tau_{a1} = 11$, $\tau_{a2} = 12$, and $\tau_{a3} = 13$.

5. Conclusions

This study examines the asynchronous control problem for discrete time delay switched linear systems based on MDADT. In order to address the independent switching delay of the sub-controller in relation to the subsystem, a classification analysis is conducted, and distinct Lyapunov functions are chosen for the matching and mismatching intervals between the subsystem and the controller. According to the MDADT technique, the stability of the asynchronous switching system can be achieved by modifying the proportion between the matching period and the mismatching period. Ultimately, the simulation of a discrete time delay switching system with three subsystems under the ADT technique and the MDADT technique is given. The analysis of the data confirms the effectiveness of the designed asynchronous control method.

Author Contributions: Conceptualization and writing—original draft preparation, J.Y. and X.Q.; funding acquisition, J.Y.; software, X.Q.; writing—review and editing, X.Q. and Y.S. All authors have read and agreed to the published version of the manuscript.

Funding: This work is supported by National Natural Science Foundation of China (No. 61673079).

Data Availability Statement: The data that support the results of this study are available on request from the corresponding author upon reasonable request.

Conflicts of Interest: The authors declare no conflict of interest.

References

1. Liu, X.; Tong, X.; Wang, Z.; Zhang, M. Uniform non-degeneracy discrete chaotic system and its application in image encryption. *Nonlinear Dyn.* **2022**, *108*, 653–682. [CrossRef]
2. Diekmann, O.; Othmer, H.G.; Planqué, R.; Bootsma, M.C. The discrete-time Kermack–McKendrick model: A versatile and computationally attractive framework for modeling epidemics. *Proc. Natl. Acad. Sci. USA* **2021**, *118*, e2106332118. [CrossRef]
3. Catania, L.; Di Mari, R.; Santucci de Magistris, P. Dynamic discrete mixtures for high-frequency prices. *J. Bus. Econ. Stat.* **2022**, *40*, 559–577. [CrossRef]
4. Heidler, F. H.; Paul, C. On the use of high-power diodes as crowbar switch for capacitive high-current generators. *IEEE Trans. Electromagn. Compat.* **2021**, *64*, 166–171. [CrossRef]
5. Wu, D.; Zhou, J.; Ye, H. Disturbance observer–based neural flight control for aircraft with switched time-varying distributed delays. *Proc. Inst. Mech. Eng. Part G J. Aerosp. Eng.* **2021**, *235*, 2451–2465. [CrossRef]
6. Laurini, M.; Consolini, L.; Locatelli, M. A graph-based algorithm for optimal control of switched systems: An application to car parking. *IEEE Trans. Autom. Control* **2021**, *66*, 6049–6055. [CrossRef]
7. Jin, Y.; Zhang, Y.; Jing, Y.; Fu, J. An average dwell-time method for fault-tolerant control of switched time-delay systems and its application. *IEEE Trans. Ind. Electron.* **2018**, *66*, 3139–3147. [CrossRef]
8. Liu, L.; Li, Z.; Liu, Y.J.; Tong, S. Adaptive fuzzy output feedback control of switched uncertain nonlinear systems with constraint conditions related to historical states. *IEEE Trans. Fuzzy Syst.* **2022**, *30*, 5091–5103. [CrossRef]
9. Pepe, P. On Lyapunov methods for nonlinear discrete-time switching systems with dwell-time ranges. *IEEE Trans. Autom. Control* **2021**, *67*, 1574–1581. [CrossRef]

10. Gunasekaran, N.; Ali, M.S.; Arik, S.; Ghaffar, H.A.; Diab, A.A.Z. Finite-time and sampled-data synchronization of complex dynamical networks subject to average dwell-time switching signal. *Neural Netw.* **2022**, *149*, 137–145. [CrossRef]
11. Chen, W.; Fei, Z.; Zhao, X.; Basin, M.V. Generic stability criteria for switched nonlinear systems with switching-signal-based Lyapunov functions using Takagi–Sugeno fuzzy model. *IEEE Trans. Fuzzy Syst.* **2022**, *30*, 4239–4248. [CrossRef]
12. Wang, J.; Wang, H.; Yan, H.; Wang, Y.; Shen, H. Fuzzy H_∞ sliding mode control of persistent dwell-time switched nonlinear systems. *IEEE Trans. Fuzzy Syst.* **2022**, *30*, 5143–5151. [CrossRef]
13. Fei, Z.; Chen, W.; Zhao, X.; Ren, S. Stabilization of switched linear neutral systems with time-scheduled feedback control strategy. *IEEE Trans. Autom. Control* **2022**, *68*, 1093–1100. [CrossRef]
14. Li, Z.; Cao, G.; Xie, W.; Gao, R.; Zhang, W. Switched-observer-based adaptive neural networks tracking control for switched nonlinear time-delay systems with actuator saturation. *Inf. Sci.* **2023**, *621*, 36–57. [CrossRef]
15. Sobhanipour, H.; Rezaie, B. Enhanced exponential stability analysis for switched linear time-varying delay systems under admissible edge-dependent average dwell-time strategy. *IEEE Trans. Syst. Man Cybern. Syst.* **2023**. [CrossRef]
16. Chen, H.; Lim, C.C.; Shi, P. Robust H_∞-based control for uncertain stochastic fuzzy switched time-delay systems via integral sliding mode strategy. *IEEE Trans. Fuzzy Syst.* **2020**, *30*, 382–393. [CrossRef]
17. Lyu, Z.; Liu, Z.; Zhang, Y.; Chen, C.P. Adaptive neural control for switched nonlinear systems with unstable dynamic uncertainties: A small gain-based approach. *IEEE Trans. Cybern.* **2020**, *52*, 5654–5667. [CrossRef]
18. Qi, Y.; Yuan, S.; Niu, B. Asynchronous control for switched T–S fuzzy systems subject to data injection attacks via adaptive event-triggering schemes. *IEEE Trans. Syst. Man Cybern. Syst.* **2021**, *52*, 4658–4670. [CrossRef]
19. Eddoukali, Y.; Benzaouia, A.; Ouladsine, M. Integrated fault detection and control design for continuous-time switched systems under asynchronous switching. *ISA Trans.* **2019**, *84*, 12–19. [CrossRef]
20. Qi, W.; Zong, G.; Ahn, C.K. Input–output finite-time asynchronous SMC for nonlinear semi-Markov switching systems with application. *IEEE Trans. Syst. Man Cybern. Syst.* **2021**, *52*, 5344–5353. [CrossRef]
21. Zheng, Q.; Xu, S.; Du, B. Asynchronous nonfragile guaranteed cost control for impulsive switched fuzzy systems with quantizations and its applications. *IEEE Trans. Fuzzy Syst.* **2022**, *30*, 4471–4483. [CrossRef]
22. Huang, J.; Hao, X.; Pan, X. Asynchronous switching control of discrete-time linear system based on mode-dependent average dwell time. *Int. J. Control Autom. Syst.* **2020**, *18*, 1705–1714. [CrossRef]
23. Wang, Y.; Tang, R.; Su, H.; Sun, Y.; Yang, X. Asynchronous control of switched discrete-time positive systems with delay. *IEEE Trans. Syst. Man Cybern. Syst.* **2022**, *52*, 7193–7200. [CrossRef]
24. Shi, S.; Fei, Z.; Shi, P.; Ahn, C.K. Asynchronous filtering for discrete-time switched T–S fuzzy systems. *IEEE Trans. Fuzzy Syst.* **2019**, *28*, 1531–1541. [CrossRef]
25. He, S.; Ai, Q.; Ren, C.; Dong, J.; Liu, F. Finite-time resilient controller design of a class of uncertain nonlinear systems with time-delays under asynchronous switching. *IEEE Trans. Syst. Man Cybern. Syst.* **2018**, *49*, 281–286. [CrossRef]
26. Raza, M.T.; Khan, A.Q.; Mustafa, G.; Abid, M. Design of fault detection and isolation filter for switched control systems under asynchronous switching. *IEEE Trans. Control Syst. Technol.* **2015**, *24*, 13–23. [CrossRef]
27. Qi, Y.; Zhao, X.; Fu, J.; Zeng, P.; Yu, W. Event-triggered control for switched systems under multiasynchronous switching. *IEEE Trans. Syst. Man Cybern. Syst.* **2021**, *52*, 4685–4696. [CrossRef]
28. Chekakta, I.; Belkhiat, D.E.; Guelton, K.; Jabri, D.; Manamanni, N. Asynchronous observer design for switched T–S systems with unmeasurable premises and switching mismatches. *Eng. Appl. Artif. Intell.* **2021**, *104*, 104371. [CrossRef]
29. Zhao, X.; Zhang, L.; Shi, P.; Liu, M. Stability and stabilization of switched linear systems with mode-dependent average dwell time. *IEEE Trans. Autom. Control* **2011**, *57*, 1809–1815. [CrossRef]
30. Zhang, L.; Boukas, E.K.; Shi, P. Exponential H_∞ filtering for uncertain discrete-time switched linear systems with average dwell time: A μ-dependent approach. *Int. J. Robust Nonlinear Control. IFAC-Affiliated J.* **2008**, *18*, 1188–1207. [CrossRef]
31. Xiong, J.; Lam, J. Stabilization of networked control systems with a logic ZOH. *IEEE Trans. Autom. Control* **2009**, *54*, 358–363. [CrossRef]

axioms

MDPI

Article

Solvability, Approximation and Stability of Periodic Boundary Value Problem for a Nonlinear Hadamard Fractional Differential Equation with p-Laplacian

Kaihong Zhao

Department of Mathematics, School of Electronics & Information Engineering, Taizhou University, Taizhou 318000, China; zhaokaihongs@126.com

Abstract: The fractional order p-Laplacian differential equation model is a powerful tool for describing turbulent problems in porous viscoelastic media. The study of such models helps to reveal the dynamic behavior of turbulence. Therefore, this article is mainly concerned with the periodic boundary value problem (BVP) for a class of nonlinear Hadamard fractional differential equation with p-Laplacian operator. By virtue of an important fixed point theorem on a complete metric space with two distances, we study the solvability and approximation of this BVP. Based on nonlinear analysis methods, we further discuss the generalized Ulam-Hyers (GUH) stability of this problem. Eventually, we supply two example and simulations to verify the correctness and availability of our main results. Compared to many previous studies, our approach enables the solution of the system to exist in metric space rather than normed space. In summary, we obtain some sufficient conditions for the existence, uniqueness, and stability of solutions in the metric space.

Keywords: Hadamard fractional calculus; p-Laplacian operator; boundary value conditions; dynamical behavior; complete metric space

MSC: 34A08; 34A37; 34D20

Citation: Zhao, K. Solvability, Approximation and Stability of Periodic Boundary Value Problem for a Nonlinear Hadamard Fractional Differential Equation with p-Laplacian. *Axioms* **2023**, *12*, 733. https://doi.org/10.3390/axioms12080733

Academic Editor: Tianwei Zhang

Received: 23 June 2023
Revised: 23 July 2023
Accepted: 26 July 2023
Published: 27 July 2023

1. Introduction

The p-Laplacian differential equation is one of the famous and important second-order nonlinear ordinary differential equations (ODEs). This equation first appeared in Leibenson's study [1] of turbulence in porous media in 1983. The underlying form of p-Laplacian differential equation is written as

$$\Phi_{p}(u'(t))' = f(t, u(t)),\ t \in (0,1),$$

where $\Phi_{p} : x \to |x|^{p-2}x(p > 1)$ is called the p-Laplacian operator. Its inverse is $\Phi_{p}^{-1} = \Phi_{q}$ with $\frac{1}{p} + \frac{1}{q} = 1$. Due to its description of fundamental mechanical problems in turbulence, p-Laplacian differential equations have been extensively and deeply studied. In recent years, some scholars have begun to focus on the nonlinear fractional differential system with p-Laplacian. For example, the authors in [2] investigated the multiple positive solutions of a nonlinear high order Riemann-Liouville fractional p-Laplacian equation with integral boundary value conditions. In [3], the author explored the existence and GUH-stability of a nonlinear Caputo-Fabrizio fractional coupled Laplacian equations. In [4], based on the Guo-Krasnosel'skii fixed point theorem, the authors probed into the multiple positive solutions of a system of mixed Hadamard fractional BVP with (p_1, p_2)-Laplacian. In fact, some articles have been disposed of the BVP of p-Laplacian system involving Riemann-Liouville or Caputo fractional derivatives (see [5–13]).

Hadamard [14] raised a novel fractional integral and derivative in 1892, which was later named Hadamard-type fractional calculus. There are some obvious differences between Hadamard fractional calculus and Riemann-Liouville fractional calculus. For example, $k_H(t,s) = (\log \frac{t}{s})^{\gamma-1}$ is the integral kernel corresponding to γ-order Hadamard fractional derivative, while $k_R(t,s) = (t-s)^{\gamma-1}$ is the integral kernel corresponding to γ-order Riemann-Liouville fractional derivative. Furthermore, for any $\lambda > 0$, $k_H(\lambda t, \lambda s) = k_H(t,s)$ is different from $k_R(\lambda t, \lambda s) = \lambda^{\gamma-1} k_R(t,s) \neq k_R(t,s)$. The study on Hadamard fractional differential equations has attracted the attention of many scholars. There have been a series of fruitful achievements (see [15–21]). In 1940s, Ulam and Hyers [22,23] put forward a new stability that describes the stationarity of the exact and approximate solutions of system. Subsequently, extensive and in-depth research was conducted on the Ulam-Hyers stability of various systems. Especially, many excellent research results have emerged regarding the Ulam-Hyers stability of fractional order differential systems (see some of them [3,21,24–32]). Moreover, it is rare to combine the Hadamard fractional derivative with Laplacian operator. Therefore, it is novel and interesting to probe these problems.

Illuminated by the above arguments, this manuscript deals with the periodic BVP of a nonlinear Hadamard fractional differential equation with p-Laplacian operator as follows:

$$\begin{cases} {}^{\mathrm{H}}\mathscr{D}_{1^+}^{\alpha}\left[\Phi_p\left({}^{\mathrm{H}}\mathscr{D}_{1^+}^{\beta} u(t)\right)\right] = f(t, u(t)), \ t \in (1, e], \\ u(1) = u(e), \ {}^{\mathrm{H}}\mathscr{D}_{1^+}^{\beta} u(1) = {}^{\mathrm{H}}\mathscr{D}_{1^+}^{\beta} u(e), \end{cases} \tag{1}$$

where $0 < \alpha \leq 1$, $1 < \beta \leq 2$, $p > 1$, ${}^{\mathrm{H}}\mathscr{D}_{1^+}^{*}$ is the $*$-order Hadamard fractional derivative, $\Phi_p = |x|^{p-2}x$, and its inverse $\Phi_p^{-1} = \Phi_q$ with $\frac{1}{p} + \frac{1}{q} = 1$, $f \in C([1,e] \times \mathbb{R}, \mathbb{R})$. In addition, our study has also been inspired by the latest achievements in fractional differential equations, such as numerical algorithms and simulations [33–38], as well as the application of some nonsingular fractional derivative models [34,37–43].

The paper aims to discuss the approximation and GUH-stability of BVP (1). The novelty of this paper is mainly reflected as follows: (a) Since there is no paper dealing with the approximation problem of nonlinear Hadamard fractional differential systems with Laplace operator, we first consider the system (1) to fill this gap. (b) By applying a fixed point theorem on complete metric space with two kinds of distance, we obtain some sufficient conditions to ensure that system (1) has a unique solution. In addition, we build the generalized Ulam-Hyers stability of system (1) based on nonlinear analysis methods and inequality techniques. (c) Many previous papers (see [2–13,17–19,24,25]) usually used some fixed-point theorems on Banach spaces to study the existence of solutions of fractional differential equations. However, we handle the existence of solutions to fractional order differential equations by defining two different distances on a complete distance space. This allows for the discussion of the existence of solutions in a broader space, and there are relatively few restrictions on the existence of solutions. Therefore, our research methods and results are novel and interesting.

The rest sections of this paper are organized as follows. In Section 2, we recollect the definition of Hadamard fractional integrals and derivatives and some necessary lemmas. In Section 3, we discuss the existence, uniqueness, and approximation of solutions to BVP (1) by constructing two different distances and applying an important fixed point theorem on metric space. Furthermore, we use nonlinear analysis methods and inequality techniques to establish the GUH-stability of BVP (1) in Section 4. Section 5 provides the numerical solutions and simulations for two examples by means of ODE113 toolbox in MATLAB. Finally, we have made a brief summary in Section 6.

2. Preliminaries

This portion mainly introduces some important concepts and lemmas.

Definition 1 ([44]). *For $a > 0$, the left-sided Hadamard fractional integral of order $\gamma > 0$ for a function $\xi : [a, \infty) \to \mathbb{R}$ is defined by*

$${}^{\mathrm{H}}\mathscr{I}_{a^+}^{\gamma} \xi(t) = \frac{1}{\Gamma(\gamma)} \int_a^t \left(\log \frac{t}{s}\right)^{\gamma-1} \xi(s) \frac{ds}{s},$$

provided the integral exists, where $\Gamma(\gamma) = \int_0^\infty t^{\gamma-1}e^{-t}dt$ *and* $\log(\cdot) = \log_e(\cdot)$.

Definition 2 ([44])**.** *Let* $a, \gamma > 0$ *and* $\xi \in C^m[a,\infty)$*, the* γ*-order left-sided Hadamard fractional derivative is defined by*

$$^{\mathrm{H}}\mathscr{D}^{\alpha}_{a^+}\xi(t) = \frac{1}{\Gamma(m-\gamma)}\left(t\frac{d}{dt}\right)^m \int_a^t \left(\log\frac{t}{s}\right)^{m-\gamma-1}\xi(s)\frac{ds}{s},$$

where $m-1 < \alpha \le m$, $m = [\gamma]+1$*, and* $[\cdot]$ *is the Gaussian truncating integer function.*

Lemma 1 ([44])**.** *Let* $a, b, \gamma > 0$ *and* $\xi \in C^m(a,b) \cap L^1(a,b)$*, then*

$$^{\mathrm{H}}\mathscr{I}^{\gamma}_{a^+}(^{\mathrm{H}}\mathscr{D}^{\gamma}_{a^+}\xi(t)) = \xi(t) + \sum_{i=1}^{m} c_i\left(\log\frac{t}{a}\right)^{\gamma-i},$$

where $c_1, c_2, \ldots, c_m$ *are some real constants, and* $m = [\gamma]+1$.

Lemma 2. *Let* $p > 1$*. The* p*-Laplacian operator* $\Phi_p(z) = |z|^{p-2}z$ *has the followings:*

(i) *If* $z \ge 0$*, then* $\Phi_p(z) = z^{p-1}$*, and* $\Phi_p(z)$ *is increasing with respect to* z*;*
(ii) *For all* $z, w \in \mathbb{R}$, $\Phi_p(zw) = \Phi_p(z)\Phi_p(w)$*;*
(iii) *If* $\frac{1}{p} + \frac{1}{q} = 1$*, then* $\Phi_q[\Phi_p(z)] = \Phi_p[\Phi_q(z)] = z$*, for all* $z \in \mathbb{R}$*;*
(iv) *For all* $z, w \ge 0$, $z \le w \Leftrightarrow \Phi_q(z) \le \Phi_q(w)$*;*
(v) $0 \le z \le \Phi_q^{-1}(w) \Leftrightarrow 0 \le \Phi_q(z) \le w$*;*
(vi) $|\Phi_q(z) - \Phi_q(w)| \le \begin{cases} (q-1)\overline{M}^{q-2}|z-w|, & q \ge 2,\ 0 \le z, w \le \overline{M}, \\ (q-1)\underline{M}^{q-2}|z-w|, & 1 < q < 2,\ z, w \ge \underline{M} \ge 0. \end{cases}$

Now we introduce the following important fixed point theorem on a complete metric space involving two different distances, which will be used to prove the existence and uniqueness of solution to BVP (1).

Lemma 3 ([45])**.** *Let* ρ *and* ϱ *be two different metrics on a nonempty set* $\mathbb{X}$*, and define an operator* $\mathscr{T} : \mathbb{X} \to \mathbb{X}$*. Assume that*

(a1) *For all* $x, y \in \mathbb{X}$*, there has a constant* $\iota > 0$ *such that* $\varrho(\mathscr{T}x, \mathscr{T}y) \le \iota\rho(x,y)$*;*
(a2) $(\mathbb{X}, \varrho)$ *is a complete metric space;*
(a3) $\mathscr{T} : (\mathbb{X}, \varrho) \to (\mathbb{X}, \varrho)$ *is continuous;*
(a4) *For all* $x, y \in \mathbb{X}$*, there has a constant* $0 < \kappa < 1$ *such that* $\rho(\mathscr{T}x, \mathscr{T}y) \le \kappa\rho(x,y)$.

Then there has a unique $x^* \in \mathbb{X}$ *such that* $\mathscr{T}x^* = x^*$*, and* $\lim_{k\to\infty}\mathscr{T}^k x_0 = x^*$ *for any* $x_0 \in \mathbb{X}$.

It is worth noting that the application techniques and related generalization of Lemma 3 can also be found in [46–49] and the references therein.

3. Solvability and Approximation

In this portion, we will prove the existence of a unique solution for system (1) based on Lemma 3. To this end, we need the following important lemma.

Lemma 4. *Assume that* $0 < \alpha \le 1$, $1 < \beta \le 2$ *and* $p > 1$ *are some constants,* $f \in C([1,e] \times \mathbb{R}, \mathbb{R})$*. Then BVP (1) is equivalent to the following integral equation*

$$u(t) = -A_u(e)(\log t)^{\beta-1} + A_u(t), \tag{2}$$

where $A_u(t) = {}^{\mathrm{H}}\mathscr{I}^{\beta}_{1^+}[\Phi_q(^{\mathrm{H}}\mathscr{I}^{\alpha}_{1^+}f(t,u(t)))]$.

Proof. If $u(t) \in C((1,e],\mathbb{R})$ is a solution of system (1), then it follows from Lemma 1 that

$$\Phi_{p}({}^{\mathrm{H}}\mathscr{D}^{\beta}_{1^+}u(t)) = c(\log t)^{\alpha-1} + {}^{\mathrm{H}}\mathscr{I}^{\alpha}_{1^+}f(t,u(t)), \tag{3}$$

which implies that

$${}^{\mathrm{H}}\mathscr{D}^{\beta}_{1^+}u(t) = \Phi_{q}[c(\log t)^{\alpha-1} + {}^{\mathrm{H}}\mathscr{I}^{\alpha}_{1^+}f(t,u(t))]. \tag{4}$$

According to the existence of ${}^{\mathrm{H}}\mathscr{D}^{\beta}_{1^+}u(1)$ and (4), we know that $c = 0$ and ${}^{\mathrm{H}}\mathscr{D}^{\beta}_{1^+}u(1) = 0$. By Lemma 1 and (4), we have

$$u(t) = d_1(\log t)^{\beta-1} + d_2(\log t)^{\beta-2} + {}^{\mathrm{H}}\mathscr{I}^{\beta}_{1^+}[\Phi_{q}({}^{\mathrm{H}}\mathscr{I}^{\alpha}_{1^+}f(t,u(t)))]. \tag{5}$$

Similarly, we drive from $u(1) = u(e)$ and (5) that $d_2 = 0$ and

$$d_1 = -{}^{\mathrm{H}}\mathscr{I}^{\beta}_{1^+}[\Phi_{q}({}^{\mathrm{H}}\mathscr{I}^{\alpha}_{1^+}f(t,u(t)))]\Big|_{t=e} = -A_u(e). \tag{6}$$

In view of (5) and (6), we have

$$u(t) = -A_u(e)(\log t)^{\beta-1} + A_u(t). \tag{7}$$

Thus, $u(t) \in C((1,e],\mathbb{R})$ is a solution of system (2). Vice versa, if $u(t) \in C((1,e],\mathbb{R})$ is a solution of (2), then it is also a solution of (1) because the above derivation is completely reversible. The proof is completed. □

Let $\mathbb{X} = C([1,e],\mathbb{R})$, two different distances $\rho, \varrho : \mathbb{X} \to \mathbb{X}$ are respectively defined by

$$\rho(u(t), v(t)) = \sup_{t\in[1,e]} |u(t) - v(t)|, \quad \varrho(u(t), v(t)) = \int_1^e |u(t) - v(t)|dt, \tag{8}$$

for all $u(t), v(t) \in \mathbb{X}$. It is easy to prove that $(\mathbb{X}, \rho)$ and $(\mathbb{X}, \varrho)$ are all complete metric spaces. In addition, we need the following underlying assumptions in the whole paper.

(H1) $0 < \alpha \le 1, 1 < \beta \le 2$ and $1 < p \le 2$ are some constants, $f \in C([1,e] \times \mathbb{R}, \mathbb{R})$.
(H2) There has a constant $M > 0$ such that

$$0 \le f(t,u) \le M, \ \forall\, t \in [1,e], \ u \in \mathbb{R}.$$

(H3) There has a function $0 \le \ell(t) \in C[1,e]$ such that, for all $t \in [1,e]$ and $u, v \in \mathbb{R}$,

$$|f(t,u) - f(t,v)| \le \ell(t)|u - v|.$$

(H4) $\kappa = \frac{2(q-1)}{\Gamma(\alpha+\beta+1)}\left(\frac{M}{\Gamma(\alpha+1)}\right)^{q-2}\|\ell\|_e < 1$, where $\|\ell\|_e = \max_{1\le t\le e}\{\ell(t)\}$.

Theorem 1. *If* (H1)–(H4) *are fulfilled, then BVP* (1) *has a unique solution* $u^*(t) \in \mathbb{X}$.

Proof. In what follows, we will apply Lemma 3 to prove Theorem 1. Two different distances $\rho, \varrho : \mathbb{X} \to \mathbb{X}$ are defined as (8), then $(\mathbb{X}, \rho)$ and $(\mathbb{X}, \varrho)$ are all complete metric spaces, which indicates that the condition (a2) holds. According to Lemma 4, for all $u(t) \in \mathbb{X}$, an operator $\mathscr{T} : \mathbb{X} \to \mathbb{X}$ is defined by

$$\mathscr{T}(u(t)) = -A_u(e)(\log t)^{\beta-1} + A_u(t), \tag{9}$$

where $A_u(t) = {}^{\mathrm{H}}\mathscr{I}^{\beta}_{1^+}[\Phi_{q}({}^{\mathrm{H}}\mathscr{I}^{\alpha}_{1^+}f(t,u(t)))]$.

From the continuity of Φ_{q} and Hadamard fractional integral, we know that $\mathscr{T}:(\mathbb{X},\varrho) \to (\mathbb{X},\varrho)$ is continuous, which means that the condition (a3) holds. By (H2), we have

$$0 \leq {}^{\mathrm{H}}\mathscr{J}_{1^+}^{\alpha} f(t,u(t),u(t-\tau(t))) \leq \frac{M}{\Gamma(\alpha+1)}(\log t)^{\alpha} \leq \frac{M}{\Gamma(\alpha+1)},\ t\in[1,e]. \tag{10}$$

For all $u,v\in\mathbb{X}$, $t\in[1,e]$, we derive from (vi) in Lemma 2, (H3) and (10) that

$$\begin{aligned}
&|A_u(t)-A_v(t)| = |{}^{\mathrm{H}}\mathscr{J}_{1^+}^{\beta}[\Phi_{q}({}^{\mathrm{H}}\mathscr{J}_{1^+}^{\alpha} f(t,u(t)))-\Phi_{q}({}^{\mathrm{H}}\mathscr{J}_{1^+}^{\alpha} f(t,v(t)))]|\\
\leq&{}^{\mathrm{H}}\mathscr{J}_{1^+}^{\beta}|\Phi_{q}({}^{\mathrm{H}}\mathscr{J}_{1^+}^{\alpha} f(t,u(t)))-\Phi_{q}({}^{\mathrm{H}}\mathscr{J}_{1^+}^{\alpha} f(t,v(t)))|\\
\leq&(q-1)\left(\frac{M}{\Gamma(\alpha+1)}\right)^{q-2}{}^{\mathrm{H}}\mathscr{J}_{1^+}^{\beta}|{}^{\mathrm{H}}\mathscr{J}_{1^+}^{\alpha} f(t,u(t))-{}^{\mathrm{H}}\mathscr{J}_{1^+}^{\alpha} f(t,v(t))|\\
\leq&(q-1)\left(\frac{M}{\Gamma(\alpha+1)}\right)^{q-2}{}^{\mathrm{H}}\mathscr{J}_{1^+}^{\beta}[{}^{\mathrm{H}}\mathscr{J}_{1^+}^{\alpha}|f(t,u(t))-f(t,v(t))|]\\
\leq&(q-1)\left(\frac{M}{\Gamma(\alpha+1)}\right)^{q-2}{}^{\mathrm{H}}\mathscr{J}_{1^+}^{\alpha+\beta}[\ell(t)|u(t)-v(t)|]\\
\leq&(q-1)\left(\frac{M}{\Gamma(\alpha+1)}\right)^{q-2}\frac{1}{\Gamma(\alpha+\beta+1)}\|\ell\|_e\cdot\rho(u,v).
\end{aligned}\tag{11}$$

It follows from (9) and (11) that

$$\begin{aligned}
&|\mathscr{T}(u(t))-\mathscr{T}(v(t))| = |-(A_u(e)-A_v(e))(\log t)^{\beta-1}+(A_u(t)-A_v(t))|\\
\leq&|A_u(e)-A_v(e)|(\log t)^{\beta-1}+|(A_u(t)-A_v(t))|\\
\leq&\frac{2(q-1)}{\Gamma(\alpha+\beta+1)}\left(\frac{M}{\Gamma(\alpha+1)}\right)^{q-2}\|\ell\|_e\cdot\rho(u,v)=\kappa\rho(u,v).
\end{aligned}\tag{12}$$

In light of (12), we have

$$\rho(\mathscr{T}(u),\mathscr{T}(v))\leq\kappa\rho(u,v),\ \forall\, u,v\in\mathbb{X},\ t\in[1,e]. \tag{13}$$

According to (H4) and (13), we know that (a4) in Lemma 3 holds.

Similar to (11), noticing that $(\log\frac{t}{s})^{\alpha+\beta-1}$ and $\frac{1}{s}$ are monotonically decreasing with respect to s in $[1,e]$, we have

$$\begin{aligned}
&|A_u(t)-A_v(t)| \leq (q-1)\left(\frac{M}{\Gamma(\alpha+1)}\right)^{q-2}{}^{\mathrm{H}}\mathscr{J}_{1^+}^{\alpha+\beta}[\ell(t)|u(t)-v(t)|]\\
=&(q-1)\left(\frac{M}{\Gamma(\alpha+1)}\right)^{q-2}\frac{1}{\Gamma(\alpha+\beta)}\|\ell\|_e\int_1^t\left(\log\frac{t}{s}\right)^{\alpha+\beta-1}|u(s)-v(s)|\frac{ds}{s}\\
\leq&(q-1)\left(\frac{M}{\Gamma(\alpha+1)}\right)^{q-2}\frac{1}{\Gamma(\alpha+\beta)}\|\ell\|_e\cdot(\log t)^{\alpha+\beta-1}\int_1^t|u(s)-v(s)|ds\\
\leq&\frac{q-1}{\Gamma(\alpha+\beta)}\left(\frac{M}{\Gamma(\alpha+1)}\right)^{q-2}\|\ell\|_e\cdot(\log e)^{\alpha+\beta-1}\int_1^e|u(s)-v(s)|ds\\
=&\frac{q-1}{\Gamma(\alpha+\beta)}\left(\frac{M}{\Gamma(\alpha+1)}\right)^{q-2}\|\ell\|_e\cdot\varrho(u,v).
\end{aligned}\tag{14}$$

Similar to (12), we derive from (14) that

$$|\mathscr{T}(u(t))-\mathscr{T}(v(t))|\leq\frac{2(q-1)}{\Gamma(\alpha+\beta)}\left(\frac{M}{\Gamma(\alpha+1)}\right)^{q-2}\|\ell\|_e\cdot\varrho(u,v). \tag{15}$$

From (15), we get

$$\varrho(\mathscr{T}(u),\mathscr{T}(v)) = \int_1^e |\mathscr{T}(u(t)) - \mathscr{T}(v(t))|dt$$
$$\leq \frac{2(q-1)e}{\Gamma(\alpha+\beta)}\left(\frac{M}{\Gamma(\alpha+1)}\right)^{q-2} \|\ell\|_e \cdot \varrho(u,v). \tag{16}$$

Equation (16) indicates that (a1) in Lemma 3 also holds. Thus, it follows from Lemma 3 that $\mathscr{T}$ exists a unique fixed point $u^*(t) \in \mathbb{X}$, which is the unique solution of (1). The proof is completed. □

Next, we shall discuss the approximation of solution for system (1). In fact, from Lemma 3, we conclude that the unique solution $u^*(t) \in \mathbb{X}$ of (1) satisfies $u^*(t) = \lim_{n\to\infty} \mathscr{T}^n u_0$ for any $u_0 \in \mathbb{X}$. Denote $u_n(t) = \mathscr{T}^n u_0$, then $\{u_n(t)\}$ is a approximation sequence of solution to system (1). Based on (9), $u_n(t)$ can be represented as

$$u_n(t) = -A_{u_{n-1}}(e)(\log t)^{\beta-1} + A_{u_{n-1}}(t), \tag{17}$$

where $A_{u_{n-1}}(t) = {}^{\mathrm{H}}\mathscr{I}^{\beta}_{1^+}\left[\Phi_{q}\left({}^{\mathrm{H}}\mathscr{I}^{\alpha}_{1^+} f(t,u_{n-1}(t))\right)\right]$.

Similar to (12), we derive from (17) that

$$|u_{n+1}(t) - u_n(t)| \leq \kappa |u_n(t) - u_{n-1}(t)|,$$

which implies that

$$\rho(u_{n+1}, u_n) \leq \kappa\rho(u_n, u_{n-1}). \tag{18}$$

By virtue of (H4) and (18), we know that $\{u_n(t)\}$ converges exponentially on $(\mathbb{X},\rho)$.

4. Generalized Ulam-Hyers Stability

This section centres on the GUH-stability of BVP (1). We first provide the concept of GUH-stability for BVP (1).

For all $\delta > 0$, consider the following fractional differential inequality

$$\begin{cases} {}^{\mathrm{H}}\mathscr{D}^{\alpha}_{1^+}\left[\Phi_{p}\left({}^{\mathrm{H}}\mathscr{D}^{\beta}_{1^+} u(t)\right)\right] - f(t,u(t)) \leq \delta,\ t \in (1,e], \\ u(1) = u(e),\ {}^{\mathrm{H}}\mathscr{D}^{\beta}_{1^+} u(1) = {}^{\mathrm{H}}\mathscr{D}^{\beta}_{1^+} u(e). \end{cases} \tag{19}$$

Definition 3. *BVP (1) is said to be generalized Ulam-Hyers (GUH) stable on the metric space $(\mathbb{X},\rho)$, provided that, for all $\delta > 0$ and any solution $u \in \mathbb{X}$ of (19), there have an $\omega \in C(\mathbb{R},\mathbb{R}^+)$ with $\omega(0) = 0$ and a unique solution $u^* \in \mathbb{X}$ of (1) such that*

$$\rho(u,u^*) \leq \omega(\delta).$$

Remark 1. *$u(t) \in \mathbb{X}$ solves the inequality (19) iff there has a continuous function $\varphi(t)$ such that*

$$\begin{cases} |\varphi(t)| \leq \delta,\ t \in (1,e], \\ {}^{\mathrm{H}}\mathscr{D}^{\alpha}_{1^+}\left[\Phi_{p}\left({}^{\mathrm{H}}\mathscr{D}^{\beta}_{1^+} u(t)\right)\right] = f(t,u(t)) + \varphi(t),\ t \in (1,e], \\ u(1) = u(e),\ {}^{\mathrm{H}}\mathscr{D}^{\beta}_{1^+} u(1) = {}^{\mathrm{H}}\mathscr{D}^{\beta}_{1^+} u(e). \end{cases} \tag{20}$$

Theorem 2. *If (H1)–(H4) are satisfied, then BVP (1) is GUH-stable.*

Proof. On the basis of Lemma 4 and Remark 1, the solution $u(t)$ of inequality (19) is written by

$$u(t) = -A_u^{\varphi}(e)(\log t)^{\beta-1} + A_u^{\varphi}(t), \tag{21}$$

where $A_u^{\varphi}(t) = {}^{\mathrm{H}}\mathcal{J}_{1^+}^{\beta}\left[\Phi_{q}\left({}^{\mathrm{H}}\mathcal{J}_{1^+}^{\alpha}[f(t,u(t)) + \varphi(t)]\right)\right]$. In the light of Theorem 1 and Lemma 4, the unique solution $u^*(t)$ of BVP (1) is read as

$$u^*(t) = -A_{u^*}(e)(\log t)^{\beta-1} + A_{u^*}(t), \tag{22}$$

where $A_{u^*}(t) = {}^{\mathrm{H}}\mathcal{J}_{1^+}^{\beta}\left[\Phi_{q}\left({}^{\mathrm{H}}\mathcal{J}_{1^+}^{\alpha} f(t,u^*(t))\right)\right]$.

Similar to (11), we obtain

$$\begin{aligned}
&|A_u^{\varphi}(t) - A_{u^*}(t)| = \left|{}^{\mathrm{H}}\mathcal{J}_{1^+}^{\beta}\left[\Phi_{q}\left({}^{\mathrm{H}}\mathcal{J}_{1^+}^{\alpha}[f(t,u(t)) + \varphi(t)]\right) - \Phi_{q}\left({}^{\mathrm{H}}\mathcal{J}_{1^+}^{\alpha} f(t,u^*(t))\right)\right]\right| \\
\leq &{}^{\mathrm{H}}\mathcal{J}_{1^+}^{\beta}\left|\Phi_{q}\left({}^{\mathrm{H}}\mathcal{J}_{1^+}^{\alpha}[f(t,u(t)) + \varphi(t)]\right) - \Phi_{q}\left({}^{\mathrm{H}}\mathcal{J}_{1^+}^{\alpha} f(t,u^*(t))\right)\right| \\
\leq &(q-1)\left(\frac{M+\delta}{\Gamma(\alpha+1)}\right)^{q-2} {}^{\mathrm{H}}\mathcal{J}_{1^+}^{\beta}\left|{}^{\mathrm{H}}\mathcal{J}_{1^+}^{\alpha}[f(t,u(t)) + \varphi(t)] - {}^{\mathrm{H}}\mathcal{J}_{1^+}^{\alpha} f(t,u^*(t))\right| \\
\leq &(q-1)\left(\frac{M+\delta}{\Gamma(\alpha+1)}\right)^{q-2} {}^{\mathrm{H}}\mathcal{J}_{1^+}^{\beta}\left[{}^{\mathrm{H}}\mathcal{J}_{1^+}^{\alpha}[|f(t,u(t)) - f(t,u^*(t))| + |\varphi(t)|]\right] \\
\leq &(q-1)\left(\frac{M+\delta}{\Gamma(\alpha+1)}\right)^{q-2} {}^{\mathrm{H}}\mathcal{J}_{1^+}^{\alpha+\beta}[\ell(t)|u(t) - u^*(t)| + |\varphi(t)|] \\
\leq &(q-1)\left(\frac{M+\delta}{\Gamma(\alpha+1)}\right)^{q-2} \frac{1}{\Gamma(\alpha+\beta+1)}[\|\ell\|_e \cdot \rho(u,\, u^*) + \delta].
\end{aligned} \tag{23}$$

By the same manner of (12), we derive from (21)–(23) that

$$\begin{aligned}
&|u(t) - u^*(t)| = |-(A_u^{\varphi}(e) - A_{u^*}(e))(\log t)^{\beta-1} + (A_u^{\varphi}(t) - A_{u^*}(t))| \\
\leq &|A_u^{\varphi}(e) - A_{u^*}(e)|(\log t)^{\beta-1} + |(A_u^{\varphi}(t) - A_{u^*}(t))| \\
\leq &\frac{2(q-1)}{\Gamma(\alpha+\beta+1)}\left(\frac{M+\delta}{\Gamma(\alpha+1)}\right)^{q-2}[\|\ell\|_e \cdot \rho(u,\, u^*) + \delta] \\
= &\kappa(\delta)\rho(u,\, u^*) + \lambda(\delta),
\end{aligned} \tag{24}$$

where $\kappa(\delta) = \frac{2(q-1)}{\Gamma(\alpha+\beta+1)}\left(\frac{M+\delta}{\Gamma(\alpha+1)}\right)^{q-2}\|\ell\|_e$, $\lambda(\delta) = \frac{2(q-1)\delta}{\Gamma(\alpha+\beta+1)}\left(\frac{M+\delta}{\Gamma(\alpha+1)}\right)^{q-2}$.

For any sufficiently small $\delta > 0$, the condition (H4) ensures that $0 < \kappa(\delta) < 1$. Thus, we know from (24) that

$$\rho(u,\, u^*) \leq \frac{\lambda(\delta)}{1-\kappa(\delta)} = \omega(\delta). \tag{25}$$

Obviously, $\kappa(0) = \kappa < 1$, $\lambda(0) = 0$ and $\omega(\delta) = \frac{\lambda(\delta)}{1-\kappa(\delta)} > 0$ with $\omega(0) = 0$. By virtue of Definition 3, (25) shows that BVP (1) is GUH-stable. The proof is completed. □

5. Two Examples and Simulations

This section provides two examples and simulations to inspect the correctness and validity of our main results. Consider the following nonlinear Hadamard fractional differential equation with p-Laplacian operator

$$\begin{cases} {}^{\mathrm{H}}\mathscr{D}_{1^+}^{\alpha}\left[\Phi_{p}\left({}^{\mathrm{H}}\mathscr{D}_{1^+}^{\beta} u(t)\right)\right] = f(t,u(t)),\ t \in (1,e], \\ u(1) = u(e),\ {}^{\mathrm{H}}\mathscr{D}_{1^+}^{\beta} u(1) = {}^{\mathrm{H}}\mathscr{D}_{1^+}^{\beta} u(e), \end{cases} \tag{26}$$

Example 1. *In (26), we take* $p = \frac{5}{4}$, $\alpha = 0.2$, $\beta = 1.4$, $f(t,u) = \frac{2+\sin(3t)}{20}[\frac{3\pi}{4} + \arctan(u)]$, *then a simple computation gives that* $q = 5 > 2$, *and*

$$\frac{\pi}{80} \leq f(t,u) \leq \frac{3\pi}{16},\ |f(t,u) - f(t,v)| \leq \frac{2+\sin(3t)}{20}|u-v|.$$

In consequent, the conditions (H1)–(H3) *are fulfilled. In addition,* $M = \frac{3\pi}{16}$, $\ell(t) = \frac{2+\sin(3t)}{20}$, $\|\ell\|_e = \frac{3}{20}$, *and*

$$\kappa = \frac{2(q-1)}{\Gamma(\alpha+\beta+1)}\left(\frac{M}{\Gamma(\alpha+1)}\right)^{q-2}\|\ell\|_e \approx 0.1716 < 1.$$

Thus, (H4) *holds. From Theorem 1 and Theorem 2, we claim that Example 1 has a unique solution, which is GUH-stable.*

Remark 2. *In Example 1,* p, α, β *are all rational number.* $\alpha = 0.2$ *is close to 0, and* $\beta = 1.4$ *is close to 1.5. To further verify the correctness of our results and the sensitivity of numerical simulation to parameters, we choose* p, α, β *as irrational number satisfying* α *close to 1 and* β *close to 2 in the following example.*

Example 2. *In (26), Choose* $p = \frac{\sqrt{15}}{2}$, $\alpha = \sqrt{0.9}$, $\beta = \sqrt{3.9}$, *and* $f(t,u)$ *be same as Example 1. Then* $q = 2.0678 > 2$, *and the conditions* (H1)–(H3) *also hold.* M, $\ell(t)$ *and* $\|\ell\|_e$ *are same as Example 1. In addition,*

$$\kappa = \frac{2(q-1)}{\Gamma(\alpha+\beta+1)}\left(\frac{M}{\Gamma(\alpha+1)}\right)^{q-2}\|\ell\|_e \approx 0.0567 < 1.$$

Thus, (H4) *is also true. From Theorem 1 and Theorem 2, we claim that Example 2 also has a unique GUH-stable solution.*

To perform the numerical simulation on Examples 1 and 2, we need to give a concise algorithm below. Let $v(t) = {}^{H}\mathscr{D}^{\beta}_{1^+}u(t)$, then the Equation (2) can be rewritten as

$$\begin{cases} u(t) = -\frac{1}{\Gamma(\beta)}\int_1^e \left(\log\frac{e}{s}\right)^{\beta-1} v(s)\frac{ds}{s}\cdot(\log t)^{\beta-1} \\ \qquad + \frac{1}{\Gamma(\beta)}\int_1^t \left(\log\frac{t}{s}\right)^{\beta-1} v(s)\frac{ds}{s}, \\ v(t) = \left[\frac{1}{\Gamma(\alpha)}\int_1^t \left(\log\frac{t}{s}\right)^{\alpha-1} f(s,u(s))\frac{ds}{s}\right]^{q-1}. \end{cases} \tag{27}$$

Taking the derivative at both sides of (27), we get

$$\begin{cases} \frac{du(t)}{dt} = -\frac{\beta-1}{\Gamma(\beta)}\int_1^e \left(\log\frac{e}{s}\right)^{\beta-1} v(s)\frac{ds}{s}\cdot\frac{(\log t)^{\beta-2}}{t} \\ \qquad + \frac{\beta-1}{t\Gamma(\beta)}\int_1^t \left(\log\frac{t}{s}\right)^{\beta-2} v(s)\frac{ds}{s}, \\ \frac{dv(t)}{dt} = (q-1)\left[\frac{1}{\Gamma(\alpha)}\int_1^t \left(\log\frac{t}{s}\right)^{\alpha-1} f(s,u(s))\frac{ds}{s}\right]^{q-2} \\ \qquad \times\frac{\alpha-1}{t\Gamma(\alpha)}\int_1^t \left(\log\frac{t}{s}\right)^{\alpha-2} f(s,u(s))\frac{ds}{s}. \end{cases} \tag{28}$$

For (28), we can apply the appropriate ODE toolbox in MATLAB to perform numerical solutions and simulations.

Based on the above algorithm, we employ the ODE113 toolbox in MATLAB R2019b on two examples to give their numerical solutions and simulations. Example 1 is shown as Tables 1 and 2, Figures 1 and 2. Example 2 is shown as Tables 3 and 4, Figures 3 and 4. Figure 2 and Tables 1 and 2 show that Example 1 is GUH-stable. Figure 4 and Tables 3 and 4 show that Example 2 is GUH-stable.

Table 1. The numerical solution $u(t)$ to Example 1 which needs to multiply by 10^{10}.

u \ t	**1.2**	**1.4**	**1.6**	**1.8**	**2.0**	**2.2**	**2.4**	**2.6**	**2.7183**
$\delta = 0$	0.0079	0.0314	0.0497	0.0645	0.0786	0.0963	0.1210	0.1448	0.1501
$\delta = 0.001$	0.0080	0.0318	0.0501	0.0650	0.0790	0.0971	0.1218	0.1447	0.1498

Table 2. The numerical solution $v(t)$ to Example 1 which needs to multiply by -10^{10}.

u \ t	**1.2**	**1.4**	**1.6**	**1.8**	**2.0**	**2.2**	**2.4**	**2.6**	**2.7183**
$\delta = 0$	0.1653	0.2690	0.3344	0.4302	0.7319	1.7307	4.0310	7.5843	9.7746
$\delta = 0.001$	0.1671	0.2720	0.3355	0.4327	0.7319	1.7749	3.9019	7.2621	9.3765

Table 3. The numerical solution $u(t)$ to Example 2.

u \ t	**1.2**	**1.4**	**1.6**	**1.8**	**2.0**	**2.2**	**2.4**	**2.6**	**2.7183**
$\delta = 0$	0.0018	0.0121	0.0252	0.0384	0.0507	0.0614	0.0699	0.0749	0.0757
$\delta = 0.001$	0.0019	0.0122	0.0254	0.0387	0.0511	0.0619	0.0704	0.0754	0.0763

Table 4. The numerical solution $v(t)$ to Example 2 which needs to multiply by -1.

u \ t	**1.2**	**1.4**	**1.6**	**1.8**	**2.0**	**2.2**	**2.4**	**2.6**	**2.7183**
$\delta = 0$	0.0818	0.1947	0.2757	0.3530	0.4481	0.5721	0.7189	0.8741	0.9639
$\delta = 0.001$	0.0824	0.1960	0.2779	0.3556	0.4516	0.5767	0.7244	0.8828	0.9723

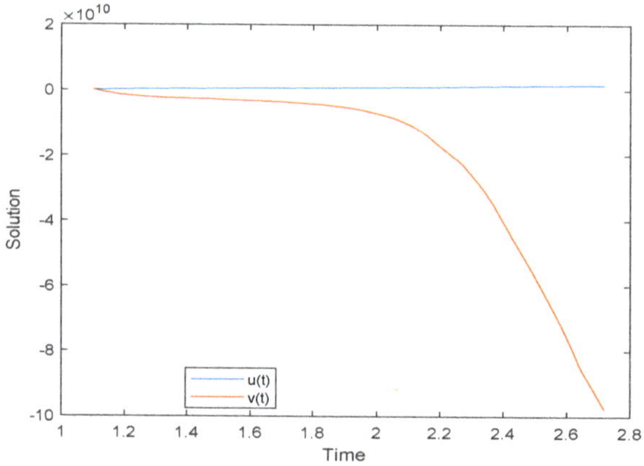

Figure 1. Simulation of solutions to Example 1.

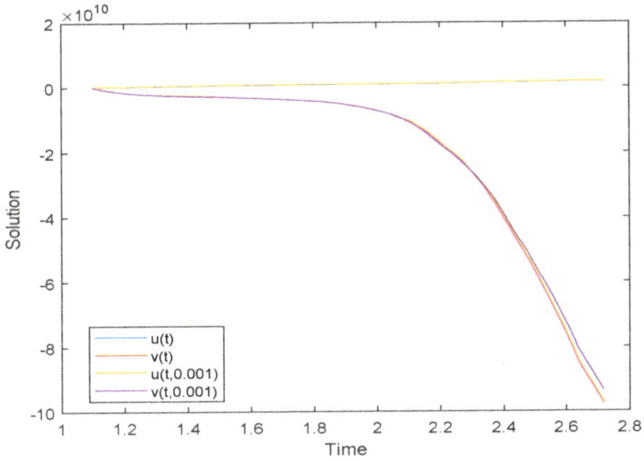

Figure 2. Evolution of the GUH-stability of Example 1.

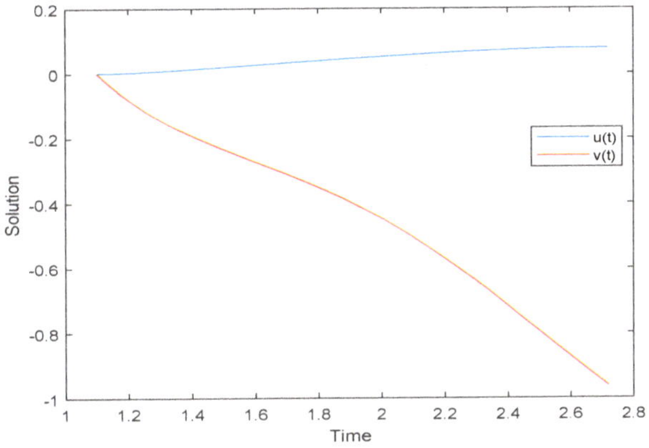

Figure 3. Simulation of solutions to Example 2.

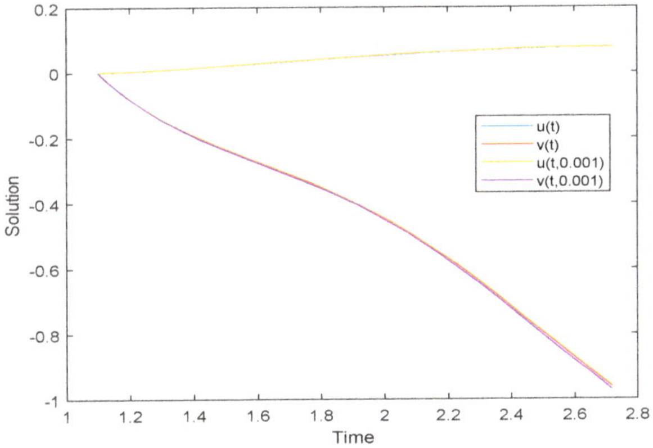

Figure 4. Evolution of the GUH-stability of Example 2.

6. Summaries

It is well known that the p-Laplacian differential equation arises from the turbulence problem in porous medium. In viscoelastic mechanics, some studies have shown that fractional order differential equation models are more accurate than integer order differential equation models. Therefore, the fractional p-Laplacian differential model has greater advantages in the study of viscoelastic porous medium turbulence. In this article, we study BVP (1) of a nonlinear p-Laplacian Hadamard fractional differential equation. Unlike many published papers, we have established the existence, uniqueness, stability, and sequence approximation of solutions for fractional order differential equations on a wide range of complete metric spaces rather than Banach spaces. We have obtained some concise and easily verifiable sufficient criteria. Examples 1 and 2 and simulations demonstrate that our main results are correct and available. Meanwhile, Figures 1 and 2 also indicate that the solution of BVP (1) is sensitive and dependent on parameters p, α and β. Our results provide theoretical support for revealing the mechanical problems of viscoelastic porous medium turbulence. The mathematical theories and methods used in the article have certain generality in solving similar problems. In addition, based on our recent research findings [50–53], we plan to study some ecosystems involving fractional derivatives or reaction diffusion effects in the future.

Funding: The APC was funded by research start-up funds for high-level talents of Taizhou University.

Data Availability Statement: Not applicable.

Acknowledgments: The author would like to express his heartfelt gratitude to the reviewers for their constructive comments.

Conflicts of Interest: The author declares no conflict of interest.

References

1. Leibenson, L. General problem of the movement of a compressible uid in a porous medium. *Izv. Akad. Nauk Kirg. SSR Ser. Biol. Nauk* **1983**, *9*, 7–10.
2. Alsaedi, A.; Luca, R.; Ahmad, B. Existence of positive solutions for a system of singular fractional boundary value problems with p-Laplacian operators. *Mathematics* **2020**, *8*, 1890. [CrossRef]
3. Zhao, K.H. Solvability and GUH-stability of a nonlinear CF-fractional coupled Laplacian equations. *AIMS Math.* **2023**, *8*, 13351–13367.
4. Rao, S.; Ahmadini, A. Multiple positive solutions for system of mixed Hadamard fractional boundary value problems with (p_1, p_2)-Laplacian operator. *AIMS Math.* **2023**, *8*, 14767–14791. [CrossRef]
5. Alsaedi, A.; Alghanmi, M.; Ahmad, B.; Alharbi, B. Uniqueness of solutions for a ψ-Hilfer fractional integral boundary value problem with the p-Laplacian operator. *Demonstr. Math.* **2023**, *56*, 20220195.
6. Sun, B.; Zhang, S.; Jiang, W. Solvability of fractional functional boundary-value problems with p-Laplacian operator on a half-line at resonance. *J. Appl. Anal. Comput.* **2023**, *13*, 11–33.
7. Ahmadkhanlu, A. On the existence and multiplicity of positive solutions for a p-Laplacian fractional boundary value problem with an integral boundary condition. *Filomat* **2023**, *37*, 235–250.
8. Chabane, F.; Benbachir, M.; Hachama, M.; Samei, M.E. Existence of positive solutions for p-Laplacian boundary value problems of fractional differential equations. *Bound. Value Probl.* **2022**, *2022*, 65. [CrossRef]
9. Rezapour, S.; Abbas, M.; Etemad, S.; Minh Dien, N. On a multi-point p-Laplacian fractional differential equation with generalized fractional derivatives. *Math. Method. Appl. Sci.* **2023**, *46*, 8390–8407. [CrossRef]
10. Boutiara, A.; Abdo, M.; Almalahi, M.; Shah, K.; Abdalla, B.; Abdeljawad, T. Study of Sturm-Liouville boundary value problems with p-Laplacian by using generalized form of fractional order derivative. *AIMS Math.* **2022**, *7*, 18360–18376. [CrossRef]
11. Salem, A.; Almaghamsi, L.; Alzahrani, F. An infinite system of fractional order with p-Laplacian operator in a tempered sequence space via measure of noncompactness technique. *Fractal Fract.* **2021**, *5*, 182. [CrossRef]
12. Jong, K.; Choi, H.; Kim, M.; Kim, K.; Jo, S.; Ri, O. On the solvability and approximate solution of a one-dimensional singular problem for a p-Laplacian fractional differential equation. *Chaos Soliton Fract.* **2021**, *147*, 110948.
13. Li, S.; Zhang, Z.; Jiang, W. Multiple positive solutions for four-point boundary value problem of fractional delay differential equations with p-Laplacian operator. *Appl. Numer. Math.* **2021**, *165*, 348–356. [CrossRef]
14. Hadamard, J. Essai sur l'étude des fonctions données par leur développment de Taylor. *J. Math. Pures Appl.* **1892**, *8*, 101–186.
15. Kilbas, A.A. Hadamard-type fractional calculus. *J. Korean Math. Soc.* **2001**, *38*, 1191–1204.
16. Butzer, P.L.; Kilbas, A.A.; Trujillo, J.J. Compositions of Hadamard-type fractional integration operators and the semigroup property. *J. Math. Anal. Appl.* **2002**, *269*, 387–400. [CrossRef]

17. Ahmad, B.; Ntouyas, S.K. On Hadamard fractional integro-differential boundary value problems. *J. Appl. Math. Comput.* **2015**, *47*, 119–131. [CrossRef]
18. Aljoudi, S.; Ahmad, B.; Nieto, J.J.; Alsaedi, A. A coupled system of Hadamard type sequential fractional differential equations with coupled strip conditions. *Chaos Soliton Fract.* **2016**, *91*, 39–46.
19. Benchohra, M.; Bouriah, S.; Graef, J.R. Boundary value problems for nonlinear implicit Caputo-Hadamard-type fractional differential equations with impulses. *Mediterr. J. Math.* **2017**, *14*, 206.
20. Huang, H.; Zhao, K.H.; Liu, X.D. On solvability of BVP for a coupled Hadamard fractional systems involving fractional derivative impulses. *AIMS Math.* **2022**, *7*, 19221–19236. [CrossRef]
21. Zhao, K.H. Existence and UH-stability of integral boundary problem for a class of nonlinear higher-order Hadamard fractional Langevin equation via Mittag-Leffler functions. *Filomat* **2023**, *37*, 1053–1063. [CrossRef]
22. Ulam, S. *A Collection of Mathematical Problems-Interscience Tracts in Pure and Applied Mathmatics*; Interscience: New York, NY, USA, 1906.
23. Hyers, D. On the stability of the linear functional equation. *Proc. Natl. Acad. Sci. USA* **1941**, *27*, 2222–2240. [CrossRef]
24. Zada, A.; Waheed, H.; Alzabut, J.; Wang, X. Existence and stability of impulsive coupled system of fractional integrodifferential equations. *Demonstr. Math.* **2019**, *52*, 296–335. [CrossRef]
25. Yu, X. Existence and β-Ulam-Hyers stability for a class of fractional differential equations with non-instantaneous impulses. *Adv. Differ. Equ.* **2015**, *2015*, 104. [CrossRef]
26. Zhao, K.H. Stability of a nonlinear fractional Langevin system with nonsingular exponential kernel and delay control. *Discret. Dyn. Nat. Soc.* **2022**, *2022*, 9169185. [CrossRef]
27. Chen, C.; Li, M. Existence and Ulam type stability for impulsive fractional differential systems with pure delay. *Fractal Fract.* **2022**, *6*, 742. [CrossRef]
28. Zhao, K.H. Existence, stability and simulation of a class of nonlinear fractional Langevin equations involving nonsingular Mittag-Leffler kernel. *Fractal Fract.* **2022**, *6*, 469. [CrossRef]
29. Zhao, K.H. Stability of a nonlinear Langevin system of ML-type fractional derivative affected by time-varying delays and differential feedback control. *Fractal Fract.* **2022**, *6*, 725. [CrossRef]
30. Mehmood, M.; Abbas, A.; Akgul, A.; Asjad, M.I.; Eldin, S.M.; Abd El-Rahman, M.; Baleanu, D. Existence and stability results for coupled system of fractional differential equations involving AB-caputo derivative. *Fractals* **2023**, *31*, 2340023. [CrossRef]
31. Yaghoubi, H.; Zare, A.; Rasouli, M.; Alizadehsani, R. Novel frequency-based approach to analyze the stability of polynomial fractional differential equations. *Axioms* **2023**, *12*, 147. [CrossRef]
32. Alqahtani, R.; Ntonga, J.; Ngondiep, E. Stability analysis and convergence rate of a two-step predictor-corrector approach for shallow water equations with source terms. *AIMS Math.* **2023**, *8*, 9265–9289.
33. Salama, F.; Ali, N.; Hamid, N. Fast $O(N)$ hybrid Laplace transform-finite difference method in solving 2D time fractional diffusion equation. *J. Math. Comput. Sci.* **2021**, *23*, 110–123. [CrossRef]
34. Jassim, H.; Hussain, M. On approximate solutions for fractional system of differential equations with Caputo-Fabrizio fractional operator. *J. Math. Comput. Sci.* **2021**, *23*, 58–66. [CrossRef]
35. Can, N.; Nikan, O.; Rasoulizadeh, M.; Jafari, H.; Gasimov, Y.S. Numerical computation of the time non-linear fractional generalized equal width model arising in shallow water channel. *Therm. Sci.* **2020**, *24*, 49–58. [CrossRef]
36. Akram, T.; Abbas, M.; Ali, A. A numerical study on time fractional Fisher equation using an extended cubic B-spline approximation. *J. Math. Comput. Sci.* **2021**, *22*, 85–96. [CrossRef]
37. Ahmad, I.; Ahmad, H.; Thounthong, P.; Chu, Y.M.; Cesarano, C. Solution of multi-term time-fractional PDE models arising in mathematical biology and physics by local meshless method. *Symmetry* **2020**, *12*, 1195. [CrossRef]
38. Murtaza, S.; Ahmad, Z.; Ali, I.; Chu, Y.M.; Cesarano, C. Analysis and numerical simulation of fractal-fractional order non-linear couple stress nanofluid with cadmium telluride nanoparticles. *J. King Saud Univ. Sci.* **2023**, *35*, 102618. [CrossRef]
39. Zhao, K.H. Generalized UH-stability of a nonlinear fractional coupling (p_1, p_2)-Laplacian system concerned with nonsingular Atangana-Baleanu fractional calculus. *J. Inequal. Appl.* **2023**, *accepted*.
40. Ahmad, Z.; Bonanomi, G.; di Serafino, D.; Giannino, F. Transmission dynamics and sensitivity analysis of pine wilt disease with asymptomatic carriers via fractal-fractional differential operator of Mittag-Leffler kernel. *Appl. Numer. Math.* **2023**, *185*, 446–465. [CrossRef]
41. Ahmad, Z.; El-Kafrawy, S.; Alandijany, T.; Mirza, A.A.; El-Daly, M.M.; Faizo, A.A.; Bajrai, L.H.; Kamal, M.A.; Azhar, E.I. A global report on the dynamics of COVID-19 with quarantine and hospitalization: A fractional order model with non-local kernel. *Comput. Biol. Chem.* **2022**, *98*, 107645. [CrossRef]
42. Ahmad, Z.; Ali, F.; Khan, N.; Khan, I. Dynamics of fractal-fractional model of a new chaotic system of integrated circuit with Mittag-Leffler kernel. *Chaos Soliton. Fract.* **2021**, *153*, 111602. [CrossRef]
43. Wang, F.; Asjad, M.; Zahid, M.; Iqbal, A.; Ahmad, H.; Alsulami, M.D. Unsteady thermal transport flow of Casson nanofluids with generalized Mittag-Leffler kernel of Prabhakar's type. *J. Mater. Res. Technol.* **2021**, *14*, 1292–1300. [CrossRef]
44. Kilbas, A.A.; Srivastava, H.M.; Trujillo, J.J. *Theory and Applications of Fractional Differential Equations*; Elsevier: Amsterdam, The Netherlands, 2006.
45. Rus, I.A. On a fixed point theorem of Maia. *Stud. Univ. Babes-Bolyai Math.* **1977**, *22*, 40–42.

46. Wardowski, D. Fixed points of a new type of contractive mappings in complete metric spaces. *Fixed Point Theory Appl.* **2012**, *2012*, 94. [CrossRef]
47. Agarwal, R.; O'Regan, D. Fixed point theory for generalized contractions on spaces with two metrics. *J. Math. Anal. Appl.* **2000**, *248*, 402–414. [CrossRef]
48. Karapinar, E.; Fulga, A.; Agarwal, R. A survey: F-contractions with related fixed point results. *J. Fixed Point Theory Appl.* **2020**, *22*, 69. [CrossRef]
49. Mehmood, N.; Khan, I.; Nawaz, M.; Ahmad, N. Existence results for ABC-fractional BVP via new fixed point results of F-Lipschitzian mappings. *Demonstr. Math.* **2022**, *55*, 452–469. [CrossRef]
50. Zhao, K.H. Local exponential stability of several almost periodic positive solutions for a classical controlled GA-predation ecosystem possessed distributed delays. *Appl. Math. Comput.* **2023**, *437*, 127540. [CrossRef]
51. Zhao, K.H. Existence and stability of a nonlinear distributed delayed periodic AG-ecosystem with competition on time scales. *Axioms* **2023**, *12*, 315. [CrossRef]
52. Zhao, K.H. Global stability of a novel nonlinear diffusion online game addiction model with unsustainable control. *AIMS Math.* **2022**, *7*, 20752–20766. [CrossRef]
53. Zhao, K.H. Attractor of a nonlinear hybrid reaction-diffusion model of neuroendocrine transdifferentiation of human prostate cancer cells with time-lags. *AIMS Math.* **2023**, *8*, 14426–14448. [CrossRef]

axioms

Article

Weighted Pseudo-θ-Almost Periodic Sequence and Finite-Time Guaranteed Cost Control for Discrete-Space and Discrete-Time Stochastic Genetic Regulatory Networks with Time Delays

Shumin Sun [1], Tianwei Zhang [2,*] and Zhouhong Li [3,*]

[1] City College, Kunming University of Science and Technology, Kunming 650051, China; hnsmsun@hotmail.com
[2] Department of Mathematics, Yunnan University, Kunming 650091, China
[3] Department of Mathematics, Yuxi Normal University, Yuxi 653100, China
* Correspondence: zhang@kust.edu.cn (T.Z.); mathzhli@163.com (Z.L.)

Abstract: This paper considers the dual hybrid effects of discrete-time stochastic genetic regulatory networks and discrete-space stochastic genetic regulatory networks in difference formats of exponential Euler difference and second-order central finite difference. The existence of a unique-weight pseudo-θ-almost periodic sequence solution for discrete-time and discrete-space stochastic genetic regulatory networks on the basis of discrete constant variation formulation is discussed, as well as the theory of semi-flow and metric dynamical systems. Furthermore, a finite-time guaranteed cost controller is constructed to reach global exponential stability of these discrete networks via establishing a framework of drive, response, and error networks. The results indicate that spatial diffusions of non-negative dense coefficients have no influence on the global existence of the unique weighted pseudo-θ-almost periodic sequence solution of the networks. The present study is a basic work in the consideration of discrete spatial diffusion in stochastic genetic regulatory networks and serves as a foundation for further study.

Keywords: discrete spatial diffusion; discrete time; stochastic; weighted pseudo-θ-almost periodicity; finite-time guaranteed cost controller; finite difference method

MSC: 35B15

Citation: Sun, S.; Zhang, T.; Li, Z. Weighted Pseudo-θ-Almost Periodic Sequence and Finite-Time Guaranteed Cost Control for Discrete-Space and Discrete-Time Stochastic Genetic Regulatory Networks with Time Delays. *Axioms* **2023**, *12*, 682. https://doi.org/10.3390/axioms12070682

Academic Editor: Feliz Manuel Minhós

Received: 28 April 2023
Revised: 30 June 2023
Accepted: 6 July 2023
Published: 11 July 2023

1. Introduction

Genetic regulatory networks (GRNs) have been widely recognized due to their possible usages [1]. GRNs are actually a complex dynamical system that describes the regulatory mechanisms of DNA, mRNA, and protein interactions in biological systems at the molecular level [2,3]. The analysis of genetic regulatory networks is not only an important way to understand and grasp the operation mechanisms of the activity of cellular life [4], but also has promising applications in the fields of disease genetic prediction and drug target screening [5–8]. For this reason, it is necessary and valuable to propose suitable mathematical models to represent expression mechanisms and signal transduction pathways. Currently, GRNs are generally modeled by Boolean models, Bayesian models, and differential equation models. Two of the most widely used models are Boolean models and differential equation models [9–11]. In particular, differential equations describe the concentration changes in proteins and mRNA [12,13]. This model has received more attention because of its higher accuracy and its ability to accurately describe the nonlinear dynamic behaviour of biological systems.

In general, the majority of models utilised to characterize GRNs in the currently available literature suppose that the concentrations of mRNAs and proteins are spatially homogeneous at all times. However, this assumption has some limitations, for example the diffusion phenomenon should be considered for the case of non-uniform distributions of gene product concentrations [14]. Therefore, the issue of kinetic analysis of GRNs with reaction–diffusion effects is worth investigating. Moreover, time delay is often inevitable due to the finite processing time of interactions among agents and may influence system performance. As of recently, a great deal of results on GRNs with time delays can be found in the literature, see, e.g., Han et al. [14], who established an asymptotic stability criterion for reaction–diffusion delayed GRNs under Dirichlet and Neumann boundary conditions, respectively, insightfully recognizing that diffusion–reaction information can reduce the conservation of the system. Robust state estimation of delayed genetic regulatory networks with reaction–diffusion terms and uncertainty terms under the Dirichlet boundary condition is considered by Zou et al. in [15]. Xie et al. [16] discuss the stability of genetic regulatory networks, centralised spatial diffusion, and discrete and infinite distribution delays.

During the processes of both computational simulation and analysis, engineers often use discrete-time continuous models to evaluate their structural behaviour. The signals received and operated in digital networks are dependent on discrete-time rather than continuous-time. Therefore, discrete-time GRNs have been studied by many authors. For example, Xue et al. [17] investigate the problems of state boundary description and reachable set estimation for discrete-time delayed genetic regulatory networks with bounded perturbations. Liu et al. [18] study the problem of exponential stability analysis of discrete genetic regulatory networks with time-varying discrete-time delays and unbounded distributed time delays. Yue et al. [19] investigate the dynamics of discrete-time genetic models and obtain conditions for the existence and stability of fixed points. It is shown that the discrete-time genetic network undergoes fold bifurcation, flip bifurcation, and Neimark–Sacker bifurcation, illuminating the richer dynamical properties of the discrete-time genetic model than the original continuous-time model. It is worth noting that most of the results on GRNs only concern discrete-time GRNs [17–22], while the results on spatial discrete GRNs have not received sufficient attention in existing studies, probably owing to the partial ineffectiveness of traditional methods in space–time continuous networks, such as the Lyapunov–Krasovskii general functions in discrete-space and -time networks, and the difficulty of computing the difference. To date, there are several reports referring to space–time discrete models [23–25]; nevertheless, the models of stochastic space–time discrete GRNs have not been deeply addressed.

It is well known that stochastic uncertainty is inevitable in various dynamical systems, with reference to its ability to alter the mechanical properties of genetic regulatory networks in practical applications. Therefore, the dynamic behaviour of delayed stochastic genetic regulatory networks has been extensively studied, see the literature [26–29]. For example, Xu et al. [26] investigate the input state stability problem of stochastic gene regulation networks with multiple time delays, and give sufficient conditions for the mean square exponential input state stability of the system using the Lyapunov generalization, Ito's formula, and Dynkin's formula. Wang [29] investigates the dual effects of discrete space and discrete time in stochastic genetic regulatory networks by means of exponential Eulerian differences and central finite differences. In addition, finite-time guaranteed cost control is a very effective method in the engineering field due to its many advantages in practical applications, see references [30–37]. The advantages of finite-time guaranteed cost controllers are listed below: (1) Stability. A finite-time guaranteed cost controller is a feedback controller that adjusts the system to remain stable when it is subject to external disturbances or internal changes. (2) Reliability. It can adjust the control strategy adaptively depending on the state of the system, so as to increase the reliability of the system. In summary, the finite-time cost-preserving controller is an advanced control method for genetic regulatory networks with many advantages that can assist the system to be more stable, reliable, and robust, and optimise the performance index of the system.

On the other hand, the global exponential stability and almost periodic nature of GRNs are significant and necessary dynamical behaviours that have been extensively researched by many authors in the last two decades, see the literature [18,38–42]. Particularly in stochastic models, the notion of θ-almost periodicity was first introduced in the paper [43] on the basis of semi-flow and metric dynamical system theories, and the existence of θ-almost periodicity for several continuous-time stochastic models was investigated [44,45]. First, pseudo-almost periodicity was introduced in the early 1990s by Zhang [46] as a natural extension of classical probability periodicity. Since then, pseudo-approximate periodic solutions of differential equations have attracted a lot of attention. In the literature [47], Diagana extended pseudo-almost periodicity to weighted pseudo-almost periodicity and reported a number of excellent contributions on weighted pseudo-almost periodicity, see references [48–50]. However, the study of the θ-almost periodicity of stochastic discrete-time GRNs, not to mention weighted pseudo-θ-almost periodicity, influenced by spatial diffusion, has not been addressed in depth so far.

Based on the above motivation, the main purpose of this paper is to establish discrete-time stochastic genetic regulatory networks (SGRNs) for discrete-space diffusion using exponential Euler difference and central finite difference methods. On this ground, a discrete constant variation formula for discrete SGRNs is derived. On the basis of the discrete constant variation formula, the weighted pseudo-θ-almost periodicity of discrete SGRNs with discrete spatial diffusion is investigated by combining the theory of semi-fluid dynamical systems and metric dynamical systems. In the end, a finite-time guaranteed cost controller for this type of SGRN is designed by the construction of a drive, response, and error network framework. The main studies and innovations of this paper are briefly summarised in turn as follows.

(1) Discrete-time and discrete-space SGRNs are newly introduced, which extends the studied models in reports [18,40].
(2) The weighted pseudo-θ-almost periodicity of this class of SGRNs is considered for the first time, which complements the works on the almost periodicity of GRNs in references [12,38].
(3) Finite-time cost-preserving controllers are designed for this class of SGRNs.

Plan of this paper: In Section 2, a formula for discrete-time and discrete-space SGRNs is given and the concept of weighted pseudo-θ-almost periodicity is presented. Section 3 discusses the global existence of unique weighted pseudo-θ-almost periodic sequence solutions for discrete-time and discrete-space SGRNs on the basis of the theory of semifluid and metric dynamical systems, the discrete constant variation formula, and the fixed-point theorem. Furthermore, in Section 4, finite-time cost-preserving controllers are designed by constructing a framework of drive, response, and error networks for discrete-time and discrete-space SGRNs. Section 5 gives numerical examples of discrete-time and discrete-space SGRNs achieving weight pseudo-θ-almost periodicity, finite-time guaranteed cost control, and global exponential stability. The conclusions and main points of the paper are given in Section 6.

Symbols: $\mathbb{R}^n$ denotes the space of n-dimensional real vectors; $\mathbb{Z}$ is the field of integral numbers; $\mathbb{N}_0 = \{0,1,2,\ldots\}$; $\mathbb{N} = \mathbb{N}_0 \setminus \{0\}$; $\mathbb{N}_a^b = \{a, a+1, \ldots, b\}$ for any $a, b \in \mathbb{Z}$; $I_J = I \cap J$, $\forall I, J \subseteq \mathbb{R}$. Let $\xi_1 = (1,0,\ldots,0)^T$, $\xi_2 = (0,1,\ldots,0)^T, \ldots \xi_m = (0,0,\ldots,1)^T$.

Define $N_p \in \mathbb{N}$ for $p \in \mathbb{N}_1^m$, $\mho_\nu := \left\{\nu = (\nu_1,\ldots,\nu_m)^T : (\nu_p, p) \in (\mathbb{N}_1^{N_p-1}, \mathbb{N}_1^m)\right\}$, $\partial\mho_\nu := \bar{\mho}_\nu \setminus \mho_\nu$, $\bar{\mho}_\nu = \left\{\nu = (\nu_1,\ldots,\nu_m)^T : (\nu_p, p) \in (\mathbb{N}_0^{N_p}, \mathbb{N}_1^m)\right\}$.

For any function $f : \bar{\mho}_\nu \times \mathbb{Z}$ to $\mathbb{R}^n$, we denote as $f := f_k^{\langle\nu\rangle} = (f_{1,k}^{\langle\nu\rangle}, \ldots, f_{n,k}^{\langle\nu\rangle})^T$, where $(\nu, k) \in \bar{\mho}_\nu \times \mathbb{Z}$. Sometimes, $f = (f_1, \ldots, f_n)^T$ is used for simplicity.

2. Problem Formulation

In this section, firstly, discrete-time and discrete-space SGRNs are presented, which can be considered as discrete formats of continuous-time SGRNs with reaction diffusion. Secondly, the constant variation formula of the discrete network is obtained by dividing the discrete network into two discrete sub-networks based on the theory of difference equations. In the next step, important inequalities are given, such as the Minkowski inequality in Lemma 2. Finally, the definition of weighted pseudo-θ-almost periodicity is presented.

2.1. Space–Time Discrete Stochastic GRNs

This article considers the following space–time discrete stochastic genetic regulatory networks (GRNs) in the Euler form of

$$\begin{cases} \mathbf{m}_{i,k+1}^{\langle v\rangle} = e^{-a_{i,k}h}\mathbf{m}_{i,k}^{\langle v\rangle} + \dfrac{1-e^{-a_{i,k}h}}{a_{i,k}}\Bigg[\sum_{q=1}^{n}\Theta_{iq}\tilde{\Delta}_{\hbar_q}^{2}\mathbf{m}_{i,k}^{\langle v\rangle} \\ \quad + \sum_{j=1}^{m} b_{ij,k}f_j(\mathbf{p}_{j,k-\sigma_{j,k}}^{\langle v\rangle}) + \sum_{j=1}^{m}\gamma_{ij,k}g_j(\mathbf{p}_{j,k-\mu_{j,k}}^{\langle v\rangle})w_{1j,k} + I_{i,k}\Bigg], \\ \mathbf{p}_{i,k+1}^{\langle v\rangle} = e^{-c_{i,k}h}\mathbf{p}_{i,k}^{\langle v\rangle} + \dfrac{1-e^{-c_{i,k}h}}{c_{i,k}}\Bigg[\sum_{q=1}^{n}\Pi_{iq}\tilde{\Delta}_{\hbar_q}^{2}\mathbf{p}_{i,k}^{\langle v\rangle} + d_{i,k}\mathbf{m}_{i,k}^{\langle v\rangle} + \sum_{j=1}^{m}\varpi_{ij,k}\eta_j(\mathbf{m}_{j,k-\nu_{j,k}}^{\langle v\rangle})w_{2j,k}\Bigg] \end{cases} \tag{1}$$

for $(v,k) \in \mho_v \times \mathbb{Z}$ and $i = 1,2,\ldots,m$; $\mathbf{m}_i$ and $\mathbf{p}_i$ denote the concentrations of the ith mRNA and ith protein, respectively;

$$\tilde{a}_i = a_i - 2\sum_{q=1}^{n}\frac{\Theta_{iq}}{\hbar^2}, \quad \tilde{c}_i = c_i - 2\sum_{q=1}^{n}\frac{\Pi_{iq}}{\hbar^2},$$

$\tilde{a}_i > 0$ and $\tilde{c}_i > 0$ are the decay rates of the ith mRNA and ith protein, respectively; Θ_{iq} and Π_{iq} represent the transmission diffusion matrixes, where $\tilde{\Delta}_{\hbar_q}^{2}$ means the discrete-space operator denoted by

$$\tilde{\Delta}_{\hbar_q}^{2}\mathbf{m}_{i,\cdot}^{\langle\cdot\rangle} := \frac{\mathbf{m}_{i,\cdot}^{\langle v+\xi_q\rangle} + \mathbf{m}_{i,\cdot}^{\langle v-\xi_q\rangle}}{\hbar^2}, \quad \tilde{\Delta}_{\hbar_q}^{2}\mathbf{p}_{i,\cdot}^{\langle\cdot\rangle} := \frac{\mathbf{p}_{i,\cdot}^{\langle v+\xi_q\rangle} + \mathbf{p}_{i,\cdot}^{\langle v-\xi_q\rangle}}{\hbar^2}, \quad q \in \mathbb{N}_1^n;$$

$\hbar$ and h denote the length of the space and time steps in order; γ_{ij} and ϖ_{ij} stand for noise intensities; $d_i > 0$ is the translation rate; $I_i = \sum_{j\in\mathbf{I}_i} w_{ij}, w_{ij} \geq 0$ is bounded and $\mathbf{I}_i$ is the set of all the j which is a repressor of gene i; $b_{ij} = w_{ij}$ if transcription factor j is an activator of gene i, $b_{ij} = 0$ if there is no link from node j to i, and $b_{ij} = -w_{ij}$ if transcription factor j is a repressor of gene i; f_j, g_j, and η_j are Hill functions; $w_{1j,k} := \frac{1}{h}[\mathbf{w}_{1j}(kh+h) - \mathbf{w}_{1j}(kh)]$, $w_{2j,k} := \frac{1}{h}[\mathbf{w}_{2j}(kh+h) - \mathbf{w}_{2j}(kh)]$, and $i,j = 1,2,\ldots,m$; $\mathbf{w}_{11},\ldots,\mathbf{w}_{1m},\mathbf{w}_{21},\ldots,\mathbf{w}_{2m}$ are scalar mutually independent two-sided standard Brown motions on complete probability space $(\Omega,\mathcal{F},\mathscr{F}_\cdot,\mathbf{P})$ with filtration

$$\mathscr{F}_k = \sigma\big\{(w_{11,q},\ldots,w_{1m,q},w_{21,q},\ldots,w_{2m,q}) : q \in (-\infty,k)_{\mathbb{Z}}\big\}, \forall k \in \mathbb{Z}.$$

The Dirichlet boundary conditions of GRNs Equation (1) are described as

$$\mathbf{m}_{i,k}^{\langle v\rangle}\Big|_{v\in\partial\mho_v} = 0 = \mathbf{p}_{i,k}^{\langle v\rangle}\Big|_{v\in\partial\mho_v}, \quad \forall k \in \mathbb{Z}. \tag{2}$$

Herein, $\mho_v$ can be regarded as a discrete form of the rectangle area $\mho$ in $\mathbb{R}^m$, which is described by

$$\mho = \Big\{x = (x_1,x_2,\ldots,x_m)^T \in \mathbb{R}^m : 0 < x_p < L_p := \hbar N_p, p \in \mathbb{N}_1^m\Big\}.$$

Let $\mathbf{m}_{i,k}^{\langle \nu \rangle} = M_i(\nu\hbar, kh)$ and $\mathbf{p}_{i,k}^{\langle \nu \rangle} = P_i(\nu\hbar, kh)$ for $(\nu, k) \in \mho_\nu \times \mathbb{Z}$. Then, GRNs Equation (1) is a full discretization scheme of the following stochastic GRNs with reaction diffusions

$$\begin{cases} \frac{\partial}{\partial t} M_i(x,t) = \sum_{q=1}^{n} \frac{\partial}{\partial x_q}\left[\Theta_{iq}\frac{\partial M_i(x,t)}{\partial x_q}\right] - \tilde{a}_i(t)M_i(x,t) \\ \qquad + \sum_{j=1}^{m} b_{ij}(t)f_j(P_j(x,t-\sigma_j(t))) + I_i(t) + \sum_{j=1}^{m}\gamma_{ij}(x,t)g_j(P_j(x,t-\mu_j(t)))\frac{\mathrm{d}}{\mathrm{d}t}\mathbb{W}_{1j}(t), \\ \frac{\partial}{\partial t} P_i(x,t) = \sum_{q=1}^{n} \frac{\partial}{\partial x_q}\left[\Pi_{iq}\frac{\partial P_i(x,t)}{\partial x_q}\right] - \tilde{c}_i(t)P_i(x,t) \\ \qquad + d_i(x,t)M_i(x,t) + \sum_{j=1}^{m}\varpi_{ij}(x,t)\eta_j(M_j(x,t-\nu_j(t)))\frac{\mathrm{d}}{\mathrm{d}t}\mathbb{W}_{2j}(t), \\ M_i(x,t)\Big|_{x\in\partial\mho} = 0 = P_i(x,t)\Big|_{x\in\partial\mho}, \end{cases} \tag{3}$$

where $x = (x_1, \ldots, x_n)^T \in \mho \subseteq \mathbb{R}^n$ refers to a space variable.

The discrete techniques in SGRNs Equation (1) are therefore Eulerian difference (ED) for Brownian motion, exponential Eulerian difference (EED) for time variables, and central finite difference (CFD) for spatial variables, respectively. For more information on ED, EED, and CFD, please see the literature [51–55].

Remark 1. *By using Euler differences, reports [18,40] considered discrete-time GRNs without spatial diffusions. In this article, SGRNs Equation (1) extends the models in reports [18,40].*

Lemma 1. *GRNs Equation (1) can be expressed as*

$$\begin{cases} \mathbf{m}_{i,k}^{\langle \nu \rangle} = \prod_{s=k_0}^{k-1} e^{-a_{i,s}h}\mathbf{m}_{i,k_0}^{\langle \nu \rangle} + \sum_{v=k_0}^{k-1}\prod_{s=v+1}^{k-1}\frac{e^{-a_{i,s}h}(1-e^{-a_{i,v}h})}{a_{i,v}} \\ \qquad \times\left[\sum_{q=1}^{n}\Theta_{iq}\tilde{\Delta}_{\hbar_q}^2\mathbf{m}_{i,v}^{\langle \nu \rangle} + \sum_{j=1}^{m} b_{ij,v}f_j(\mathbf{p}_{j,v-\sigma_{j,v}}^{\langle \nu \rangle}) + \sum_{j=1}^{m}\gamma_{ij,v}g_j(\mathbf{p}_{j,v-\mu_{j,v}}^{\langle \nu \rangle})w_{1j,v} + I_{i,v}\right], \\ \mathbf{p}_{i,k}^{\langle \nu \rangle} = \prod_{s=k_0}^{k-1} e^{-c_{i,s}h}\mathbf{p}_{i,k_0}^{\langle \nu \rangle} + \sum_{v=k_0}^{k-1}\prod_{s=v+1}^{k-1}\frac{e^{-c_{i,s}h}(1-e^{-c_{i,v}h})}{c_{i,v}} \\ \qquad \times\left[\sum_{q=1}^{n}\Pi_{iq}\tilde{\Delta}_{\hbar_q}^2\mathbf{p}_{i,v}^{\langle \nu \rangle} + d_{i,v}\mathbf{m}_{i,v}^{\langle \nu \rangle} + \sum_{j=1}^{m}\varpi_{ij,v}\eta_j(\mathbf{m}_{j,v-\nu_{j,v}}^{\langle \nu \rangle})w_{2j,v}\right], \end{cases} \tag{4}$$

where $(\nu, k) \in \mho_\nu \times [k_0, \infty)_{\mathbb{Z}}$ with some initial point $k_0 \in \mathbb{Z}$, $i = 1, 2, \ldots, m$. Moreover, it holds that

$$\mathbf{m}_{i,k}^{\langle \nu \rangle}\Big|_{\nu\in\partial\mho_\nu} = 0 = \mathbf{p}_{i,k}^{\langle \nu \rangle}\Big|_{\nu\in\partial\mho_\nu}, \quad \forall k \in [k_0,\infty)_{\mathbb{Z}}, i = 1,2,\ldots,m.$$

Lemma 2 ([56] (Minkowski inequality))**.** *If $X, Y \in L^2(\Omega, \mathbb{R})$, then*

$$\left(\mathbf{E}|X+Y|^2\right)^{\frac{1}{2}} \le \left(\mathbf{E}|X|^2\right)^{\frac{1}{2}} + \left(\mathbf{E}|Y|^2\right)^{\frac{1}{2}}.$$

Lemma 3 ([56] (Hölder inequality))**.** *Let $a_k, b_k : \mathbb{Z} \to \mathbb{R}$. Then,*

$$\left|\sum_k a_k b_k\right|^2 \le \sum_k |a_k| \sum_k |a_k||b_k|^2.$$

Lemma 4. $\mathbf{E}|w_{1j,k}|^2 = \mathbf{E}|w_{2j,k}|^2 = \frac{1}{h}$ *for $j = 1, 2, \ldots, n$.*

Proof. By the definition of $w_{1j,k}$ and Ito formula, it is derived that

$$\mathbf{E}|w_{1j,k}|^2 = \frac{1}{h^2}\mathbf{E}\left(\int_{kh}^{kh+h} \mathrm{d}\mathbb{W}_{1j}(s)\right)^2 = \frac{1}{h^2}\mathbf{E}\int_{kh}^{kh+h} \mathrm{d}s = \frac{1}{h}, \quad \forall j = 1, 2, \dots, n.$$

This completes the proof. □

2.2. Weighted Pseudo-Almost Periodicity

In the following, assume that $(\mathbb{X}, \|\cdot\|_{\mathbb{X}})$ is a norm linear space, and $L^p(\Omega, \mathbb{R}^n)$ denotes the set of all pth integrable $\mathbb{R}^n$-valued random variables with the norm

$$\|u\|_p = \max_{1\le i\le n} [\mathbf{E}|u_i|^p]^{1/p}, \quad \forall u = (u_1, \dots, u_n)^T \in L^p(\Omega, \mathbb{R}^n), p > 0,$$

in which $\mathbf{E}$ denotes the expectation operator with respect to probability space $(\Omega, \mathcal{F}, \mathbf{P})$.

Definition 1. *Let $X \in \mathbb{X}$ and $\epsilon > 0$ be arbitrary. If $v = v_\epsilon$ and $\tau \in [a, a + v_\epsilon]_{\mathbb{Z}}$ for any $a \in \mathbb{Z}$, ensuring that*

$$\|X_{k+\tau} - X_k\|_{\mathbb{X}} < \epsilon, \quad \forall k \in \mathbb{Z},$$

then $\{X_k\}$ is an almost periodic sequence. Herein, τ is called an ϵ-almost period of X. $AP(\mathbb{Z}, \mathbb{X})$ denotes the set of the whole almost periodic sequences.

Let $\mathbb{U}$ be the set of all weight sequences $\alpha : \mathbb{Z} \to (0, +\infty)$ satisfying

$$\frac{\alpha_{k+s}}{\alpha_k} \le \bar{\alpha}, \quad \forall k \in \mathbb{Z}, s \in [0, \sigma_0]_{\mathbb{Z}};$$

$$\mu_k(\alpha) := \sum_{s=-k}^{k} \alpha_s \to +\infty, \quad \frac{1}{\mu_k(\alpha)} \sum_{s=-k-\sigma_0}^{-k} \alpha_s \to 0, \quad \text{as } k \to +\infty,$$

where $\sigma_0 = \max_{1\le j\le m} \sup_{k\in\mathbb{Z}}\{\sigma_{j,k}, \mu_{j,k}, \nu_{j,k}\}$.

Define $\mathbb{B}(\mathbb{Z}, \mathbb{X})$ as the set of all bounded sequences from $\mathbb{Z}$ to $\mathbb{X}$ and

$$PAP_0^\mu(\mathbb{Z}, \mathbb{X}, \alpha) := \left\{X \in \mathbb{B}(\mathbb{Z}, \mathbb{X}) : \lim_{k\to+\infty} \frac{1}{\mu_k(\alpha)} \sum_{s=-k}^{k} \alpha_s \|X_s\|_{\mathbb{X}} = 0\right\}.$$

When $\mathbb{X} = L^2(\Omega, \mathbb{R}^n)$ or $\mathbb{R}^n$, we use $PAP_0^\mu(\mathbb{Z}, \mathbb{R}^n, \alpha)$ to denote $PAP_0^\mu(\mathbb{Z}, \mathbb{X}, \alpha)$.

Definition 2. *Sequence $X \in \mathbb{B}(\mathbb{Z}, \mathbb{X})$ is said to be a weighted pseudo-almost periodic sequence or an α-pseudo-almost periodic sequence in the case $X = Y + Z$, where $Y \in AP(\mathbb{Z}, \mathbb{X})$, $Z \in PAP_0^\mu(\mathbb{Z}, \mathbb{X}, \alpha)$, and $\alpha \in \mathbb{U}$. The space of all α-pseudo-almost periodic sequences is represented by $PAP^\mu(\mathbb{Z}, \mathbb{X}, \alpha)$.*

Supposing that $(\Omega, \mathcal{F}, \mathbf{P}, \theta)$ is a metric dynamical system, see the pioneering work in [57]. It holds that $\theta_k : \Omega \to \Omega$ is $\mathcal{F}$-measurable, $\mathbf{P}(\theta_k^{-1}(A)) = \mathbf{P}(A)$ for any $A \in \mathcal{F}$, and $\theta_{s+k} = \theta_s \circ \theta_k$, $\forall s, k \in \mathbb{Z}$.

Definition 3. *The translation to a sequential process X_k is defined as*

$$\mathcal{L}_\tau X_k(\omega) := X_{k+\tau}(\theta_{-\tau}\omega), \quad \forall \omega \in \Omega, s, k, \tau \in \mathbb{Z}.$$

Definition 4. *If $X_k \in \mathbb{X}$, $\forall k \in \mathbb{Z}$, then X is said to be θ-almost periodic in the case that for each $\epsilon > 0$ we can find at least one positive integer $\nu = \nu(\epsilon)$ and it has a constant $\tau = \tau(\epsilon) \in (a, a+\nu)_{\mathbb{Z}}$ for arbitrary $a \in \mathbb{Z}$, ensuring that*

$$\|\mathcal{L}_\tau X_k - X_k\|_{\mathbb{X}} \leq \epsilon, \quad \forall k \in \mathbb{Z}.$$

Herein, τ is called an ϵ-θ-almost period of X. The space of all θ-almost periodic sequences is represented by $AP^\theta(\mathbb{Z}, \mathbb{X})$. If $\mathcal{L}_\tau X = X$ with $\tau \in \mathbb{Z}$, then X is said to be θ-periodic.

When $\mathbb{X} = L^p(\Omega, \mathbb{R}^n)$ with $p > 0$, then X is said to be θ-almost periodic in p-mean. If $p = 2$, the elements in $PAP^\theta(\mathbb{Z}, L^p(\Omega, \mathbb{R}^n))$ are called a mean square θ-almost periodic sequence. Hereby, we use a simplified symbol $PAP^\theta(\mathbb{Z}, \mathbb{R}^n)$ to denote $PAP^\theta(\mathbb{Z}, L^2(\Omega, \mathbb{R}^n))$.

Definition 5. *Sequence $X : \mathbb{Z} \to \mathbb{X}$ is said to be a weighted pseudo-θ-almost periodic sequence or α-pseudo-θ-almost periodic sequence in the case $X = Y + Z$, where $Y \in AP^\theta(\mathbb{Z}, \mathbb{X})$, $Z \in PAP_0^\mu(\mathbb{Z}, \mathbb{X}, \alpha)$, and $\alpha \in \mathbb{U}$. The space of all α-pseudo-θ-almost periodic sequences is represented by $PAP^{\theta,\mu}(\mathbb{Z}, \mathbb{X}, \alpha)$. If Y is θ-periodic, then X is said to be a weighted pseudo-θ-periodic sequence or an α-pseudo-θ-periodic sequence.*

When $\mathbb{X} = L^p(\Omega, \mathbb{R}^n)$ with $p > 0$, then X is said to be a weighted pseudo-θ-almost periodic sequence or an α-pseudo-θ-almost periodic sequence in p-mean. If $p = 2$, the elements in $PAP^{\theta,\mu}(\mathbb{Z}, L^p(\Omega, \mathbb{R}^n), \alpha)$ are called a weighted pseudo mean square θ-almost periodic sequence or an α-pseudo mean square θ-almost periodic sequence. Hereby, a simplified symbol $PAP^{\theta,\mu}(\mathbb{Z}, \mathbb{R}^n, \alpha) := PAP^{\theta,\mu}(\mathbb{Z}, L^2(\Omega, \mathbb{R}^n), \alpha)$.

3. Mean Square α-Pseudo-θ-Almost Periodic Sequence

This section focuses on weighted pseudo-θ-almost periodic sequence solutions in the mean square sense of SGRNs Equation (1) based on stochastic calculus theory, the constant variation formula, and the Banach contraction mapping principle.

For any $\mathbf{u} = (\mathbf{m}, \mathbf{p})^T \in PAP^{\theta,\mu}(\mho_\nu \times \mathbb{Z}, \mathbb{R}^{2m}, \alpha)$ with $\mathbf{m} = (\mathbf{m}_1, \cdots, \mathbf{m}_m)^T$ and $\mathbf{p} = (\mathbf{p}_1, \cdots, \mathbf{p}_m)^T$, define $\Gamma : PAP^{\theta,\mu}(\mho_\nu \times \mathbb{Z}, \mathbb{R}^{2m}, \alpha) \to \mathbb{R}^{2m}$ by

$$\Gamma\mathbf{u} = \Big((\Phi\mathbf{u}_1), \cdots, (\Phi\mathbf{u})_m, (\Psi\mathbf{u})_1, \cdots, (\Psi\mathbf{u})_m\Big)^T,$$

where

$$\begin{cases} (\Phi\mathbf{u})_{i,k}^{\langle\nu\rangle} = \sum\limits_{v=-\infty}^{k-1} \prod\limits_{s=v+1}^{k-1} \dfrac{e^{-a_{i,s}h}(1-e^{-a_{i,v}h})}{a_{i,v}} \Bigg[\sum\limits_{q=1}^{n} \Theta_{iq}\tilde{\Delta}_{\hbar_q}^2 \mathbf{m}_{i,v}^{\langle\nu\rangle} \\ \qquad + \sum\limits_{j=1}^{m} b_{ij,v} f_j(\mathbf{p}_{j,v-\sigma_{j,v}}^{\langle\nu\rangle}) + \sum\limits_{j=1}^{m} \gamma_{ij,v} g_j(\mathbf{p}_{j,v-\mu_{j,v}}^{\langle\nu\rangle}) w_{1j,v} + I_{i,v}\Bigg], \\ (\Psi\mathbf{u})_{i,k}^{\langle\nu\rangle} = \sum\limits_{v=-\infty}^{k-1} \prod\limits_{s=v+1}^{k-1} \dfrac{e^{-c_{i,s}h}(1-e^{-c_{i,v}h})}{c_{i,v}} \Bigg[\sum\limits_{q=1}^{n} \Pi_{iq}\tilde{\Delta}_{\hbar_q}^2 \mathbf{p}_{i,v}^{\langle\nu\rangle} \\ \qquad + \sum\limits_{j=1}^{m} \varpi_{ij,v} \eta_j(\mathbf{m}_{j,v-\nu_{j,v}}^{\langle\nu\rangle}) w_{2j,v} + d_{i,v}\mathbf{m}_{i,v}^{\langle\nu\rangle}\Bigg], \quad \forall(\nu, k) \in \mho_\nu \times \mathbb{Z}; \end{cases} \tag{5}$$

$(\Phi\mathbf{u})_{i,k}^{\langle\nu\rangle}\Big|_{\nu\in\partial\mho_\nu} = 0 = (\Psi\mathbf{u})_{i,k}^{\langle\nu\rangle}\Big|_{\nu\in\partial\mho_\nu}$, $\forall k \in \mathbb{Z}, i = 1, 2, \ldots, m.$

For $\forall\mathbf{u} = (\mathbf{m}, \mathbf{p}) \in PAP^{\theta,\mu}(\mho_\nu \times \mathbb{Z}, \mathbb{R}^{2m}, \alpha)$, define the norm as follows:

$$\|\mathbf{u}\|_\infty = \sup_{(\nu,k)\in\mho_\nu\times\mathbb{Z}} \max_{1\leq i\leq m} \Big\{\big\|\mathbf{m}_{i,k}^{\langle\nu\rangle}\big\|_2, \big\|\mathbf{p}_{i,k}^{\langle\nu\rangle}\big\|_2\Big\},$$

in which $\left\|\mathbf{m}_{i,k}^{\langle\nu\rangle}\right\|_2 = \left[\mathbf{E}\left(\mathbf{m}_{i,k}^{\langle\nu\rangle}\right)^2\right]^{\frac{1}{2}}$ and $\left\|\mathbf{p}_{i,k}^{\langle\nu\rangle}\right\|_2 = \left[\mathbf{E}\left(\mathbf{p}_{i,k}^{\langle\nu\rangle}\right)^2\right]^{\frac{1}{2}}$ for all $(\nu,k) \in \mho_\nu \times \mathbb{Z}$, $i = 1,2,\ldots,m$.

Define

$$\underline{a}_i := \inf_{k\in\mathbb{Z}} a_{i,k}, \quad \underline{c}_i := \inf_{k\in\mathbb{Z}} c_{i,k}, \quad \bar{d}_i := \sup_{k\in\mathbb{Z}} |d_{i,k}|,$$

$$\bar{I}_i := \sup_{k\in\mathbb{Z}} |I_{i,k}|, \quad \bar{b}_{ij} := \sup_{k\in\mathbb{Z}} |b_{ij,k}|, \quad \bar{\gamma}_{ij} := \sup_{k\in\mathbb{Z}} |\gamma_{ij,k}|, \quad \bar{\varpi}_{ij} := \sup_{k\in\mathbb{Z}} |\varpi_{ij,k}|,$$

where $i,j = 1,2,\ldots,m$.

In the later discussion of this paper, the following assumptions are necessary:

($\mathbf{g}_1$) a_i and c_i are $\mathbb{R}$-valued almost periodic sequences; σ_j, μ_j, and ν_j are $\mathbb{Z}_0$-valued almost periodic sequences; b_{ij}, γ_{ij}, ϖ_{ij}, I_i, and d_i are $\mathbb{R}$-valued α-pseudo-almost periodic sequences.

($\mathbf{g}_2$) $f_j(0) = g_j(0) = \eta_j(0) = 0$ and there exist positive numbers L_j^f, L_j^g and L_j^η such that

$$|f_j(u) - f_j(v)| \le L_j^f |u-v|, \quad |g_j(u) - g_j(v)| \le L_j^g |u-v|, \quad |\eta_j(u) - \eta_j(v)| \le L_j^\eta |u-v|$$

for any $u,v \in \mathbb{R}$, $j = 1,2,\ldots,m$.

($\mathbf{g}_3$) $\min_{1\le i\le m}\{\underline{a}_i, \underline{c}_i\} > 0$.

3.1. α-Pseudo-θ-Almost Periodicity of Operator Γ

Define a coordinate function $\mathbf{w}_{pj,k}(\omega) := \mathbf{w}_{pj}(kh,\omega) := \omega_{pj,k}$ and $\theta = (\theta_k)_{k\in\mathbb{Z}}$, which is the dynamical system on $(\Omega,\mathcal{F},\mathbf{P})$, as

$$\theta_k\omega(s) = \left(\mathbf{w}_{11,k+s} - \mathbf{w}_{11,k}, \ldots, \mathbf{w}_{1m,k+s} - \mathbf{w}_{1m,k}, \mathbf{w}_{21,k+s} - \mathbf{w}_{21,k}, \ldots, \mathbf{w}_{2m,k+s} - \mathbf{w}_{2m,k}\right)^T,$$

where $\omega = (\omega_{11},\ldots,\omega_{1m},\omega_{21},\ldots,\omega_{2m})^T \in \Omega$, $k,s \in \mathbb{Z}$, $p = 1,2$, $j = 1,2,\ldots,m$.

For any $k,\tau \in \mathbb{Z}$ and $\omega \in \Omega$, it holds that

$$\mathbf{w}_{pj,k+\tau}(\theta_{-\tau}\omega) = \mathbf{w}_{pj,k}(\omega) - \mathbf{w}_{pj,-\tau}(\omega), \quad p = 1,2, j = 1,2,\ldots,m. \tag{6}$$

Lemma 5. *Let $\sigma : \mathbb{Z} \to [0,\sigma_0]_{\mathbb{Z}}$ with $\sigma_0 > 0$ and $\Delta\sigma < 1$. If $\mathbf{x} \in PAP_0^\mu(\mathbb{Z},\mathbb{X},\alpha)$, then $\mathbf{x}_{k-\sigma_k} \in PAP_0^\mu(\mathbb{Z},\mathbb{X},\alpha)$, $\forall k \in \mathbb{Z}$.*

Proof. By the definition of $PAP_0^\mu(\mathbb{Z},\mathbb{X},\alpha)$, we obtain

$$\begin{aligned}\frac{1}{\mu_k(\alpha)}\sum_{s=-k}^{k}\alpha_s\|\mathbf{x}_{s-\sigma_s}\|_{\mathbb{X}} &\le \frac{\bar{\alpha}}{\mu_k(\alpha)}\sum_{q=-k-\sigma_{-k}}^{k-\sigma_k}\alpha_q\|\mathbf{x}_q\|_{\mathbb{X}} \\ &\le \frac{\bar{\alpha}}{\mu_k(\alpha)}\sum_{q=-k}^{k}\alpha_q\|\mathbf{x}_q\|_{\mathbb{X}} + \frac{\bar{\alpha}}{\mu_k(\alpha)}\sum_{q=-k-\sigma_0}^{-k}\alpha_q\|\mathbf{x}_q\|_{\mathbb{X}} \to 0,\end{aligned}$$

as $k \to \infty$. This completes the proof. □

Corollary 1. *If $\mathbf{x} \in PAP_0^\mu(\mathbb{Z},\mathbb{X},\alpha)$, then $\mathbf{x}_{k-1} \in PAP_0^\mu(\mathbb{Z},\mathbb{X},\alpha)$ for each $k \in \mathbb{Z}$.*

Lemma 6. *Let $\sigma : \mathbb{Z} \to [0,\sigma_0]_{\mathbb{Z}}$ be an almost periodic sequence, which satisfies the conditions in Lemma 5. If $\mathbf{x} \in PAP^{\theta,\mu}(\mathbb{Z},\mathbb{X},\alpha)$, then $\mathbf{x}_{k-\sigma_k} \in PAP^{\theta,\mu}(\mathbb{Z},\mathbb{X},\alpha)$, $\forall k \in \mathbb{Z}$.*

Proof. Owing to $\mathbf{x} \in PAP^{\theta,\mu}(\mathbb{Z},\mathbb{X},\alpha)$, then $\mathbf{x} = \hat{\mathbf{x}} + \check{\mathbf{x}}$, where $\hat{\mathbf{x}} \in AP^\theta(\mathbb{Z},\mathbb{R})$ and $\check{\mathbf{x}} \in PAP_0^\mu(\mathbb{Z},\mathbb{R},\alpha)$. From Lemma 5, $\check{\mathbf{x}}_{k-\sigma_k} \in PAP_0^\mu(\mathbb{Z},\mathbb{X},\alpha)$, $\forall k \in \mathbb{Z}$. It suffices to prove $\hat{\mathbf{x}}_{k-\sigma_k} \in AP^\theta(\mathbb{Z},\mathbb{X})$, $\forall k \in \mathbb{Z}$.

Let $\tau \in \mathbb{Z}$ be an ϵ-θ-almost period of σ and $\hat{\mathbf{x}}$, $\epsilon \in (0,1)$. Noting that $\sigma : \mathbb{Z} \to \mathbb{Z}$, so

$$|\sigma_{k+\tau} - \sigma_k| = 0 < \epsilon, \quad \forall k \in \mathbb{Z},$$

which derives

$$\|\mathcal{L}_\tau \hat{\mathbf{x}}_{k-\sigma_k} - \hat{\mathbf{x}}_{k-\sigma_k}\|_{\mathbb{X}} \leq \left\|\hat{\mathbf{x}}_{k+\tau-\sigma_{k+\tau}} - \hat{\mathbf{x}}_{k-\sigma_{k+\tau}}\right\|_{\mathbb{X}} + \left\|\hat{\mathbf{x}}_{k-\sigma_{k+\tau}} - \hat{\mathbf{x}}_{k-\sigma_k}\right\|_{\mathbb{X}} < \epsilon, \quad \forall k \in \mathbb{Z}.$$

Then, $\hat{\mathbf{x}}_{k-\sigma_k} \in AP^\theta(\mathbb{Z}, \mathbb{X})$, $\forall k \in \mathbb{Z}$. This completes the proof. □

Lemma 7. *If $b \in PAP^\mu(\mathbb{Z}, \mathbb{R}, \alpha)$, $\mathbf{x} \in PAP^{\theta,\mu}(\mathbb{Z}, \mathbb{X}, \alpha)$ is bounded, $f(0) = 0$, and $f : \mathbb{R} \to \mathbb{R}$ meets the Lipschitz condition with Lipschitz constant $L_f > 0$, then $bf(\mathbf{x}) \in PAP^{\theta,\mu}(\mathbb{Z}, \mathbb{X}, \alpha)$.*

Proof. Under the assumptions in Lemma 7, there exist $\hat{b} \in AP(\mathbb{Z}, \mathbb{R})$, $\check{b} \in PAP_0^\mu(\mathbb{Z}, \mathbb{R}, \alpha)$, $\hat{\mathbf{x}} \in AP^\theta(\mathbb{Z}, \mathbb{X})$, and $\check{\mathbf{x}} \in PAP_0^\mu(\mathbb{Z}, \mathbb{X}, \alpha)$ such that

$$b = \hat{b} + \check{b}, \quad \mathbf{x} = \hat{\mathbf{x}} + \check{\mathbf{x}}.$$

For any $\tau \in \mathbb{Z}$,

$$\begin{aligned} \left\|\mathcal{L}_\tau \hat{b}_k f(\hat{\mathbf{x}}_k) - \hat{b}_k f(\hat{\mathbf{x}}_k)\right\|_{\mathbb{X}} &= \left\|\hat{b}_{k+\tau} f(\mathcal{L}_\tau \hat{\mathbf{x}}_k) - \hat{b}_k f(\hat{\mathbf{x}}_k)\right\|_{\mathbb{X}} \\ &\leq \left|\hat{b}_{k+\tau} - \hat{b}_k\right| L_f \|\hat{\mathbf{x}}_{k+\tau}(\theta_{-\tau}\omega)\|_{\mathbb{X}} + |\hat{b}_k| L_f \|\mathcal{L}_\tau \hat{\mathbf{x}}_k - \hat{\mathbf{x}}_k\|_{\mathbb{X}}, \quad \forall k \in \mathbb{Z}, \end{aligned}$$

which implies $\hat{b} f(\hat{\mathbf{x}}) \in AP^\theta(\mathbb{Z}, \mathbb{X})$. Meanwhile,

$$\left\|bf(\mathbf{x}) - \hat{b}f(\hat{\mathbf{x}})\right\|_{\mathbb{X}} \leq |\check{b}| L_f \|\mathbf{x}\|_2 + |\hat{b}| L_f \|\check{\mathbf{x}}\|_{\mathbb{X}},$$

which induces $bf(\mathbf{x}) - \hat{b}f(\hat{\mathbf{x}}) \in PAP_0^\mu(\mathbb{Z}, \mathbb{X}, \alpha)$. This completes the proof. □

Lemma 8. *If $a \in AP(\mathbb{Z}, \mathbb{R})$ with $\underline{a} = \inf_{k \in \mathbb{Z}} a_k > 0$, $\mathbf{x} \in PAP^{\theta,\mu}(\mathbb{Z}, \mathbb{R}, \alpha)$ is bounded and $\mathbf{x}_k$ is $\mathscr{F}_k$-adaptive for each $k \in \mathbb{Z}$, then*

$$\sum_{v=-\infty}^{k-1} \prod_{s=v+1}^{k-1} e^{-a_s h} \mathbf{x}_v \in PAP^{\theta,\mu}(\mathbb{Z}, \mathbb{R}, \alpha), \quad \sum_{v=-\infty}^{k-1} \prod_{s=v+1}^{k-1} e^{-a_s h} \mathbf{x}_v w_{pj,v} \in PAP^{\theta,\mu}(\mathbb{Z}, \mathbb{R}, \alpha), \quad \forall k \in \mathbb{Z},$$

where $p = 1, 2$, $j = 1, 2, \ldots, m$.

Proof. Similar to Lemma 7, there exist $\hat{\mathbf{x}} \in AP^\theta(\mathbb{Z}, \mathbb{R})$ and $\check{\mathbf{x}} \in PAP_0^\mu(\mathbb{Z}, \mathbb{R}, \alpha)$ such that $\mathbf{x} = \hat{\mathbf{x}} + \check{\mathbf{x}}$.

Let $\bar{a} = \sup_{k \in \mathbb{Z}} a_k$, $\tau \in \mathbb{Z}$ be an ϵ-θ-almost period of a and $\hat{\mathbf{x}}$,

$$\hat{\mathcal{I}}_{pj,k} := \sum_{v=-\infty}^{k-1} \prod_{s=v+1}^{k-1} e^{-a_s h} \hat{\mathbf{x}}_v w_{pj,v}, \quad \check{\mathcal{I}}_{pj,k} := \sum_{v=-\infty}^{k-1} \prod_{s=v+1}^{k-1} e^{-a_s h} \check{\mathbf{x}}_v w_{pj,v}, \quad \forall k \in \mathbb{Z},$$

where $p = 1, 2$, $j = 1, 2, \ldots, m$. By using Equation (6) and the Minkowski and Hölder inequalities in Lemmas 2 and 3, we have

$$\begin{aligned} \|\mathcal{L}_\tau \hat{\mathcal{I}}_{pj,k} - \hat{\mathcal{I}}_{pj,k}\|_2 &= \left\{ \mathbf{E}\left[\sum_{v=-\infty}^{k-1} \prod_{s=v+1}^{k-1} e^{-a_s h} \left(e^{a_s h} (e^{-a_{s+\tau} h} - e^{-a_s h}) \hat{\mathbf{x}}_{v+\tau} + (\hat{\mathbf{x}}_{v+\tau} - \hat{\mathbf{x}}_v) \right) w_{pj,v} \right]^2 \right\}^{\frac{1}{2}} \\ &\leq \left\{ \sum_{v=-\infty}^{k-1} e^{-\underline{a}(k-v-1)h} \sum_{v=-\infty}^{k-1} e^{-\underline{a}(k-v-1)h} \mathbf{E}\left[\left(e^{(\bar{a}-\underline{a})h} \epsilon h |\hat{\mathbf{x}}_{v+\tau}| + |\hat{\mathbf{x}}_{v+\tau} - \hat{\mathbf{x}}_v| \right) w_{pj,v} \right]^2 \right\}^{\frac{1}{2}} \\ &\leq \frac{1}{1 - e^{-\underline{a}h}} \left(e^{(\bar{a}-\underline{a})h} h \sup_{k \in \mathbb{Z}} \|\hat{\mathbf{x}}_k\|_2 + 1 \right) h^{-\frac{1}{2}} \epsilon, \quad \forall k \in \mathbb{Z}, \end{aligned}$$

which implies $\hat{\mathcal{I}}_{pj} \in AP^\theta(\mathbb{Z}, \mathbb{R})$, $p = 1, 2$, $j = 1, 2, \ldots, m$.

On the other hand, similar to the before derivation, we attain

$$\begin{aligned}\left\|\check{\mathcal{I}}_{pj,k}\right\|_2 &= \left\{\mathbf{E}\left[\sum_{v=-\infty}^{k-1}\prod_{s=v+1}^{k-1} e^{-a_s h}\check{\mathbf{x}}_v w_{pj,v}\right]^2\right\}^{\frac{1}{2}} \\ &\leq \left[\sum_{v=-\infty}^{k-1} e^{-\underline{a}(k-v-1)h}\sum_{v=-\infty}^{k-1} e^{-\underline{a}(k-v-1)h}\mathbf{E}\left(\check{\mathbf{x}}_v^2 w_{pj,v}^2\right)\right]^{\frac{1}{2}} \\ &\leq \left[\frac{1}{1-e^{-\underline{a}h}}\sum_{v=-\infty}^{k-1}\frac{1}{h}e^{-\underline{a}(k-v-1)h}\|\check{\mathbf{x}}_v\|_2^2\right]^{\frac{1}{2}}, \quad \forall k\in\mathbb{Z},\end{aligned}$$

which implies

$$\begin{aligned}\lim_{k\to+\infty}\frac{1}{\mu_k(\alpha)}\sum_{s=-k}^{k}\alpha_s\|\check{\mathcal{I}}_{pj,s}\|_2 &\leq \lim_{k\to+\infty}\frac{1}{\mu_k(\alpha)}\left[\sum_{s=-k}^{k}\alpha_s\sum_{s=-k}^{k}\alpha_s\|\check{\mathcal{I}}_{pj,s}\|_2^2\right]^{\frac{1}{2}} \\ &\leq \lim_{k\to+\infty}\left[\frac{1}{\mu_k(\alpha)(1-e^{-\underline{a}h})}\sum_{s=-k}^{k}\alpha_s\sum_{v=-\infty}^{s-1}\frac{1}{h}e^{-\underline{a}(s-v-1)h}\|\check{\mathbf{x}}_v\|_2^2\right]^{\frac{1}{2}} \\ &\leq \left[\frac{\sup_{k\in\mathbb{Z}}\|\check{\mathbf{x}}_k\|_2}{1-e^{-\underline{a}h}}\sum_{q=0}^{\infty}e^{-\underline{a}qh}\frac{1}{h}\lim_{k\to+\infty}\frac{1}{\mu_k(\alpha)}\sum_{s=-k}^{k}\alpha_s\|\check{\mathbf{x}}_{s-q-1}\|_2\right]^{\frac{1}{2}}\ (q=s-v-1) \\ &= 0, \quad p=1,2, j=1,2,\ldots,m.\end{aligned}$$

In the above computations, Corollary 1 and the principle of uniform convergence are employed. Thus, $\sum_{v=-\infty}^{k-1}\prod_{s=v+1}^{k-1}e^{-a_s h}\mathbf{x}_v w_{\cdot\cdot,v}\in PAP^{\theta,\mu}(\mathbb{Z},\mathbb{R},\alpha)$, $\forall k\in\mathbb{Z}$. Furthermore, $\sum_{v=-\infty}^{k-1}\prod_{s=v+1}^{k-1}e^{-a_s h}\mathbf{x}_v\in PAP^{\theta,\mu}(\mathbb{Z},\mathbb{R},\alpha)$ can be similarly addressed, and $\forall k\in\mathbb{Z}$. This completes the proof. □

Together with Lemmas 5–8, we derive the following:

Theorem 1. *Supposing that* $(\mathbf{g}_1)$–$(\mathbf{g}_3)$ *hold. Then,* Γ *maps* $PAP^{\theta,\mu}(\mho_\nu\times\mathbb{Z},\mathbb{R}^{2m},\alpha)$ *to* $PAP^{\theta,\mu}(\mho_\nu\times\mathbb{Z},\mathbb{R}^{2m},\alpha)$.

3.2. Weighted Pseudo-Almost Periodic Sequence Solution to GRNs Equation (1)

Define

$$PAP_b^{\theta,\mu}(\mho_\nu\times\mathbb{Z},\mathbb{R}^{2m},\alpha)=\left\{\mathbf{u}\in PAP^{\theta,\mu}(\mho_\nu\times\mathbb{Z},\mathbb{R}^{2m},\alpha):\|\mathbf{u}-\varphi\|_\infty\leq\frac{\varsigma\varphi_0}{1-\varsigma}\right\},$$

where

$$\varphi=(\varphi_1,\varphi_2,\cdots,\varphi_m,0,\cdots,0)^T,\quad \varphi_{i,k}^{\langle\nu\rangle}=\sum_{v=-\infty}^{k-1}\prod_{s=v+1}^{k-1}\frac{e^{-a_{i,s}h}(1-e^{-a_{i,v}h})}{a_{i,v}}I_{i,v}$$

for all $(\nu,k)\in\mho_\nu\times\mathbb{Z}$, $i=1,2,\ldots,m$. From the definition of φ, we derive

$$\|\varphi\|_\infty=\max_{1\leq i\leq m}\sup_{(\nu,k)\in\mho_\nu\times\mathbb{Z}}\left\|\varphi_{i,k}^{\langle\nu\rangle}\right\|_2=\max_{1\leq i\leq m}\sup_{(\nu,k)\in\mho_\nu\times\mathbb{Z}}\sum_{v=-\infty}^{k-1}\prod_{s=v+1}^{k-1}\frac{e^{-a_{i,s}h}(1-e^{-a_{i,v}h})}{a_{i,v}}I_{i,v}\leq\max_{1\leq i\leq m}\frac{\bar{I}_i}{\underline{a}_i}=\varphi_0,$$

which induces

$$\|\mathbf{u}\|_\infty\leq\|\mathbf{u}-\varphi\|_\infty+\|\varphi\|_\infty\leq\frac{\varsigma\varphi_0}{1-\varsigma}+\varphi_0=\frac{\varphi_0}{1-\varsigma},\quad\forall\mathbf{u}\in PAP_b^{\theta,\mu}(\mho_\nu\times\mathbb{Z},\mathbb{R}^{2m},\alpha).$$

Theorem 2. *Let* $(\mathbf{g}_1)$–$(\mathbf{g}_3)$ *be valid. GRNs Equation (1) possesses a unique weighted pseudo- or* α*-pseudo-almost periodic sequence solution if the following condition holds.*

($\mathbf{g}_4$) $\varsigma = \max\{\varsigma_1, \varsigma_2\} < 1$, *where*

$$\varsigma_1 = \max_{1\le i\le m} \frac{1}{\underline{a}_i}\left[\sum_{q=1}^{n} \frac{2|\Theta_{iq}|}{\hbar^2} + \sum_{j=1}^{m} \bar{b}_{ij}L_j^f + \sum_{j=1}^{m} \bar{\gamma}_{ij}L_j^g h^{-\frac{1}{2}}\right],$$

$$\varsigma_2 = \max_{1\le i\le m} \frac{1}{\underline{c}_i}\left[\sum_{q=1}^{n} \frac{2|\Pi_{iq}|}{\hbar^2} + \sum_{j=1}^{m} \bar{\varpi}_{ij}L_j^\eta h^{-\frac{1}{2}} + \bar{d}_i\right].$$

Proof. Let us prove that the operator Γ is self-mapping from $PAP_b^{\theta,\mu}(\mho_\nu \times \mathbb{Z}, \mathbb{R}^{2m}, \alpha)$ to $PAP_b^{\theta,\mu}(\mho_\nu \times \mathbb{Z}, \mathbb{R}^{2m}, \alpha)$. Supposing that $\mathbf{u} = (\mathbf{m}, \mathbf{p})^T = (\mathbf{m}_1, \cdots, \mathbf{m}_m, \mathbf{p}_1, \cdots, \mathbf{p}_m)^T \in PAP_b^{\theta,\mu}(\mho_\nu \times \mathbb{Z}, \mathbb{R}^{2m}, \alpha)$. In view of Equation (5) and by utilizing the Minkowski and Hölder inequalities in Lemmas 2 and 3, we have

$$\begin{aligned}
\left\|(\Phi\mathbf{u})_{i,k}^{\langle\nu\rangle} - \varphi_{i,k}^{\langle\nu\rangle}\right\|_2 &= \Bigg\{\mathbf{E}\Bigg(\sum_{v=-\infty}^{k-1}\prod_{s=v+1}^{k-1}\frac{e^{-a_{i,s}h}(1-e^{-a_{i,v}h})}{a_{i,v}}\Bigg[\sum_{q=1}^{n}\Theta_{iq}\tilde{\Delta}_{\hbar_q}^2\mathbf{m}_{i,v}^{\langle\nu\rangle} \\
&\quad + \sum_{j=1}^{m} b_{ij,v}f_j(\mathbf{p}_{j,v-\sigma_{j,v}}^{\langle\nu\rangle}) + \sum_{j=1}^{m}\gamma_{ij,v}g_j(\mathbf{p}_{j,v-\mu_{j,v}}^{\langle\nu\rangle})w_{1j,v}\Bigg]\Bigg)^2\Bigg\}^{\frac{1}{2}} \\
&\le \frac{1-e^{-\underline{a}_i h}}{\underline{a}_i}\Bigg\{\mathbf{E}\Bigg(\sum_{v=-\infty}^{k-1}e^{-\underline{a}_i(k-v-1)h}\Bigg[\sum_{q=1}^{n}|\Theta_{iq}||\tilde{\Delta}_{\hbar_q}^2\mathbf{m}_{i,v}^{\langle\nu\rangle}| \\
&\quad + \sum_{j=1}^{m}\bar{b}_{ij}L_j^f|\mathbf{p}_{j,v-\sigma_{j,v}}^{\langle\nu\rangle}| + \sum_{j=1}^{m}\bar{\gamma}_{ij}L_j^g|\mathbf{p}_{j,v-\mu_{j,v}}^{\langle\nu\rangle}||w_{1j,v}|\Bigg]\Bigg)^2\Bigg\}^{\frac{1}{2}} \\
&\le \frac{1-e^{-\underline{a}_i h}}{\underline{a}_i}\Bigg\{\sum_{v=-\infty}^{k-1}e^{-\underline{a}_i(k-v-1)h}\sum_{v=-\infty}^{k-1}e^{-\underline{a}_i(k-v-1)h} \\
&\quad \times \mathbf{E}\Bigg[\sum_{q=1}^{n}|\Theta_{iq}||\tilde{\Delta}_{\hbar_q}^2\mathbf{m}_{i,v}^{\langle\nu\rangle}| + \sum_{j=1}^{m}\bar{b}_{ij}L_j^f|\mathbf{p}_{j,v-\sigma_{j,v}}^{\langle\nu\rangle}| + \sum_{j=1}^{m}\bar{\gamma}_{ij}L_j^g|\mathbf{p}_{j,v-\mu_{j,v}}^{\langle\nu\rangle}||w_{1j,v}|\Bigg]^2\Bigg\}^{\frac{1}{2}} \\
&\le \frac{1-e^{-\underline{a}_i h}}{\underline{a}_i}\Bigg\{\frac{1}{1-e^{-\underline{a}_i h}}\sum_{v=-\infty}^{k-1}e^{-\underline{a}_i(k-v-1)h}\Bigg\{\Bigg(\mathbf{E}\Bigg[\sum_{q=1}^{n}|\Theta_{iq}||\tilde{\Delta}_{\hbar_q}^2\mathbf{m}_{i,v}^{\langle\nu\rangle}| \\
&\quad + \sum_{j=1}^{m}\bar{b}_{ij}L_j^f|\mathbf{p}_{j,v-\sigma_{j,v}}^{\langle\nu\rangle}| + \sum_{j=1}^{m}\bar{\gamma}_{ij}L_j^g|\mathbf{p}_{j,v-\mu_{j,v}}^{\langle\nu\rangle}||w_{1j,v}|\Bigg]^2\Bigg)^{\frac{1}{2}}\Bigg\}^2\Bigg\}^{\frac{1}{2}} \qquad (7)\\
&\le \frac{1-e^{-\underline{a}_i h}}{\underline{a}_i}\Bigg\{\frac{1}{1-e^{-\underline{a}_i h}}\sum_{v=-\infty}^{k-1}e^{-\underline{a}_i(k-v-1)h}\Bigg\{\Bigg(\mathbf{E}\Bigg(\sum_{q=1}^{n}|\Theta_{iq}||\tilde{\Delta}_{\hbar_q}^2\mathbf{m}_{i,v}^{\langle\nu\rangle}|\Bigg)^2\Bigg) \\
&\quad + \Bigg(\mathbf{E}\Bigg(\sum_{j=1}^{m}\bar{b}_{ij}L_j^f|\mathbf{p}_{j,v-\sigma_{j,v}}^{\langle\nu\rangle}|\Bigg)^2\Bigg)^{\frac{1}{2}} + \Bigg(\mathbf{E}\sum_{j=1}^{m}\bar{\gamma}_{ij}L_j^g|\mathbf{p}_{j,v-\mu_{j,v}}^{\langle\nu\rangle}||w_{1j,v}|\Bigg)^2\Bigg)^{\frac{1}{2}}\Bigg\}^2\Bigg\}^{\frac{1}{2}} \\
&\le \frac{1-e^{-\underline{a}_i h}}{\underline{a}_i}\Bigg\{\frac{1}{1-e^{-\underline{a}_i h}}\sum_{v=-\infty}^{k-1}e^{-\underline{a}_i(k-v-1)h}\Bigg\{\sum_{q=1}^{n}|\Theta_{iq}|\frac{2}{\hbar}\|\mathbf{u}\|_\infty \\
&\quad + \sum_{j=1}^{m}\bar{b}_{ij}L_j^f\|\mathbf{u}\|_\infty + \sum_{j=1}^{m}\bar{\gamma}_{ij}L_j^g\frac{1}{\sqrt{h}}\|\mathbf{u}\|_\infty\Bigg\}^2\Bigg\}^{\frac{1}{2}} \\
&\le \frac{1-e^{-\underline{a}_i h}}{\underline{a}_i}\Bigg\{\frac{1}{1-e^{-\underline{a}_i h}}\frac{1}{1-e^{-\underline{a}_i h}}\Bigg\{\sum_{q=1}^{n}|\Theta_{iq}|\frac{2}{\hbar}\|\mathbf{u}\|_\infty \\
&\quad + \sum_{j=1}^{m}\bar{b}_{ij}L_j^f\|\mathbf{u}\|_\infty + \sum_{j=1}^{m}\bar{\gamma}_{ij}L_j^g\frac{1}{\sqrt{h}}\|\mathbf{u}\|_\infty\Bigg\}^2\Bigg\}^{\frac{1}{2}} \\
&\le \frac{1}{\underline{a}_i}\Bigg(\sum_{q=1}^{n}|\Theta_{iq}|\frac{2}{\hbar} + \sum_{j=1}^{m}\bar{b}_{ij}L_j^f + \sum_{j=1}^{m}\bar{\gamma}_{ij}L_j^g\frac{1}{\sqrt{h}}\Bigg)\|\mathbf{u}\|_\infty \\
&\le \frac{\varsigma\varphi_0}{1-\varsigma}, \quad i = 1, 2, \ldots, m,
\end{aligned}$$

as well as

$$
\begin{aligned}
\left\|(\Psi\mathbf{u})_{i,k}^{\langle\nu\rangle}-0\right\|_2 &= \left\{\mathbf{E}\left(\sum_{v=-\infty}^{k-1}\prod_{s=v+1}^{k-1}\frac{e^{-c_{i,s}h}(1-e^{-c_{i,v}h})}{c_{i,v}}\left[\sum_{q=1}^{n}\Pi_{iq}\tilde{\Delta}_{\hbar_q}^2\mathbf{p}_{i,v}^{\langle\nu\rangle}\right.\right.\right.\\
&\quad\left.\left.\left.+d_{i,v}\mathbf{m}_{i,v}^{\langle\nu\rangle}+\sum_{j=1}^{m}\varpi_{ij,v}\eta_j(\mathbf{m}_{j,v-\nu_{j,v}}^{\langle\nu\rangle})w_{2j,v}\right]\right)^2\right\}^{\frac{1}{2}}\\
&\le \frac{1-e^{-\underline{c}_ih}}{\underline{c}_i}\left\{\mathbf{E}\left(\sum_{v=-\infty}^{k-1}e^{-\underline{c}_i(k-v-1)h}\left[\sum_{q=1}^{n}|\Pi_{iq}||\tilde{\Delta}_{\hbar_q}^2\mathbf{p}_{i,v}^{\langle\nu\rangle}|\right.\right.\right.\\
&\quad\left.\left.\left.+\bar{d}_i|\mathbf{m}_{i,v}^{\langle\nu\rangle}|+\sum_{j=1}^{m}\bar{\varpi}_{ij}L_j^{\eta}|\mathbf{m}_{j,v-\nu_{j,v}}^{\langle\nu\rangle}||w_{2j,v}|\right]\right)^2\right\}^{\frac{1}{2}}\\
&\le \frac{1-e^{-\underline{c}_ih}}{\underline{c}_i}\left\{\sum_{v=-\infty}^{k-1}e^{-\underline{c}_i(k-v-1)h}\sum_{v=-\infty}^{k-1}e^{-\underline{c}_i(k-v-1)h}\right.\\
&\quad\left.\times\mathbf{E}\left[\sum_{q=1}^{n}|\Pi_{iq}||\tilde{\Delta}_{\hbar_q}^2\mathbf{p}_{i,v}^{\langle\nu\rangle}|+\bar{d}_i|\mathbf{m}_{i,v}^{\langle\nu\rangle}|+\sum_{j=1}^{m}\bar{\varpi}_{ij}L_j^{\eta}|\mathbf{m}_{j,v-\nu_{j,v}}^{\langle\nu\rangle}||w_{2j,v}|\right]^2\right\}^{\frac{1}{2}}\\
&\le \frac{1-e^{-\underline{c}_ih}}{\underline{c}_i}\left\{\frac{1}{1-e^{-\underline{c}_ih}}\sum_{v=-\infty}^{k-1}e^{-\underline{c}_i(k-v-1)h}\left\{\left(\mathbf{E}\left[\sum_{q=1}^{n}|\Pi_{iq}||\tilde{\Delta}_{\hbar_q}^2\mathbf{p}_{i,v}^{\langle\nu\rangle}|\right.\right.\right.\right.\\
&\quad\left.\left.\left.\left.+\bar{d}_i|\mathbf{m}_{i,v}^{\langle\nu\rangle}|+\sum_{j=1}^{m}\bar{\varpi}_{ij}L_j^{\eta}|\mathbf{m}_{j,v-\nu_{j,v}}^{\langle\nu\rangle}||w_{2j,v}|\right]^2\right)^{\frac{1}{2}}\right\}^2\right\}^{\frac{1}{2}}\\
&\le \frac{1-e^{-\underline{c}_ih}}{\underline{c}_i}\left\{\frac{1}{1-e^{-\underline{c}_ih}}\sum_{v=-\infty}^{k-1}e^{-\underline{c}_i(k-v-1)h}\left\{\left(\mathbf{E}\left(\sum_{q=1}^{n}|\Pi_{iq}||\tilde{\Delta}_{\hbar_q}^2\mathbf{p}_{i,v}^{\langle\nu\rangle}|\right)\right)^2\right.\right.\\
&\quad\left.\left.+\left(\mathbf{E}\left(\bar{d}_i|\mathbf{m}_{j,v}^{\langle\nu\rangle}|\right)\right)^{2}{}^{\frac{1}{2}}+\left(\mathbf{E}\sum_{j=1}^{m}\bar{\varpi}_{ij}L_j^{\eta}|\mathbf{m}_{j,v-\nu_{j,v}}^{\langle\nu\rangle}||w_{2j,v}|\right)\right)^2{}^{\frac{1}{2}}\right\}^2\right\}^{\frac{1}{2}}\\
&\le \frac{1-e^{-\underline{c}_ih}}{\underline{c}_i}\left\{\frac{1}{1-e^{-\underline{c}_ih}}\sum_{v=-\infty}^{k-1}e^{-\underline{c}_i(k-v-1)h}\right.\\
&\quad\left.\times\left\{\sum_{q=1}^{n}|\Pi_{iq}|\frac{2}{\hbar}\|\mathbf{u}\|_\infty+\bar{d}_i\|\mathbf{u}\|_\infty+\sum_{j=1}^{m}\bar{\varpi}_{ij}L_j^{\eta}\frac{1}{\sqrt{h}}\|\mathbf{u}\|_\infty\right\}^2\right\}^{\frac{1}{2}}\\
&\le \frac{1-e^{-\underline{c}_ih}}{\underline{c}_i}\left\{\frac{1}{1-e^{-\underline{c}_ih}}\frac{1}{1-e^{-\underline{c}_ih}}\right.\\
&\quad\left.\times\left\{\sum_{q=1}^{n}|\Pi_{iq}|\frac{2}{\hbar}\|\mathbf{u}\|_\infty+\bar{d}_i\|\mathbf{u}\|_\infty+\sum_{j=1}^{m}\bar{\varpi}_{ij}L_j^{\eta}\frac{1}{\sqrt{h}}\|\mathbf{u}\|_\infty\right\}^2\right\}^{\frac{1}{2}}\\
&\le \frac{1}{\underline{c}_i}\left(\sum_{q=1}^{n}|\Pi_{iq}|\frac{2}{\hbar}+\bar{d}_i+\sum_{j=1}^{m}\bar{\varpi}_{ij}L_j^{\eta}\frac{1}{\sqrt{h}}\right)\|\mathbf{u}\|_\infty\\
&\le \frac{\varsigma\varphi_0}{1-\varsigma},\quad i=1,2,\ldots,m.
\end{aligned}
\tag{8}
$$

In the calculations of the stochastic terms of Equations (7) and (8), Lemma 4 has been employed.

Together with Equations (7) and (8), $\|\Gamma\mathbf{u}-\varphi\|_\infty \le \dfrac{\varsigma\varphi_0}{1-\varsigma}$ and $\Gamma\mathbf{u}$ is well defined in space $\left(PAP_b^{\theta,\mu}(\mho_\nu\times\mathbb{Z},\mathbb{R}^{2m},\alpha),\|\cdot\|_\infty\right)$ for any $\mathbf{u}\in PAP_b^{\theta,\mu}(\mho_\nu\times\mathbb{Z},\mathbb{R}^{2m},\alpha)$.

In the end, the property of contraction to the operator Γ in space $PAP_b^{\theta,\mu}(\mho_\nu\times\mathbb{Z},\mathbb{R}^{2m},\alpha)$ will be demonstrated. Let $\mathbf{u}=(\mathbf{m}_1,\cdots,\mathbf{m}_m,\mathbf{p}_1,\cdots,\mathbf{p}_m)^T$ and $\tilde{\mathbf{u}}=(\tilde{\mathbf{m}}_1,\cdots,\tilde{\mathbf{m}}_m,\tilde{\mathbf{p}}_1,\cdots,\tilde{\mathbf{p}}_m)^T$ belong to space $PAP_b^{\theta,\mu}(\mho_\nu\times\mathbb{Z},\mathbb{R}^{2m},\alpha)$, it follows that

$$
\begin{aligned}
\left\|(\Phi\mathbf{u})_{i,k}^{\langle\nu\rangle}-(\Phi\tilde{\mathbf{u}})_{i,k}^{\langle\nu\rangle}\right\|_2 =\ & \Bigg\{\mathbf{E}\Bigg(\sum_{v=-\infty}^{k-1}\prod_{s=v+1}^{k-1}\frac{e^{-a_{i,s}h}(1-e^{-a_{i,v}h})}{a_{i,v}}\Bigg[\sum_{q=1}^{n}\Theta_{iq}\tilde{\Delta}^2_{\hbar_q}(\mathbf{m}_{i,v}^{\langle\nu\rangle}-\tilde{\mathbf{m}}_{i,v}^{\langle\nu\rangle}) \\
& +\sum_{j=1}^{m}b_{ij,v}\Big(f_j(\mathbf{p}_{j,v-\sigma_{j,v}}^{\langle\nu\rangle})-f_j(\tilde{\mathbf{p}}_{j,v-\sigma_{j,v}}^{\langle\nu\rangle})\Big) \\
& +\sum_{j=1}^{m}\gamma_{ij,v}\Big(g_j(\mathbf{p}_{j,v-\mu_{j,v}}^{\langle\nu\rangle})-g_j(\tilde{\mathbf{p}}_{j,v-\mu_{j,v}}^{\langle\nu\rangle})\Big)w_{1j,v}\Bigg]\Bigg)^2\Bigg\}^{\frac{1}{2}} \\
\leq\ & \frac{1-e^{-\underline{a}_ih}}{\underline{a}_i}\Bigg\{\mathbf{E}\Bigg(\sum_{v=-\infty}^{k-1}e^{-\underline{a}_i(k-v-1)h}\Bigg[\sum_{q=1}^{n}|\Theta_{iq}||\tilde{\Delta}^2_{\hbar_q}(\mathbf{m}_{i,v}^{\langle\nu\rangle}-\tilde{\mathbf{m}}_{i,v}^{\langle\nu\rangle})| \\
& +\sum_{j=1}^{m}\bar{b}_{ij}L_j^f|\mathbf{p}_{j,v-\sigma_{j,v}}^{\langle\nu\rangle}-\tilde{\mathbf{p}}_{j,v-\sigma_{j,v}}^{\langle\nu\rangle}|+\sum_{j=1}^{m}\bar{\gamma}_{ij}L_j^g|\mathbf{p}_{j,v-\mu_{j,v}}^{\langle\nu\rangle}-\tilde{\mathbf{p}}_{j,v-\mu_{j,v}}^{\langle\nu\rangle}||w_{1j,v}|\Bigg]\Bigg)^2\Bigg\}^{\frac{1}{2}} \\
\leq\ & \frac{1-e^{-\underline{a}_ih}}{\underline{a}_i}\Bigg\{\sum_{v=-\infty}^{k-1}e^{-\underline{a}_i(k-v-1)h}\sum_{v=-\infty}^{k-1}e^{-\underline{a}_i(k-v-1)h}\mathbf{E}\Bigg[\sum_{q=1}^{n}|\Theta_{iq}||\tilde{\Delta}^2_{\hbar_q}(\mathbf{m}_{i,v}^{\langle\nu\rangle}-\tilde{\mathbf{m}}_{i,v}^{\langle\nu\rangle})| \\
& +\sum_{j=1}^{m}\bar{b}_{ij}L_j^f|\mathbf{p}_{j,v-\sigma_{j,v}}^{\langle\nu\rangle}-\tilde{\mathbf{p}}_{j,v-\sigma_{j,v}}^{\langle\nu\rangle}|+\sum_{j=1}^{m}\bar{\gamma}_{ij}L_j^g|\mathbf{p}_{j,v-\mu_{j,v}}^{\langle\nu\rangle}-\tilde{\mathbf{p}}_{j,v-\mu_{j,v}}^{\langle\nu\rangle}||w_{1j,v}|\Bigg]^2\Bigg\}^{\frac{1}{2}} \\
\leq\ & \frac{1-e^{-\underline{a}_ih}}{\underline{a}_i}\Bigg\{\frac{1}{1-e^{-\underline{a}_ih}}\sum_{v=-\infty}^{k-1}e^{-\underline{a}_i(k-v-1)h}\Bigg\{\Bigg(\mathbf{E}\Bigg[\sum_{q=1}^{n}|\Theta_{iq}||\tilde{\Delta}^2_{\hbar_q}(\mathbf{m}_{i,v}^{\langle\nu\rangle}-\tilde{\mathbf{m}}_{i,v}^{\langle\nu\rangle})| \\
& +\sum_{j=1}^{m}\bar{b}_{ij}L_j^f|\mathbf{p}_{j,v-\sigma_{j,v}}^{\langle\nu\rangle}-\tilde{\mathbf{p}}_{j,v-\sigma_{j,v}}^{\langle\nu\rangle}|+\sum_{j=1}^{m}\bar{\gamma}_{ij}L_j^g|\mathbf{p}_{j,v-\mu_{j,v}}^{\langle\nu\rangle}-\tilde{\mathbf{p}}_{j,v-\mu_{j,v}}^{\langle\nu\rangle}||w_{1j,v}|\Bigg]^2\Bigg)^{\frac{1}{2}}\Bigg\}^2\Bigg\}^{\frac{1}{2}} \\
\leq\ & \frac{1-e^{-\underline{a}_ih}}{\underline{a}_i}\Bigg\{\frac{1}{1-e^{-\underline{a}_ih}}\sum_{v=-\infty}^{k-1}e^{-\underline{a}_i(k-v-1)h}\Bigg\{\Bigg(\mathbf{E}\Bigg(\sum_{q=1}^{n}|\Theta_{iq}||\tilde{\Delta}^2_{\hbar_q}(\mathbf{m}_{i,v}^{\langle\nu\rangle}-\tilde{\mathbf{m}}_{i,v}^{\langle\nu\rangle})|\Bigg)^2\Bigg)^{\frac{1}{2}} \\
& +\Bigg(\mathbf{E}\Bigg(\sum_{j=1}^{m}\bar{b}_{ij}L_j^f|\mathbf{p}_{j,v-\sigma_{j,v}}^{\langle\nu\rangle}-\tilde{\mathbf{p}}_{j,v-\sigma_{j,v}}^{\langle\nu\rangle}|\Bigg)^2\Bigg)^{\frac{1}{2}} \\
& +\Bigg(\mathbf{E}\sum_{j=1}^{m}\bar{\gamma}_{ij}L_j^g|\mathbf{p}_{j,v-\mu_{j,v}}^{\langle\nu\rangle}-\tilde{\mathbf{p}}_{j,v-\mu_{j,v}}^{\langle\nu\rangle}||w_{1j,v}|\Bigg)^2\Bigg)^{\frac{1}{2}}\Bigg\}^2\Bigg\}^{\frac{1}{2}} \\
\leq\ & \frac{1-e^{-\underline{a}_ih}}{\underline{a}_i}\Bigg\{\frac{1}{1-e^{-\underline{a}_ih}}\sum_{v=-\infty}^{k-1}e^{-\underline{a}_i(k-v-1)h}\Bigg\{\sum_{q=1}^{n}|\Theta_{iq}|\frac{2}{\hbar}\|\mathbf{u}-\tilde{\mathbf{u}}\|_\infty \\
& +\sum_{j=1}^{m}\bar{b}_{ij}L_j^f\|\mathbf{u}-\tilde{\mathbf{u}}\|_\infty+\sum_{j=1}^{m}\bar{\gamma}_{ij}L_j^g\frac{1}{\sqrt{h}}\|\mathbf{u}-\tilde{\mathbf{u}}\|_\infty\Bigg\}^2\Bigg\}^{\frac{1}{2}} \\
\leq\ & \frac{1-e^{-\underline{a}_ih}}{\underline{a}_i}\Bigg\{\frac{1}{(1-e^{-\underline{a}_ih})^2}\Bigg\{\sum_{q=1}^{n}|\Theta_{iq}|\frac{2}{\hbar}\|\mathbf{u}-\tilde{\mathbf{u}}\|_\infty \\
& +\sum_{j=1}^{m}\bar{b}_{ij}L_j^f\|\mathbf{u}-\tilde{\mathbf{u}}\|_\infty+\sum_{j=1}^{m}\bar{\gamma}_{ij}L_j^g\frac{1}{\sqrt{h}}\|\mathbf{u}-\tilde{\mathbf{u}}\|_\infty\Bigg\}^2\Bigg\}^{\frac{1}{2}} \\
\leq\ & \frac{1}{\underline{a}_i}\Bigg(\sum_{q=1}^{n}|\Theta_{iq}|\frac{2}{\hbar}+\sum_{j=1}^{m}\bar{b}_{ij}L_j^f+\sum_{j=1}^{m}\bar{\gamma}_{ij}L_j^g\frac{1}{\sqrt{h}}\Bigg)\|\mathbf{u}-\tilde{\mathbf{u}}\|_\infty \\
\leq\ & \varsigma\|\mathbf{u}-\tilde{\mathbf{u}}\|_\infty,\quad i=1,2,\ldots,m,
\end{aligned}
\tag{9}
$$

as well as

$$
\begin{aligned}
\left\|(\Psi\mathbf{u})_{i,k}^{\langle\nu\rangle}-(\Psi\tilde{\mathbf{u}})_{i,k}^{\langle\nu\rangle}\right\|_2 =& \Bigg\{\mathbf{E}\Bigg(\sum_{v=-\infty}^{k-1}\prod_{s=v+1}^{k-1}\frac{e^{-c_{i,s}h}(1-e^{-c_{i,v}h})}{c_{i,v}}\Bigg[\sum_{q=1}^{n}\Pi_{iq}\tilde{\Delta}_{\hbar_q}^2(\mathbf{p}_{i,v}^{\langle\nu\rangle}-\tilde{\mathbf{p}}_{i,v}^{\langle\nu\rangle}) \\
&+d_{i,v}(\mathbf{m}_{i,v}^{\langle\nu\rangle}-\tilde{\mathbf{m}}_{i,v}^{\langle\nu\rangle})+\sum_{j=1}^{m}\varpi_{ij,v}\eta_j(\mathbf{m}_{j,v-\nu_{j,v}}^{\langle\nu\rangle}-\tilde{\mathbf{m}}_{j,v-\nu_{j,v}}^{\langle\nu\rangle})w_{2j,v}\Bigg]\Bigg)^2\Bigg\}^{\frac{1}{2}} \\
\le& \frac{1-e^{-\underline{c}_ih}}{\underline{c}_i}\Bigg\{\mathbf{E}\Bigg(\sum_{v=-\infty}^{k-1}e^{-\underline{c}_i(k-v-1)h}\Bigg[\sum_{q=1}^{n}|\Pi_{iq}||\tilde{\Delta}_{\hbar_q}^2(\mathbf{p}_{i,v}^{\langle\nu\rangle}-\tilde{\mathbf{p}}_{i,v}^{\langle\nu\rangle})| \\
&+\bar{d}_i|\mathbf{m}_{i,v}^{\langle\nu\rangle}-\tilde{\mathbf{m}}_{i,v}^{\langle\nu\rangle}|+\sum_{j=1}^{m}\bar{\varpi}_{ij}L_j^{\eta}|\mathbf{m}_{j,v-\nu_{j,v}}^{\langle\nu\rangle}-\tilde{\mathbf{m}}_{j,v-\nu_{j,v}}^{\langle\nu\rangle}||w_{2j,v}|\Bigg]\Bigg)^2\Bigg\}^{\frac{1}{2}} \\
\le& \frac{1-e^{-\underline{c}_ih}}{\underline{c}_i}\Bigg\{\sum_{v=-\infty}^{k-1}e^{-\underline{c}_i(k-v-1)h}\sum_{v=-\infty}^{k-1}e^{-\underline{c}_i(k-v-1)h}\mathbf{E}\Bigg[\sum_{q=1}^{n}|\Pi_{iq}||\tilde{\Delta}_{\hbar_q}^2(\mathbf{p}_{i,v}^{\langle\nu\rangle}-\tilde{\mathbf{p}}_{i,v}^{\langle\nu\rangle})| \\
&+\bar{d}_i|\mathbf{m}_{i,v}^{\langle\nu\rangle}-\tilde{\mathbf{m}}_{i,v}^{\langle\nu\rangle}|+\sum_{j=1}^{m}\bar{\varpi}_{ij}L_j^{\eta}|\mathbf{m}_{j,v-\nu_{j,v}}^{\langle\nu\rangle}-\tilde{\mathbf{m}}_{j,v-\nu_{j,v}}^{\langle\nu\rangle}||w_{2j,v}|\Bigg]^2\Bigg\}^{\frac{1}{2}} \\
\le& \frac{1-e^{-\underline{c}_ih}}{\underline{c}_i}\Bigg\{\frac{1}{1-e^{-\underline{c}_ih}}\sum_{v=-\infty}^{k-1}e^{-\underline{c}_i(k-v-1)h}\Bigg\{\Bigg(\Bigg(\mathbf{E}\Bigg[\sum_{q=1}^{n}|\Pi_{iq}||\tilde{\Delta}_{\hbar_q}^2(\mathbf{p}_{i,v}^{\langle\nu\rangle}-\tilde{\mathbf{p}}_{i,v}^{\langle\nu\rangle})| \\
&+\bar{d}_i|\mathbf{m}_{i,v}^{\langle\nu\rangle}-\tilde{\mathbf{m}}_{i,v}^{\langle\nu\rangle}|+\sum_{j=1}^{m}\bar{\varpi}_{ij}L_j^{\eta}|\mathbf{m}_{j,v-\nu_{j,v}}^{\langle\nu\rangle}-\tilde{\mathbf{m}}_{j,v-\nu_{j,v}}^{\langle\nu\rangle}||w_{2j,v}|\Bigg]^2\Bigg)^{\frac{1}{2}}\Bigg)^2\Bigg\}\Bigg\}^{\frac{1}{2}} \\
\le& \frac{1-e^{-\underline{c}_ih}}{\underline{c}_i}\Bigg\{\frac{1}{1-e^{-\underline{c}_ih}}\sum_{v=-\infty}^{k-1}e^{-\underline{c}_i(k-v-1)h}\Bigg\{\Bigg(\Bigg(\mathbf{E}\Bigg(\sum_{q=1}^{n}|\Pi_{iq}||\tilde{\Delta}_{\hbar_q}^2(\mathbf{p}_{i,v}^{\langle\nu\rangle}-\tilde{\mathbf{p}}_{i,v}^{\langle\nu\rangle})|\Bigg)^2\Bigg)^{\frac{1}{2}} \\
&+\Bigg(\mathbf{E}\Bigg(\bar{d}_i|\mathbf{m}_{j,v}^{\langle\nu\rangle}-\tilde{\mathbf{m}}_{j,v}^{\langle\nu\rangle}|\Bigg)^2\Bigg)^{\frac{1}{2}}+\Bigg(\mathbf{E}\sum_{j=1}^{m}\bar{\varpi}_{ij}L_j^{\eta}|\mathbf{m}_{j,v-\nu_{j,v}}^{\langle\nu\rangle}-\tilde{\mathbf{m}}_{j,v-\nu_{j,v}}^{\langle\nu\rangle}||w_{2j,v}|\Bigg)^2\Bigg)^{\frac{1}{2}}\Bigg)^2\Bigg\}\Bigg\}^{\frac{1}{2}} \\
\le& \frac{1-e^{-\underline{c}_ih}}{\underline{c}_i}\Bigg\{\frac{1}{1-e^{-\underline{c}_ih}}\sum_{v=-\infty}^{k-1}e^{-\underline{c}_i(k-v-1)h}\Bigg\{\sum_{q=1}^{n}|\Pi_{iq}|\frac{2}{\hbar}\|\mathbf{u}-\tilde{\mathbf{u}}\|_\infty \\
&+\bar{d}_i\|\mathbf{u}-\tilde{\mathbf{u}}\|_\infty+\sum_{j=1}^{m}\bar{\varpi}_{ij}L_j^{\eta}\frac{1}{\sqrt{h}}\|\mathbf{u}-\tilde{\mathbf{u}}\|_\infty\Bigg\}^2\Bigg\}^{\frac{1}{2}} \\
\le& \frac{1-e^{-\underline{c}_ih}}{\underline{c}_i}\Bigg\{\frac{1}{(1-e^{-\underline{c}_ih})^2}\Bigg\{\sum_{q=1}^{n}|\Pi_{iq}|\frac{2}{\hbar}\|\mathbf{u}-\tilde{\mathbf{u}}\|_\infty \\
&+\bar{d}_i\|\mathbf{u}-\tilde{\mathbf{u}}\|_\infty+\sum_{j=1}^{m}\bar{\varpi}_{ij}L_j^{\eta}\frac{1}{\sqrt{h}}\|\mathbf{u}-\tilde{\mathbf{u}}\|_\infty\Bigg\}^2\Bigg\}^{\frac{1}{2}} \\
\le& \frac{1}{\underline{c}_i}\Bigg(\sum_{q=1}^{n}|\Pi_{iq}|\frac{2}{\hbar}+\bar{d}_i+\sum_{j=1}^{m}\bar{\varpi}_{ij}L_j^{\eta}\frac{1}{\sqrt{h}}\Bigg)\|\mathbf{u}-\tilde{\mathbf{u}}\|_\infty \\
\le& \varsigma\|\mathbf{u}-\tilde{\mathbf{u}}\|_\infty,\quad i=1,2,\ldots,m.
\end{aligned}
\tag{10}
$$

The inequalities in Equations (9) and (10) exhibit $\|\Gamma\mathbf{u}-\Gamma\tilde{\mathbf{u}}\|_\infty\le\varsigma\|\mathbf{u}-\tilde{\mathbf{u}}\|_\infty$, $\forall\mathbf{u},\tilde{\mathbf{u}}\in PAP_b^{\theta,\mu}(\mho_\nu\times\mathbb{Z},\mathbb{R}^{2m},\alpha)$. In line with assumption $(\mathbf{g}_1)$, the operator Γ is a contraction mapping. Consequently, Γ possess a unique fixed point $\hat{\mathbf{u}}=(\hat{\mathbf{m}},\hat{\mathbf{p}})^T\in PAP_b^{\theta,\mu}(\mho_\nu\times\mathbb{Z},\mathbb{R}^{2m},\alpha)$, i.e., $\Gamma\hat{\mathbf{u}}=\hat{\mathbf{u}}$. Hence, $\hat{\mathbf{u}}$ is a unique weighted pseudo-almost periodic sequence to GRNs Equation (1). This completes the proof. □

Remark 2. *Articles [12,38] studied the existence of a unique (weighted pseudo) almost periodic solution of continuous-time GRNs without spatial diffusions. However, this paper not only regards the spatial diffusions, but also studies the corollary responding to multi-variable discrete GRNs. So Theorem 2 complements the works of [12,38].*

4. Finite-Time Guaranteed Cost Controls in Exponential Form

In this section, finite-time guaranteed cost controllers for SGRNs Equation (1) are designed based on the drive network, response network, and error network. The global exponential stability of SGRNs Equation (1) in the mean square sense is also discussed.

4.1. The Frame of Controlling GRNs

Let $\hat{\mathbf{u}} = (\hat{\mathbf{m}}, \hat{\mathbf{p}})^T \in PAP_b^{\theta,\mu}(\mho_\nu \times \mathbb{Z}, \mathbb{R}^{2m}, \alpha)$ be the unique weighted pseudo-almost periodic sequence to GRNs Equation (1), where $\hat{\mathbf{m}} = (\hat{\mathbf{m}}_1, \ldots, \hat{\mathbf{m}}_m)^T$ and $\hat{\mathbf{p}} = (\hat{\mathbf{p}}_1, \ldots, \hat{\mathbf{p}}_m)^T$. That is,

$$\begin{cases} \hat{\mathbf{m}}_{i,k+1}^{\langle\nu\rangle} = e^{-a_{i,k}h}\hat{\mathbf{m}}_{i,k}^{\langle\nu\rangle} + \dfrac{1-e^{-a_{i,k}h}}{a_{i,k}}\Bigg[\sum\limits_{q=1}^{n}\Theta_{iq}\tilde{\Delta}_{\hbar_q}^2\hat{\mathbf{m}}_{i,k}^{\langle\nu\rangle} \\ \quad + \sum\limits_{j=1}^{m} b_{ij,k}f_j(\hat{\mathbf{p}}_{j,k-\sigma_{j,k}}^{\langle\nu\rangle}) + \sum\limits_{j=1}^{m}\gamma_{ij,k}g_j(\hat{\mathbf{p}}_{j,k-\mu_{j,k}}^{\langle\nu\rangle})w_{1j,k} + I_{i,k}\Bigg], \\ \hat{\mathbf{p}}_{i,k+1}^{\langle\nu\rangle} = e^{-c_{i,k}h}\hat{\mathbf{p}}_{i,k}^{\langle\nu\rangle} + \dfrac{1-e^{-c_{i,k}h}}{c_{i,k}}\Bigg[\sum\limits_{q=1}^{n}\Pi_{iq}\tilde{\Delta}_{\hbar_q}^2\hat{\mathbf{p}}_{i,k}^{\langle\nu\rangle} \\ \quad + \sum\limits_{j=1}^{m}\varpi_{ij,k}\eta_j(\hat{\mathbf{m}}_{j,k-\nu_{j,k}}^{\langle\nu\rangle})w_{2j,k} + d_{i,k}\hat{\mathbf{m}}_{i,k}^{\langle\nu\rangle}\Bigg], \quad \forall(\nu,k) \in \mho_\nu \times \mathbb{Z}_0, \end{cases} \tag{11}$$

where $i = 1, 2, \ldots, m$. The initial and boundary values of GRNs Equation (11) can be described as

$$\hat{\mathbf{m}}_{i,s}^{\langle\cdot\rangle} = \hat{\varphi}_{i,s}^{\langle\cdot\rangle}, \quad \hat{\mathbf{p}}_{i,s}^{\langle\cdot\rangle} = \hat{\phi}_{i,s}^{\langle\cdot\rangle}, \quad \forall s \in [-\sigma_0, 0]_{\mathbb{Z}}; \quad \hat{\mathbf{m}}_{i,k}^{\langle\nu\rangle}\Big|_{\nu\in\partial\mho_\nu} = 0 = \hat{\mathbf{p}}_{i,k}^{\langle\nu\rangle}\Big|_{\nu\in\partial\mho_\nu}, \quad \forall k \in \mathbb{Z}_0,$$

where $i = 1, 2, \ldots, m$.

A controlling network is constructed as below:

$$\begin{cases} \mathbf{m}_{i,k+1}^{\langle\nu\rangle} = e^{-a_{i,k}h}\mathbf{m}_{i,k}^{\langle\nu\rangle} + \dfrac{1-e^{-a_{i,k}h}}{a_{i,k}}\Bigg[\sum\limits_{q=1}^{n}\Theta_{iq}\tilde{\Delta}_{\hbar_q}^2\mathbf{m}_{i,k}^{\langle\nu\rangle} \\ \quad + \sum\limits_{j=1}^{m} b_{ij,k}f_j(\mathbf{p}_{j,k-\sigma_{j,k}}^{\langle\nu\rangle}) + \sum\limits_{j=1}^{m}\gamma_{ij,k}g_j(\mathbf{p}_{j,k-\mu_{j,k}}^{\langle\nu\rangle})w_{1j,k} + I_{i,k}\Bigg] + \rho_{i,k}^{\langle\nu\rangle}, \\ \mathbf{p}_{i,k+1}^{\langle\nu\rangle} = e^{-c_{i,k}h}\mathbf{p}_{i,k}^{\langle\nu\rangle} + \dfrac{1-e^{-c_{i,k}h}}{c_{i,k}}\Bigg[\sum\limits_{q=1}^{n}\Pi_{iq}\tilde{\Delta}_{\hbar_q}^2\mathbf{p}_{i,k}^{\langle\nu\rangle} \\ \quad + \sum\limits_{j=1}^{m}\varpi_{ij,k}\eta_j(\mathbf{m}_{j,k-\nu_{j,k}}^{\langle\nu\rangle})w_{2j,k} + d_{i,k}\mathbf{m}_{i,k}^{\langle\nu\rangle}\Bigg] + \varrho_{i,k}^{\langle\nu\rangle}, \quad (\nu,k) \in \mho_\nu \times \mathbb{Z}_0, \end{cases} \tag{12}$$

where $i = 1, 2, \ldots, m$. The initial and boundary values of GRNs Equation (12) are given by

$$\mathbf{m}_{i,s}^{\langle\cdot\rangle} = \varphi_{i,s}^{\langle\cdot\rangle}, \quad \mathbf{p}_{i,s}^{\langle\cdot\rangle} = \phi_{i,s}^{\langle\cdot\rangle}, \quad \forall s \in [-\sigma_0, 0]_{\mathbb{Z}}; \quad \mathbf{m}_{i,k}^{\langle\nu\rangle}\Big|_{\nu\in\partial\mho_\nu} = 0 = \mathbf{p}_{i,k}^{\langle\nu\rangle}\Big|_{\nu\in\partial\mho_\nu}, \quad \forall k \in \mathbb{Z}_0,$$

where $i = 1, 2, \ldots, m$.

Let $\mathbf{e}_i = \mathbf{m}_i - \hat{\mathbf{m}}_i$ and $\mathbf{w}_i = \mathbf{p}_i - \hat{\mathbf{p}}_i$, $i = 1, 2, \ldots, m$. Together with GRNs Equations (12) and (11), it yields

$$\begin{cases} \mathbf{e}_{i,k+1}^{\langle v \rangle} &= e^{-a_{i,k}h}\mathbf{e}_{i,k}^{\langle v \rangle} + \dfrac{1-e^{-a_{i,k}h}}{a_{i,k}}\Big[\sum_{q=1}^{n}\Theta_{iq}\tilde{\Delta}_{\hbar_q}^2\mathbf{e}_{i,k}^{\langle v \rangle} \\ &\quad + \sum_{j=1}^{m} b_{ij,k}\tilde{f}_j(\mathbf{w}_{j,k-\sigma_{j,k}}^{\langle v \rangle}) + \sum_{j=1}^{m}\gamma_{ij,k}\tilde{g}_j(\mathbf{w}_{j,k-\mu_{j,k}}^{\langle v \rangle})w_{1j,k}\Big] + \rho_{i,k}^{\langle v \rangle}, \\ \mathbf{w}_{i,k+1}^{\langle v \rangle} &= e^{-c_{i,k}h}\mathbf{w}_{i,k}^{\langle v \rangle} + \dfrac{1-e^{-c_{i,k}h}}{c_{i,k}}\Big[\sum_{q=1}^{n}\Pi_{iq}\tilde{\Delta}_{\hbar_q}^2\mathbf{w}_{i,k}^{\langle v \rangle} \\ &\quad + \sum_{j=1}^{m}\varpi_{ij,k}\tilde{\eta}_j(\mathbf{e}_{j,k-\nu_{j,k}}^{\langle v \rangle})w_{2j,k} + d_{i,k}\mathbf{e}_{i,k}^{\langle v \rangle}\Big] + \varrho_{i,k}^{\langle v \rangle}, \end{cases} \tag{13}$$

where

$$\tilde{f}_j(\mathbf{w}_j) = f_j(\mathbf{p}_j) - f_j(\hat{\mathbf{p}}_j), \quad \tilde{g}_j(\mathbf{w}_j) = g_j(\mathbf{p}_j) - g_j(\hat{\mathbf{p}}_j), \quad \tilde{\eta}_j(\mathbf{e}_j) = g_j(\mathbf{m}_j) - g_j(\hat{\mathbf{m}}_j),$$

in which $(v, k) \in \mho_v \times \mathbb{Z}_0$, $i, j = 1, 2, \ldots, m$.

The state feedback controller is designed:

$$\rho_{i,k}^{\langle \cdot \rangle} = \kappa_i \mathbf{e}_{i,k}^{\langle \cdot \rangle}, \quad \varrho_{i,k}^{\langle \cdot \rangle} = \varkappa_i \mathbf{w}_{i,k}^{\langle \cdot \rangle}, \quad \forall k \in \mathbb{Z}_0, \tag{14}$$

where κ_i and $\varkappa_i$ denote the controller gains to be determined later, $i = 1, 2, \ldots, m$.

Substituting controller Equation (14) into the error network Equation (13) leads to

$$\begin{cases} \mathbf{e}_{i,k+1}^{\langle v \rangle} &= (e^{-a_{i,k}h} + \kappa_i)\mathbf{e}_{i,k}^{\langle v \rangle} + \dfrac{1-e^{-a_{i,k}h}}{a_{i,k}}\Big[\sum_{q=1}^{n}\Theta_{iq}\tilde{\Delta}_{\hbar_q}^2\mathbf{e}_{i,k}^{\langle v \rangle} \\ &\quad + \sum_{j=1}^{m} b_{ij,k}\tilde{f}_j(\mathbf{w}_{j,k-\sigma_{j,k}}^{\langle v \rangle}) + \sum_{j=1}^{m}\gamma_{ij,k}\tilde{g}_j(\mathbf{w}_{j,k-\mu_{j,k}}^{\langle v \rangle})w_{1j,k}\Big], \\ \mathbf{w}_{i,k+1}^{\langle v \rangle} &= (e^{-c_{i,k}h} + \varkappa_i)\mathbf{w}_{i,k}^{\langle v \rangle} + \dfrac{1-e^{-c_{i,k}h}}{c_{i,k}}\Big[\sum_{q=1}^{n}\Pi_{iq}\tilde{\Delta}_{\hbar_q}^2\mathbf{w}_{i,k}^{\langle v \rangle} \\ &\quad + \sum_{j=1}^{m}\varpi_{ij,k}\tilde{\eta}_j(\mathbf{e}_{j,k-\nu_{j,k}}^{\langle v \rangle})w_{2j,k} + d_{i,k}\mathbf{e}_{i,k}^{\langle v \rangle}\Big], \quad (v,k) \in \mho_v \times \mathbb{Z}_0, \end{cases} \tag{15}$$

where $i = 1, 2, \ldots, m$.

Similar to the derivation of Formula (4), we achieve

$$\begin{cases} \mathbf{e}_{i,k}^{\langle v \rangle} &= \prod_{s=0}^{k-1}(e^{-a_{i,s}h} + \kappa_i)\mathbf{e}_{i,0}^{\langle v \rangle} + \sum_{v=0}^{k-1}\prod_{s=v+1}^{k-1}\dfrac{(e^{-a_{i,s}h} + \kappa_i)(1-e^{-a_{i,v}h})}{a_{i,v}} \\ &\quad \times\Big[\sum_{q=1}^{n}\Theta_{iq}\tilde{\Delta}_{\hbar_q}^2\mathbf{e}_{i,v}^{\langle v \rangle} + \sum_{j=1}^{m} b_{ij,v}\tilde{f}_j(\mathbf{w}_{j,v-\sigma_{j,v}}^{\langle v \rangle}) + \sum_{j=1}^{m}\gamma_{ij,v}\tilde{g}_j(\mathbf{w}_{j,v-\mu_{j,v}}^{\langle v \rangle})w_{1j,v}\Big], \\ \mathbf{w}_{i,k}^{\langle v \rangle} &= \prod_{s=0}^{k-1}(e^{-c_{i,s}h} + \varkappa_i)\mathbf{w}_{i,0}^{\langle v \rangle} + \sum_{v=0}^{k-1}\prod_{s=v+1}^{k-1}\dfrac{(e^{-c_{i,s}h} + \varkappa_i)(1-e^{-c_{i,v}h})}{c_{i,v}} \\ &\quad \times\Big[\sum_{q=1}^{n}\Pi_{iq}\tilde{\Delta}_{\hbar_q}^2\mathbf{w}_{i,v}^{\langle v \rangle} + d_{i,v}\mathbf{e}_{i,v}^{\langle v \rangle} + \sum_{j=1}^{m}\varpi_{ij,v}\tilde{\eta}_j(\mathbf{e}_{j,v-\nu_{j,v}}^{\langle v \rangle})w_{2j,v}\Big], \quad (v,k) \in \mho_v \times \mathbb{Z}_0, \end{cases} \tag{16}$$

where $i = 1, 2, \ldots, m$. Moreover, it holds that

$$\mathbf{e}_{i,s}^{\langle \cdot \rangle} = \varphi_{i,s}^{\langle \cdot \rangle} - \hat{\varphi}_{i,s}^{\langle \cdot \rangle}, \quad \mathbf{w}_{i,s}^{\langle \cdot \rangle} = \phi_{i,s}^{\langle \cdot \rangle} - \hat{\phi}_{i,s}^{\langle \cdot \rangle}, \quad \forall s \in [-\sigma_0, 0]_{\mathbb{Z}}; \quad \mathbf{e}_{i,k}^{\langle v \rangle}\Big|_{v \in \partial\mho_v} = 0 = \mathbf{w}_{i,k}^{\langle v \rangle}\Big|_{v \in \partial\mho_v}, \quad \forall k \in \mathbb{Z}_0,$$

where $i = 1, 2, \ldots, m$.

Definition 6. *State feedback controller Equation (14) finite-time stabilises GRNs Equation (12) with a finite-time exponential convergent form in case the error networks Equation (15) achieves finite-time exponential stability, i.e., for any* $\epsilon \in (0,1)$ *there exists* $\delta > 0$, $\mu > 0$ *and integer* $K > 0$, *ensuring that*

$$\varphi_0 := \max_{1 \le i \le m} \max_{(\nu,s) \in \mho_\nu \times [-\sigma_0, 0]_{\mathbb{Z}}} \left\{ \left\| \mathbf{e}_{i,s}^{\langle \nu \rangle} \right\|_2, \left\| \mathbf{w}_{i,s}^{\langle \nu \rangle} \right\|_2 \right\} < \delta$$

implies that

$$\max_{1 \le i \le m} \max_{\nu \in \mho_\nu} \left\{ \left\| \mathbf{e}_{i,k}^{\langle \nu \rangle} \right\|_2, \left\| \mathbf{w}_{i,k}^{\langle \nu \rangle} \right\|_2 \right\} \le \epsilon e^{-\mu k h}, \quad \forall k \in [0, K]_{\mathbb{Z}}. \tag{17}$$

Herein, K is called the settling time.

Define a performance index J_c^K associated with the error networks Equation (15) by

$$J_c^K = \mathbf{E} \sum_{k=0}^{K} \max_{\nu \in \mho_\nu} \mathbf{U}_k^{\langle \nu \rangle T} F \mathbf{U}_k^{\langle \nu \rangle},$$

where

$$\mathbf{U} = \mathrm{col}(\mathbf{e}, \rho, \mathbf{w}, \varrho), \quad F = \mathrm{diag}(P_1, Q_1, P_2, Q_2),$$
$$\mathbf{e} = \mathrm{col}(\mathbf{e}_1, \ldots, \mathbf{e}_m), \quad \mathbf{w} = \mathrm{col}(\mathbf{w}_1, \ldots, \mathbf{w}_m),$$
$$\rho = \mathrm{col}(\rho_1, \ldots, \rho_m), \quad \varrho = \mathrm{col}(\varrho_1, \ldots, \varrho_m),$$

$P_\imath = P_\imath^T > 0, Q_\imath = Q_\imath^T > 0, \imath = 1, 2.$

Definition 7. *State feedback controller Equation (14) is said to be a finite-time guaranteed cost controller to GRNs Equation (12) in case it finite-time stabilises GRNs Equation (12) with an exponential convergent form and meets*

$$J_c^K \le \lambda,$$

where $\lambda > 0$ *is a constant.*

4.2. Design of Finite-Time Guaranteed Cost Controllers

From the first equation of the error networks Equation (16), we obtain

$$\begin{aligned} \left\| \mathbf{e}_{i,k}^{\langle \nu \rangle} \right\|_2 = \left[\mathbf{E} | \mathbf{e}_{i,k}^{\langle \nu \rangle} |^2 \right]^{\frac{1}{2}} \le\ & (e^{-\underline{a}_i h} + \kappa_i)^k \| \mathbf{e}_{i,0}^{\langle \nu \rangle} \|_2 + \sum_{v=0}^{k-1} (e^{-\underline{a}_i h} + \kappa_i)^{k-v-1} \tfrac{(1 - e^{-\underline{a}_i h})}{\underline{a}_i} \\ & \times \left[\sum_{q=1}^{n} |\Theta_{iq}| \| \tilde{\Delta}_{\hbar_q}^2 \mathbf{e}_{i,v}^{\langle \nu \rangle} \|_2 + \sum_{j=1}^{m} \bar{b}_{ij} L_j^f \| \mathbf{w}_{j,v-\sigma_{j,v}}^{\langle \nu \rangle} \|_2 + \sum_{j=1}^{m} \bar{\gamma}_{ij} L_j^g \| \mathbf{w}_{j,v-\mu_{j,v}}^{\langle \nu \rangle} \|_2 h^{-\frac{1}{2}} \right], \end{aligned} \tag{18}$$

where $\nu \in \mho_\nu, i = 1, 2, \ldots, m$. Similarly,

$$\begin{aligned} \left\| \mathbf{w}_{i,k}^{\langle \nu \rangle} \right\|_2 = \left[\mathbf{E} | \mathbf{w}_{i,k}^{\langle \nu \rangle} |^2 \right]^{\frac{1}{2}} \le\ & (e^{-\underline{c}_i h} + \varkappa_i)^k \| \mathbf{w}_{i,0}^{\langle \nu \rangle} \|_2 + \sum_{v=0}^{k-1} (e^{-\underline{c}_i h} + \varkappa_i)^{k-v-1} \tfrac{(1 - e^{-\underline{c}_i h})}{\underline{c}_i} \\ & \times \left[\sum_{q=1}^{n} |\Pi_{iq}| \| \tilde{\Delta}_{\hbar_q}^2 \mathbf{w}_{i,v}^{\langle \nu \rangle} \|_2 + \bar{d}_i \| \mathbf{e}_{i,v}^{\langle \nu \rangle} \|_2 + \sum_{j=1}^{m} \bar{\varpi}_{ij} L_j^\eta \| \mathbf{e}_{j,v-\nu_{j,v}}^{\langle \nu \rangle} \|_2 h^{-\frac{1}{2}} \right], \end{aligned} \tag{19}$$

where $\nu \in \mho_\nu, i = 1, 2, \ldots, m$.

Equations (18) and (19) are equal to

$$\max_{\nu\in\mho_\nu}\left\|\mathbf{e}_{i,k}^{\langle\nu\rangle}\right\|_2 \leq (e^{-\underline{a}_i h}+\kappa_i)^k \max_{\nu\in\mho_\nu}\|\mathbf{e}_{i,0}^{\langle\nu\rangle}\|_2+\sum_{v=0}^{k-1}(e^{-\underline{a}_i h}+\kappa_i)^{k-v-1}\frac{(1-e^{-\underline{a}_i h})}{\underline{a}_i} \times\left[\sum_{q=1}^{n}|\Theta_{iq}|\max_{\nu\in\mho_\nu}\|\tilde{\Delta}_{\hbar_q}^2\mathbf{e}_{i,v}^{\langle\nu\rangle}\|_2+\sum_{j=1}^{m}\bar{b}_{ij}L_j^f\max_{\nu\in\mho_\nu}\|\mathbf{w}_{j,v-\sigma_{j,v}}^{\langle\nu\rangle}\|_2 + \sum_{j=1}^{m}\bar{\gamma}_{ij}L_j^g\max_{\nu\in\mho_\nu}\|\mathbf{w}_{j,v-\mu_{j,v}}^{\langle\nu\rangle}\|_2 h^{-\frac{1}{2}}\right], \tag{20}$$

and

$$\max_{\nu\in\mho_\nu}\left\|\mathbf{w}_{i,k}^{\langle\nu\rangle}\right\|_2 \leq (e^{-\underline{c}_i h}+\varkappa_i)^k \max_{\nu\in\mho_\nu}\|\mathbf{w}_{i,0}^{\langle\nu\rangle}\|_2+\sum_{v=0}^{k-1}(e^{-\underline{c}_i h}+\varkappa_i)^{k-v-1}\frac{(1-e^{-\underline{c}_i h})}{\underline{c}_i} \times\left[\sum_{q=1}^{n}|\Pi_{iq}|\max_{\nu\in\mho_\nu}\|\tilde{\Delta}_{\hbar_q}^2\mathbf{w}_{i,v}^{\langle\nu\rangle}\|_2+\bar{d}_i\max_{\nu\in\mho_\nu}\|\mathbf{e}_{i,v}^{\langle\nu\rangle}\|_2 + \sum_{j=1}^{m}\bar{\varpi}_{ij}L_j^\eta\max_{\nu\in\mho_\nu}\|\mathbf{e}_{j,v-\nu_{j,v}}^{\langle\nu\rangle}\|_2 h^{-\frac{1}{2}}\right], \quad i=1,2,\ldots,m. \tag{21}$$

Theorem 3. *If* $(\mathbf{g}_2)$ *and the following assumptions are fulfilled,*

$(\mathbf{g}_5)$ *The control gains* $\kappa_i = e^{-\hat{a}_i h} - e^{-\underline{a}_i h}$ *and* $\varkappa_i = e^{-\hat{c}_i h} - e^{-\underline{c}_i h}$, *where* $\hat{a}_i$ *and* $\hat{c}_i$ *are positive constants,* $i = 1,2,\ldots,m$.

$(\mathbf{g}_6)$ *It holds that* $1 - e^{-\underline{\alpha} h} < \max\{v_1, v_2\} < \dfrac{1-e^{-\underline{\alpha} h}}{1-e^{-\bar{\alpha} h}}$, *where* $\underline{\alpha} = \min_{1\leq i\leq m}\{\hat{a}_i, \hat{c}_i\}$ *and* $\bar{\alpha} = \max_{1\leq i\leq m}\{\hat{a}_i, \hat{c}_i\}$,

$$v_1 = \max_{1\leq i\leq m}\frac{(1-e^{-\underline{a}_i h})}{\underline{a}_i}\left[\sum_{q=1}^{n}\frac{2|\Theta_{iq}|}{\hbar^2}+\sum_{j=1}^{m}\bar{b}_{ij}L_j^f+\sum_{j=1}^{m}\bar{\gamma}_{ij}L_j^g h^{-\frac{1}{2}}\right],$$

$$v_2 = \max_{1\leq i\leq m}\frac{(1-e^{-\underline{c}_i h})}{\underline{c}_i}\left[\sum_{q=1}^{n}\frac{2|\Pi_{iq}|}{\hbar^2}+\bar{d}_i+\sum_{j=1}^{m}\bar{\varpi}_{ij}L_j^\eta h^{-\frac{1}{2}}\right].$$

then state feedback controller Equation (14) is a finite-time guaranteed cost controller for GRNs Equation (12) with the settling time K satisfying

$$K < -\frac{1}{\bar{\alpha}h}\ln\left(1-\frac{1-e^{-\underline{\alpha}h}}{\max\{v_1,v_2\}}\right).$$

Proof. In accordance with $(\mathbf{g}_6)$, for any $\epsilon > 0$, we can select $\delta > 0$ and $0 < \mu < \underline{\alpha}$ to be small enough, causing

$$\frac{\delta}{\epsilon}+\max_{1\leq i\leq m}\frac{1-e^{-(\hat{a}_i-\mu)Kh}}{1-e^{-(\hat{a}_i-\mu)h}}\frac{(1-e^{-\underline{a}_i h})e^{\mu(\sigma_0+1)h}}{\underline{a}_i}\left[\sum_{q=1}^{n}\frac{2|\Theta_{iq}|}{\hbar^2}+\sum_{j=1}^{m}\bar{b}_{ij}L_j^f+\sum_{j=1}^{m}\bar{\gamma}_{ij}L_j^g h^{-\frac{1}{2}}\right] < 1,$$

$$\frac{\delta}{\epsilon}+\max_{1\leq i\leq m}\frac{1-e^{-(\hat{c}_{i_1}-\mu)Kh}}{1-e^{-(\hat{c}_{i_1}-\mu)h}}\frac{(1-e^{-\underline{c}_i h})e^{\mu(\sigma_0+1)h}}{\underline{c}_i}\left[\sum_{q=1}^{n}\frac{2|\Pi_{iq}|}{\hbar^2}+\bar{d}_i+\sum_{j=1}^{m}\bar{\varpi}_{ij}L_j^\eta h^{-\frac{1}{2}}\right] < 1.$$

A method of reduction to absurdity will be adapted here, supposing that Equation (17) holds. If not, then one of the following two cases must be valid.

(*a*) There exist $k_0 \in (0, T]_{\mathbb{Z}}$ and $i_0 \in \{1,2,\ldots,m\}$ such that

$$\max_{1\leq i\leq m}\max_{\nu\in\mho_\nu}\left\{\left\|\mathbf{e}_{i,k}^{\langle\nu\rangle}\right\|_2,\left\|\mathbf{w}_{i,k}^{\langle\nu\rangle}\right\|_2\right\}\leq\epsilon e^{-\mu kh},\quad\forall k\in[0,k_0)_{\mathbb{Z}};\quad\max_{\nu\in\mho_\nu}\left\|\mathbf{e}_{i_0,k_0}^{\langle\nu\rangle}\right\|_2>\epsilon e^{-\mu k_0 h}.$$

(*b*) There exist $k_1 \in (0,T]_{\mathbb{Z}}$ and $i_1 \in \{1,2,\ldots,m\}$ ensuring

$$\max_{1\leq i\leq m}\max_{\nu\in\mho_\nu}\left\{\left\|\mathbf{e}_{i,k}^{\langle\nu\rangle}\right\|_2,\left\|\mathbf{w}_{i,k}^{\langle\nu\rangle}\right\|_2\right\}\leq\epsilon e^{-\mu kh},\quad\forall k\in[0,k_1)_{\mathbb{Z}};\quad\max_{\nu\in\mho_\nu}\left\|\mathbf{w}_{i_1,k_1}^{\langle\nu\rangle}\right\|_2>\epsilon e^{-\mu k_1 h}.$$

If (a) holds, from Equation (20) and $(\mathbf{g}_5)$ we obtain

$$\begin{aligned}
\max_{\nu\in\mho_\nu}\left\|\mathbf{e}_{i_0,k_0}^{\langle\nu\rangle}\right\|_2 \leq\ & (e^{-\underline{a}_{i_0}h}+\kappa_{i_0})^{k_0}\delta+\sum_{v=0}^{k_0-1}(e^{-\underline{a}_{i_0}h}+\kappa_{i_0})^{k_0-v-1}\frac{(1-e^{-\underline{a}_{i_0}h})}{\underline{a}_{i_0}}\\
&\times\left[\sum_{q=1}^{n}\frac{2|\Theta_{i_0q}|}{\hbar^2}+\sum_{j=1}^{m}\bar{b}_{i_0j}L_j^f+\sum_{j=1}^{m}\bar{\gamma}_{i_0j}L_j^g h^{-\frac{1}{2}}\right]e^{\mu\sigma_0 h}\epsilon e^{-\mu v h}\\
\leq\ & e^{-\hat{a}_{i_0}k_0h}\delta+\sum_{v=0}^{k_0-1}e^{-\hat{a}_{i_0}h(k_0-v-1)}\frac{(1-e^{-\underline{a}_{i_0}h})}{\underline{a}_{i_0}}\\
&\times\left[\sum_{q=1}^{n}\frac{2|\Theta_{i_0q}|}{\hbar^2}+\sum_{j=1}^{m}\bar{b}_{i_0j}L_j^f+\sum_{j=1}^{m}\bar{\gamma}_{i_0j}L_j^g h^{-\frac{1}{2}}\right]e^{\mu\sigma_0 h}\epsilon e^{-\mu v h}\\
=\ & e^{-\hat{a}_{i_0}k_0h}\delta+\sum_{v=0}^{k_0-1}e^{-(\hat{a}_{i_0}-\mu)h(k_0-v-1)}\frac{(1-e^{-\underline{a}_{i_0}h})}{\underline{a}_{i_0}}e^{\mu(\sigma_0+1)h}\\
&\times\left[\sum_{q=1}^{n}\frac{2|\Theta_{i_0q}|}{\hbar^2}+\sum_{j=1}^{m}\bar{b}_{i_0j}L_j^f+\sum_{j=1}^{m}\bar{\gamma}_{i_0j}L_j^g h^{-\frac{1}{2}}\right]\epsilon e^{-\mu k_0 h}\\
\leq\ & \left(\frac{\delta}{\epsilon}e^{-(\hat{a}_{i_0}-\mu)k_0h}+\frac{1-e^{-(\hat{a}_{i_0}-\mu)k_0h}}{1-e^{-(\hat{a}_{i_0}-\mu)h}}\frac{(1-e^{-\underline{a}_{i_0}h})e^{\mu(\sigma_0+1)h}}{\underline{a}_{i_0}}\right.\\
&\left.\times\left[\sum_{q=1}^{n}\frac{2|\Theta_{i_0q}|}{\hbar^2}+\sum_{j=1}^{m}\bar{b}_{i_0j}L_j^f+\sum_{j=1}^{m}\bar{\gamma}_{i_0j}L_j^g h^{-\frac{1}{2}}\right]\right)\epsilon e^{-\mu k_0 h}\\
\leq\ & \left\{\frac{\delta}{\epsilon}+\frac{1-e^{-(\hat{a}_{i_0}-\mu)Kh}}{1-e^{-(\hat{a}_{i_0}-\mu)h}}\frac{(1-e^{-\underline{a}_{i_0}h})e^{\mu(\sigma_0+1)h}}{\underline{a}_{i_0}}\right.\\
&\left.\times\left[\sum_{q=1}^{n}\frac{2|\Theta_{i_0q}|}{\hbar^2}+\sum_{j=1}^{m}\bar{b}_{i_0j}L_j^f+\sum_{j=1}^{m}\bar{\gamma}_{i_0j}L_j^g h^{-\frac{1}{2}}\right]\right\}\epsilon e^{-\mu k_0 h}\\
\leq\ & \epsilon e^{-\mu k_0 h},
\end{aligned}$$

which contradicts fact (a).

On the other hand, if (b) holds, from Equation (21), we can likewise compute

$$\begin{aligned}
\max_{\nu\in\mho_\nu}\left\|\mathbf{w}_{i_1,k_1}^{\langle\nu\rangle}\right\|_2 \leq\ & (e^{-\underline{c}_{i_1}h}+\varkappa_{i_1})^{k_1}\delta+\sum_{v=0}^{k_1-1}(e^{-\underline{c}_{i_1}h}+\varkappa_{i_1})^{k_1-v-1}\frac{(1-e^{-\underline{c}_{i_1}h})}{\underline{c}_{i_1}}\\
&\times\left[\sum_{q=1}^{n}\frac{2|\Pi_{i_1q}|}{\hbar^2}+\bar{d}_{i_1}+\sum_{j=1}^{m}\bar{\varpi}_{i_1j}L_j^\eta h^{-\frac{1}{2}}\right]e^{\mu\sigma_0 h}\epsilon e^{-\mu v h}\\
\leq\ & e^{-\hat{c}_{i_1}k_1h}\delta+\sum_{v=0}^{k_1-1}e^{-\hat{c}_{i_1}h(k_1-v-1)}\frac{(1-e^{-\underline{c}_{i_1}h})}{\underline{c}_{i_1}}\\
&\times\left[\sum_{q=1}^{n}\frac{2|\Pi_{i_1q}|}{\hbar^2}+\bar{d}_{i_1}+\sum_{j=1}^{m}\bar{\varpi}_{i_1j}L_j^\eta h^{-\frac{1}{2}}\right]e^{\mu\sigma_0 h}\epsilon e^{-\mu v h}\\
=\ & e^{-\hat{c}_{i_1}k_1h}\delta+\sum_{v=0}^{k_1-1}e^{-(\hat{c}_{i_1}-\mu)h(k_1-v-1)}\frac{(1-e^{-\underline{c}_{i_1}h})}{\underline{c}_{i_1}}e^{\mu(\sigma_0+1)h}\\
&\times\left[\sum_{q=1}^{n}\frac{2|\Pi_{i_1q}|}{\hbar^2}+\bar{d}_{i_1}+\sum_{j=1}^{m}\bar{\varpi}_{i_1j}L_j^\eta h^{-\frac{1}{2}}\right]\epsilon e^{-\mu k_1 h}\\
\leq\ & \left(\frac{\delta}{\epsilon}e^{-(\hat{c}_{i_1}-\mu)k_1h}+\frac{1-e^{-(\hat{c}_{i_1}-\mu)k_1h}}{1-e^{-(\hat{c}_{i_1}-\mu)h}}\frac{(1-e^{-\underline{c}_{i_1}h})e^{\mu(\sigma_0+1)h}}{\underline{c}_{i_1}}\right.\\
&\left.\times\left[\sum_{q=1}^{n}\frac{2|\Pi_{i_1q}|}{\hbar^2}+\bar{d}_{i_1}+\sum_{j=1}^{m}\bar{\varpi}_{i_1j}L_j^\eta h^{-\frac{1}{2}}\right]\right)\epsilon e^{-\mu k_1 h}\\
\leq\ & \left\{\frac{\delta}{\epsilon}+\frac{1-e^{-(\hat{c}_{i_1}-\mu)Kh}}{1-e^{-(\hat{c}_{i_1}-\mu)h}}\frac{(1-e^{-\underline{c}_{i_1}h})e^{\mu(\sigma_0+1)h}}{\underline{c}_{i_1}}\right.\\
&\left.\times\left[\sum_{q=1}^{n}\frac{2|\Pi_{i_1q}|}{\hbar^2}+\bar{d}_{i_1}+\sum_{j=1}^{m}\bar{\varpi}_{i_1j}L_j^\eta h^{-\frac{1}{2}}\right]\right\}\epsilon e^{-\mu k_1 h}\\
\leq\ & \epsilon e^{-\mu k_1 h},
\end{aligned}$$

which contradicts fact (b). As a consequence, state feedback controller Equation (14) with the control gains in $(\mathbf{g}_5)$ stabilises GRNs Equation (12) in finite time.

In light of Definition 7, the finite-time guaranteed cost control will be displayed as follows. It holds that

$$\begin{aligned} \mathbf{U}^T\mathbf{U} &= \begin{pmatrix} \mathbf{e}\, \rho\, \mathbf{w}\, \varrho \end{pmatrix} \begin{pmatrix} \mathbf{e} \\ \rho \\ \mathbf{w} \\ \varrho \end{pmatrix} \\ &= \sum_{i=1}^{m} (\mathbf{e}_i^2 + \rho_i^2 + \mathbf{w}_i^2 + \varrho_i^2) \\ &= \sum_{i=1}^{m} [(1+\kappa_i^2)\mathbf{e}_i^2 + (1+\varkappa_i^2)\mathbf{w}_i^2] \\ &\le \sum_{i=1}^{m} (2+\kappa_i^2+\varkappa_i^2)\max\{\mathbf{e}_i^2, \mathbf{w}_i^2\}, \end{aligned}$$

which induces

$$J_c^K = \mathbf{E}\sum_{k=0}^{K} \max_{\nu\in\mho_\nu} \mathbf{U}_k^{\langle\nu\rangle T}\mathbf{U}_k^{\langle\nu\rangle} \le \vartheta \sum_{k=0}^{K} \max_{1\le i\le m}\max_{\nu\in\mho_\nu}\Big\{\left\|\mathbf{e}_{i,k}^{\langle\nu\rangle}\right\|_2, \left\|\mathbf{w}_{i,k}^{\langle\nu\rangle}\right\|_2\Big\} \le \vartheta\sum_{k=0}^{K}\epsilon e^{-\mu k h} \le \lambda,$$

where $\vartheta = \sum_{i=1}^{m}\left(2+\kappa_i^2+\varkappa_i^2\right)$ and $\lambda = \dfrac{\vartheta}{1-e^{-\mu h}}$. Therefore, state feedback controller Equation (14) is a finite-time guaranteed cost controller for GRNs Equation (12). This completes the proof. □

If $\kappa_i = 0 = \varkappa_i$ in feedback controller Equation (14), then $\rho_{i,k}^{\langle\nu\rangle}$ and $\varrho_{i,k}^{\langle\nu\rangle}$ are vanished from GRNs Equation (12), $\forall(\nu,k)\in\mho_\nu\times\mathbb{N}_0$ and $i=1,2,\ldots,m$. Based upon the proof of Theorem 3, we can easily obtain

Corollary 2. *Let assumptions $(\mathbf{g}_2)$–$(\mathbf{g}_4)$ hold. Then, GRNs Equation (1) is finite-time exponentially stable in a mean-square sense. Further, if $(\mathbf{g}_1)$ holds, then GRNs Equation (1) admits a unique weighted pseudo almost periodic sequence solution, which is finite-time exponentially stable in a mean-square sense.*

5. Example

This section gives an experimental example to verify the feasibility of the main results for discrete-space and -time stochastic GRNs, which have been addressed in the previous sections of this article.

Considering the following discrete-time stochastic GRNs with discrete spatial diffusions

$$\begin{cases} \begin{pmatrix} \mathbf{m}_{1,k+1}^{\langle\nu\rangle} \\ \mathbf{m}_{2,k+1}^{\langle\nu\rangle} \end{pmatrix} = \begin{pmatrix} e^{-9h} & 0 \\ 0 & e^{-10h} \end{pmatrix}\begin{pmatrix} \mathbf{m}_{1,k}^{\langle\nu\rangle} \\ \mathbf{m}_{2,k}^{\langle\nu\rangle} \end{pmatrix} + \begin{pmatrix} \frac{1-e^{-9h}}{9} & 0 \\ 0 & \frac{1-e^{-10h}}{10} \end{pmatrix}\Bigg[\begin{pmatrix} 0.2 & 0 \\ 0 & 0.2 \end{pmatrix}\tilde{\Delta}_{\hbar}^2\begin{pmatrix} \mathbf{m}_{1,k}^{\langle\nu\rangle} \\ \mathbf{m}_{2,k}^{\langle\nu\rangle} \end{pmatrix} \\ \quad + \begin{pmatrix} 1.2\cos(k\pi+\frac{\pi}{4})+e^{-|k|} & 0.5 \\ 0.3 & 1.8\sin(k\pi+\frac{\pi}{4})+e^{-|k|} \end{pmatrix}\begin{pmatrix} f_1(\mathbf{p}_{1,k-2}^{\langle\nu\rangle}) \\ f_2(\mathbf{p}_{2,k-1}^{\langle\nu\rangle}) \end{pmatrix} \\ \quad + \begin{pmatrix} 0.2 & 0.1 \\ 0 & 0.15 \end{pmatrix}\begin{pmatrix} g_1(\mathbf{p}_{1,k-1}^{\langle\nu\rangle})w_{11,k} \\ g_2(\mathbf{p}_{2,k-1}^{\langle\nu\rangle})w_{12,k} \end{pmatrix} + \begin{pmatrix} 1+0.2\cos(k\pi+\frac{\pi}{4}) \\ 0.5+0.5\sin(k\pi+\frac{\pi}{4}) \end{pmatrix}\Bigg], \\ \begin{pmatrix} \mathbf{p}_{1,k+1}^{\langle\nu\rangle} \\ \mathbf{p}_{2,k+1}^{\langle\nu\rangle} \end{pmatrix} = \begin{pmatrix} e^{-12h} & 0 \\ 0 & e^{-15h} \end{pmatrix}\begin{pmatrix} \mathbf{p}_{1,k}^{\langle\nu\rangle} \\ \mathbf{p}_{2,k}^{\langle\nu\rangle} \end{pmatrix} + \begin{pmatrix} \frac{1-e^{-12h}}{12} & 0 \\ 0 & \frac{1-e^{-15h}}{15} \end{pmatrix}\Bigg[\begin{pmatrix} 0.1 & 0 \\ 0 & 0.1 \end{pmatrix}\tilde{\Delta}_{\hbar}^2\begin{pmatrix} \mathbf{p}_{1,k}^{\langle\nu\rangle} \\ \mathbf{p}_{2,k}^{\langle\nu\rangle} \end{pmatrix} \\ \quad + 0.1\begin{pmatrix} |\mathbf{m}_{1,k}^{\langle\nu\rangle}| \\ |\mathbf{m}_{2,k}^{\langle\nu\rangle}| \end{pmatrix} + \begin{pmatrix} \cos(k\pi+\frac{\pi}{3})+e^{-|k|} & 0.1 \\ 0 & \sin(k\pi+\frac{\pi}{5})+e^{-|k|} \end{pmatrix}\begin{pmatrix} \eta_1(\mathbf{m}_{1,k-1}^{\langle\nu\rangle})w_{21,k} \\ \eta_2(\mathbf{m}_{2,k-2}^{\langle\nu\rangle})w_{22,k} \end{pmatrix}\Bigg], \end{cases} \tag{22}$$

where $(\nu,k)\in(0,10)\times\mathbb{Z}_0$,

$$\mathbf{m}_{i,k}^{\langle\nu\rangle}\Big|_{\nu=0}=\mathbf{m}_{i,k}^{\langle\nu\rangle}\Big|_{\nu=10}=0,\quad \mathbf{p}_{i,k}^{\langle\nu\rangle}\Big|_{\nu=0}=\mathbf{p}_{i,k}^{\langle\nu\rangle}\Big|_{\nu=10}=0,\quad \forall k\in\mathbb{Z}_0, i=1,2.$$

Taking $h=0.1$ and $\hbar=0.5$. Corresponding to GRNs Equation (1),

$$a_{1,k}=9,\quad a_{2,k}=10,\quad c_{1,k}=12,\quad c_{2,k}=15,\quad \Theta_{11}=\Theta_{22}=0.2,\quad \Pi_{11}=\Pi_{22}=0.1,$$

$$\Theta_{12}=\Theta_{21}=\Pi_{12}=\Pi_{21}=0,\quad b_{11,k}=1.2\cos(k\pi+\frac{\pi}{4})+e^{-|k|},\quad b_{12,k}=0.5,\quad b_{21,k}=0.3,$$

$$b_{22,k}=1.8\sin(k\pi+\frac{\pi}{4})+e^{-|k|},\quad \sigma_{1,k}=2,\quad \sigma_{2,k}=1,\quad \gamma_{11,k}=0.2,\quad \gamma_{12,k}=0.1,\quad \gamma_{21,k}=0,$$

$$\gamma_{22,k}=0.15,\quad I_{1,k}=1+0.2\cos(k\pi+\frac{\pi}{4}),\quad I_{2,k}=0.5+0.5\sin(k\pi+\frac{\pi}{4}),\quad d_{1,k}=d_{2,k}=0.1,$$

$$\varpi_{11,k}=\cos(k\pi+\frac{\pi}{3})+e^{-|k|},\quad \varpi_{12,k}=0.1,\quad \varpi_{21,k}=0,\quad \varpi_{22,k}=\sin(k\pi+\frac{\pi}{5})+e^{-|k|},$$

$$f_1(\mathbf{p}_{1,k-2}^{\langle\nu\rangle})=\frac{\left(\frac{\mathbf{p}_{1,k-2}^{\langle\nu\rangle}}{15}\right)^2}{1+\left(\frac{\mathbf{p}_{1,k-2}^{\langle\nu\rangle}}{15}\right)^2},\quad f_2(\mathbf{p}_{2,k-1}^{\langle\nu\rangle})=\frac{\left(\frac{\mathbf{p}_{2,k-1}^{\langle\nu\rangle}}{15}\right)^2}{1+\left(\frac{\mathbf{p}_{2,k-1}^{\langle\nu\rangle}}{15}\right)^2},\quad g_i(\mathbf{p}_{i,k-1}^{\langle\nu\rangle})=\frac{\left(\frac{\mathbf{p}_{i,k-1}^{\langle\nu\rangle}}{20}\right)^2}{1+\left(\frac{\mathbf{p}_{i,k-1}^{\langle\nu\rangle}}{20}\right)^2},$$

$$\eta_1(\mathbf{m}_{1,k-1}^{\langle\nu\rangle})=\frac{\left(\frac{\mathbf{m}_{1,k-1}^{\langle\nu\rangle}}{10}\right)^2}{1+\left(\frac{\mathbf{m}_{1,k-1}^{\langle\nu\rangle}}{10}\right)^2},\quad \eta_2(\mathbf{m}_{2,k-2}^{\langle\nu\rangle})=\frac{\left(\frac{\mathbf{m}_{2,k-2}^{\langle\nu\rangle}}{10}\right)^2}{1+\left(\frac{\mathbf{m}_{2,k-2}^{\langle\nu\rangle}}{10}\right)^2},\qquad i=1,2,\forall(\nu,k)\in(0,10)\times\mathbb{Z}_0.$$

Obviously, $L_1^f=L_2^f=\frac{1}{15}$, $L_1^g=L_2^g=0.05$, $L_1^\eta=L_2^\eta=0.1$. It follows from the direct calculation that $\max\{\varsigma_1,\varsigma_2\}<1$. Therefore, assumptions $(\mathbf{g}_1)$–$(\mathbf{g}_4)$ in Theorem 2 are valid, i.e., GRNs Equation (22) possesses a unique weighted pseudo- or α-pseudo-almost periodic sequence solution, see Figures 1 and 2. Let $\hat{a}_1=1.25$, $\hat{a}_2=12$, $\hat{c}_1=14$, and $\hat{c}_2=7$. Then, the state feedback controllers corresponding to Equation (14) are listed as follows:

$$\rho_{1,k}^{\langle\cdot\rangle}=0.4983\mathbf{e}_{1,k}^{\langle\cdot\rangle},\quad \rho_{2,k}^{\langle\cdot\rangle}=-0.0667\mathbf{e}_{2,k}^{\langle\cdot\rangle},\quad \varrho_{1,k}^{\langle\cdot\rangle}=-0.0546\mathbf{w}_{1,k}^{\langle\cdot\rangle},\quad \varrho_{2,k}^{\langle\cdot\rangle}=0.2735\mathbf{w}_{2,k}^{\langle\cdot\rangle},\qquad (23)$$

where $k\in\mathbb{Z}_0$. Moreover, assumptions $(\mathbf{g}_2)$ and $(\mathbf{g}_5)$–$(\mathbf{g}_6)$ in Theorem 3 hold. Then, the state feedback controller Equation (23) is a finite-time guaranteed cost controller for GRNs Equation (22) with the settling time K satisfying $K<4.0294$, see Figures 3–6. Finally, the trajectories of the finite-time exponential stability of GRNs Equation (22) in three-dimensional and two-dimensional spaces are shown in Figures 7–10.

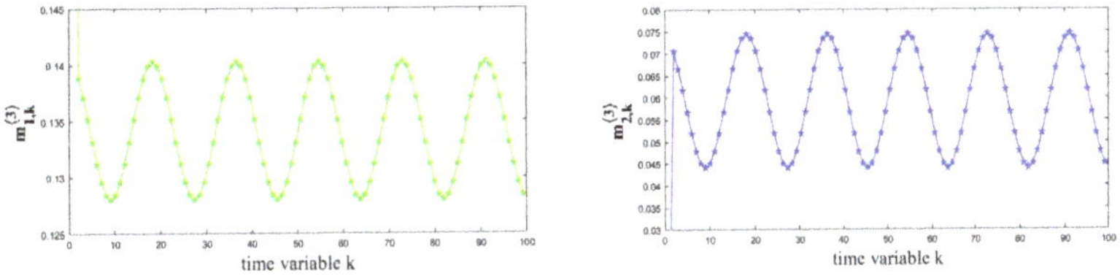

Figure 1. Weighted pseudo-almost periodic sequence solution of $\mathbf{m}_{1,k}^{\langle 3\rangle}$ and $\mathbf{m}_{2,k}^{\langle 3\rangle}$.

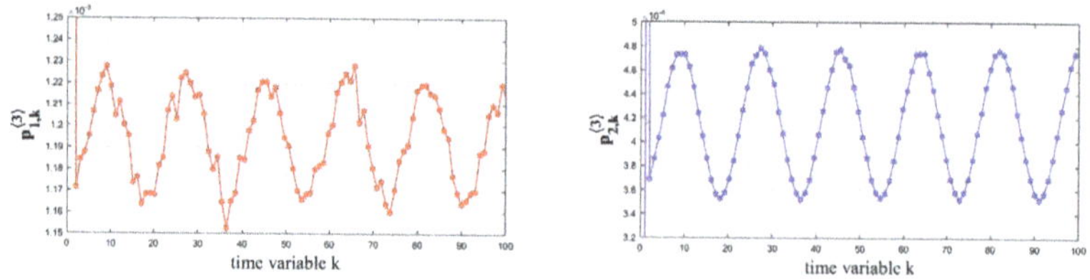

Figure 2. Weighted pseudo-almost periodic sequence solution of $\mathbf{p}^{\langle 3\rangle}_{1,k}$ and $\mathbf{p}^{\langle 3\rangle}_{2,k}$.

In Figures 1 and 2, the pictures show the weighted pseudo-almost periodicity of **m** and **p** in GRNs Equation (22). From these pictures, we can observe that the solution of GRNs Equation (22) is not weighted pseudo-almost periodic at the beginning of the time, but it becomes almost periodic as the time increases.

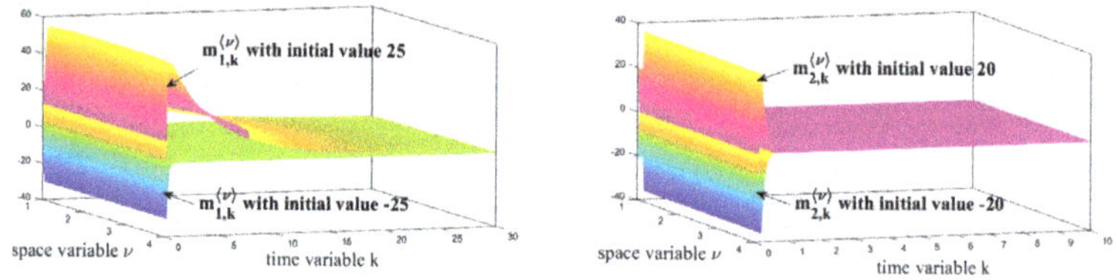

Figure 3. Finite-time guaranteed cost controller for $\mathbf{m}^{\langle v\rangle}_{1,k}$ and $\mathbf{m}^{\langle v\rangle}_{2,k}$ with the settling time K satisfying $K < 4.0294$.

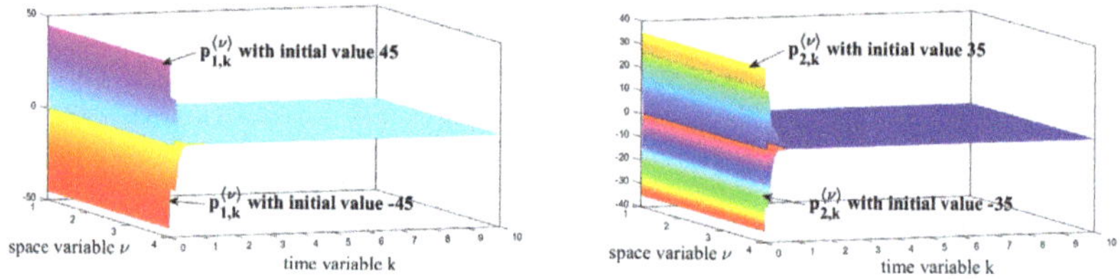

Figure 4. Finite-time guaranteed cost controller for $\mathbf{p}^{\langle v\rangle}_{1,k}$ and $\mathbf{p}^{\langle v\rangle}_{2,k}$ with the settling time K satisfying $K < 4.0294$.

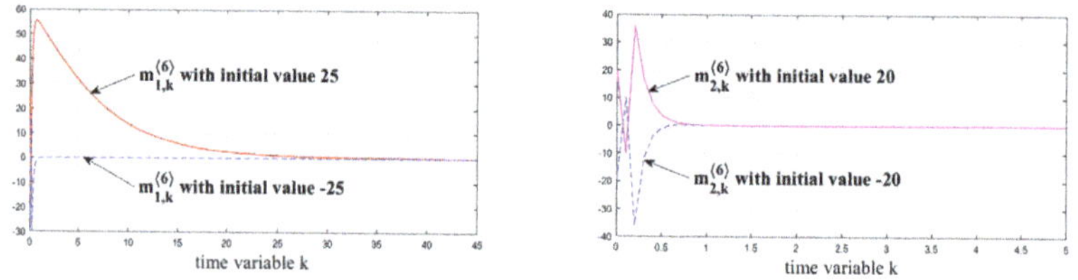

Figure 5. Finite-time guaranteed cost controller for $\mathbf{m}^{\langle 6\rangle}_{1,k}$ and $\mathbf{m}^{\langle 6\rangle}_{2,k}$ with the settling time K satisfying $K < 4.0294$.

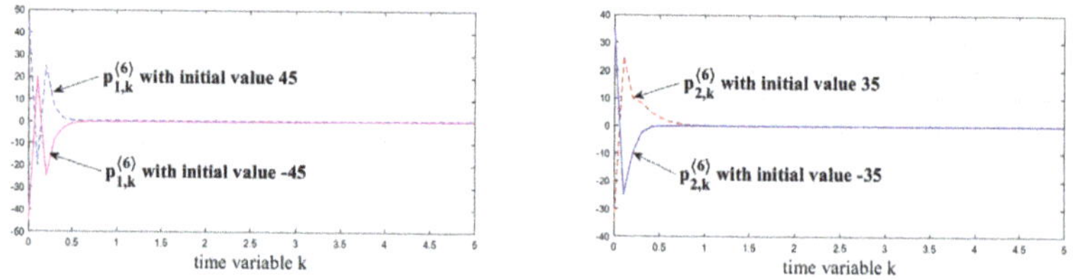

Figure 6. Finite-time guaranteed cost controller for $\mathbf{p}^{\langle 6\rangle}_{1,k}$ and $\mathbf{p}^{\langle 6\rangle}_{2,k}$ with the settling time K satisfying $K < 4.0294$.

In Figures 3 and 4, the pictures show the trajectories of **m** and **p** in GRNs Equation (22) with feedback controls in the closed loop. By observing these pictures, we can observe that the solutions of GRNs Equation (22) with different initial values realise finite-time exponential stability in three-dimensional space. Figures 5 and 6 give the trajectories of **m** and **p** of GRNs Equation (22) with feedback controls in the closed loop when $\nu = 6$.

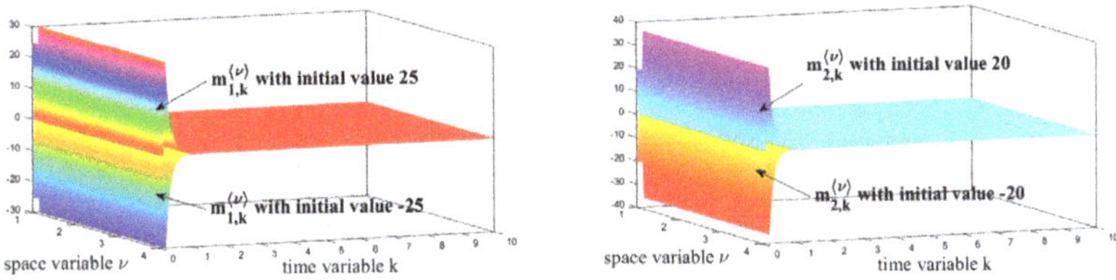

Figure 7. Finite-time exponential stability of $\mathbf{m}_{1,k}^{\langle\nu\rangle}$ and $\mathbf{m}_{2,k}^{\langle\nu\rangle}$.

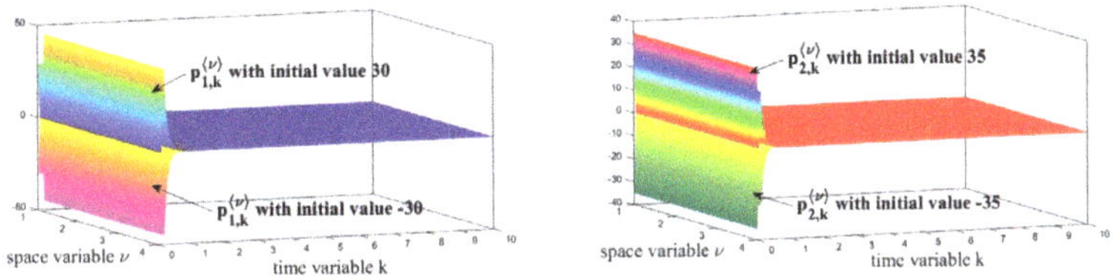

Figure 8. Finite-time exponential stability of $\mathbf{p}_{1,k}^{\langle\nu\rangle}$ and $\mathbf{p}_{2,k}^{\langle\nu\rangle}$.

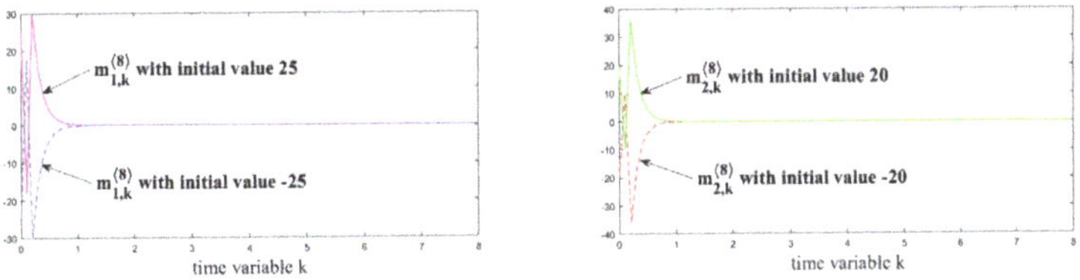

Figure 9. Finite-time exponential stability of $\mathbf{m}_{1,k}^{\langle 8\rangle}$ and $\mathbf{m}_{2,k}^{\langle 8\rangle}$.

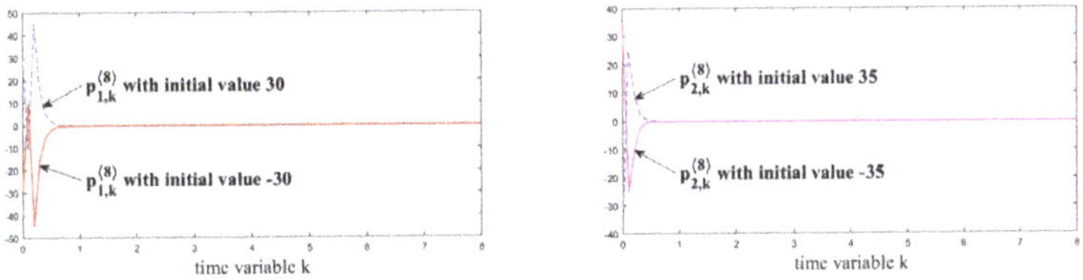

Figure 10. Finite-time exponential stability of $\mathbf{p}_{1,k}^{\langle 8\rangle}$ and $\mathbf{p}_{2,k}^{\langle 8\rangle}$.

Figures 7 and 8 show the solutions of GRNs Equation (22) without feedback control, realising finite-time exponential stability in three-dimensional space. Figures 9 and 10 draw the solutions of GRNs Equation (22) without feedback control, realising finite-time exponential stability when $\nu = 8$.

6. Conclusions and Perspectives

Utilizing EED and CFT techniques, discrete stochastic genetic regulatory networks with discrete spatial diffusion are presented, which can be considered as fully discrete configurations of stochastic genetic regulatory networks with reaction diffusion. Based on the constant variable formulation in discrete form, the existence uniqueness, the finite-time guaranteed cost control, and the exponential stability of the weighted pseudo-θ-almost periodic sequence of such discrete stochastic genetic regulatory networks in the mean-square sense are discussed. In addition, Lemmas 2 and 3, among others, have been crucial to the discussion in this paper over the course of the study. Notably, the work in this paper will initiate the development of qualitative problems in discrete-time and discrete-space models, laying the theoretical and practical foundations for future work in this area.

Author Contributions: Conceptualization, S.S. and T.Z.; Methodology, S.S. and T.Z.; Formal analysis, S.S., T.Z. and Z.L.; Investigation, S.S., T.Z. and Z.L.; Writing-original draft, S.S., T.Z. and Z.L.; Writing—review and editing, S.S., T.Z. and Z.L. All authors have read and agreed to the published version of the manuscript.

Funding: This work was supported by the Key Laboratory of Complex Dynamics System and Application Analysis of Department of Education of Yunnan Province.

Data Availability Statement: Not applicable.

Conflicts of Interest: The authors declare no conflict of interest.

References

1. Alon, U. *An Introductin to Systems Biology: Design Principles of Biological Circuits*; CRC: London, UK, 2006.
2. Thieffry, D.; Thomas, R. Qualitative analysis of gene networks. *Proc. Pac. Symp. Biocomput.* **1998**, *3*, 77–88.
3. Bao, W.Z.; Yuan, C.A.; Zhang, Y.H. Mutli-features prediction of protein translational modification sites. *IEEE/ACM Trans. Comput. Biol. Bioinf.* **2018**, *15*, 1453–1460. [CrossRef] [PubMed]
4. Somogyi, R.; Sniegoski, C. Modeling the complexity of genetic networks: Understanding multigenic and pleiotropic regulation. *Complexity* **1996**, *1*, 45–63. [CrossRef]
5. de Jong, H. Modeling and simuation of genetic regulatory systems: A literature review. *J. Comput. Biol.* **2002**, *9*, 67–103. [CrossRef] [PubMed]
6. Barabási, A.; Gulbahce, N.; Loscalzo, J. Network medicien: A network-based approach to human disease. *Nat. Rev. Genet.* **2011**, *12*, 56–68. [CrossRef] [PubMed]
7. Song, Q.; Long, L.; Zhao, Z.; Liu, Y.; Alsaadi, F.E. Stability criteria of quatemion-valued neutral-type delayed neural networks. *Neurocomputing* **2020**, *412*, 287–294. [CrossRef]
8. Hood, L.; Health, J.; Phelps, M.; Lin, B. Systems biology and new technologies enable predictive and preventative medicine. *Science* **2004**, *306*, 640–643. [CrossRef]
9. Liu, R.J.; Lu, J.Q.; Lou, J.G.; Alsaedi, A.; Alsaedi, F.E. Set stabiliation of Boolean networks under pinning contril strategy. *Neurocomputing* **2017**, *260*, 142–148. [CrossRef]
10. Possieri, C.; Teel, A.R. Asymptotic stability in probability for stochastic Boolean Networks. *Automatica* **2017**, *83*, 1–9. [CrossRef]
11. Zhang, X.Y.; Wang, Y.T.; Zhang, X. Improved stochastic integral inequalities to stability analysis of stochastic genetic regulatory networks with mixed time-varying delays. *IET Control Theory Appl.* **2020**, *14*, 2439–2448. [CrossRef]
12. Ayachi, M. Existence and exponential stability of weighted pseudo-almost periodic solutions for genetic regulatory networks with time-varying delays. *Int. J. Biomath.* **2021**, *14*, 2150006. [CrossRef]
13. Chen, T.; He, H.Y.; Church, G.M. Modeling gene expression with differential equations. *Pac. Symp. Biocomput.* **1999**, *4*, 29–40.
14. Han, Y.Y.; zhang, X.; Wang, Y.T. Asymptotic Stability Criteria for genetic regulatory networks with time-varying delays and reaction-diffusion terms. *Circ. Syst. Signal Process* **2015**, *34*, 3161–3190. [CrossRef]
15. Zou, C.Y.; Zhou, C.J.; Zhang, Q.; He, V.Y.; Huang, C. State emstimation for delayed genetic regulatory networks with reaction diffusion terms and Markovian jump. *Complex Intell. Syst.* **2023**, 1–15. [CrossRef]
16. Xie, Y.P.; Xiao, L.; Wang, L.M.; Wang, G.H. Algebriaic Stability Criteria of Reaction Diffusion Genetic Regulatory Neteorks With Discrete and Distrubted Delays. *IEEE Access* **2021**, *9*, 16410–16418. [CrossRef]
17. Xue, Y.; Liu, C.Y.; Zhang, X. State bounding description and reachable set estimation for discrete-time genetic regulatory networks with time-varying delays and bounded disturbances. *IEEE Trans. Syst. Man Cybern. Syst.* **2022**, *52*, 6652–6661. [CrossRef]
18. Liu, C.Y.; Wang, X.; Xue, Y. Global exponential stability analysis of discrete-time genetic regulatory networks with time-varying discrete delays and unbounded distributed delays. *Neurocomputing* **2020**, *372*, 100–108. [CrossRef]
19. Yue, D.D.; Guan, Z.H.; Chen, J.; Ling, G.; Wu, Y. Bifurcations and chaos of a discrete-time model in genetic regulatory networks. *Nonlinear Dyn.* **2017**, *87*, 567–586. [CrossRef]
20. Zhang, T.W.; Li, Y.K. Global exponential stability of discrete-time almost automorphic Caputo—Fabrizio BAM fuzzy neural networks via exponential Euler technique. *Knowl.-Based Syst.* **2022**, *246*, 108675. [CrossRef]
21. Huang, Z.K.; Mohamad, S.; Gao, F. Multi-almost periodicity in semi-discretizations of a general class of neural networks. *Math. Comput. Simul.* **2014**, *101*, 43–60. [CrossRef]

22. Zhang, T.W.; Han, S.F.; Zhou, J.W. Dynamic behaviours for semi-discrete stochastic Cohen-Grossberg neural networks with time delays. *J. Frankl. Inst.* **2020**, *357*, 13006–13040. [CrossRef]
23. Zhang, T.W.; Qu, H.Z.; Liu, Y.T.; Zhou, J.W. Weighted pseudo θ-almost periodic sequence solution and guaranteed cost control for discrete-time and discrete-space stochastic inertial neural networks. *Chaos Solitons Fractals* **2023**, *173*, 113658. [CrossRef]
24. Zhang, T.W.; Li, Z.H. Switching clusters' synchronization for discrete space-time complex dynamical networks via boundary feedback controls. *Pattern Recognit.* **2023**, *143*, 109763. [CrossRef]
25. Zhang, T.W.; Liu, Y.T.; Qu, H.Z. Global mean-square exponential stability and random periodicity of discrete-time stochastic inertial neural networks with discrete spatial diffusions and Dirichlet boundary condition. *Comput. Math. Appl.* **2023**, *141*, 116–128. [CrossRef]
26. Xu, G.X.; Bao, H.B.; Cao, J.D. Mean-square exponential input-to-state stability of stochastic gene regulatory networks with maltiple time delays. *Neural Process. Lett.* **2020**, *51*, 271–286. [CrossRef]
27. Zhou, J.; Xu, S.; Shen, H. Finite-time robust stochastic stability of uncertain stochastic delayed reaction-diffusion genetic regulatory networks. *Neurocomputing* **2011**, *74*, 2790–2796. [CrossRef]
28. Wang, W.Q.; Zhong, S.M.; Liu, F. Robust filtering of uncertain stochastic genetic regulatory networks with time-varying delays. *Chaos Solitons Fract.* **2012**, *45*, 915–929. [CrossRef]
29. Wang, B. Random periodic sequence of globally mean-square exponentially stable discrete-time stochastic genetic regulatory networks with discrete spatial diffusions. *Electron. Res. Arch.* **2023**, *31*, 3097–3122. [CrossRef]
30. Zhang, G.P.; Zhu, Q.X. Finite-time guaranteed cost control for uncertain delayed switched nonlinear stochastic systems. *J. Frankl. Institeu* **2022**, *359*, 8802–8818. [CrossRef]
31. Gao, H.; Zhang, H.B.; Shi, K.B.; Zhou, K. Event-triggered finite-time guaranteed cost control for networked Takagi-Sugeno (T-S) fuzzy switched systems under denial of service attacks. *Int. J. Robust Nolinear Control* **2022**, *32*, 5764–5775. [CrossRef]
32. Liu, L.P.; Di, Y.F.; Shang, Y.L.; Fu, Z.M.; Fan, B. Guaranteed Cost and Finite-Time Non-fragile Control of Fractional-Order Positive Switched Systems with Asynchronous Switching and Impulsive Moments. *Circuits Syst. Signal Process.* **2021**, *40*, 3143–3160. [CrossRef]
33. Liu, M.X.; Wu, B.W.; Wang, Y.E.; Liu, L.L. Dynamic Output Feedback Control and Guaranteed Cost Finite-time Boundedness for Uncertain Switched Linear Systems. *Int. J. Control Autom. Syst.* **2023**, *21*, 400–409. [CrossRef]
34. Liu, M.X.; Wu, B.W.; Wang, Y.E.; Liu, L.L. Dynamic Output Feedback control and Guaranteed Cost Finite-Time Boundedness for Switched Linear Systems. *Circuits Syst. Signal Process.* **2022**, *41*, 2653–2668. [CrossRef]
35. Liu, X.K.; Li, W.C.; Yao, C.X.; Li, Y. Finite-Time Guaranteed Cost Control for Markovian Jump Systems with Time-Varying Delays. *Mathematics* **2022**, *10*, 2028. [CrossRef]
36. Zhang, X.; Yin, Y.Y.; Wang, H.; He, S.P. Finite-time dissipative control for time-delay Markov jump systems with conic-type non-linearities under guaranteed cost controller and quantiser. *IET Control Theory Appl.* **2021**, *15*, 489–498. [CrossRef]
37. Luo, Y.P.; Wang, X.E.; Cao, J.D. Guaranteed-cost finite-time consensus of multi-agent systems via intermittent control. *Math. Methods Appl. Sci.* **2022**, *45*, 697–717. [CrossRef]
38. Duan, L.; Di, F.J.; Wang, Z.Y. Existence and global exponential stability of almost periodic solutions of genetic regulatory networks with time-varying delays. *J. Exp. Theor. Artif. Intell.* **2020**, *32*, 453–463. [CrossRef]
39. Luo, Q.; Zhang, R.B.; Liao, X.X. Unconditional global exponential stability in Lagrange sense of genetic regulatory networks with SUM regulatory logic. *Cogn. Neurodyn.* **2010**, *4*, 251–261. [CrossRef]
40. Li, Y.J.; Zhang, X.; Tan, C. Global exponential stability analysis of discrete-time genetic regulatory networks with time delays. *Asian J. Control* **2013**, *15*, 1448–1475. [CrossRef]
41. Xie, Y.P.; Xiao, L.; Ge, M.F.; Wang, L.M.; Wang, G.H. New results on global exponential stability of genetic regulatory networks with diffusion effect and time-varying hybird delays. *Neural Process. Lett.* **2021**, *53*, 3947–3963. [CrossRef]
42. Liu, Z.X.; Yang, X.; Yu, T.T.; Zhang, X.; Wang, X. Global Exponential Satbility Analysis of Coupled Cyclic Genentic Regulatory Networks With Constant Delays. *IEEE Trans. Control Netw. Syst.* **2021**, *8*, 1811–1821. [CrossRef]
43. Zhang, W.L.; Zheng, Z.H. Random almost periodic solutions of random dynamical systems. *arXiv* **2019**, arXiv:1909.01586.
44. de Fitte, P.R. Almost periodicity and periodicity for nonautonomous random dynamical systems. *Stochastics Dyn.* **2020**, *21*, 2150034. [CrossRef]
45. Marie, N.; Fitte, P.R.D. Almost periodic and periodic solutions of differential equations driven by the fractional Brownian motion with statistical application. *Stochastics* **2020**, *93*, 886–906. [CrossRef]
46. Zhang, C. Pseudo almost periodic solutions of some differential equations. *J. Math. Anal. Appl.* **1994**, *181*, 62–76. [CrossRef]
47. Diagana, T. Weighted pseudo-almost periodic functions and applications. *Comptes Rendus Math.* **2006**, *343*, 643–646. [CrossRef]
48. Es-saiydy, M.; Zitane, M. New composition theorem for weighted stepanov-like pseudo almost periodic functions on time scales and applications. *Bol. Soc. Parana. Mat.* 2023, *in press*. [CrossRef]
49. Yan, Z. Sensitivity analysis for a fractional stochastic differential equation with S-p-weighted pseudo almost periodic coefficients and infinite delay. *Fract. Calc. Appl. Anal.* **2022**, *25*, 2356–2399. [CrossRef]
50. M'Hamdi, M.S. On the weighted pseudo almost-periodic solutions of static DMAM neural network. *Neural Process. Lett.* **2022**, *54*, 4443–4464. [CrossRef]

51. Hu, P.; Huang, C.M. Delay dependent asymptotic mean square stability analysis of the stochastic exponential Euler method. *J. Comput. Appl. Math.* **2021**, *382*, 113068. [CrossRef]
52. Zhang, T.W.; Li, Y.K. Exponential Euler scheme of multi-delay Caputo-Fabrizio fractional-order differential equations. *Appl. Math. Lett.* **2022**, *124*, 107709. [CrossRef]
53. Bessaih, H.; Garrido-Atienza, M.J.; Köpp, V.; Schmalfuß, B.; Yang, M. Synchronization of stochastic lattice equations. *Nonlinear Differ. Equ. Appl. Nodea* **2020**, *27*, 36. [CrossRef]
54. Han, X.Y.; Kloeden, P.E. Sigmoidal approximations of Heaviside functions in neural lattice models. *J. Differ. Equ.* **2020**, *268*, 5283–5300. [CrossRef]
55. Han, X.Y.; Kloden, P.E.; Usman, B. Upper semi-continuous convergence of attractors for a Hopfield-type lattice model. *Nonlinearity* **2020**, *33*, 1881–1906. [CrossRef]
56. Kuang, J.C. *Applied Inequalities*; Shandong Science and Technology Press: Shandong, China, 2012.
57. Arnold, L. *Random Dynamical Systems*; Springer: Berlin, Germany, 1998.

axioms

Article

On the Crossing Bridge between Two Kirchhoff–Love Plates

Alexander Khludnev [1,2]

[1] Institute of Hydrodynamics of SB RAS, 630090 Novosibirsk, Russia; khlud@hydro.nsc.ru
[2] Sobolev Institute of Mathematics of SB RAS, 630090 Novosibirsk, Russia

Abstract: The paper is concerned with equilibrium problems for two elastic plates connected by a crossing elastic bridge. It is assumed that an inequality-type condition is imposed, providing a mutual non-penetration between the plates and the bridge. The existence of solutions is proved, and passages to limits are justified as the rigidity parameter of the bridge tends to infinity and to zero. Limit models are analyzed. The inverse problem is investigated when both the displacement field and the elasticity tensor of the plate are unknown. In this case, additional information concerning a displacement of a given point of the plate is assumed be given. A solution existence of the inverse problem is proved.

Keywords: elastic plate; crossing bridge; rigidity parameter; inverse problem; solution existence

MSC: 35B30; 35J88

Citation: Khludnev, A. On the Crossing Bridge between Two Kirchhoff–Love Plates. *Axioms* **2023**, *12*, 120. https://doi.org/10.3390/axioms12020120

Academic Editor: Adrian Petrusel

Received: 2 December 2022
Revised: 13 January 2023
Accepted: 18 January 2023
Published: 26 January 2023

1. Introduction

Bridged structures are very popular for solving connecting problems. Such structures may be different in type, and their quality depends on the purposes addressed. In this paper, we analyze the structure consisting of two Kirchhoff–Love elastic plates and a junction (bridge) that is in contact with the plates. To describe the behavior of the bridge, we use the Euler–Bernoulli beam model. The junction has the displacement coinciding with the displacement of the plates at two fixed points. Moreover, an inequality-type restriction is assumed to be imposed for the solution to provide a mutual non-penetration between the plates and the bridge. This approach implies that the problem is formulated as a free boundary one.

During the last years, boundary-value problems in elasticity with inequality-type boundary conditions have been under active study. We can refer the reader to the books [1,2] containing results for crack models with the non-penetration boundary conditions for a wide class of elasticity problems. There are many papers related to thin inclusions incorporated into elastic bodies. In the case of delamination of the surrounding elastic body from the inclusion, one more difficulty appears since we obtain an interfacial crack. We pay attention to the paper [3] where an equilibrium problem for two elastic plates is analyzed in the case of thin incorporated inclusion and Neumann type boundary conditions for the plate. Different properties of solutions in equilibrium problems for elastic bodies with thin rigid, semi-rigid, and elastic inclusions and cracks are analyzed in [4–13] and many other papers. In [14–16], one can find models for the analysis of non-homogeneous elastic bodies. Note that a derivation of models for elastic bodies with thin inclusions usually takes into account changing physical and geometrical parameters [17–19]. Contact problems for elastic plates with thin elastic structures were analyzed in [20,21]. We can also mention a number of applied studies related to thin inclusions of different nature in elastic bodies [22–29]. An application of the finite element method for planar mechanical elastic systems can be found in [30]. As for inverse problems in elasticity, the literature in this field is very vast. We will only mention the articles [31,32] and the links in them.

The structure of the paper is as follows. Section 2 addresses variational and differential formulations of the equilibrium problem. Passages to limits, as a rigidity parameter of the bridge tends to infinity and to zero, are investigated in Sections 3 and 4. We provide a justification of the limit procedure and analyze the limit models. Section 5 is concerned with the analysis of the inverse problem.

2. Setting the Problem

Let $\Omega_1, \Omega_2 \subset \mathbb{R}^2$ be bounded domains with Lipschitz boundaries Γ^1, Γ^2, respectively, such that $\bar{\Omega}_1 \cap \bar{\Omega}_2 = \emptyset$. Assume that Γ^i is divided into two smooth parts Γ^i_N and Γ^i_D, meas $\Gamma^i_D > 0$, $i = 1,2$. We set $b = (-2,2) \times \{0\}$, $b_1 = (-2,-1) \times \{0\}$, $b_2 = (1,2) \times \{0\}$, $b_0 = (-1,1) \times \{0\}$. Moreover, we assume that $b_i \subset \Omega_i$, and b crosses Γ^i_N, $b_0 \cap \Omega_i = \emptyset$, $i = 1,2$, see Figure 1. Denote by $\nu = (0,1)$, $n = (n_1, n_2)$ unit normal vectors to b, Γ^i, respectively, and set $\Omega = \Omega_1 \cup \Omega_2$, $\Omega_b = \Omega \setminus \bar{b}$.

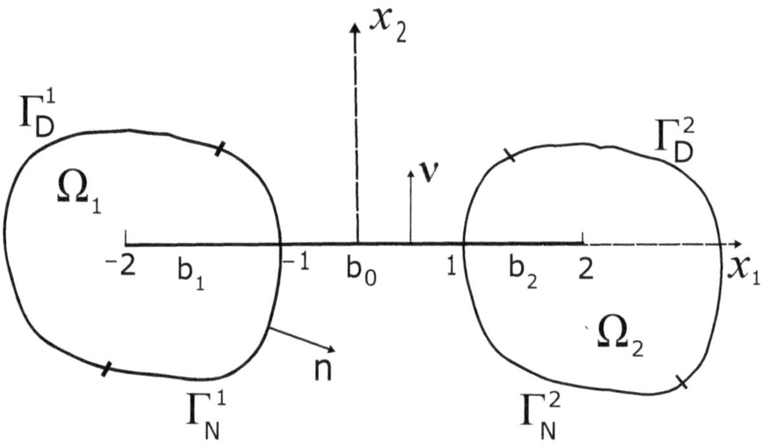

Figure 1. Elastic plates Ω_1, Ω_2 with crossing bridge b.

The set Ω corresponds to two elastic plates, and b fits to a thin elastic crossing bridge between two plates. We describe b in the frame of the Euler–Bernoulli beam model. In what follows, the crossing bridge b will be characterized by a rigidity parameter $\alpha > 0$. At the first step, this parameter is fixed being equal to 1, and in the sequel we analyze passages to the limit as α goes to infinity and to zero.

Let w be a scalar-valued function. We use the notations $w_n = \frac{\partial w}{\partial n}$, $w_\nu = \frac{\partial w}{\partial \nu}$. If $M = \{M_{ij}\}, i,j = 1,2$, then $\nabla\nabla M = M_{ij,ij}$. We also put $\nabla\nabla w = \{w_{,ij}\}, i,j = 1,2$. Summation convention over repeated indices is used; all functions with two lower indices are assumed to be symmetric in those indices.

In the domains Ω_1, Ω_2, elasticity tensors $A = \{a_{ijkl}\}, B = \{b_{ijkl}\}$, $i,j,k,l = 1,2$, are considered with the usual properties of symmetry and positive definiteness,

$$a_{ijkl} \in L^\infty(\Omega_1), \tag{1}$$
$$A\xi \cdot \xi \geq c_0 |\xi|^2 \quad \forall \xi = \{\xi_{ij}\},\ \xi_{ji} = \xi_{ij},\ c_0 = const > 0\,.$$

Similar properties are fulfilled for the tensor B on Ω_2.

We introduce notations for a bending moment M_n and a transverse force $T^n = T^n(M)$ on the boundaries of the plates,

$$M_n = -M_{ij} n_j n_i;\ T^n = -M_{ij,j} n_i - M_{ij,k} \tau_k \tau_j n_i\,,\ (\tau_1, \tau_2) = (-n_2, n_1). \tag{2}$$

In this case, for smooth functions $w, M = \{M_{ij}\}, i,j = 1,2$, the following Green's formula holds, see [2], Section 1.2.3,

$$-\int_{\Omega_i} M \cdot \nabla\nabla w = -\int_{\Omega_i} w\nabla\nabla M + \int_{\Gamma^i} M_n w_n - \int_{\Gamma^i} T^n w,\ i = 1,2.$$

Since the domain Ω_b with the cut $b_1 \cup b_2$ is a union of the domains $\Omega_1 \setminus b_1$ and $\Omega_2 \setminus b_2$, the above Green's formula allows us to write Green's formula for Ω_b,

$$-\int_{\Omega_b} M \cdot \nabla\nabla w = -\int_{\Omega_b} w\nabla\nabla M - \int_{b_1\cup b_2} [M_\nu] w_\nu + \int_{b_1\cup b_2} [T^\nu] w + \int_{\Gamma^1\cup\Gamma^2} M_n w_n - \int_{\Gamma^1\cup\Gamma^2} T^n w, \tag{3}$$

where $[h] = h^+ - h^-$ is a jump of a function h on b_i; $h^\pm$ are the traces of h on the crack faces $b_i^\pm$, $i = 1,2$. The signs $\pm$ fit to positive and negative directions of ν; the values M_ν, T^ν with the normal vector ν are defined on b similar to (2).

In view of the above notations, an equilibrium problem for the plates Ω_1, Ω_2 and the crossing bridge b is formulated as follows. Given external forces $f \in L^2(\Omega), g \in L^2(b)$ acting on the plates and the crossing bridge, respectively, we have to find a displacement of the plates w,; a moment tensor $M = \{M_{ij}\}, i,j = 1,2$, defined in Ω, Ω_b, respectively; and a crossing bridge displacement v defined on b such that

$$\nabla\nabla M + f = 0 \ \text{ in } \ \Omega_b, \tag{4}$$

$$M + E\nabla\nabla w = 0 \ \text{ in } \Omega_b, \tag{5}$$

$$v_{,1111} = g \text{ on } b_0;\ \ v_{,1111} = -[T^\nu] + g \text{ on } b_1 \cup b_2\ , \tag{6}$$

$$w = w_n = 0 \text{ on } \Gamma_D^1 \cup \Gamma_D^2;\ M_n = T^n = 0 \text{ on } \Gamma_N^1 \cup \Gamma_N^2, \tag{7}$$

$$w(\pm 2, 0) = 0;\ v = v_{,11} = 0 \text{ as } x_1 = -2, 2, \tag{8}$$

$$v - w \geq 0,\ [T^\nu] \leq 0,\ (v - w)[T^\nu] = 0 \text{ on } \ b_1 \cup b_2, \tag{9}$$

$$[w] = [w_\nu] = 0,\ [M_\nu] = 0 \ \text{ on } \ b_1 \cup b_2, \tag{10}$$

$$[v(\pm 1)] = [v_{,1}(\pm 1)] = 0,\ \ [v_{,11}(\pm 1)] = [v_{,111}(\pm 1)] = 0. \tag{11}$$

Here, $[h(a)] = h(a+0) - h(a-0)$; $w_{,1} = \frac{\partial w}{\partial x_1}$, $(x_1, x_2) \in \Omega$. The tensor E is equal to A, B in Ω_1, Ω_2, respectively. Functions defined on b we identify with functions of the variable x_1.

Relations (4) and (5) are the equilibrium equations for the Kirchhoff–Love elastic plates Ω_1, Ω_2 and the constitutive law; (6) is the Euler–Bernoulli equilibrium equations for the crossing bridge parts b_i, see [1,2]. The right-hand side $-[T^\nu]$ in (6) describes forces acting on $b_1 \cup b_2$ from the elastic plates. The first inequality in (9) provides a non-penetration between the plates and the bridge. Relation (11) provides glue conditions at the points where the bridge b crosses the external boundaries of the elastic plates. Note that, by (9), the contact set between the plates and the bridge is unknown.

We can provide a variational formulation of the problem (4)–(11). Introduce the space

$$W = H^{2,0}(b) \times H_D^{2,0}(\Omega)$$

with the norm

$$\|(v,w)\|_W^2 = \|v\|_{H^{2,0}(b)}^2 + \|w\|_{H_D^{2,0}(\Omega)}^2,$$

where $H^{2,0}(b)$, $H_D^{2,0}(\Omega)$ are the usual Sobolev spaces,

$$H_D^{2,0}(\Omega) = \{w \in H^2(\Omega) \mid w = w_n = 0 \text{ on } \Gamma_D^1 \cup \Gamma_D^2;\ w(\pm 2, 0) = 0\},$$

$$H^{2,0}(b) = \{v \in H^2(b) \mid v(\pm 2) = 0\},$$

and consider the energy functional $\Pi: W \to \mathbb{R}$,

$$\Pi(v, w) = \frac{1}{2}C(w, w) - \int\limits_{\Omega} fw + \frac{1}{2}\int\limits_{b} v_{,11}^2 - \int\limits_{b} gv.$$

Here,

$$C(w, \bar{w}) = \int\limits_{\Omega_1} a_{ijkl} w_{,kl} \bar{w}_{,ij} + \int\limits_{\Omega_2} b_{ijkl} w_{,kl} \bar{w}_{,ij}.$$

Denote by S the set of admissible displacements,

$$S = \{(v, w) \in W \mid v - w \geq 0 \text{ on } b_1 \cup b_2\}$$

and consider the problem:

$$\text{Find } (v, w) \in S \text{ such that } \Pi(v, w) = \inf_S \Pi.$$

This minimization problem has a unique solution since the functional Π is weakly lower semicontinuous and coercive. The coercivity of the functional Π follows from the Dirichlet boundary conditions on the sets Γ_D^i for the function w and conditions $v(\pm 2) = 0$. The set S is weakly closed. The solution of the problem satisfies the following variational inequality

$$(v, w) \in S, \tag{12}$$

$$C(w, \bar{w} - w) - \int\limits_{\Omega} f(\bar{w} - w) \tag{13}$$

$$+ \int\limits_{b} v_{,11}(\bar{v}_{,11} - v_{,11}) - \int\limits_{b} g(\bar{v} - v) \geq 0 \;\; \forall\, (\bar{v}, \bar{w}) \in S.$$

Theorem 1. *Problem formulations* (4)–(13) *are equivalent for smooth solutions.*

Proof. Assume that (12) and (13) hold. We can substitute in (13) test functions of the form $(\bar{v}, \bar{w}) = (v, w) \pm (0, \varphi)$, $\varphi \in C_0^\infty(\Omega_b)$. This provides the equilibrium Equation (4) fulfilled in the distributional sense. Next, test functions of the form $(\bar{v}, \bar{w}) = (v, w + \varphi)$ can be substituted in (13), where $\varphi \in C_0^\infty(\Omega)$, $\varphi \leq 0$ on $b_1 \cup b_2$; $\varphi(\pm 2, 0) = 0$. Taking into account the equilibrium Equation (4) and Green Formula (3), we obtain

$$-\int\limits_{b_1 \cup b_2} [M_\nu] \varphi_\nu + \int\limits_{b_1 \cup b_2} [T^\nu] \varphi \geq 0.$$

From here, it follows

$$[M_\nu] = 0, \; [T^\nu] \leq 0 \text{ on } b_1 \cup b_2. \tag{14}$$

Now, test functions of the form $(\bar{v}, \bar{w}) = (v + \psi, w + \varphi)$ are substituted in (13), $(\psi, \varphi) \in S$, supp $\psi \subset (b_1 \cup b_2)$. This gives

$$C(w, \varphi) - \int\limits_{\Omega} f\varphi + \int\limits_{b} v_{,11}\psi_{,11} - \int\limits_{b} g\psi \geq 0.$$

Consequently, by using the Green Formula (3), in view of (4), (14), we derive

$$\int\limits_{b_1 \cup b_2} [T^\nu]\varphi + \int\limits_{b} v_{,1111}\psi - \int\limits_{b} g\psi \geq 0.$$

Choosing the above inequality $\psi = \varphi$ on $b_1 \cup b_2$,, the following equation

$$v_{,1111} = -[T^\nu] + g \text{ on } b_1 \cup b_2 \tag{15}$$

is derived. To proceed, take test functions of the form $(\bar{v}, \bar{w}) = (v \pm \psi, w)$ in (3), supp $\psi \subset b_0$. The following relation is obtained:

$$\int_{b_0} v_{,11}\psi_{,11} - \int_{b_0} g\psi = 0.$$

Thus,

$$v_{,1111} = g \text{ on } b_0. \tag{16}$$

Now, we are aiming to derive the last relation of (9). Assume that the inequality $v(x_0) - w(x_0) > 0$ holds at a point $x_0 \in b_1 \cup b_2$. In this case, we can take $(\bar{v}, \bar{w}) = (v, w) \pm \varepsilon(\psi, \varphi)$ as a test function in (13), where the support of ψ belongs to a small neighborhood of x_0; the support of φ belongs to a small neighborhood of the point $(x_0, 0)$, and ε is small. This implies

$$C(w, \varphi) - \int_\Omega f\varphi + \int_b v_{,11}\psi_{,11} - \int_b g\psi = 0.$$

By (3), (4), and (14), we obtain the relation

$$\int_{b_1 \cup b_2} [T^\nu]\varphi + \int_b v_{,1111}\psi - \int_b g\psi = 0.$$

In particular, this provides

$$[T^\nu] = 0 \text{ in a neighborhood of the point } x_0.$$

This means that

$$(v - w)[T^\nu] = 0 \text{ on } b_1 \cup b_2.$$

The next step of our reasoning is to derive boundary conditions for v at the points $\pm 1, \pm 2$ and the last condition of (7). To this end, we take test function in (13) of the form $(\bar{v}, \bar{w}) = (v, w) \pm (\psi, \varphi)$, $(\psi, \varphi) \in W$, $\varphi = \psi$ on $b_1 \cup b_2$. It provides the equality

$$C(w, \varphi) - \int_\Omega f\varphi + \int_{b_0} v_{,11}\psi_{,11} + \int_{b_1 \cup b_2} v_{,11}\psi_{,11} - \int_b g\psi = 0.$$

Applying the Green Formula (3), this relation implies

$$\begin{aligned} &- \int_{\Omega_b} \nabla\nabla M \cdot \varphi - \int_{\Omega_b} f\varphi + \int_{b_0} v_{,1111}\psi + \int_{b_1 \cup b_2} v_{,1111}\psi \\ &- \int_{b_1 \cup b_2} [M_\nu]\varphi_\nu + \int_{b_1 \cup b_2} [T^\nu]\varphi + \int_{\Gamma^1 \cup \Gamma^2} M_n \varphi_n - \int_{\Gamma^1 \cup \Gamma^2} T^n \varphi \\ &- \int_{b_0} g\psi - \int_{b_1 \cup b_2} g\psi - v_{,111}\psi|_{x_1=-1}^{x_1=1} + v_{,11}\psi_{,1}|_{x_1=-1}^{x_1=1} \\ &- v_{,111}\psi|^{x_1=-1} + v_{,11}\psi_{,1}|_{x_1=-2}^{x_1=-1} - v_{,111}\psi|_{x_1=1} + v_{,11}\psi_{,1}|_{x_1=1}^{x_1=2} = 0. \end{aligned} \tag{17}$$

From here, it follows that

$$M_n = T^n = 0 \text{ on } \Gamma_N^1 \cup \Gamma_N^2. \tag{18}$$

Taking into account (4), (14)–(16), from (17) we obtain

$$\begin{aligned} -v_{,11}\psi_{,1}(-2) + v_{,11}\psi_{,1}(2) - [v_{,11}(1)]\psi_{,1}(1) \\ +[v_{,111}(1)]\psi(1) - [v_{,11}(-1)]\psi_{,1}(-1) + [v_{,111}(-1)]\psi(-1) = 0. \end{aligned} \tag{19}$$

Consequently,

$$v_{,11}(\pm 2) = 0, \; [v_{,11}(\pm 1)] = [v_{,111}(\pm 1)] = 0.$$

Hence, we derived all relations (4)–(11) from (12) and (13).

Let us prove the converse. Assume that (4)–(11) are fulfilled. Then, we have for all $(\bar{v}, \bar{w}) \in S$,

$$\begin{aligned} -\int_{\Omega_b} (\nabla\nabla M + f)(\bar{w} - w) + \int_{b_0} (v_{,1111} - g)(\bar{v} - v) \\ + \int_{b_1 \cup b_2} (v_{,1111} + [T^\nu] - g)(\bar{v} - v) = 0. \end{aligned} \tag{20}$$

Integrating by parts in the second and the third integrals of (20) and using the Formula (3), it follows that

$$\begin{aligned} -\int_{\Omega_b} M\nabla\nabla(\bar{w} - w) - \int_{\Omega_b} f(\bar{w} - w) + \int_{b_0} v_{,11}(\bar{v}_{,11} - v_{,11}) - \int_{b} g(\bar{v} - v) \\ + \int_{b_1 \cup b_2} v_{,11}(\bar{v}_{,11} - v_{,11}) + \int_{b_1 \cup b_2} [M_\nu](\bar{w}_\nu - w_\nu) - \int_{b_1 \cup b_2} [T^\nu](\bar{w} - w) \\ - \int_{\Gamma^1 \cup \Gamma^2} M_n(\bar{w}_n - w_n) + \int_{\Gamma^1 \cup \Gamma^2} T^n(\bar{w} - w) + \int_{b_1 \cup b_2} [T^\nu](\bar{v} - v) \\ + v_{,111}(\bar{v} - v)|_{x_1=-1}^{x_1=1} - v_{,11}(\bar{v}_{,1} - v_{,1})|_{x_1=-1}^{x_1=1} + v_{,111}(\bar{v} - v)|_{x_1=-2}^{x_1=-1} \\ - v_{,11}(\bar{v}_{,1} - v_{,1})|_{x_1=-2}^{x_1=-1} + v_{,111}(\bar{v} - v)|_{x_1=1}^{x_1=2} - v_{,11}(\bar{v}_{,1} - v_{,1})|_{x_1=1}^{x_1=2} = 0. \end{aligned} \tag{21}$$

We can change the integration over Ω_b by integration over Ω in the first two integrals of (21) and use boundary conditions for $w, \bar{w}, M_n, T^n$. To derive the variational inequality (12) and (13) from (21), it suffices to check that

$$\begin{aligned} -\int_{b_1 \cup b_2} [T^\nu](\bar{w} - w) + \int_{b_1 \cup b_2} [T^\nu](\bar{v} - v) \\ + v_{,111}(\bar{v} - v)|_{x_1=-1}^{x_1=1} - v_{,11}(\bar{v}_{,1} - v_{,1})|_{x_1=-1}^{x_1=1} + v_{,111}(\bar{v} - v)|^{x_1=-1} \\ - v_{,11}(\bar{v}_{,1} - v_{,1})|^{x_1=-1} + v_{,111}(\bar{v} - v)|_{x_1=1} - v_{,11}(\bar{v}_{,1} - v_{,1})|_{x_1=1} \le 0. \end{aligned} \tag{22}$$

However, the inequality (22) easily follows from (6)–(11). Hence, we proved that (4)–(11) imply (12) and (13). Theorem 1 is proved . □

3. Convergence of Rigidity Parameter α to Infinity

In this section, we introduce a positive bridge rigidity parameter α into the model (12) and (13) and analyze a passage to the limit as $\alpha \to \infty$. Our aim is to justify this passage to the limit and investigate the limit model. Instead of (12) and (13), for any $\alpha > 0$, consider the following problem

$$(v^\alpha, w^\alpha) \in S, \tag{23}$$

$$C(w^\alpha, \bar{w} - w^\alpha) - \int_\Omega f(\bar{w} - w^\alpha) \tag{24}$$

$$+\alpha \int_b v^\alpha_{,11}(\bar{v}_{,11} - v^\alpha_{,11}) - \int_b g(\bar{v} - v^\alpha) \geq 0 \ \ \forall (\bar{v}, \bar{w}) \in S.$$

The solution (v^α, w^α) of this problem is supplied with the index α. Note that we can write an equivalent differential formulation of the problem (23) and (24) similar to (4)–(11). In this case, instead of (6) we have the following equations for the crossing bridge

$$\alpha v^\alpha_{,1111} = g \text{ on } b_0; \ \ \alpha v^\alpha_{,1111} = -[T^\nu] + g \text{ on } b_1 \cup b_2.$$

In what follows, we justify a passage to the limit as $\alpha \to \infty$ in (23) and (24). At the first step, a priori estimates of the solutions are derived.

From (23) and (24), the following relation is obtained:

$$C(w^\alpha, w^\alpha) - \int_\Omega f w^\alpha + \alpha \int_b (v^\alpha_{,11})^2 - \int_b g v^\alpha = 0. \tag{25}$$

From (25), we derive the estimate being uniform in $\alpha \geq \alpha_0 > 0$,

$$\|(v^\alpha, w^\alpha)\|_W \leq c, \tag{26}$$

moreover, the relation (25) implies

$$\int_b (v^\alpha_{,11})^2 \leq \frac{c}{\alpha}. \tag{27}$$

By estimates (26) and (27), we can assume that as $\alpha \to \infty$

$$(v^\alpha, w^\alpha) \to (v, w) \ \text{ weakly in } \ W, \tag{28}$$

$$v(x_1) = a_0 + a_1 x_1, \ x_1 \in (-2, 2); \ a_0, a_1 \in \mathbb{R}. \tag{29}$$

On the other hand, since $v \in H^{2,0}(b)$, consequently, $v = 0$ on b.

Then introduce the set of admissible displacements for the limit problem,

$$S_\infty = \{w \in H^{2,0}_D(\Omega) \mid w \leq 0 \text{ on } b_1 \cup b_2\}.$$

We take any element $\tilde{w} \in S_\infty$. Then, $(0, \tilde{w}) \in S$. Substitute this function in (24). By (28) and (29), it is possible to pass to the limit in (23) and (24) as $\alpha \to \infty$. The limit relations are of the form

$$w \in S_\infty, \tag{30}$$

$$C(w, \tilde{w} - w) - \int_\Omega f(\tilde{w} - w) \geq 0 \ \ \forall \tilde{w} \in S_\infty. \tag{31}$$

Thus, we have shown the following result.

Theorem 2. *As $\alpha \to \infty$, the solutions of the problem* (23) *and* (24) *converge in the sense* (28) *and* (29) *to the solution of* (30) *and* (31).

To conclude this section, we provide a differential formulation of the problem (30) and (31): find functions w, $M = \{M_{ij}\}, i,j = 1,2$, defined in Ω, Ω_b, respectively, such that

$$\nabla\nabla M + f = 0 \text{ in } \Omega_b, \tag{32}$$

$$M + E\nabla\nabla w = 0 \text{ in } \Omega_b, \tag{33}$$

$$w = w_n = 0 \text{ on } \Gamma_D^1 \cup \Gamma_D^2;\ M_n = T^n = 0 \text{ on } \Gamma_N^1 \cup \Gamma_N^2, \tag{34}$$

$$w \le 0,\ [T^\nu] \le 0,\ w[T^\nu] = 0 \text{ on } b_1 \cup b_2, \tag{35}$$

$$[w] = [w_\nu] = 0,\ [M_\nu] = 0 \text{ on } b_1 \cup b_2;\ w(\pm 2, 0) = 0. \tag{36}$$

The following statement takes place providing a connection between problems (30)–(36).

Theorem 3. *Problem formulations* (30)–(36) *are equivalent provided that the solutions are smooth.*

Proof. Let (32)–(36) be fulfilled. Then, we have

$$\int_{\Omega_b} (\nabla\nabla M + f)(\bar{w} - w) = 0,\ \bar{w} \in S_\infty.$$

From this relation, by (3), it follows that

$$\int_{\Omega} M\nabla\nabla(\bar{w} - w) + \int_{b_1 \cup b_2} [T^\nu](\bar{w} - w) + \int_{\Omega} f(\bar{w} - w) = 0. \tag{37}$$

In so doing, we changed the integration domain Ω_b by Ω since $[M_\nu] = 0$, $[w] = [w_\nu] = 0$ on $b_1 \cup b_2$. Thus, to obtain (30) and (31) from (37) it suffices to check that

$$\int_{b_1 \cup b_2} [T^\nu](\bar{w} - w) \ge 0. \tag{38}$$

However, the inequality (38) easily follows from (35).

Conversely, assume that (30) and (31) hold. We take a test function of the form $\bar{w} = w + \varphi$, $\varphi \in C_0^\infty(\Omega_b)$ and substitute it in (31). This implies the equilibrium Equation (32). The other arguments are reminiscent of those used in the proof of Theorem 1, and we omit them. Theorem 3 is proved. □

4. Convergence of Rigidity Parameter of b_0 to Zero

In this section, we assume that $g = 0$ on b_0. A convergence to zero of the rigidity parameter α will be analyzed when assuming that a change of this parameter happens at b_0. In this case, the rigidity parameter at b_1, b_2 is fixed and is equal to 1.

We first provide a formulation of the equilibrium problem such as (4)–(11) for this case: find functions w^α, $M = \{M_{ij}\}, i,j = 1,2$, defined in Ω, Ω_b, respectively, and functions v^α defined on b such that

$$\nabla\nabla M + f = 0 \text{ in } \Omega_b, \tag{39}$$

$$M + E\nabla\nabla w^\alpha = 0 \text{ in } \Omega_b, \tag{40}$$

$$\alpha v^\alpha_{,1111} = 0 \text{ on } b_0;\ v^\alpha_{,1111} = -[T^\nu] + g \text{ on } b_1 \cup b_2, \tag{41}$$

$$w^\alpha = w^\alpha_n = 0 \text{ on } \Gamma_D^1 \cup \Gamma_D^2;\ M_n = T^n = 0 \text{ on } \Gamma_N^1 \cup \Gamma_N^2, \tag{42}$$

$$v^\alpha = v^\alpha_{,11} = 0 \text{ as } x_1 = -2, 2;\ w(\pm 2, 0) = 0, \tag{43}$$

$$[w^\alpha] = [w^\alpha_\nu] = 0,\ [M_\nu] = 0 \text{ on } b_1 \cup b_2, \tag{44}$$

$$v^\alpha - w^\alpha \ge 0,\ [T^\nu] \le 0,\ (v^\alpha - w^\alpha)[T^\nu] = 0 \text{ on } b_1 \cup b_2, \tag{45}$$

$$[v^\alpha(\pm 1)] = [v^\alpha_{,1}(\pm 1)] = 0,\ v^\alpha_{,11}(\pm 1 \pm 0) = \alpha v^\alpha_{,11}(\pm 1 \mp 0), \tag{46}$$

$$v^\alpha_{,111}(\pm 1 \pm 0) = \alpha v^\alpha_{,111}(\pm 1 \mp 0). \tag{47}$$

In relations (46) and (47), we should simultaneously take upper or lower signs.

The problem (39)–(47) can be formulated in a variational form. Indeed, consider the energy functional $\pi_\alpha : W \to \mathbb{R}$,

$$\pi_\alpha(v,w) = \frac{1}{2}C(w,w) - \int_\Omega fw + \frac{\alpha}{2}\int_{b_0} v_{,11}^2 + \frac{1}{2}\int_{b_1\cup b_2} v_{,11}^2 - \int_{b_1\cup b_2} gv.$$

Then, the problem

$$\text{find } (v^\alpha, w^\alpha) \in S \text{ such that } \pi_\alpha(v^\alpha, w^\alpha) = \inf_S \pi_\alpha$$

has a solution satisfying the variational inequality

$$(v^\alpha, w^\alpha) \in S,\ \ C(w^\alpha, \bar{w} - w^\alpha) - \int_\Omega f(\bar{w} - w^\alpha) \tag{48}$$

$$+\alpha\int_{b_0} v^\alpha_{,11}(\bar{v}_{,11} - v^\alpha_{,11}) + \int_{b_1\cup b_2} v^\alpha_{,11}(\bar{v}_{,11} - v^\alpha_{,11}) \tag{49}$$

$$- \int_{b_1\cup b_2} g(\bar{v} - v^\alpha) \geq 0 \ \ \forall(\bar{v}, \bar{w}) \in S.$$

In what follows, we aim to justify a passage to the limit in (48) and (49) as $\alpha \to 0$. From (48) and (49), the following relation is obtained:

$$C(w^\alpha, w^\alpha) - \int_\Omega fw^\alpha + \alpha\int_{b_0}(v^\alpha_{,11})^2 + \int_{b_1\cup b_2}(v^\alpha_{,11})^2 - \int_{b_1\cup b_2} gv^\alpha = 0. \tag{50}$$

This relation provides the following estimate being uniform in α

$$\|v^\alpha\|^2_{H^2(b_1\cup b_2)} + \|w^\alpha\|^2_{H^{2,0}_D(\Omega)} \leq c, \tag{51}$$

moreover, the relation (50) implies

$$\alpha\int_{b_0}(v^\alpha_{,11})^2 \leq c. \tag{52}$$

By estimates (51) and (52), we can assume that, as $\alpha \to 0$,

$$v^\alpha \to v \text{ weakly in } H^2(b_1 \cup b_2),\ w^\alpha \to w \ \text{ weakly in } \ H^{2,0}_D(\Omega). \tag{53}$$

From (51) it follows that uniformly in α,

$$v^\alpha(\pm 1 \pm 0),\ v^\alpha_{,1}(\pm 1 \pm 0) \text{ are bounded.} \tag{54}$$

Here, and in (55) below, we should take upper or below signs simultaneously. Taking into account the conditions

$$[v^\alpha] = [v^\alpha_{,1}] = 0 \text{ as } \ x_1 = \pm 1$$

we obtain for small α that

$$\sqrt{\alpha}v^\alpha(\pm 1 \mp 0),\ \sqrt{\alpha}v^\alpha_{,1}(\pm 1 \mp 0) \text{ are bounded.} \tag{55}$$

Consequently, relations (52), (55) imply for small α that

$$\sqrt{\alpha}v^\alpha \text{ are bounded in } H^2(b_0).$$

Thus, we can assume that as $\alpha \to 0$,

$$\sqrt{\alpha} v^{\alpha} \to \bar{v} \text{ weakly in } H^2(b_0). \tag{56}$$

Now, introduce the set of admissible displacements for the limit problem

$$S_0 = \{(v,w) \in H^2(b_1 \cup b_2) \times H_D^{2,0}(\Omega) \mid v - w \geq 0 \text{ on } b_1 \cup b_2; \\ v(\pm 2) = 0\}.$$

Take $(\bar{v}, \bar{w}) \in S_0$ and extend the function $\bar{v}$ to b_0 assuming that the extension belongs to the space $H^{2,0}(b)$. In this case $(\bar{v}, \bar{w}) \in S$, and we can substitute $(\bar{v}, \bar{w})$ in (48) and (49) as a test function. Passing to the limit as $\alpha \to 0$, by (53), (56), the following variational inequality is obtained:

$$(v,w) \in S_0, \tag{57}$$

$$C(w, \bar{w} - w) - \int_{\Omega} f(\bar{w} - w) + \int_{b_1 \cup b_2} v_{,11}(\bar{v}_{,11} - v_{,11}) \\ - \int_{b_1 \cup b_2} g(\bar{v} - v) \geq 0 \;\; \forall (\bar{v}, \bar{w}) \in S_0. \tag{58}$$

Thus, the following statement is proved.

Theorem 4. *As $\alpha \to 0$, the solutions of the problem* (48) *and* (49) *converge in the sense* (53) *to the solution of* (57) *and* (58).

To conclude the section, we provide a differential formulation of the problem (57) and (58): find a displacement of the elastic plates w, a moment tensor $M = \{M_{ij}\}, i,j = 1,2$, defined in Ω, Ω_b, respectively, and a function v defined on $b_1 \cup b_2$ such that

$$\nabla\nabla M + f = 0 \;\text{ in }\; \Omega_b, \tag{59}$$

$$M + E\nabla\nabla w = 0 \;\text{ in } \Omega_b, \tag{60}$$

$$v_{,1111} = -[T^{\nu}] + g \text{ on } b_1 \cup b_2\,, \tag{61}$$

$$w = w_n = 0 \text{ on } \Gamma_D^1 \cup \Gamma_D^2;\; M_n = T^n = 0 \text{ on } \Gamma_N^1 \cup \Gamma_N^2, \tag{62}$$

$$w(\pm 2, 0) = 0;\; v = v_{,11} = 0 \text{ as } x_1 = -2, 2, \tag{63}$$

$$v - w \geq 0,\; [T^{\nu}] \leq 0,\; (v - w)[T^{\nu}] = 0 \text{ on } \; b_1 \cup b_2, \tag{64}$$

$$[w] = [w_{\nu}] = 0,\; [M_{\nu}] = 0 \;\text{ on }\; b_1 \cup b_2, \tag{65}$$

$$v_{,11}(\pm 1) = v_{,111}(\pm 1) = 0. \tag{66}$$

The following statement is valid.

Theorem 5. *Problem formulations* (57)–(59) *and* (66) *are equivalent provided that the solutions are smooth.*

We omit the proof of this theorem since it is reminiscent of that of Theorem 1. The only step we have to take is to provide a proof that from (57) and (58) the boundary conditions (66) follow. Indeed, take in (57) and (58) test functions of the form $(\bar{v}, \bar{w}) = (v,w) \pm (\tilde{v}, \tilde{w})$, $(\tilde{v}, \tilde{w}) \in S_0$, $\tilde{v} = \tilde{w}$ on $b_1 \cup b_2$. This gives

$$C(w, \tilde{w}) - \int_{\Omega} f\tilde{w} + \int_{b_1 \cup b_2} v_{,11}\tilde{v}_{,11} - \int_{b_1 \cup b_2} g\tilde{v} = 0. \tag{67}$$

Since

$$C(w,\bar{w}) = -\int_{\Omega} M_{ij}(w)\bar{w}_{,ij},$$

we can integrate by parts in the third term of (67) and use Green's Formula (3). This implies

$$-\int_{\Omega_b} \nabla\nabla M \cdot \bar{w} - \int_{\Omega_b} f\bar{w} + \int_{b_1\cup b_2} v_{,1111}\bar{v} \tag{68}$$
$$-\int_{b_1\cup b_2} [M_\nu]\bar{w}_\nu + \int_{b_1\cup b_2} [T^\nu]\bar{w} + \int_{\Gamma^1\cup\Gamma^2} M_n\bar{w}_n - \int_{\Gamma^1\cup\Gamma^2} T^n\bar{w}$$
$$-\int_{b_1\cup b_2} g\bar{v} - v_{,111}\bar{v}|^{x_1=-1} + v_{,11}\bar{v}_{,1}|^{x_1=-1} - v_{,111}\bar{v}|_{x_1=1} + v_{,11}\bar{v}_{,1}|_{x_1=1} = 0.$$

Since the equilibrium equations (59), (61) hold, and since $[M_\nu] = 0$ on $b_1 \cup b_2$, the relation (68) implies boundary conditions (66) and the second group of boundary conditions (62).

Theorem 5 is proved.

To conclude this section, we note that the problems (59) and (66) describe an equilibrium state for two plates occupying the domains Ω_1, Ω_2. In fact, we have two independent problems (for each plate) since there is no connection between the plates.

5. Analysis of Inverse Problem

In this section, we analyze an inverse problem related to the equilibrium problem (12) and (13). Elasticity tensors A, B are assumed to be constant. The inverse problem consists in finding displacement fields of the plates and the bridge together with an elasticity tensor A when assuming that additional data are provided by measurement. More precisely, it is assumed that for a given continuous function ξ, a value $\xi(w(x_0))$ is known, where $w(x_0)$ is the displacement of the plate at a given point $x_0 \in \Omega_2$, $x_0 \neq (2,0)$. In particular, we can assume that $\xi(w(x_0)) = w(x_0)$. Note that from a practical standpoint, it is no problem to provide measurements for finding a displacement $w(x_0)$ of the point x_0,; consequently, $\xi(w(x_0))$. We first introduce the 6D space with the Euclidean metric,

$$\mathbb{R}_{sym} = \{A = \{a_{ijkl}\} \mid a_{ijkl} = a_{jikl} = a_{klij},\ i,j,k,l = 1,2;\ a_{ijkl} \in \mathbb{R}\}.$$

Let $G \subset \mathbb{R}_{sym}$ be a bounded domain with a smooth boundary whose elements satisfy the inequality (1). Then, for any $A \in \bar{G}$ and the fixed tensor B it is possible to find a solution of the variational inequality

$$(v^A, w^A) \in S, \tag{69}$$

$$C_A(w^A, \bar{w} - w^A) - \int_{\Omega} f(\bar{w} - w^A) \tag{70}$$
$$+\int_b v^A_{,11}(\bar{v}_{,11} - v^A_{,11}) - \int_b g(\bar{v} - v^A) \geq 0 \ \ \forall (\bar{v},\bar{w}) \in S,$$

where $C_A = C$ with the given tensor A.

Now, we assume that the elasticity tensor A is unknown in the problems (69) and (70). On the other hand, the plate displacement of the point x_0 is known. Namely, $w(x_0)$ is known from a measurement. Then, the precise formulation of the inverse problem is as follows. Let $d \in \mathbb{R}$ be given. We have to find (v^A, w^A), $A \in \bar{G}$ such that

$$(v^A, w^A) \in S, \tag{71}$$

$$C_A(w^A, \bar{w} - w^A) - \int_\Omega f(\bar{w} - w^A) \tag{72}$$
$$+ \int_b v^A_{,11}(\bar{v}_{,11} - v^A_{,11}) - \int_b g(\bar{v} - v^A) \geq 0 \;\; \forall (\bar{v}, \bar{w}) \in S,$$

$$\xi(w^A(x_0)) = d. \tag{73}$$

Below, we prove the existence of a solution of the inverse problem (71)–(73).

Theorem 6. *$d_1, d_2 \in \mathbb{R}, d_1 \leq d_2$, exist such that for any fixed $d \in [d_1, d_2]$, the inverse problem* (71)–(73) *has a solution.*

Proof. We introduce a function L defined on the closed set $\bar{G}$,

$$L : \bar{G} \to \mathbb{R}, \; L(A) = \xi(w^A(x_0)), \tag{74}$$

where (v^A, w^A) is the solution of the direct problem (69) and (70) with the given elasticity tensor A. In what follows, we prove that this function is continuous on the set $\bar{G}$. Indeed, let $A^p \in \bar{G}$,

$$A^p \to A, \; A \in \bar{G}, \; p \to \infty, \tag{75}$$

where we use the convergence in the Euclidean norm $|\cdot|$. For any p, we can find the unique solution of the problem

$$(v^p, w^p) \in S, \tag{76}$$

$$C_p(w^p, \bar{w} - w^p) - \int_\Omega f(\bar{w} - w^p) \tag{77}$$
$$+ \int_b v^p_{,11}(\bar{v}_{,11} - v^p_{,11}) - \int_b g(\bar{v} - v^p) \geq 0 \;\; \forall (\bar{v}, \bar{w}) \in S,$$

where C_p fits the elasticity tensor A^p. The variational inequality (76) and (77) implies

$$C_p(w^p, w^p) - \int_\Omega f w^p + \int_b (v^p_{,11})^2 - \int_b g v^p = 0. \tag{78}$$

From (78), by the uniformity of this estimate in p, it follows that

$$\|(v^p, w^p)\|_W \leq c. \tag{79}$$

Choosing a subsequence, if necessary, we can assume that as $p \to \infty$,

$$(v^p, w^p) \to (v, w) \text{ weakly in } W. \tag{80}$$

By (75), (80), a passage to the limit in (76) and (77), as $p \to \infty$, is possible, and the limit relation reads as follows:

$$(v, w) \in S,$$

$$C_A(w, \bar{w} - w) - \int_\Omega f(\bar{w} - w)$$
$$+ \int_b v_{,11}(\bar{v}_{,11} - v_{,11}) - \int_b g(\bar{v} - v) \geq 0 \;\; \forall (\bar{v}, \bar{w}) \in S.$$

Consequently, we have $(v, w) = (v^A, w^A)$,

$$(v^A, w^A) \in S,$$

$$C_A(w^A, \bar{w} - w^A) - \int_\Omega f(\bar{w} - w^A)$$

$$+ \int_b v^A_{,11}(\bar{v}_{,11} - v^A_{,11}) - \int_b g(\bar{v} - v^A) \geq 0 \;\; \forall\, (\bar{v}, \bar{w}) \in S.$$

Moreover, by (80), we can assume that $w^p(x_0) \to w^A(x_0)$ as $p \to \infty$; consequently,

$$\xi(w^p(x_0)) \to \xi(w^A(x_0)).$$

We proved, therefore, that the function L is continuous on the compact set $\bar{G}$. By the Weierstrass extreme value theorem, this means that we can find

$$d_1 = \min_{A \in \bar{G}} L(A), \; d_2 = \max_{A \in \bar{G}} L(A).$$

Taking into account the intermediate value theorem for continuous functions, we conclude that for any $d \in [d_1, d_2]$ $A \in \bar{G}$ exists such that

$$L(A) = d.$$

This implies that the inverse problems (71) and (73) have a solution. Theorem 6 is proved. □

Note that similar arguments can be used for proving a solution existence to an inverse boundary problem with a different additional information compared to (73). In particular, instead of (73), we can consider

$$\xi(v^A(y_0)) = d,$$

where $y_0 \in (1, 2)$ is a given point, and v^A is the displacement of the bridge.

6. Conclusions

The paper presents a rigorous mathematical analysis of the elastic structure consisting of two Kirchhoff–Love plates and the crossing 1D bridge. An inequality-type restriction is imposed on the solution, which provides a mutual non-penetration between the plates and the bridge. This restriction implies that the boundary-value problem as a whole refers to the problem with unknown set of a contact. The solution existence of the problem is established, and asymptotic analysis is fulfilled with respect to the rigidity parameter of the bridge as this parameter tends to infinity and to zero. Therefore, in the frame of the high-level mathematical model, we provide a correctness of the boundary-value problem and analyze the limit mathematical models. Moreover, the existence of a solution to the inverse problem is proved, which allows us to find both the displacement field and the elasticity tensor of one plate provided that a displacement of the other plate at a given point is known.

Funding: This work was supported by Mathematical Center in Akademgorodok under agreement No. 075-15-2019-1613 with the Ministry of Science and Higher Education of the Russian Federation.

Data Availability Statement: Not applicable.

Conflicts of Interest: The authors declare no conflict of interest.

References

1. Khludnev, A.M.; Kovtunenko, V.A. *Analysis of Cracks in Solids*; WIT Press: Southampton, UK ; Boston, MA, USA, 2000.
2. Khludnev, A.M. *Elasticity Problems in Nonsmooth Domains*; Fizmatlit: Moscow, Russia, 2010.
3. Khludnev, A.M. Asymptotics of solutions for two elastic plates with thin junction. *Sib. Electr. Math. Rep.* **2022**, *19*, 484–501.
4. Caillerie, D. The effect of a thin inclusion of high rigidity in an elastic body. *Math. Methods Appl. Sci.* **1980**, *2*, 251–270. [CrossRef]
5. El Jarroudi, M. Homogenization of an elastic material reinforced with thin rigid von Karman ribbons. *Math. Mech. Solids* **2018**, *24*, 1–27. [CrossRef]
6. Lazarev, N.; Itou, H. Optimal location of a rigid inclusion in equilibrium problems for inhomogeneous Kirchhoff–Love plates with a crack. *Math. Mech. Solids* **2019**, *24*, 3743–3752. [CrossRef]
7. Khludnev, A.M.; Popova, T.S. Semirigid inclusions in elastic bodies: Mechanical interplay and optimal control. *Comp. Math. Appl. 2019*, *77*, 253–262. [CrossRef]
8. Lazarev, N. Shape sensitivity analysis of the energy integrals for the Timoshenko-type plate containing a crack on the boundary of a rigid inclusion. *Z. Angew. Math. Phys.* **2015**, *66*, 2025–2040. [CrossRef]
9. Rudoy, E.M. Domain decomposition method for crack problems with nonpenetration condition. *ESAIM Math. Model. Numer. Anal.* **2016**, *50*, 995–1009. [CrossRef]
10. Rudoy, E.M. On numerical solving a rigid inclusions problem in 2D elasticity. *Z. Angew Math. Phys.* **2017**, *68*, 19. [CrossRef]
11. Shcherbakov, V.V. Shape optimization of rigid inclusions in elastic plates with cracks. *Z. Angew. Math. Phys.* **2016**, *67*, 71. [CrossRef]
12. Shcherbakov, V.V. Energy release rates for interfacial cracks in elastic bodies with thin semirigid inclusions. *Z. Angew. Math. Phys.* **2017**, *68*, 26. [CrossRef]
13. Khludnev, A.M.; Leugering, G.R. Delaminated thin elastic inclusion inside elastic bodies. *Math. Mech. Complex Syst.* **2014**, *2*, 1–21. [CrossRef]
14. Mallick, P. *Fiber-Reinforced Composites: Materials, Manufacturing, and Design*; Marcel Dekker: New York, NY, USA, 1993.
15. Kozlov, V.A.; Ma'zya, V.G.; Movchan, A.B. *Asymptotic Analysis of Fields in a Multi-Structure*; Oxford Mathematical Monographs; Oxford University Press: New York, NY, USA, 1999.
16. Panasenko, G. *Multi-Scale Modelling for Structures and Composites*; Springer: New York, NY, USA, 2005.
17. Rudoy, E. Asymptotic justification of models of plates containing inside hard thin inclusions. *Technologies* **2020**, *8*, 59. [CrossRef]
18. Furtsev, A.; Rudoy, E. Variational approach to modeling soft and stiff interfaces in the Kirchhoff–Love theory of plates. *Int. J. Solids Struct.* **2020**, *202*, 562–574. [CrossRef]
19. Gaudiello, A.; Sili, A. Limit models for thin heterogeneous structures with high contrast. *J. Diff. Equat.* **2021**, *302*, 37–63. [CrossRef]
20. Furtsev, A.I. On contact between a thin obstacle and a plate containing a thin inclusion. *J. Math. Sci.* **2019**, *237*, 530–545. [CrossRef]
21. Furtsev, A.I. Differentiation of the energy functional with respect to the length of delamination in the problem of the contact of a plate and a beam. *Sib. Electr Math Rep.* **2018**, *15*, 935–949.
22. Pasternak, I.M. Plane problem of elasticity theory for anisotropic bodies with thin elastic inclusions. *J. Math. Sci.* **2012**, *186*, 31–47. [CrossRef]
23. Ballarini, R. Elastic stress diffusion around a thin corrugated inclusion. *IMA J. Appl. Math.* **2011**, *76*, 633–641. [CrossRef]
24. Dong, C.Y.; Kang, Y.L. Numerical analysis of doubly periodic array of cracks/rigid-line inclusions in an infinite isotropic medium using the boundary integral equation method. *Int. J. Fract.* **2005**, *133*, 389–405. [CrossRef]
25. Goudarzi, M.; Dal Corso, F.; Bigoni, D.; Simone, A. Dispersion of rigid line inclusions as stiffeners and shear band instability triggers. *Int. J. Solids Struct.* **2021**, *210–211*, 255–272. [CrossRef]
26. Saccomandi, G.; Beatty, M. Universal relations for fiber-reinforced elastic materials. *Math. Mech. Solids* **2002**, *7*, 99–110. [CrossRef]
27. Hu, K.X.; Chandra, A.; Huang, Y. On crack, rigid-line fiber, and interface interactions. *Mech. Mater.* **1994**, *19*, 15–28. [CrossRef]
28. Bellieud, M.; Bouchitte, G. Homogenization of a soft elastic material reinforced by fibers. *Asymptot. Anal.* **2002**, *32*, 153–183.
29. Pingle, P.; Sherwood, J.; Gorbatikh, L. Properties of rigid-line inclusions as building blocks of naturally occurring composites. *Compos. Sci. Technol.* **2008**, *68*, 2267–2272. [CrossRef]
30. Scutaru, M.L.; Vlase, S.; Marin M.; Modrea, A. New analytical method based on dynamic response of planar mechanical elastic systems. *Bound Value Probl.* **2020**, *1*, 104. [CrossRef]
31. Khludnev, A.M. Inverse problem for elastic body with thin elastic inclusion. *J. Inverse Ill-Posed Probl.* **2020**, *28*, 195–209. [CrossRef]
32. Khludnev, A.M.; Fankina, I.V. Equilibrium problem for elastic plate with thin rigid inclusion crossing an external boundary. *Z. Angew. Math. Phys.* **2021**, *72*, 121. [CrossRef]

axioms

Article

Monotonically Iterative Method for the Cantilever Beam Equations

Yujun Cui, Huiling Chen and Yumei Zou *

College of Mathematics and Systems Science, Shandong University of Science and Technology, Qingdao 266590, China
* Correspondence: skd993330@sdust.edu.cn

Abstract: In this paper, we consider the existence of extremal solutions for the nonlinear fourth-order differential equation. By use of a new comparison result, some sufficient conditions for the existence of extremal solutions are established by combining the monotone iterative technique and the methods of lower and upper solutions. Finally, an example is given to illustrate the validity of our main results.

Keywords: boundary value problem; comparison result; monotone iterative technique; lower and upper solutions

check for updates

Citation: Cui, Y.; Chen, H.; Zou, Y. Monotonically Iterative Method for the Cantilever Beam Equations. *Axioms* **2023**, *12*, 178. https://doi.org/10.3390/axioms12020178

Academic Editor: Tianwei Zhang

Received: 23 December 2022
Revised: 3 February 2023
Accepted: 6 February 2023
Published: 8 February 2023

1. Introduction

In this paper, we shall establish the existence of extremal solutions for the nonlinear fourth-order differential equation

$$\begin{cases} u^{(4)}(t) = f(t, u(t), u'(t)), \\ u(0) = u'(0) = u''(1) = u'''(1) = 0, \end{cases} \tag{1}$$

where $f \in C([0,1] \times \mathbb{R} \times \mathbb{R}, \mathbb{R})$.

Recently, differential equations of fourth-order have received more and more attention due to their various applications in science and engineering such as physics, control of dynamical systems etc. For example, The cantilever beam equation of problem (1) is a simplified mechanical model. This cantilever beam equation models the deformations of an elastic beam in equilibrium state, whose one end-point is fixed and the other is free [1,2]. Owing to its significance in physics, a number of works are devoted to the existence of solutions of fourth-order differential equations with different boundary conditions [3–14]. The methods used in these works are the Krasnosel'skii's fixed point theorem [3,4], critical point theorem [5], the contraction mapping principle [6–8], the topological degree theory [9,10] the fixed point index [10–12], the Ekeland variational principle [13], and bifurcation theory [14].

The existence of positive solutions for the simply fourth-order boundary value problem

$$\begin{cases} u^{(4)}(t) = f(t, u(t)), \ t \in (0,1), \\ u(0) = u'(0) = u''(1) = u'''(1) = 0, \end{cases} \tag{2}$$

which f does not contain any derivative terms has been discussed by several authors, see [2,15–17]. In References [15–17], (2) appears as a special case of the $(p, n-p)$ focal boundary value problems for $p = 2$ and $n = 4$. In all these works the Krasnoselskii's fixed point theorem are applied.

For the cantilever beam equation with a nonlinear boundary condition of third-order derivative

$$\begin{cases} u^{(4)}(t) = f(t, u(t)), \ t \in (0,1), \\ u(0) = u'(0) = u''(1), \ u'''(1) = g(u(1)), \end{cases} \tag{3}$$

the existence of solutions was considered by Ma [18] and Ma et al. [19] respectively based on variational methods and the contraction principle. The boundary condition in (3) may be interpreted in a material sense as the beam having a clamped end at $x = 0$ and a shear force resting on the bearing g at $x = 1$.

For the nonlinear fourth-order boundary value problem

$$\begin{cases} u^{(4)}(t) = f(t, u(t), u'(t)), \ t \in (0,1), \\ u(0) = u'(0) = u''(1) = u'''(1) = 0, \end{cases}$$

the existence of positive solutions has also been discussed by making use of the monotonically iterative technique and applying the successively approximate method, see [20].

Alves et al. [21] considered the cantilever beam equation

$$\begin{cases} u^{(4)}(t) = f(t, u(t), u'(t)), \ t \in (0,1), \\ u(0) = u'(0) = u''(1), \ u'''(1) = g(u(1)), \end{cases}$$

where $f : [0,1] \times [0, +\infty) \times [0, +\infty) \to [0, +\infty)$ is continuous. The existence of monotone positive solutions is obtained by using the monotone iteration method.

Many scholars have considered the case of the fourth-order boundary value problem that f contains the fully derivative terms

$$\begin{cases} u^{(4)}(t) = f(t, u, u', u'', u'''), \ t \in (0,1), \\ u(0) = u'(0) = u''(1) = u'''(1) = 0. \end{cases} \tag{4}$$

In [22], Li used the fixed point index theory in cones to obtain the existence results of problem (16) when $f(t, u_0, u_1, u_2, u_3)$ is superlinear or sublinear growth on u_0, u_1, u_2, u_3. In [23], Li and Chen extended the existence result by letting f may be superlinear growth and have negative value. Using the method of lower and upper solutions and the monotone iterative technique, some existence results are obtained in [24]. For fully fourth-order nonlinear BVPs with other boundary conditions, the existence of solutions has been discussed by the use of nonlinear analysis method such as the lower and upper solution method [25], Rus's contraction mapping [26], the monotone iterative technique [27], the Fourier analysis method and Leray-Schauder fixed point theorem [28]. However, the key to the application of the monotone iterative technique use in [21,24,27] is the monotonicity assumptions on nonlinearity f.

Inspired by the work mentioned above, the aim of this paper is to discuss the existence of extremal solutions to the boundary value problem of the nonlinear differential Equation (1) by the monotone iterative technique and the upper and lower solution method. According to the author's knowledge, it is the first application of this method to such problems under nomonotonicity assumptions on unknown function and monotonicity assumptions on the first order derivative of unknown function in nonlinearity. The paper is organized as follows. In Section 2, we present here the necessary lemmas and establish two new comparison results. In Section 3, we give the definitions of the upper and lower solutions and obtain the existence results of extremal solutions of the problems (1) and (2).

2. Preliminaries

In this sections, we present Green's function, some lemmas and comparison results that will be used to prove our main results.

Let $E = C[0,1]$ be a Banach space endowed with the maximum norm $\|u\| = \max_{0 \le t \le 1} |u(t)|$.

Lemma 1 ([21]). *For $\sigma \in C[0,1]$, the linear boundary value problem*

$$\begin{cases} u^{(4)}(t) = \sigma(t), \ t \in (0,1), \\ u(0) = a, u'(0) = b, u''(1) = c, u'''(1) = -d, \end{cases} \tag{5}$$

has the unique solution

$$u(t) = \int_0^1 G(t,s)\sigma(s)ds + d(\frac{t^2}{2} - \frac{t^3}{6}) + \frac{ct^2}{2} + bt + a,$$

where $G(t,s)$ is the Green's function defined by

$$G(t,s) = \begin{cases} \frac{1}{6}s^2(3t-s), & 0 \le s \le t \le 1, \\ \frac{1}{6}t^2(3s-t), & 0 \le t < s \le 1. \end{cases}$$

From the expression of G, we easily verify that $G_t(t,s)$, the partial derivative of $G(t,s)$ to t, is given by

$$G_t(t,s) = \begin{cases} \frac{1}{2}s^2, & 0 \le s \le t \le 1, \\ ts - \frac{1}{2}t^2, & 0 \le t < s \le 1. \end{cases}$$

Lemma 2 ([19,22]). *The following inequalities hold true.*

(1) $G(t,s) \le \frac{1}{2}s^2 t$ *and* $G(t,s) \le \frac{1}{2}t^2 s, \forall\, t,s \in [0,1]$,

(2) $G(t,s) \ge \frac{1}{3}t^2 s^2, \forall\, t,s \in [0,1]$,

(3) $G_t(t,s) \le ts, \forall\, t,s \in [0,1]$,

(4) $G_t(t,s) \ge \frac{1}{2}ts^2, \forall\, t,s \in [0,1]$.

Lemma 3. *Assume that the nonnegative constant M satisfies*

$$\frac{1}{8}M < 1, \tag{6}$$

the boundary value problem

$$\begin{cases} u^{(4)}(t) = -Mu(t) + \sigma(t), \ t \in (0,1), \\ u(0) = a, u'(0) = b, u''(1) = c, u'''(1) = -d \end{cases} \tag{7}$$

has the unique solution

$$u(t) = \psi(t) + \int_0^1 H(t,s)\sigma(s)ds + \int_0^1 Q(t,s)\psi(s)ds,$$

where

$$\psi(t) = d(\frac{t^2}{2} - \frac{t^3}{6}) + \frac{ct^2}{2} + bt + a,$$
$$K_1(t,s) = -MG(t,s),$$
$$K_m(t,s) = -M\int_0^1 G(t, r_{m-1})K_{m-1}(r_{m-1}, s)ds$$
$$= (-M)^m \int_0^1 \cdots \int_0^1 G(t, r_{m-1}) \cdots G(r_1, s)dr_1 \cdots dr_{m-1}, m \geq 2,$$
$$Q(t,s) = \sum_{m=1}^{+\infty} K_m(t,s),$$
$$H(t,s) = \int_0^1 Q(t,\tau)G(\tau,s)d\tau + G(t,s).$$

Proof. By Lemma 1, we know the solution of problem (7) as follows

$$u(t) = \int_0^1 G(t,s)(-Mu(s) + \sigma(s))ds + d(\frac{t^2}{2} - \frac{t^3}{6}) + \frac{ct^2}{2} + bt + a. \tag{8}$$

Define the operator $T : E \to E$ given by

$$(Tu)(t) = M\int_0^1 G(t,s)u(s)ds, \tag{9}$$

and let

$$\varphi(t) = \int_0^1 G(t,s)\sigma(s)ds.$$

It is clear that the operator T is a positive linear continuous operator, and we can rewrite (8) as

$$(I + T)u = \varphi + \psi, \tag{10}$$

where I stands for the identity operator. For any $u \in E$, by the definition of operator norm, it follows that

$$\begin{aligned} \|Tu\| &= \max_{t\in[0,1]} |Tu(t)| \leq \max_{t\in[0,1]} M\int_0^1 G(t,s)|u(s)|ds \\ &\leq \max_{t\in[0,1]} M\int_0^1 G(t,s)ds\|u\| = \max_{t\in[0,1]} M\Big(\frac{1}{24}t^4 - \frac{1}{6}t^3 + \frac{1}{4}t^2\Big)\|u\| \\ &= \frac{1}{8}M\|u\|. \end{aligned}$$

Note that $0 < \frac{1}{8}M < 1$, then we get

$$\|T\| \leq \frac{1}{8}M < 1.$$

Thus, the operator T is a contraction mapping. By Banach fixed-point theorem, T has a unique fixed point in E, or equivalently, the problem (7) has a unique solution $u \in E$.

It follows from the perturbation theorem of identity operator that $I + T$ has a bounded inverse operator

$$\begin{aligned} (I+T)^{-1} &= \sum_{i=0}^{+\infty}(-1)^i(T)^i \\ &= I - T + T^2 - \cdots + (-1)^i(T)^i + \cdots . \end{aligned}$$

Though direct calculation, we have

$$\begin{aligned}
(I\varphi)(t) &= \int_0^1 G(t,s)\sigma(s)ds,\\
(T\varphi)(t) &= M\int_0^1 G(t,\tau)d\tau\int_0^1 G(\tau,s)\sigma(s)ds = (-1)\int_0^1\left[\int_0^1 K_1(t,\tau)G(\tau,s)d\tau\right]\sigma(s)ds\\
(T^2\varphi)(t) &= M\int_0^1 G(t,r_1)(T\varphi)(r_1)dr_1\\
&= M^2\int_0^1 G(t,r_1)dr_1\int_0^1 G(r_1,\tau)d\tau\int_0^1 G(\tau,s)\sigma(s)ds\\
&= M^2\int_0^1\left[\int_0^1\left[\int_0^1 G(t,r_1)G(r_1,\tau)dr_1\right]G(\tau,s)d\tau\right]\sigma(s)ds\\
&= (-1)^2\int_0^1\left[\int_0^1 K_2(t,\tau)G(\tau,s)d\tau\right]\sigma(s)ds,
\end{aligned}$$

then, we can obtain

$$\begin{aligned}
(T^m\varphi)(t) &= M\int_0^1 G(t,r_{m-1})(T^{m-1}\varphi)(r_{m-1})dr_{m-1}\\
&= M^m\int_0^1 G(t,r_{m-1})dr_{m-1}\cdots\int_0^1 G(r_2,r_1)dr_1\int_0^1 G(r_1,\tau)d\tau\int_0^1 G(\tau,s)\sigma(s)ds\\
&= (-1)^m\int_0^1\left[\int_0^1 K_m(t,\tau)G(\tau,s)d\tau\right]\sigma(s)ds.
\end{aligned}$$

Thus, we have

$$\begin{aligned}
&[(I - T + T^2 + \cdots + (-1)^m T^m + \cdots)\varphi](t)\\
= &\int_0^1\left[G(t,s) + \int_0^1\sum_{m=1}^{+\infty} K_m(t,\tau)G(\tau,s)d\tau\right]\sigma(s)ds\\
= &\int_0^1 H(t,s)\sigma(s)ds.
\end{aligned}$$

Similarly, we can obtain

$$\begin{aligned}
(I\psi)(t) &= d\left(\frac{t^2}{2} - \frac{t^3}{6}\right) + \frac{ct^2}{2} + bt + a,\\
(T\psi)(t) &= M\int_0^1 G(t,s)\psi(s)ds = (-1)\int_0^1 K_1(t,s)\psi(s)ds,\\
(T^2\psi)(t) &= M^2\int_0^1\int_0^1 G(t,t_1)G(t_1,s)\psi(s)dt_1ds = (-1)^2\int_0^1 K_2(t,s)\psi(s)ds
\end{aligned}$$

and

$$\begin{aligned}
(T^m\psi)(t) &= M^m\int_0^1\cdots\int_0^1 G(t,t_{m-1})\cdots G(t_1,s)\psi(s)dt_{m-1}\cdots dt_1ds\\
&= (-1)^m\int_0^1 K_m(t,s)\psi(s)ds, \quad m \geq 2.
\end{aligned}$$

This is,

$$
\begin{aligned}
& [(I - T + T^2 + \cdots + (-1)^m T^m + \cdots)\psi](t) \\
= \; & \psi(t) + \int_0^1 \sum_{m=1}^{+\infty} K_m(t,s)\psi(s)ds, \\
= \; & \psi(t) + \int_0^1 Q(t,s)\psi(s)ds.
\end{aligned}
$$

Thus, we get the solution of problem (4)

$$u(t) = \psi(t) + \int_0^1 H(t,s)\sigma(s)ds + \int_0^1 Q(t,s)\psi(s)ds.$$

□

Remark 1. It follows from the proof of Lemma 3 that the series $\sum_{m=1}^{+\infty} K_m(t,s)$ converges uniformly on $[0,1] \times [0,1]$ and all functions $K_n(t,s)$, $Q(t,s)$, $H(t,s)$ are continuous on $[0,1] \times [0,1]$. Furthermore, by the differentiability of parametrized integrals, we obtain

$$
\begin{aligned}
Q_t(t,s) &= \sum_{m=1}^{+\infty} \frac{\partial K_m}{\partial t}(t,s) \\
&= -MG_t(t,s) - M \sum_{m=2}^{+\infty} \int_0^1 G_t(t, r_{m-1}) K_{m-1}(r_{m-1}, s)ds
\end{aligned}
$$

and

$$H_t(t,s) = \int_0^1 Q_t(t,\tau)G(\tau,s)d\tau + G_t(t,s).$$

This together with the expression of G_t implies that $Q_t(t,s)$, $H_t(t,s)$ are continuous on $[0,1] \times [0,1]$.

Define $F : C[0,1] \to C^1[0,1]$ by

$$(Fu)(t) = \int_0^1 H(t,s)u(s)ds. \tag{11}$$

Based on the continuity of functions H and H_t, standard arguments show that the following lemma hold.

Lemma 4. *F is complete continuous.*

Lemma 5. *(Comparison result) Assume $u \in C^4[0,1]$ satisfies*

$$
\begin{cases}
u^{(4)}(t) \geq -Mu(t), \; t \in (0,1), \\
u(0) = 0, u'(0) \geq 0, u''(1) \geq 0, u'''(1) \leq 0,
\end{cases}
$$

where the nonnegative constant M satisfying (6) and

$$\frac{1}{3} - \frac{M}{12} - \frac{2(\frac{M}{8})^3}{3[1-(\frac{M}{8})^2]} + \frac{(\frac{M}{15})^2}{3[1-(\frac{M}{15})^2]} \geq 0, \tag{12}$$

$$\frac{1}{3} - \frac{M}{6} - \frac{4(\frac{M}{8})^3}{3[1-(\frac{M}{8})^2]} + \frac{13(\frac{M}{15})^2}{36[1-(\frac{M}{15})^2]} \geq 0, \tag{13}$$

$$\frac{1}{2} - \frac{M}{6} - \frac{4(\frac{M}{8})^3}{3[1-(\frac{M}{8})^2]} + \frac{(\frac{M}{15})^2}{2[1-(\frac{M}{15})^2]} \geq 0, \tag{14}$$

$$\frac{1}{2} - \frac{M}{3} - \frac{8(\frac{M}{8})^3}{3[1-(\frac{M}{8})^2]} + \frac{13(\frac{M}{15})^2}{24[1-(\frac{M}{15})^2]} \geq 0, \tag{15}$$

then $u(t) \geq 0$ *and* $u'(t) \geq 0$ *for* $t \in [0,1]$.

Proof. Let $\sigma(t) = u^{(4)}(t) + Mu(t)$ and $a = u(0)$, $b = u'(0)$, $c = u''(1)$, $d = -u'''(1)$, then $\sigma(t) \geq 0$ for $t \in [0,1]$ and $a = 0, b \geq 0, c \geq 0, d \geq 0$. By Lemma 3, the linear problem (7) has a unique solution

$$u(t) = \psi(t) + \int_0^1 H(t,s)\sigma(s)ds + \int_0^1 Q(t,s)\psi(s)ds.$$

Moreover,

$$u'(t) = \psi'(t) + \int_0^1 H_t(t,s)\sigma(s)ds + \int_0^1 Q_t(t,s)\psi(s)ds.$$

Now, we consider $\int_0^1 H(t,s)\sigma(s)ds$ for $t \in [0,1]$. Let $m = 2k+1, k = 1,2,\cdots$, by Lemma 2, we have

$$\begin{aligned}
K_{2k+1}(t,s) &= -M^{2k+1}\int_0^1 \cdots \int_0^1 G(t,r_{2k})\cdots G(r_1,s)dr_1\cdots dr_{2k} \\
&\geq -M^{2k+1}\int_0^1 \cdots \int_0^1 (\frac{1}{2}t^2 \cdot r_{2k})(\frac{1}{2}r_{2k}^2 \cdot r_{2k-1})\cdots(\frac{1}{2}r_2^2 \cdot r_1)\cdot(\frac{1}{2}r_1 \cdot s^2)dr_1\cdots dr_{2k} \\
&= -\frac{16M^{2k+1}}{3\cdot 8^{2k+1}}t^2s^2.
\end{aligned}$$

Let $m = 2k, k = 1,2,\cdots$, we have

$$\begin{aligned}
K_{2k}(t,s) &= M^{2k}\int_0^1 \cdots \int_0^1 G(t,r_{2k-1})\cdots G(r_1,s)dr_1\cdots dr_{2k-1} \\
&\geq M^{2k}\int_0^1 \cdots \int_0^1 (\frac{1}{3}t^2 \cdot r_{2k-1}^2)\cdots(\frac{1}{3}r_2^2 \cdot r_1^2)(\frac{1}{3}r_1^2 \cdot s^2)dr_1\cdots dr_{2k-1} \\
&= \frac{5M^{2k}}{15^{2k}}t^2s^2.
\end{aligned}$$

Thus, we can gain

$$\begin{aligned}
H(t,s) &= \int_0^1 Q(t,\tau)G(\tau,s)d\tau + G(t,s) \\
&= \int_0^1 \sum_{m=1}^{+\infty} K_m(t,\tau)G(\tau,s)d\tau + G(t,s) \\
&\geq G(t,s) - M\int_0^1 G(t,\tau)G(\tau,s)d\tau + \sum_{m=1}^{+\infty}\int_0^1 K_{2m+1}(t,\tau)G(\tau,s)d\tau \\
&+ \sum_{m=1}^{+\infty}\int_0^1 K_{2m}(t,\tau)G(\tau,s)d\tau \\
&\geq \frac{1}{3}t^2s^2 - M\int_0^1 \left(\frac{1}{2}t^2\tau\right)\left(\frac{1}{2}\tau s^2\right)d\tau - \sum_{m=1}^{+\infty}\frac{16M^{2m+1}}{3\cdot 8^{2m+1}}\int_0^1 t^2\tau^2\left(\frac{1}{2}\tau s^2\right)d\tau \\
&+ \sum_{m=1}^{+\infty}\frac{5M^{2m}}{15^{2m}}\int_0^1 t^2\tau^2\left(\frac{1}{3}\tau^2 s^2\right)d\tau \\
&= \frac{1}{3}t^2s^2 - \frac{M}{12}t^2s^2 - \frac{2}{3}\sum_{m=1}^{+\infty}\frac{M^{2m+1}}{8^{2m+1}}t^2s^2 + \frac{1}{3}\sum_{m=1}^{+\infty}\frac{M^{2m}}{15^{2m}}t^2s^2.
\end{aligned}$$

Since $0 < \frac{1}{8}M < 1$ and $\sum\limits_{m=1}^{+\infty} \frac{M^{2m+1}}{8^{2m+1}}, \sum\limits_{m=1}^{+\infty} \frac{M^{2m}}{15^{2m}}$ is convergence, we get

$$H(t,s) \geq \left\{\frac{1}{3} - \frac{M}{12} - \frac{2(\frac{M}{8})^3}{3[1-(\frac{M}{8})^2]} + \frac{(\frac{M}{15})^2}{3[1-(\frac{M}{15})^2]}\right\} t^2 s^2.$$

By (12), we know $\int_0^1 H(t,s)\sigma(s)ds \geq 0$ for $t \in [0,1]$.

Next, we claim that $\psi(t) + \int_0^1 Q(t,s)\psi(s)ds \geq 0$ for $t \in [0,1]$. Let $n(t) = t, p(t) = \frac{t^2}{2}, q(t) = \frac{t^2}{2} - \frac{t^3}{6}$, then we have $\psi(t) = dq(t) + cp(t) + bn(t)$. By simple calculation and deduction, we can get

$$\begin{aligned}
& n(t) + \int_0^1 Q(t,s)n(s)ds \\
= \; & n(t) + \int_0^1 \sum_{m=1}^{+\infty} K_m(t,s)n(s)ds \\
= \; & t - M\int_0^1 G(t,s)n(s)ds + \sum_{m=1}^{+\infty}\int_0^1 K_{2m+1}(t,s)n(s)ds + \sum_{m=1}^{+\infty}\int_0^1 K_{2m}(t,s)n(s)ds \\
\geq \; & t^2 - M(\frac{t^3}{120} - \frac{t}{12} + \frac{1}{6})t^2 - \sum_{m=1}^{+\infty} \frac{16M^{2m+1}}{3\cdot 8^{2m+1}}\frac{t^2}{4} + \sum_{m=1}^{+\infty}\frac{5M^{2m}}{15^{2m}}\frac{t^2}{4} \\
\geq \; & \left\{1 - \frac{M}{6} - \frac{4(\frac{M}{8})^3}{3[1-(\frac{M}{8})^2]} + \frac{5(\frac{M}{15})^2}{4[1-(\frac{M}{15})^2]}\right\} t^2 \\
= \; & n_1(t) \geq 0,
\end{aligned}$$

$$\begin{aligned}
& p(t) + \int_0^1 Q(t,s)p(s)ds \\
= \; & p(t) + \int_0^1 \sum_{m=1}^{+\infty} K_m(t,s)p(s)ds \\
= \; & \frac{1}{2}t^2 - M\int_0^1 G(t,s)p(s)ds + \sum_{m=1}^{+\infty}\int_0^1 K_{2m+1}(t,s)p(s)ds + \sum_{m=1}^{+\infty}\int_0^1 K_{2m}(t,s)p(s)ds \\
\geq \; & \frac{1}{2}t^2 - M(\frac{t^4}{720} - \frac{t}{36} + \frac{1}{16})t^2 - \sum_{m=1}^{+\infty} \frac{16M^{2m+1}}{3\cdot 8^{2m+1}}\frac{t^2}{10} + \sum_{m=1}^{+\infty}\frac{5M^{2m}}{15^{2m}}\frac{t^2}{10} \\
\geq \; & \left\{\frac{1}{2} - \frac{M}{16} - \frac{8(\frac{M}{8})^3}{15[1-(\frac{M}{8})^2]} + \frac{(\frac{M}{15})^2}{2[1-(\frac{M}{15})^2]}\right\} t^2 \\
= \; & p_1(t) \geq 0,
\end{aligned}$$

and

$$
\begin{aligned}
& q(t)+\int_0^1 Q(t,s)q(s)ds \\
= \; & q(t)+\int_0^1 \sum_{m=1}^{+\infty} K_m(t,s)q(s)ds \\
= \; & (\frac{t^2}{2}-\frac{t^3}{6})-M\int_0^1 G(t,s)q(s)ds+\sum_{m=1}^{+\infty}\int_0^1 K_{2m+1}(t,s)q(s)ds+\sum_{m=1}^{+\infty}\int_0^1 K_{2m}(t,s)q(s)ds \\
\geq \; & \frac{3-t}{6}t^2-\frac{M}{120}(-\frac{t^5}{42}+\frac{t^4}{6}-\frac{5t}{2}+\frac{11}{2})t^2-\sum_{m=1}^{+\infty}\frac{16M^{2m+1}}{3\cdot 8^{2m+1}}\frac{13t^2}{180}+\sum_{m=1}^{+\infty}\frac{5M^{2m}}{15^{2m}}\frac{13t^2}{180} \\
\geq \; & \left\{\frac{1}{3}-\frac{11M}{240}-\frac{52(\frac{M}{8})^3}{135[1-(\frac{M}{8})^2]}+\frac{13(\frac{M}{15})^2}{36[1-(\frac{M}{15})^2]}\right\}t^2 \\
= \; & q_1(t)\geq 0.
\end{aligned}
$$

By (13), we have

$$
\begin{aligned}
& \psi(t)+\int_0^1 Q(t,s)\psi(s)ds \\
= \; & [dq(t)+cp(t)+bn(t)]+\int_0^1 Q(t,s)[dq(s)+cp(s)+bn(s)]ds \\
= \; & d[q(t)+\int_0^1 Q(t,s)q(s)ds]+c[p(t)+\int_0^1 Q(t,s)p(s)ds]+b[n(t)+\int_0^1 Q(t,s)n(s)ds] \\
\geq \; & bn_1(t)+cp_1(t)+dq_1(t)\geq 0.
\end{aligned}
$$

Thus, we can obtain that $u(t)\geq 0$ for $t\in[0,1]$.

Next, we consider $\int_0^1 H_t(t,s)\sigma(s)ds$ for $t\in[0,1]$. Let $m=2k+1, k=1,2,\cdots$, we gain

$$
\begin{aligned}
\frac{\partial K_{2k+1}(t,s)}{\partial t} &= -M^{2k+1}\int_0^1\cdots\int_0^1 G_t(t,r_{2k})\cdots G(r_1,s)dr_1\cdots dr_{2k} \\
&\geq -M^{2k+1}\int_0^1\cdots\int_0^1 (t\cdot r_{2k})(\frac{1}{2}r_{2k}\cdot r_{2k-1}^2)\cdots(\frac{1}{2}r_2\cdot r_1^2)(\frac{1}{2}r_1\cdot s^2)dr_1\cdots dr_{2k} \\
&= -\frac{32}{3}\frac{M^{2k+1}}{8^{2k+1}}ts^2.
\end{aligned}
$$

Let $m=2k, k=1,2,\cdots$, we obtain

$$
\begin{aligned}
\frac{\partial K_{2k}(t,s)}{\partial t} &= M^{2k}\int_0^1\cdots\int_0^1 G_t(t,r_{2k-1})\cdots G(r_1,s)dr_1\cdots dr_{2k-1} \\
&\geq M^{2k}\int_0^1\cdots\int_0^1 (\frac{1}{2}t\cdot r_{2k-1}^2)(\frac{1}{3}r_{2k-1}^2\cdot r_{2k-2}^2)\cdots(\frac{1}{3}r_1^2\cdot s^2)dr_1\cdots dr_{2k-1} \\
&= \frac{15M^{2k}}{2\cdot 15^{2k}}ts^2.
\end{aligned}
$$

Therefore, we know

$$\begin{aligned}
H_t(t,s) &= \int_0^1 Q_t(t,\tau)G(\tau,s)d\tau + G_t(t,s) \\
&= \int_0^1 \sum_{m=1}^{+\infty} \frac{\partial K_m(t,\tau)}{\partial t} G(\tau,s)d\tau + G_t(t,s) \\
&\geq G_t(t,s) - M\int_0^1 G_t(t,\tau)G(\tau,s)d\tau + \sum_{m=1}^{+\infty}\int_0^1 \frac{\partial K_{2m+1}(t,\tau)}{\partial t}G(\tau,s)d\tau \\
&+ \sum_{m=1}^{+\infty}\int_0^1 \frac{\partial K_{2m}(t,\tau)}{\partial t}G(\tau,s)d\tau \\
&\geq \frac{1}{2}ts^2 - \frac{M}{6}ts^2 - \frac{4}{3}\sum_{m=1}^{+\infty}\frac{M^{2m+1}}{8^{2m+1}}ts^2 + \frac{1}{2}\sum_{m=1}^{+\infty}\frac{M^{2m}}{15^{2m}}ts^2.
\end{aligned}$$

Since $0 < \frac{1}{8}M < 1$ and $\sum\limits_{m=1}^{+\infty}\frac{M^{2m+1}}{8^{2m+1}}, \sum\limits_{m=1}^{+\infty}\frac{M^{2m}}{15^{2m}}$ is convergence, we get

$$H_t(t,s) \geq \left\{\frac{1}{2} - \frac{M}{6} - \frac{4(\frac{M}{8})^3}{3[1-(\frac{M}{8})^2]} + \frac{(\frac{M}{15})^2}{2[1-(\frac{M}{15})^2]}\right\}ts^2.$$

By (14), we know $\int_0^1 H_t(t,s)\sigma(s)ds \geq 0$ for $t \in [0,1]$.

Lastly, we consider $\psi'(t) + \int_0^1 Q_t(t,s)\psi(s)ds$ for $t \in [0,1]$, where $\psi_t(t) = dq'(t) + cp'(t) + bn'(t)$. Though calculation and deduction, we have

$$\begin{aligned}
& n'(t) + \int_0^1 Q_t(t,s)n(s)ds \\
= \;& n'(t) + \int_0^1 \sum_{m=1}^{+\infty}\frac{\partial K_m(t,s)}{\partial t}n(s)ds \\
= \;& 1 - M\int_0^1 G_t(t,s)sds + \sum_{m=1}^{+\infty}\int_0^1 \frac{\partial K_{2m+1}(t,s)}{\partial t}n(s)ds + \sum_{m=1}^{+\infty}\int_0^1\frac{\partial K_{2m}(t,s)}{\partial t}n(s)ds \\
\geq \;& 1 - M(\frac{t^3}{24} - \frac{t}{4} + \frac{1}{3})t - \sum_{m=1}^{+\infty}\frac{32M^{2m+1}}{3\cdot 8^{2m+1}}\frac{t}{4} + \sum_{m=1}^{+\infty}\frac{15M^{2m}}{2\cdot 15^{2m}}\frac{t}{4} \\
\geq \;& \left\{1 - \frac{M}{3} - \frac{8(\frac{M}{8})^3}{3[1-(\frac{M}{8})^2]} + \frac{15(\frac{M}{15})^2}{8[1-(\frac{M}{15})^2]}\right\}t \\
= \;& n_2(t) \geq 0,
\end{aligned}$$

$$\begin{aligned}
& p'(t) + \int_0^1 Q_t(t,s)p(s)ds \\
= \;& p'(t) + \int_0^1 \sum_{m=1}^{+\infty}\frac{\partial K_m(t,s)}{\partial t}p(s)ds \\
= \;& t - M\int_0^1 G_t(t,s)\frac{s^2}{2}ds + \sum_{m=1}^{+\infty}\int_0^1 \frac{\partial K_{2m+1}(t,s)}{\partial t}p(s)ds + \sum_{m=1}^{+\infty}\int_0^1\frac{\partial K_{2m}(t,s)}{\partial t}p(s)ds \\
\geq \;& t - M(\frac{t^4}{120} - \frac{t}{12} + \frac{1}{8})t - \sum_{m=1}^{+\infty}\frac{32M^{2m+1}}{3\cdot 8^{2m+1}}\frac{t}{10} + \sum_{m=1}^{+\infty}\frac{15M^{2m}}{2\cdot 15^{2m}}\frac{t}{10} \\
\geq \;& \{1 - \frac{M}{8} - \frac{16(\frac{M}{8})^3}{15[1-(\frac{M}{8})^2]} + \frac{3(\frac{M}{15})^2}{4[1-(\frac{M}{15})^2]}\}t \\
= \;& p_2(t) \geq 0
\end{aligned}$$

and

$$
\begin{aligned}
& q'(t) + \int_0^1 Q_t(t,s) q(s) ds \\
= \; & q'(t) + \int_0^1 \sum_{m=1}^{+\infty} \frac{\partial K_m(t,s)}{\partial t} q(s) ds \\
= \; & (t - \frac{t^2}{2}) - M \int_0^1 G_t(t,s) ds + \sum_{m=1}^{+\infty} \int_0^1 \frac{\partial K_{2m+1}(t,s)}{\partial t} q(s) ds + \sum_{m=1}^{+\infty} \int_0^1 \frac{\partial K_{2m}(t,s)}{\partial t} q(s) ds \\
\geq \; & (1 - \frac{t}{2}) t - \frac{M}{6} (-\frac{t^5}{120} + \frac{t^4}{20} - \frac{3t}{8} + \frac{11}{20}) t - \sum_{m=1}^{+\infty} \frac{32 M^{2m+1}}{3 \cdot 8^{2m+1}} \frac{13t}{180} + \sum_{m=1}^{+\infty} \frac{15 M^{2m}}{2 \cdot 15^{2m}} \frac{13t}{180} \\
\geq \; & \{ \frac{1}{2} - \frac{11M}{120} - \frac{104(\frac{M}{8})^3}{135[1 - (\frac{M}{8})^2]} + \frac{13(\frac{M}{15})^2}{24[1 - (\frac{M}{15})^2]} \} t \\
= \; & q_2(t) \geq 0.
\end{aligned}
$$

By (15), we get

$$
\begin{aligned}
& \psi'(t) + \int_0^1 Q_t(t,s) \psi(s) ds \\
& = [dq'(t) + cp'(t) + bn'(t)] + \int_0^1 Q_t(t,s) [dq'(t) + cp'(t) + bn'(t)] ds \\
& = d[q'(t) + \int_0^1 Q_t(t,s) q'(t) ds] + c[p'(t) + \int_0^1 Q_t(t,s) p'(t) ds] + b[n'(t) + \int_0^1 Q_t(t,s) n'(t) ds] \\
& \geq dq_2(t) + cp_2(t) + bn_2(t) \geq 0.
\end{aligned}
$$

Thus, we can obtain that $u'(t) \geq 0$ for $t \in [0,1]$. □

If the condition $u(0) = 0$ replaced by $u(0) \geq 0$, the result in Lemma 5 may be invalid. However, similar to the proof of Lemma 5, we have the following comparison result.

Lemma 6. *Assume $u \in C^4[0,1]$ satisfies*

$$
\begin{cases} u^{(4)}(t) \geq -Mu(t), \; t \in (0,1), \\ u(0) \geq 0, u'(0) \geq 0, u''(1) \geq 0, u'''(1) \leq 0, \end{cases}
$$

where the nonnegative constant M satisfying (6), (12) and

$$
\frac{1}{3} - \frac{M}{4} - \frac{16(\frac{M}{8})^3}{9[1 - (\frac{M}{8})^2]} + \frac{13(\frac{M}{15})^2}{36[1 - (\frac{M}{15})^2]} \geq 0, \tag{16}
$$

then $u(t) \geq 0$ for $t \in [0,1]$.

3. Main Results

Definition 1. *A function $v \in C^4[0,1]$ is called a lower solution of problem (1) if it satisfies*

$$
\begin{cases} v^{(4)}(t) \leq f(t, v(t), v'(t)), \; t \in (0,1), \\ v(0) = 0, v'(0) \leq 0, v''(1) \leq 0, v'''(1) \geq 0. \end{cases}
$$

Definition 2. *A function $w \in C^4[0,1]$ is called a upper solution of problem (1) if it satisfies*

$$
\begin{cases} w^{(4)}(t) \geq f(t, w(t), w'(t)), \; t \in (0,1), \\ w(0) = 0, w'(0) \geq 0, w''(1) \geq 0, w'''(1) \leq 0. \end{cases}
$$

For $v_0, w_0 \in C^1[0,1]$, we write $v_0 \leq w_0$ if and only if $v_0(t) \leq w_0(t)$ and $v_0'(t) \leq w_0'(t)$ for all $t \in [0,1]$. In such a case, we denote

$$
[v_0, w_0] = \{u \in C^1[0,1] : \; v_0(t) \leq u(t) \leq w_0(t), v_0'(t) \leq u'(t) \leq w_0'(t) \; t \in [0,1]\}.
$$

In the following, we list the assumptions to be used throughout our main results.

(H_1) Assume that the functions v_0, w_0 are lower and upper solutions of the problem (1) respectively, and $v_0 \leq w_0$.

(H_2) For fixed $(t, x) \in [0,1] \times [\min_{t\in[0,1]} v_0(t), \max_{t\in[0,1]} w_0(t)]$, $f(t, x, y)$ is monotone nondecreasing to y.

(H_3) The function $f \in C([0,1] \times \mathbb{R} \times \mathbb{R}, \mathbb{R})$ satisfies

$$f(t, x, z) - f(t, y, z) \geq -M(x - y)$$

where $M > 0$ satisfying Lemma 5 and $v_0(t) \leq y \leq x \leq w_0(t), v_0'(t) \leq z \leq w_0'(t), t \in [0,1]$.

Theorem 1. *Assume that M satisfies (H_1), (H_2) and (H_3). Then there exist monotone sequences $\{v_n(t)\}, \{w_n(t)\}$ which converge in $C^1[0,1]$ to the extremal solutions of the problem (1) in $[v_0, w_0]$, respectively.*

Proof. For any $\alpha \in [v_0, w_0]$, we consider the following problem:

$$\begin{cases} u^{(4)}(t) = M(\alpha(t) - u(t)) + f(t, \alpha(t), \alpha'(t)), \ \ t \in (0,1), \\ u(0) = u'(0) = u''(1) = u'''(1) = 0. \end{cases} \tag{17}$$

From the proof of Lemma 1, the problem (17) has a unique solution $u \in E$, which can be expressed as

$$u(t) = \int_0^1 H(t,s)[f(s, \alpha(s), \alpha'(s)) + M\alpha(s)]ds.$$

Define an operator $A : [v_0, w_0] \to C^1[0,1]$ written as

$$A\alpha(t) = \int_0^1 H(t,s)[f(s, \alpha(s), \alpha'(s)) + M\alpha(s)]ds.$$

So, $u \in [v_0, w_0]$ is a solution of the problem (17) if and only if $u \in [v_0, w_0]$ is the fixed point of A.

Define a Nemytsky operator $Q : [v_0, w_0] \to C[0,1]$ written as

$$Q\alpha(t) = f(t, \alpha(t), \alpha'(t)) + M\alpha(t), \ \ \alpha \in [v_0, w_0].$$

Obviously, $A = F \circ Q$ and A is compact. Moreover, the operator A has the following properties:

(i) $v_0 \leq Av_0, Aw_0 \leq w_0$;

(ii) $Ay_1 \leq Ay_2$, if $v_0 \leq y_1 \leq y_2 \leq w_0$.

To prove (i), let $\alpha = v_0, v_1 = Av_0$, and $p = v_1 - v_0$. Then from condition (H_1) and the definition of the lower solution, we obtain

$$\begin{cases} p^{(4)}(t) & \geq -Mv_1(t) + f(t, v_0(t), v_0'(t)) + Mv_0 - f(t, v_0(t), v_0'(t)) \\ & = -Mp(t), \\ p(0) & = 0, p'(0) \geq 0, p''(1) \geq 0, p'''(1) \leq 0. \end{cases}$$

Then, from Lemma 5, we get $p(t) \geq 0, p'(t) \geq 0$ for $t \in [0,1]$, that is, $v_0 \leq Av_0$. Similarly, we can prove that $Aw_0 \leq w_0$.

To prove (ii), let $y_1, y_2 \in [v_0, w_0]$ with $y_1 \leq y_2$. Suppose that $u_1 = Ay_1, u_2 = Ay_2$. Let $p = u_2 - u_1$. By condition (H_3), we get

$$\begin{cases} p^4(t) &= f(t, y_2(t), y_2'(t)) - f(t, y_1(t), y_1'(t)) + M(y_2(t) - y_1(t)) \\ & \quad -Mu_2(t) + Mu_1(t) \\ &\geq f(t, y_2(t), y_1'(t)) - f(t, y_1(t), y_1'(t)) + M(y_2(t) - y_1(t)) \\ & \quad -Mu_2(t) + Mu_1(t) \geq -Mp(t), \\ p(0) &= p'(0) = p''(1) = p'''(1) = 0. \end{cases}$$

By Lemma 5, we deduce $p(t) \geq 0, p'(t) \geq 0$ which implies $Ay_1 \leq Ay_2$. Therefore, A is a monotone operator on $[v_0, w_0]$.

Let $v_m = Av_{m-1}, w_m = Aw_{m-1}$, by (i) and (ii), we have

$$v_0(t) \leq v_1(t) \leq v_2(t) \leq \cdots \leq v_m(t) \leq \cdots \leq w_m(t) \leq \cdots \leq w_2(t) \leq w_1(t) \leq w_0(t),$$

and

$$v_0'(t) \leq v_1'(t) \leq v_2'(t) \leq \cdots \leq v_m'(t) \leq \cdots \leq w_m'(t) \leq \cdots \leq w_2'(t) \leq w_1'(t) \leq w_0'(t).$$

Note that $\{v_m(t)\}$ and $\{v_m'(t)\}$ are monotone nondecreasing and are bounded from above, and that $\{w_m(t)\}$ and $\{w_m'(t)\}$ are monotone nonincreasing and are bounded from below. Then, by the completely continuity of operator A and $v_m(0) = w_m(0) = 0$ for all $m \in \mathbb{N}$, we obtain

$$\lim_{n\to\infty} v_n(t) = v_*(t), \ \lim_{n\to\infty} w_n(t) = w^*(t)$$
$$\lim_{n\to\infty} v_n'(t) = v_*'(t), \ \lim_{n\to\infty} w_n'(t) = w^{*\prime}(t)$$

uniformly on $[0,1]$, respectively. And the limit functions $v_*, w^* \in [v_0, w_0]$ are solutions of the problem (1).

In the following, we prove v_*, w^* are extremal solutions of the problem (1) in $[v_0, w_0]$. Let $u \in [v_0, w_0]$ be a solution of the problem (1). In view of the monotonicity of A and $u = Au$, we conclude

$$v_0 \leq v_1 = Av_0 \leq Au = u \leq w_1 = Aw_0 \leq w_0,$$

which yields

$$v_0 \leq v_m \leq u \leq w_m \leq w_0, \ \ m = 1, 2, \ldots.$$

Therefore, we have $v_0 \leq v_* \leq u \leq w^* \leq w_0$. This shows v_* and w^* are minimal solution and maximal solution of the problem (1) in $[v_0, w_0]$, respectively. This ends the proof. □

For the boundary value problem (2), appears as the special case of problem (1) that f does not contain first-order derivative term, the definition of the upper and lower solutions can be weakened.

Definition 3 ([24])**.** *A function $v \in C^4[0,1]$ is called a lower solution of problem (2) if it satisfies*

$$\begin{cases} v^{(4)}(t) \leq f(t, v(t)), \ \ t \in (0,1), \\ v(0) \leq 0, v'(0) \leq 0, v''(1) \leq 0, v'''(1) \geq \ 0. \end{cases}$$

Definition 4 ([24])**.** *A function $w \in C^4[0,1]$ is called a upper solution of problem (2) if it satisfies*

$$\begin{cases} w^{(4)}(t) \geq f(t, w(t)), \ \ t \in (0,1), \\ w(0) \geq 0, w'(0) \geq 0, w''(1) \geq 0, w'''(1) \leq \ 0. \end{cases}$$

Based on Lemma 6, we present the existence of extremal solutions for problem (2).

Theorem 2. *Assume that* $f : [0,1] \times \mathbb{R} \to \mathbb{R}$ *is continuous, problem (2) has a lower solution* v_0 *and an upper solution* w_0 *with* $v_0(t) \leq w_0(t)$ *for* $t \in [0,1]$, *and* f *satisfies the following condition:*

$$f(t,x) - f(t,y) \geq -M(x-y)$$

where $M > 0$ *satisfying Lemma 6 and* $v_0(t) \leq y \leq x \leq w_0(t), t \in [0,1]$. *Then there exist monotone sequences* $\{v_n(t)\}, \{w_n(t)\}$ *which converge in* $C[0,1]$ *to the extremal solutions of the problem (2) in* $[v_0, w_0]$, *respectively.*

4. Example

Consider the problem

$$\begin{cases} u^{(4)} = -\frac{7}{15}(\frac{t^3}{6}+u)^3 + \frac{7}{30}t^4 \sin u + \frac{7}{45}(\frac{u'}{2})^6 + \frac{7}{90}t^6, \\ u(0) = u'(0) = u''(1) = u'''(1) = 0, \end{cases} \tag{18}$$

Take $f(t,u,v) = -\frac{7}{15}(\frac{t^3}{6}+u)^3 + \frac{7}{30}t^4 \sin u + \frac{7}{45}(\frac{v}{2})^6 + \frac{7}{90}t^6$, $v_0(t) = 0$ and $w_0(t) = t^2 - \frac{t^3}{6}$, then we have

$$\begin{cases} v_0^{(4)}(t) = 0 \leq \frac{7}{90}t^6(1-t^3) = f(t, v_0(t), v_0'(t)), \\ v_0(0) = 0, v_0'(0) \leq 0, v_0''(1) \leq 0, v_0'''(1) \geq 0 \end{cases}$$

and

$$\begin{cases} w_0^{(4)}(t) = 0 \geq -\frac{7}{15}t^6 + \frac{7}{30}t^4 \sin(t^2 - \frac{t^3}{6}) + \frac{7}{45}(t - \frac{t^2}{4})^6 + \frac{7}{90}t^6 = f(t, w_0(t), w_0'(t)), \\ w_0(0) = 0, w_0'(0) \geq 0, w_0''(1) \geq 0, w_0'''(1) \leq 0. \end{cases}$$

It shows that condition (H_1) of Theorem 1 holds.

Note that the definition of f, f is monotone nondecreasing to $y \in [v_0', w_0']$ for fixed $(t,x) \in [0,1] \times [v_0, w_0]$. Therefore, the condition (H_2) of Theorem 1 holds.

Let $M = \frac{7}{5}$. Then, for $v_0(t) \leq y \leq x \leq w_0(t), v_0'(t) \leq z \leq w_0'(t), t \in [0,1]$,

$$\begin{aligned} & f(t,x,z) - f(t,y,z) \\ &= -\frac{7}{15}[(\frac{t^3}{6}+x)^3 - (\frac{t^3}{6}+y)^3] + \frac{7}{30}t^4(\sin x - \sin y) \\ &\geq -\frac{7}{5}(x-y), \end{aligned}$$

where $M > 0$ satisfying Lemma 5. Thus, the condition (H_3) of Theorem 1 holds.

In consequence, the problem (18) has the extremal solutions in $[v_0, w_0]$.

5. Conclusions

In this article, on a cantilever beam equation models the deformations of an elastic beam, we use the monotone iterative technique and the methods of lower and upper solutions to investigate the existence results for extremal solutions for problems (1) and (2). At the same time, two sequences are obtained for approximating the extremal solutions of the nonlinear fourth-order differential equation. It should be noted that the proof of comparison result does depend on the the perturbation theorem of identity operator. In the future, we will continue to use the monotone iterative technique to investigate problems (1) under nomonotonicity assumptions on u and v in nonlinearity $f(t,u,v)$.

Author Contributions: Investigation and formal analysis, Y.C. and H.C.; writing-original draft, H.C.; writing-review and editing, Y.C. and Y.Z. All authors have read and agreed to the published version of the manuscript.

Funding: This project was supported by the National Natural Science Foundation of China (11571207), the Shandong Natural Science Foundation (ZR2018MA011).

Institutional Review Board Statement: Not applicable.

Informed Consent Statement: Not applicable.

Data Availability Statement: Not applicable.

Conflicts of Interest: The authors declare no conflict of interest.

References

1. Aftabizadeh, A.R. Existence and uniqueness theorems for fourth-order boundary value problems. *J. Math. Anal. Appl.* **1986**, *116*, 415–426. [CrossRef]
2. Agarwal, R.P. *Boundary Value Problems for Higher Order Differential Equations*, 3rd ed.; World Scientific: Singapore, 1986.
3. Bai, Z. Positive solutions of some nonlocal fourth-order boundary value problem. *Appl. Math. Comput.* **2010**, *215*, 4191–4197. [CrossRef]
4. Hao, X.; Xu, N.; Liu, L. Existence and uniqueness of positive solutions for fourth-order m-point boundary value problems with two parameters. *Rocky Mt. J.Math.* **2013**, *43*, 1161–1180. [CrossRef]
5. Cabada, A.; Tersian, S. Multiplicity of solutions of a two point boundary value problem for a fourth-order equation. *Appl. Math. Comput.* **2013**, *219*, 5261–5267. [CrossRef]
6. Dang, Q.A.; Ngo, K.Q. New fixed point approach for a fully nonlinear fourth order boundary value problem. *Bol. Soc. Parana. Mat.* **2018**, *36*, 209–223 .
7. Dang, Q.A.; Nguyen, T.H. The unique solvability and approximation of BVP for a nonlinear fourth order Kirchhoff type equation. *East Asian J. Appl. Math.* **2018**, *8*, 323–335.
8. Dang, Q.; Quy, N. Existence results and iterative method for solving the cantilever beam equation with fully nonlinear term. *Nonlinear Anal. RWA* **2017**, *36*, 56–68. [CrossRef]
9. Fan, W.; Hao, X.; Liu, L.; Wu, Y. Nontrivial solutions of singular fourth-order Sturm-Liouville boundary value problems with a sign-changing nonlinear term. *Appl. Math. Comput.* **2011**, *217*, 6700–6708. [CrossRef]
10. Zhang, K. Nontrivial solutions of fourth-order singular boundary value problems with sign-changing nonlinear terms. *Topol. Methods Nonl. An.* **2012**, *40*, 53–70.
11. Infante, G.; Pietramala, P. A cantilever equation with nonlinear boundary conditions. *Electron. J. Qual. Theory Differ. Equ.* **2009**, *15*, 14. [CrossRef]
12. Ma, Y.Y.; Yin, C.; Zhang, G. Positive solutions of fourth-order problems with dependence on all derivatives in nonlinearity under Stieltjes integral boundary conditions. *Bound. Value Prob.* **2019**, *2019*, 41. [CrossRef]
13. Ma, T. Existence results and numerical solutions for a beam equation with nonliear boundary conditions. *Appl. Numer. Math.* **2003**, *47*, 189–196. [CrossRef]
14. Liu, Y.; O'Regan, D. Multiplicity results for a class of fourth order semipositone m-point boundary value problems. *Appl. Anal.* **2012**, *91*, 911–921. [CrossRef]
15. Agarwal, R.P.; O'Regan, D. Twin solutions to singular boundary value problems. *Proc. Am. Math. Soc.* **2000**, *128*, 2085–2094. [CrossRef]
16. Agarwal, R.P.; O'Regan, D.; Lakshmikantham, V. Singular $(p, n-p)$ focal and (n, p) higher order boundary value problems. *Nonlinear Anal.* **2000**, *42*, 215–228. [CrossRef]
17. Agarwal, R.P. Multiplicity results for singular conjugate, focal and (n, p) problems. *J. Differ. Equ.* **2001**, *170*, 142–156. [CrossRef]
18. Ma, T.F. Positive solutions for a beam equation on a nonlinear elastic foundation. *Math. Comput. Model.* **2004**, *39*, 1195–1201.
19. Alves, E.; Ma, T.F.; Pelicer, M.L. Monotone positive solutions for a fourth order equation with nonlinear boundary conditions. *Nonlinear Anal.* **2009**, *71*, 3834–3841. [CrossRef]
20. Yao, Q. Monotonically iterative method of nonlinear cantilever beam equations. *Appl. Math. Comput.* **2008**, *205*, 432–437.
21. Ma, T.F.; da Silva, J. Iterative solutions for a beam equation with nonlinear boundary conditions of third order. *Appl. Math. Comput.* **2004**, *159*, 11–18. [CrossRef]
22. Li, Y. Existence of positive solutios for the cantilever beam equations with fully nonlinear terms. *Nonlinear Anal-Real.* **2016**, *27*, 221–237. [CrossRef]
23. Li, Y.; Chen, X. Solvability for fully cantilever beam equations with superlinear nonlinearities. *Bound. Value Probl.* **2019**, *2019*, 83. [CrossRef]
24. Li, Y.; Gao, Y. The method of lower and upper solutions for the cantilever beam equations with fully nonlinear terms. *J. Inequal. Appl.* **2019**, *2019*, 136. [CrossRef]

25. Bai, Z. The upper and lower solution method for some fourth-order boundary value problems. *Nonlinear Anal-Theor.* **2007**, *67*, 1704–1709. [CrossRef]
26. Almuthaybiri, S.S.; Tisdell, C.C. Sharper existence and uniqueness results for solutions to fourth-order boundary value problems and elastic beam analysis. *Open Math.* **2020**, *18*, 1006–1024. [CrossRef]
27. Wei, M.; Li, Y.; Li, G. Lower and upper solutions method to the fully elastic cantilever beam equation with support. *Adv. Differ. Equ.* **2021**, *2021*, 301. [CrossRef]
28. Li, Y.; Liang, Q. Existence results for a fully fourth-order boundary value problem. *J. Funct. Spaces* **2013**, *2013*, 641617. [CrossRef]

axioms

Article

Probing the Oscillatory Behavior of Internet Game Addiction via Diffusion PDE Model

Kaihong Zhao

Department of Mathematics, School of Electronics & Information Engineering, Taizhou University, Taizhou 318000, China; zhaokaihongs@126.com

Abstract: We establish a non-linear diffusion partial differential equation (PDE) model to depict the dynamic mechanism of Internet gaming disorder (IGD). By constructing appropriate super- and sub-solutions and applying Schauder's fixed point theorem and continuation method, we study the existence and asymptotic stability of traveling wave solutions to probe into the oscillating behavior of IGD. An example is numerically simulated to examine the correctness of our outcomes.

Keywords: Internet game addiction; nonlinear diffusion PDE model; super- and sub-solutions; traveling wave; existence and stability

MSC: 35B35; 35K57; 35Q92; 92D25

check for updates

Citation: Zhao, K. Probing the Oscillatory Behavior of Internet Game Addiction via Diffusion PDE Model. *Axioms* **2022**, *11*, 649. https://doi.org/10.3390/axioms11110649

Academic Editor: Tianwei Zhang

Received: 11 October 2022
Accepted: 15 November 2022
Published: 16 November 2022

1. Introduction

1.1. Background and Model

In the past decade, with the continuous popularization of the Internet, the number of Internet users has increased sharply. The convenience and other benefits of the Internet are obvious to all. However, there is also some harmful content on the Internet, such as pornography, violence, online games and so on. In particular, various types of Internet games are full of major Internet websites with legal identities. These Internet games have attracted a large number of game players, especially teenagers. Many game players become addicted to Internet games. People with Internet gaming addiction tend to be impulsive, violent, misanthropic and withdrawn. This not only brings great harm to the physical and mental health of Internet game addicts but also endangers society and their families. In recent years, the number of Internet game addicts has continued to rise. This phenomenon has been widely concerning and studied. The World Health Organization [1] has pointed out that Internet game addiction is a new disease. The disease is named Internet gaming disorder (IGD) and is characterized by "Persistent and recurrent use of the Internet to engage in games, often with other players, leading to clinically significant impairment or distress" [2]. IGD is often referred to as a mental illness. The Diagnostic and Statistical Manual of Mental Disorders [3,4] provides some classifications of IGD. In order to cure and reduce the number of people with IGD, scholars from all walks of life have begun to study IGD from various aspects. Some researchers [5–9] use mathematical theories and methods to study IGD by establishing mathematical models.

In this context, we also try to use calculus methods to establish a differential equation model to study IGD. To this end, we make the underlying assumptions as follows:

(i) Internet game players are simply divided into two categories: moderate gamers M and addictive gamers A;
(ii) Because it is very difficult to stop playing games through self-control, Internet game players M and A are treated.
(iii) The spatial distribution of the number of Internet game players is very uneven, which is concentrated in places such as Internet cafes and schools, and then gradually

decreases outward. Based on this, we assume that the population distribution of the two types of Internet game players is diffuse in space.

Below, we give the state changes in Internet game players, as shown in the Figure 1.

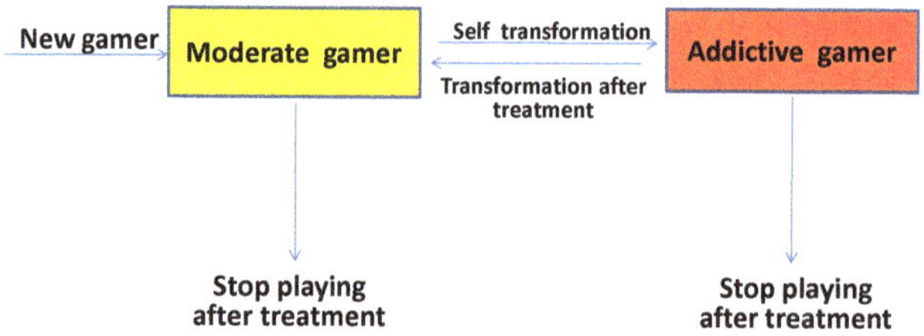

Figure 1. General scheme of the state transition of Internet gamers in our modeling.

Based on the assumptions (i)–(iii), we explain the process described in Figure 1 in detail. $M(x,t)$ and $A(x,t)$ stand for the population density of moderate gamers and addictive gamers at time t and position x, respectively. In time period Δt, the moderate gamers M have increased by $\alpha M(x,t)\Delta t$ and $\delta A(x,t)\Delta t$ because some non-gamers have become new gamers and some addictive gamers have converted to moderate gamers after treatment. In the meantime, the moderate gamers M have declined by $\beta M(x,t)A(x,t)\Delta t$ and $\gamma_1 M(x,t)\Delta t$ because some moderate gamers have become addictive gamers and another moderate gamers have converted to non-gamers after treatment. Vice versa, the addictive gamers A have only raised by $\beta M(x,t)A(x,t)\Delta t$ because of the transformation from moderate gamers to addictive gamers. At the same time, the addictive gamers M have reduced by $\delta A(x,t)\Delta t$ and $\gamma_2 A(x,t)\Delta t$ because some addictive gamers have become moderate gamers and another addictive gamers have converted to non-gamers after treatment. Furthermore, we added the diffusion terms $d_1 \frac{\partial^2 M}{\partial x^2}\Delta t$ and $d_2 \frac{\partial^2 A}{\partial x^2}\Delta t$, where d_1 and d_2 are the diffusion coefficients. Through the above analysis, we build a new model as follows:

$$\begin{cases} \frac{\partial M}{\partial t} = d_1 \frac{\partial^2}{\partial x^2} M(x,t) + \alpha - \beta M(x,t)A(x,t) - \gamma_1 M(x,t) + \delta A(x,t), \\ \frac{\partial A}{\partial t} = d_2 \frac{\partial^2}{\partial x^2} A(x,t) + \beta M(x,t)A(x,t) - (\gamma_2 + \delta)A(x,t), \end{cases} \quad (1)$$

where $(x,t) \in \mathbb{R} \times (0,\infty)$, $\alpha, \beta, \delta, \gamma_1, \gamma_2, d_1, d_2 > 0$ are some constants.

Remark 1. *In* (1)*, if there is lack of treatment and diffusion, then* $M + A = M(0) + A(0) + \alpha t \to +\infty$*, as* $t \to +\infty$*. This will lead to everyone eventually becoming a gamer. Therefore, proper treatment is necessary. Moreover, there are two kinds of healing effects on addicted gamers. One is to cure them completely and make them non-gamers. The other is to reduce their addiction and make them moderate gamers. This shows that game addiction is a stubborn psychological disease. It is difficult to eradicate completely.*

1.2. Significance and Contribution

The traveling wave solutions of non-linear reaction–diffusion equations have important applications in many disciplines, such as biological dynamics [10,11], epidemic dynamics [12–14] and tumor dynamics [15,16]. Therefore, the study of traveling wave solutions and their properties of diffusion of non-linear partial differential equation models has attracted the attention of many scholars. There have been many good works [17–23] dealing with the traveling wave of reaction–diffusion equations. Enlightened by the ideas and methods in these references, this paper focuses on the existence of traveling wave solutions to Equation (1). So, let $M(x,t) = \widetilde{M}(\xi)$, $A(x,t) = \widetilde{A}(\xi)$, $\xi = x + ct (c > 0)$, then (1) becomes

$$\begin{cases} c\widetilde{M}'(\xi) - d_1\widetilde{M}''(\xi) = \alpha - \beta\widetilde{M}(\xi)\widetilde{A}(\xi) - \gamma_1\widetilde{M}(\xi) + \delta\widetilde{A}(\xi), \\ c\widetilde{A}'(\xi) - d_2\widetilde{A}''(\xi) = \beta\widetilde{M}(\xi)\widetilde{A}(\xi) - (\gamma_2 + \delta)\widetilde{A}(\xi). \end{cases} \tag{2}$$

It is easy to verify that Equation (2) has a unique non-negative constant solution $(\widetilde{M}(\xi), \widetilde{A}(\xi)) = (\frac{\alpha}{\gamma_1}, 0)$. Let $\mathcal{M}(\xi) = \widetilde{M}(\xi) - \frac{\alpha}{\gamma_1}$, $\mathcal{A}(\xi) = \widetilde{A}(\xi)$, then Equation (2) changes into

$$\begin{cases} c\mathcal{M}'(\xi) - d_1\mathcal{M}''(\xi) = -\beta\mathcal{M}(\xi)\mathcal{A}(\xi) - \gamma_1\mathcal{M}(\xi) - (\alpha\beta\gamma_1^{-1} - \delta)\mathcal{A}(\xi), \\ c\mathcal{A}'(\xi) - d_2\mathcal{A}''(\xi) = \beta\mathcal{M}(\xi)\mathcal{A}(\xi) + (\alpha\beta\gamma_1^{-1} - \gamma_2 - \delta)\mathcal{A}(\xi). \end{cases} \tag{3}$$

The whole paper requires the following assumptions.

(A) For some given constants $\alpha, \beta, \delta, \gamma_1, \gamma_2, d_1, d_2 > 0$ and an unknown constant $c > 0$, there are $\gamma_2 + \delta < \alpha\beta\gamma_1^{-1}$ and $c > 2\sqrt{d_2(\alpha\beta\gamma_1^{-1} - \gamma_2 - \delta)}$.

The paper mainly includes the following contributions. (a) We propose a novel diffusion PDE (1) modeling Internet game addiction, which is rare in previous papers. (b) Based on Schauder's fixed point theorem and continuation method, we study the existence and asymptotic stability of traveling waves of the model (1) to reveal the oscillating behavior of IGD. (c) Our research provides some theoretical help for the study and treatment of IGD. The remaining structure of the paper is as follows. Section 2 introduces super- and sub-solutions and their properties. Section 3 gives the detailed proof process of the existence of traveling waves. Section 4 studies the global asymptotic stability of traveling waves. In Section 5, we provide an example and carry out numerical simulation to examine the validity of our results. Section 6 is a brief summary.

2. Super- and Sub-Solutions

This section provides the upper and lower solutions of (3) and their properties. Define the super-solutions $\overline{P}(\xi) = e^{\lambda\xi}$, and $\overline{Q}(\xi) = e^{\mu\xi}$, where

$$\lambda = \frac{c + \sqrt{c^2 + 4d_1\gamma_1}}{2d_1}, \quad \mu = \frac{c + \sqrt{c^2 - 4d_2(\alpha\beta\gamma_1^{-1} - \gamma_2 - \delta)}}{2d_2}.$$

By the condition (B), one has $\lambda, \mu > 0$, and

$$c\overline{P}'(\xi) - d_1\overline{P}''(\xi) = -\gamma_1\overline{P}(\xi), \quad c\overline{Q}'(\xi) - d_2\overline{Q}''(\xi) = (\alpha\beta\gamma_1^{-1} - \gamma_2 - \delta)\overline{Q}(\xi).$$

Take the sub-solutions $\underline{P}(\xi) = e^{\lambda\xi} - \mathcal{P}e^{(\lambda-\epsilon)\xi}$ and $\underline{Q}(\xi) = e^{\mu\xi} - \mathcal{Q}e^{(\mu-\epsilon)\xi}$, where $\mathcal{P}, \mathcal{Q} > 1$ and $\epsilon \in (0, \min\{\lambda, \mu\})$ are small enough such that

$$\rho = -d_1(\lambda - \epsilon)^2 + c(\lambda - \epsilon) > 0, \quad \varrho = -d_2(\mu - \epsilon)^2 + c(\mu - \epsilon) - (\alpha\beta\gamma_1^{-1} - \gamma_2 - \delta) > 0,$$

$$\underline{\xi} \triangleq \max\left\{\frac{\ln\mathcal{P}}{\epsilon}, \frac{\ln\mathcal{Q}}{\epsilon}\right\} < \min\left\{\frac{1}{\lambda}\ln\frac{\rho(\alpha\beta\gamma_1^{-1} - \delta)}{\beta\gamma_1}, \frac{1}{\mu}\ln\frac{\mathcal{P}\gamma_1}{\alpha\beta\gamma_1^{-1} - \delta}\right\} \triangleq \overline{\xi}.$$

When $\underline{\xi} < \xi < \overline{\xi}$, we obtain $\underline{P}(\xi), \underline{Q}(\xi) > 0$, and

$$\begin{aligned}
&c\underline{P}'(\xi) - d_1\underline{P}''(\xi) + \beta\underline{P}(\xi)\underline{Q}(\xi) + \gamma_1\underline{P}(\xi) + (\alpha\beta\gamma_1^{-1} - \delta)\underline{Q}(\xi) \\
=&c\left[\lambda e^{\lambda\xi} - \mathcal{P}(\lambda-\epsilon)e^{(\lambda-\epsilon)\xi}\right] - d_1\left[\lambda^2 e^{\lambda\xi} - \mathcal{P}(\lambda-\epsilon)^2 e^{(\lambda-\epsilon)\xi}\right] + \gamma_1\left[e^{\lambda\xi} - \mathcal{P}e^{(\lambda-\epsilon)\xi}\right] \\
&+\beta\left[e^{\lambda\xi} - \mathcal{P}e^{(\lambda-\epsilon)\xi}\right]\left[e^{\mu\xi} - \mathcal{Q}e^{(\mu-\epsilon)\xi}\right] + (\alpha\beta\gamma_1^{-1} - \delta)\left[e^{\mu\xi} - be^{(\mu-\epsilon)\xi}\right] \\
<&\left[\mathcal{P}d_1(\lambda-\epsilon)^2 - \mathcal{P}c(\lambda-\epsilon) - \mathcal{P}\gamma_1\right]e^{(\lambda-\epsilon)\xi} + \beta e^{\lambda\xi}e^{\mu\xi} + (\alpha\beta\gamma_1^{-1} - \delta)e^{\mu\xi} \\
<&-\left[\mathcal{P}\rho - \beta e^{\lambda\xi}e^{\mu\xi} + \mathcal{P}\gamma_1 - (\alpha\beta\gamma_1^{-1} - \delta)e^{\mu\xi}\right]e^{(\lambda-\epsilon)\xi} \\
<&-\left[\mathcal{P}\rho - \beta\cdot\frac{\rho(\alpha\beta\gamma_1^{-1} - \delta)}{\beta\gamma_1}\cdot\frac{\mathcal{P}\gamma_1}{\alpha\beta\gamma_1^{-1} - \delta} + \mathcal{P}\gamma_1 - (\alpha\beta\gamma_1^{-1} - \delta)\cdot\frac{\mathcal{P}\gamma_1}{\alpha\beta\gamma_1^{-1} - \delta}\right]e^{(\lambda-\epsilon)\xi} = 0,
\end{aligned}$$

$$\begin{aligned}
&c\underline{Q}'(\xi) - d_2\underline{Q}''(\xi) - \beta\underline{P}(\xi)\underline{Q}(\xi) - (\alpha\beta\gamma_1^{-1} - \gamma_2 - \delta)\underline{Q}(\xi) \\
=&c\left[\mu e^{\mu\xi} - \mathcal{Q}(\mu-\epsilon)e^{(\mu-\epsilon)\xi}\right] - d_2\left[\mu^2 e^{\mu\xi} - \mathcal{Q}(\mu-\epsilon)^2 e^{(\mu-\epsilon)\xi}\right] \\
&-\beta\left[e^{\lambda\xi} - \mathcal{P}e^{(\lambda-\epsilon)\xi}\right]\left[e^{\mu\xi} - \mathcal{Q}e^{(\mu-\epsilon)\xi}\right] - (\alpha\beta\gamma_1^{-1} - \gamma_2 - \delta)\left[e^{\mu\xi} - \mathcal{Q}e^{(\mu-\epsilon)\xi}\right] \\
<&-\mathcal{Q}\left[-d_2(\mu-\epsilon)^2 + c(\mu-\epsilon) - (\alpha\beta\gamma_1^{-1} - \gamma_2 - \delta)\right]e^{(\mu-\epsilon)\xi} = -\mathcal{Q}\varrho e^{(\mu-\epsilon)\xi} < 0.
\end{aligned}$$

Let $\widetilde{P}(\xi) = \max\{0, \underline{P}(\xi)\}$, $\widetilde{Q}(\xi) = \max\{0, \underline{Q}(\xi)\}$, $\xi \in \mathbb{R}$, then, we have

$$c\widetilde{P}'(\xi) - d_1\widetilde{P}''(\xi) + \beta\widetilde{P}(\xi)\widetilde{Q}(\xi) + \gamma_1\widetilde{P}(\xi) + (\alpha\beta\gamma_1^{-1} - \delta)\widetilde{Q}(\xi) \le 0,\ \forall\xi \ne \frac{\ln\mathcal{P}}{\epsilon},$$

$$c\widetilde{Q}'(\xi) - d_2\widetilde{Q}''(\xi) - \beta\widetilde{P}(\xi)\widetilde{Q}(\xi) - (\alpha\beta\gamma_1^{-1} - \gamma_2 - \delta)\widetilde{Q}(\xi) \le 0,\ \forall\xi \ne \frac{\ln\mathcal{Q}}{\epsilon}.$$

3. Existence of Traveling Wave

This section mainly discusses the existence and non-existence of traveling waves and some properties of traveling waves. We boil them down to the following theorem.

Theorem 1. *Assume that* (A) *holds, then the following assertions are true:*

(a) *For any* $c > c^* = 2\sqrt{d_2(\alpha\beta\gamma_1^{-1} - \gamma_2 - \delta)}$, *there is a traveling wave solution* $(\widetilde{M}^*(\xi), \widetilde{A}^*(\xi))$ *of model* (1) *satisfying* $\lim_{\xi\to-\infty}\widetilde{M}^*(\xi) = \frac{\alpha}{\gamma_1}$, $\lim_{\xi\to-\infty}\widetilde{A}^*(\xi) = 0$.

(b) $\exists\,\xi_0 > 0$, *when* $\xi \in (-\infty, -\xi_0)$, $\widetilde{M}^*(\xi)$ *and* $\widetilde{A}^*(\xi)$ *are monotone increasing functions.*

(c) *There is no traveling wave solution of model* (1) *provided that* $c < c^*$.

(d) $\liminf_{\xi\to+\infty}\widetilde{M}^*(\xi) > \frac{\alpha}{\gamma_1}$, $\liminf_{\xi\to+\infty}\widetilde{A}^*(\xi) > 0$.

Proof. (1) The proof of assertion (a). Here, we prove it in two steps.

Step 1: Local existence of traveling wave. For $c > 2\sqrt{d_2(\alpha\beta\gamma_1^{-1} - \gamma_2 - \delta)}$, consider a two-point BVP in $(-l, l)$ of the form

$$\begin{cases}
c\mathcal{M}'(\xi) - d_1\mathcal{M}''(\xi) = -\beta\overline{\mathcal{M}}(\xi)\overline{\mathcal{A}}(\xi) - \gamma_1\overline{\mathcal{M}}(\xi) - (\alpha\beta\gamma_1^{-1} - \delta)\overline{\mathcal{A}}(\xi) \\
\qquad\qquad\triangleq F(\overline{\mathcal{M}}(\xi), \overline{\mathcal{A}}(\xi)), \\
c\mathcal{A}'(\xi) - d_2\mathcal{A}''(\xi) = \beta\overline{\mathcal{M}}(\xi)\overline{\mathcal{M}}(\xi) + (\alpha\beta\gamma_1^{-1} - \gamma_2 - \delta)\overline{\mathcal{A}}(\xi) \triangleq G(\overline{\mathcal{M}}(\xi), \overline{\mathcal{A}}(\xi)), \\
\mathcal{M}(\pm l) = \widetilde{P}(\pm l),\ \mathcal{A}(\pm l) = \widetilde{Q}(\pm l),\ \mathcal{M}'(\pm l) = \widetilde{P}'(\pm l),\ \mathcal{A}'(\pm l) = \widetilde{Q}'(\pm l),
\end{cases} \tag{4}$$

where $l > \underline{\xi}$, and

$$\overline{\mathcal{M}}(\xi) = \begin{cases} \mathcal{M}(-l), & \xi < -l, \\ \mathcal{M}(\xi), & -l \le \xi \le l, \\ \mathcal{M}(l), & \xi > l, \end{cases} \quad \overline{\mathcal{A}}(\xi) = \begin{cases} \mathcal{A}(-l), & \xi < -l, \\ \mathcal{A}(\xi), & -l \le \xi \le l, \\ \mathcal{A}(l), & \xi > l. \end{cases} \tag{5}$$

By Section 2, for a solution $(\mathcal{M}(\xi), \mathcal{A}(\xi))$ of (4), one has $\widetilde{P}(\xi) \leq \mathcal{M}(\xi) \leq \overline{P}(\xi)$, $\widetilde{Q}(\xi) \leq \mathcal{A}(\xi) \leq \overline{Q}(\xi)$. Introducing a norm

$$\|(u,v)\| = \max\left\{ \sup_{\xi\in[-l,l]} |u(\xi)|, \sup_{\xi\in[-l,l]} |v(\xi)|, \sup_{\xi\in[-l,l]} |u'(\xi)|, \sup_{\xi\in[-l,l]} |v'(\xi)| \right\},$$

for $(u,v) \in C^2([-l,l],\mathbb{R}^2)$, then $C^2([-l,l],\mathbb{R}^2)$ is a Banach space. Let $\|(\widetilde{P},\widetilde{Q})\| = R_1$, $\|(\overline{P},\overline{Q})\| = R_2$, $R_3 = R_1 + R_1 d_1 c^{-1}(e^{\frac{2cl}{d_1}} - 1) + d_1 R_2 c^{-2}(\beta R_2 + \gamma_1 + \alpha\beta\gamma_1^{-1} - \delta)(e^{\frac{cl}{d_1}} - 1)(e^{\frac{cl}{d_1}} - e^{-\frac{cl}{d_1}})$, $R_4 = R_1 + R_1 d_1 c^{-1}(e^{\frac{2cl}{d_2}} - 1) + d_2 R_2 c^{-2}(\beta R_2 + \alpha\beta\gamma_1^{-1} - \gamma_2 - \delta)(e^{\frac{cl}{d_2}} - 1)(e^{\frac{cl}{d_2}} - e^{-\frac{cl}{d_2}})$, $R = \max\{R_1, R_2, R_3, R_4\}$, $\Omega = \{(u,v) \in C^2([-l,l],\mathbb{R}^2) : \|(u,v)\| < R+1\}$. For $(u,v) \in \Omega$, define a mapping $\mathscr{L} = (\mathscr{L}_1, \mathscr{L}_2)^T : \Omega \to \mathbb{R}^2$ as

$$(\mathscr{L}(u,v))(\xi) = \begin{pmatrix} (\mathscr{L}(u,v))(\xi) \\ (\mathscr{L}(u,v))(\xi) \end{pmatrix}, \tag{6}$$

where

$$(\mathscr{L}_1(u,v))(\xi) = u(-l) + u'(-l)e^{\frac{cl}{d_1}} \int_{-l}^{\xi} e^{\frac{c}{d_1}\tau} d\tau - \frac{1}{d_1}\int_{-l}^{\xi} [\int_{-l}^{\tau} e^{-\frac{c}{d_1}(s-\tau)} F(\overline{u}(s),\overline{v}(s)) ds] d\tau,$$

$$(\mathscr{L}_2(u,v))(\xi) = v(-l) + v'(-l)e^{\frac{cl}{d_2}} \int_{-l}^{\xi} e^{\frac{c}{d_2}\tau} d\tau - \frac{1}{d_2}\int_{-l}^{\xi} [\int_{-l}^{\tau} e^{-\frac{c}{d_2}(s-\tau)} G(\overline{u}(s),\overline{v}(s)) ds] d\tau.$$

By the boundary conditions, (A) and (6), we have

$$\begin{aligned}
&|(\mathscr{L}_1(u,v))(\xi)| \\
=&\left|\widetilde{P}(-l) + \widetilde{P}'(-l)e^{\frac{cl}{d_1}} \int_{-l}^{\xi} e^{\frac{c}{d_1}\tau} d\tau - \frac{1}{d_1}\int_{-l}^{\xi} \left[\int_{-l}^{\tau} e^{-\frac{c}{d_1}(s-\tau)} F(\overline{u}(s),\overline{v}(s)) ds\right] d\tau\right| \\
\leq&|\widetilde{P}(-l)| + |\widetilde{P}'(-l)|e^{\frac{cl}{d_1}} \int_{-l}^{l} e^{\frac{c}{d_1}\tau} d\tau + \frac{1}{d_1}\int_{-l}^{l} \left[\int_{-l}^{\tau} e^{-\frac{c}{d_1}(s-\tau)} |F(\overline{u}(s),\overline{v}(s))| ds\right] d\tau \\
\leq&R_1 + R_1\frac{d_1}{c}(e^{\frac{2cl}{d_1}} - 1) + \frac{1}{d_1}\int_{-l}^{l} \left[\int_{-l}^{l} e^{-\frac{c}{d_1}(s-\tau)} [\beta|\overline{u}(s)||\overline{v}(s))| \right. \\
&\left. + \gamma_1|\overline{u}(s)| + (\alpha\beta\gamma_1^{-1} - \delta)|\overline{v}(s)|] ds\right] d\tau \\
\leq&R_1 + R_1 d_1 c^{-1}(e^{\frac{2cl}{d_1}} - 1) + d_1 R_2 c^{-2}(\beta R_2 + \gamma_1 + \alpha\beta\gamma_1^{-1} - \delta)(e^{\frac{cl}{d_1}} - 1)(e^{\frac{cl}{d_1}} - e^{-\frac{cl}{d_1}}) \\
=&R_3 < R+1.
\end{aligned} \tag{7}$$

Similar to (7), we obtain

$$\begin{aligned}
&|(\mathscr{L}_2(u,v))(\xi)| \\
=&\left|v(-l) + v'(-l)e^{\frac{cl}{d_2}} \int_{-l}^{\xi} e^{\frac{c}{d_2}\tau} d\tau - \frac{1}{d_2}\int_{-l}^{\xi} [\int_{-l}^{\tau} e^{-\frac{c}{d_2}(s-\tau)} G(\overline{u}(s),\overline{v}(s)) ds] d\tau\right| \\
\leq&R_1 + R_1 d_1 c^{-1}(e^{\frac{2cl}{d_2}} - 1) + d_2 R_2 c^{-2}(\beta R_2 + \alpha\beta\gamma_1^{-1} - \gamma_2 - \delta)(e^{\frac{cl}{d_2}} - 1)(e^{\frac{cl}{d_2}} - e^{-\frac{cl}{d_2}}) \\
=&R_4 < R+1.
\end{aligned} \tag{8}$$

From (7) and (8), one knows that $\mathscr{L}(\Omega) \subset \Omega$. Obviously, $\mathscr{L}$ is continuous. Moreover, it is easy to prove by Arzela–Ascoli theorem that $\mathscr{L}$ is compact. Therefore, by applying Schauder's fixed point theorem, $\mathscr{L}$ exists as a fixed point $(\mathcal{M}_l^*(\xi), \mathcal{A}_l^*(\xi)) \in \Omega$, which is the solution of (4). Furthermore, $0 \leq \widetilde{P}(\xi) \leq \mathcal{M}_l^*(\xi) < R+1$ and $0 \leq \widetilde{Q}(\xi) \leq \mathcal{A}_l^*(\xi) < R+1$.

Step 2: Global continuation of traveling wave. For $(\mathcal{M}_l(\xi), \mathcal{A}_l(\xi))$, from the standard elliptic estimates, one derives that there is $N_0 > 0$ such that

$$\|\mathcal{M}_l(\xi)\|_{C^{2,\nu}(-\frac{l}{2},\frac{l}{2})} \le N_0,\ \|\mathcal{A}_l(\xi)\|_{C^{2,\nu}(-\frac{l}{2},\frac{l}{2})} \le N_0,\ \forall l > \max\left\{\frac{\ln \mathcal{P}}{\epsilon}, \frac{\ln \mathcal{Q}}{\epsilon}\right\},$$

where $\nu \in (0,1)$ is a constant. Taking $l \to +\infty$, then, one has $\mathcal{M}_l^*(\xi) \to \mathcal{M}^*(\xi)$, $\mathcal{A}_l^*(\xi) \to \mathcal{A}^*(\xi)$ in $C^2_{\text{loc}}(\mathbb{R})$, and $(\mathcal{M}^*(\xi), \mathcal{A}^*(\xi))$ satisfies Equation (3). Noticing that $0 \le \widetilde{P}(\xi) \le \mathcal{M}^*(\xi) \le e^{\lambda\xi} = \overline{P}(\xi)$ and $0 \le \widetilde{Q}(\xi) \le \mathcal{A}^*(\xi) \le e^{\mu\xi} = \overline{Q}(\xi)$, we have $\lim_{\xi\to-\infty} \mathcal{M}^*(\xi) = \lim_{\xi\to-\infty} \mathcal{A}^*(\xi) = 0$. Thus, $\widetilde{M}^*(\xi) = \mathcal{M}^*(\xi) + \frac{\alpha}{\gamma_1}$ and $\widetilde{A}^*(\xi) = \mathcal{A}^*(\xi)$ satisfy the Equation (2).

Therefore, $(\widetilde{M}^*(\xi), \widetilde{A}^*(\xi))$ is a traveling wave solution of (1) and satisfies $\lim_{\xi\to-\infty} \widetilde{M}^*(\xi) = \frac{\alpha}{\gamma_1}$ and $\lim_{\xi\to-\infty} \widetilde{A}^*(\xi) = 0$.

(2) The proof of assertion (b). For this purpose, we adopt the reduction to absurdity. Assume that, $\forall \xi > 0$, $\mathcal{M}^*(\xi)$, and $\mathcal{A}^*(\xi)$ is non-monotonic in $(-\infty, \xi)$, then, there are two infinite points sequences $\{\xi_k\}_{k=1}^{\infty}$ and $\{\eta_k\}_{k=1}^{\infty}$ satisfying $\lim_{k\to\infty} \xi_k = \lim_{k\to\infty} \eta_k = -\infty$, $\lim_{k\to\infty} \mathcal{M}^*(\xi_k) = \lim_{k\to\infty} \mathcal{A}(\eta_k) = 0$, and $\mathcal{M}^*(\xi)$ taking the maximum at $\xi = \xi_k (k \in \mathbb{N}^+)$ and $\mathcal{A}^*(\xi)$ taking the minimum at $\xi = \eta_k (k \in \mathbb{N}^+)$. Thus, we have

$$(\mathcal{M}^*)'(\xi_k) = (\mathcal{A}^*)'(\eta_k) = 0,\ (\mathcal{M}^*)''(\xi_k) < 0,\ (\mathcal{A}^*)''(\eta_k) > 0,$$

which, together with (A), implies that

$$0 < c(\mathcal{M}^*)'(\xi_k) - d_1(\mathcal{M}^*)''(\xi_k) = -\beta\mathcal{M}^*(\xi_k)\mathcal{A}^*(\xi_k) - \gamma_1\mathcal{M}^*(\xi_k) < 0, \tag{9}$$

and

$$0 > c(\mathcal{A}^*)'(\eta_k) - d_2(\mathcal{A}^*)''(\eta_k) = \beta\mathcal{M}^*(\eta_k)\mathcal{A}^*(\eta_k) + (\alpha\beta\gamma_1^{-1} - \gamma_2 - \delta)\mathcal{A}^*(\eta_k) > 0. \tag{10}$$

Obviously, (9) and (10) are contradictory in themselves. So, there is a constant $\xi_0 > 0$ such that $\mathcal{M}^*(\xi)$ and $\mathcal{A}^*(\xi)$ are all monotonous in $(-\infty, -\xi_0)$. Moreover, assume that $\mathcal{M}^*(\xi)$ and $\mathcal{A}^*(\xi)$ are all monotonically decreasing in $(-\infty, -\xi_0)$, then, for any $-\xi_0 > \xi > -\infty$, we have $0 < \mathcal{M}^*(\xi) < \mathcal{M}^*(-\infty) = 0$ and $0 < \mathcal{A}^*(\xi) < \mathcal{A}^*(-\infty) = 0$, which is an evident fallacy. Therefore, $\mathcal{M}^*(\xi)$ and $\mathcal{A}^*(\xi)$ are all monotonically increasing in $(-\infty, -\xi_0)$. By $\widetilde{M}^*(\xi) = \mathcal{M}^*(\xi) + \frac{\alpha}{\gamma_1}$ and $\widetilde{A}^*(\xi) = \mathcal{A}^*(\xi)$, one knows that $\widetilde{M}^*(\xi)$ and $\widetilde{A}^*(\xi)$ are all monotonically increasing in $(-\infty, -\xi_0)$ as well.

(3) The proof of assertion (c). We still adopt the fallacy reduction. Assume that, when $c < c^*$, the model (1) has a traveling wave solution $(\widetilde{M}(\xi), \widetilde{A}(\xi))$, then, the Equation (3) has a traveling wave solution $\mathcal{M}(\xi) = \widetilde{M}(\xi) - \frac{\alpha}{\gamma_1}$, $\mathcal{A}(\xi) = \widetilde{A}(\xi)$. Choose an infinite point sequence $\{\xi_k\}_{k=1}^{\infty}$ such that $\lim_{k\to\infty} \xi_k = -\infty$, and let $\mathcal{M}_k(\xi) = \frac{\mathcal{M}(\xi+\xi_k)}{\mathcal{M}(\xi_k)}$, $\mathcal{A}_k(\xi) = \frac{\mathcal{A}(\xi+\xi_k)}{\mathcal{A}(\xi_k)}$, $\widehat{\mathcal{M}}_k(\xi) = \mathcal{M}(\xi + \xi_k)$ and $\widehat{\mathcal{A}}_k(\xi) = \mathcal{A}(\xi + \xi_k)$, then, $\widehat{\mathcal{M}}_k(\xi)$ and $\widehat{\mathcal{A}}_k(\xi)$ satisfy the Equation (3), which yields

$$c\widehat{\mathcal{A}}_k'(\xi) - d_2\widehat{\mathcal{A}}_k''(\xi) = \beta\widehat{\mathcal{M}}_k(\xi)\widehat{\mathcal{A}}_k(\xi) + (\alpha\beta\gamma_1^{-1} - \gamma_2 - \delta)\widehat{\mathcal{A}}_k(\xi). \tag{11}$$

Dividing by $\mathcal{A}(\xi_k)$ at both ends of (11) leads to

$$c\mathcal{A}_k'(\xi) - d_2\mathcal{A}_k''(\xi) = \beta\widehat{\mathcal{M}}_k(\xi)\mathcal{A}_k(\xi) + (\alpha\beta\gamma_1^{-1} - \gamma_2 - \delta)\mathcal{A}_k(\xi). \tag{12}$$

In addition, $\mathcal{M}_k(0) = \mathcal{A}_k(0) = 1$ and $(\widehat{\mathcal{M}}_k(\xi), \widehat{\mathcal{A}}_k(\xi)) \to (0,0)$ as $k \to \infty$ because of $(\mathcal{M}(\xi), \mathcal{A}(\xi)) \to (0,0)$ as $\xi \to -\infty$. Setting $k \to \infty$ on both sides of (12), and denoting $\lim_{k\to\infty} \mathcal{A}_k(\xi) = \mathcal{A}_0(\xi)$ in $C^2_{\text{loc}}(\mathbb{R})$, then, we obtain

$$c\mathcal{A}_0'(\xi) - d_2\mathcal{A}_0''(\xi) = (\alpha\beta\gamma_1^{-1} - \gamma_2 - \delta)\mathcal{A}_0(\xi). \tag{13}$$

The general solution of ODE (13) is

$$\mathcal{A}_0(\xi) = C_1 e^{\mu_1 \xi} + C_2 e^{\mu_2 \xi}, \tag{14}$$

where C_1, C_2 are two arbitrary constants, and the characteristic roots

$$\mu_{1,2} = \frac{c \pm \sqrt{c^2 - 4d_2(\alpha\beta\gamma_1^{-1} - \gamma_2 - \delta)}}{2d_2}.$$

Moreover, $\mathcal{A}_k(0) = 1$ implies $\mathcal{A}_0(0) = 1$. Since $\mathcal{A}_k(\xi) > 0$ is monotonically increasing, $\mathcal{A}_0(\xi) > 0$ is monotonically increasing, too, which indicates that $\mu_{1,2} \in \mathbb{R}$. Thus, we obtain $c > c^* = 2\sqrt{d_2(\alpha\beta\gamma_1^{-1} - \gamma_2 - \delta)}$, which is contradictory to $c < c^*$. So, the model (1) has no traveling wave solution when $c < c^*$.

(4) The proof of assertion (d). Let us first prove that $\liminf_{\xi\to+\infty}[\mathcal{M}^*(\xi) + \mathcal{A}^*(\xi)] > 0$. Indeed, since $\mathcal{M}^*(\xi), \mathcal{A}^*(\xi) > 0$, one has $\liminf_{\xi\to+\infty}[\mathcal{M}^*(\xi) + \mathcal{A}^*(\xi)] \geq 0$. Now, we just need to prove $\liminf_{\xi\to+\infty}[\mathcal{M}^*(\xi) + \mathcal{A}^*(\xi)] \neq 0$. By application of fallacy reduction, suppose that the conclusion is not true, then, there is an infinite point sequence $\{\zeta_k\})_{k=1}^{\infty}$ such that $\lim_{k\to\infty} \zeta_k = +\infty$ and $\lim_{k\to\infty}[\mathcal{M}^*(\zeta_k) + \mathcal{A}^*(\zeta_k)] = 0$, which deduces $\lim_{k\to\infty} \mathcal{M}^*(\zeta_k) = \lim_{k\to\infty} \mathcal{A}^*(\zeta_k) = 0$. Let $\zeta_k = -\omega_k$, $\mathcal{M}^*(\zeta_k) = \widehat{\mathcal{M}}^*(-\zeta_k)$ and $\mathcal{A}^*(\zeta_k) = \widehat{\mathcal{A}}^*(-\zeta_k)$, then $\lim_{k\to\infty} \omega_k = -\infty$, $\lim_{k\to\infty} \widehat{\mathcal{M}}^*(\omega_k) = \lim_{k\to\infty} \widehat{\mathcal{A}}^*(\omega_k) = 0$, $\widehat{\mathcal{M}}^*(\omega_k)$ and $\widehat{\mathcal{A}}^*(\omega_k)$ satisfy

$$(-c)\widehat{\mathcal{A}}'(\omega_k) - d_2\widehat{\mathcal{A}}''(\omega_k) = \beta\widehat{\mathcal{M}}(\omega_k)\widehat{\mathcal{A}}(\omega_k) + (\alpha\beta\gamma_1^{-1} - \gamma_2 - \delta)\widehat{\mathcal{A}}(\omega_k). \tag{15}$$

Meanwhile, from the assertion (b), we know that $\mathcal{M}^*(\omega_k)$ and $\mathcal{A}^*(\omega_k)$ are monotonically increasing in $(-\infty, \xi_0)$. Similar to the proof process of assertion (c), only when $-c > 2\sqrt{d_2(\alpha\beta\gamma_1^{-1} - \gamma_2 - \delta)}$, $\mathcal{M}^*(\omega_k)$ and $\mathcal{A}^*(\omega_k)$ satisfying (15) are monotonically increasing in $(-\infty, \xi_0)$. Thus, we obtain $c < 2\sqrt{d_2(\alpha\beta\gamma_1^{-1} - \gamma_2 - \delta)} = c^*$, which is contradictory to the hypothesis $c > c^*$.

Next, we show that $\liminf_{\xi\to+\infty} \mathcal{M}^*(\xi) > 0$ and $\liminf_{\xi\to+\infty} \mathcal{A}^*(\xi) > 0$. One can easily obtain $\liminf_{\xi\to+\infty} \mathcal{M}^*(\xi) \geq 0$ and $\liminf_{\xi\to+\infty} \mathcal{A}^*(\xi) \geq 0$ due to $\mathcal{M}^*(\xi), \mathcal{A}^*(\xi) > 0$. Now, we apply the proof by contradiction to prove that $\liminf_{\xi\to+\infty} \mathcal{M}^*(\xi) \neq 0$ and $\liminf_{\xi\to+\infty} \mathcal{A}^*(\xi) \neq 0$. Consider $\liminf_{\xi\to+\infty} \mathcal{M}^*(\xi) \neq 0$ at first, if $\liminf_{\xi\to+\infty} \mathcal{M}^*(\xi) = 0$, there exists an infinite point $\{\xi_k\}_{k=1}^{\infty}$ such that $\lim_{k\to\infty} \xi_k = +\infty$ and $\lim_{k\to\infty} \mathcal{M}^*(\xi_k) = 0$. For $\mathcal{A}^*(\xi)$, there are two cases, namely, Case 1: $\liminf_{k\to\infty} \mathcal{A}^*(\xi_k) = 0$ and Case 2: $\liminf_{k\to\infty} \mathcal{A}^*(\xi_k) > 0$. In Case 1, there is a sub-sequence $\{\xi_k^*\} \subset \{\xi_k\}$ such that $\lim_{k\to\infty} \mathcal{A}^*(\xi_k^*) = \lim_{k\to\infty} \mathcal{M}^*(\xi_k^*) = 0$. Similar to the proof of $\liminf_{\xi\to+\infty}[\mathcal{M}^*(\xi) + \mathcal{A}^*(\xi)] > 0$, we find the contradiction between $c > c^*$ and $c < c^*$. In Case 2, there is a sub-sequence $\{\xi_k^{**}\} \subset \{\xi_k\}$ such that $\lim_{k\to\infty} \mathcal{A}^*(\xi_k^{**}) > 0$ and $\lim_{k\to\infty} \mathcal{M}^*(\xi_k^{**}) = 0$ and satisfies

$$\begin{aligned} &c(\mathcal{M}^*)'(\xi_k^{**}) - d_1(\mathcal{M}^*)''(\xi_k^{**}) \\ &= -\beta\mathcal{M}^*(\xi_k^{**})\mathcal{A}^*(\xi_k^{**}) - \gamma_1\mathcal{M}(\xi_k^{**}) - (\alpha\beta\gamma_1^{-1} - \delta)\mathcal{A}^*(\xi_k^{**}). \end{aligned} \tag{16}$$

It is worth noting that we apply $\lim_{k\to\infty} \mathcal{M}^*(\xi_k^{**}) = 0$ and Taylor expansion formula to obtain $\lim_{k\to\infty}(\mathcal{M}^*)'(\xi_k^{**}) = \lim_{k\to\infty}(\mathcal{M}^*)''(\xi_k^{**}) = 0$. So, taking the limit $k \to \infty$ at both ends of (16), we have $0 = 0 - (\alpha\beta\gamma_1^{-1} - \delta)\lim_{k\to\infty} \mathcal{A}^*(\xi_k^{**}) < 0$, which is an evident falsehood. Thus, we completed the proof of $\liminf_{\xi\to+\infty} \mathcal{M}^*(\xi) > 0$. Similar discussions can prove that $\liminf_{\xi\to+\infty} \mathcal{A}^*(\xi) > 0$ hold, and the specific proof process is omitted. Noticing the transformation $\mathcal{M}(\xi) = \widetilde{M}(\xi) - \frac{\alpha}{\gamma_1}$ and $\mathcal{A}(\xi) = \widetilde{A}(\xi)$, one obtains $\liminf_{\xi\to+\infty} \widetilde{A}^*(\xi) > \frac{\alpha}{\gamma_1}$ and $\liminf_{\xi\to+\infty} \widetilde{A}^*(\xi) > 0$.

So far, we completed the proof of all the propositions of the Theorem 1. □

4. Asymptotical Stability of Traveling Wave

This section focuses on the stability of the traveling wave solution of the model (1). Some preparatory work is necessary. According to the actual situation, our model considers the distribution and change in the number of Internet game addicts in a fixed spatial area, so we assume that there is no flow between the population in the spatial area and the outside of the area. Based on this assumption, we give the initial and boundary value conditions for the model (1) as follows:

$$\begin{cases} \frac{\partial M(x,t)}{\partial \vec{v}} = \frac{\partial A(x,t)}{\partial \vec{v}} = 0, & (x,t) \in \partial\Lambda \times \mathbb{R}^+, \\ M(x,0) = \phi_1(x),\ A(x,0) = \phi_2(x), & x \in \Lambda, \end{cases} \tag{17}$$

here, $\mathbb{R}^+ = (0,\infty)$, $\Lambda \subset \mathbb{R}$ is bounded with smooth boundary $\partial\Lambda$, $\vec{v}$ is outer normal vector of $\partial\Lambda$ and $\phi_1(x), \phi_2(x) > 0$ are continuous.

Let $\mathscr{X} = C^3(\overline{\Lambda} \times \mathbb{R}^+, \mathbb{R}^2)$ be a Banach space, then $\mathscr{X}^+ = \{(u,v) \in \mathscr{X} : u > 0, v > 0\}$ is a closed positive cone of $\mathscr{X}$. We discuss the stability of traveling wave solutions of model (1). Obviously, $(M(x,t), A(x,t)) = (\frac{\alpha}{\gamma_1}, 0)$ is a non-negative constant stationary solution of model (1). Here, we have the following result about the stability of the model (1).

Theorem 2. *If* (A) *is true, then the traveling wave solution* $(M^*(x,t), A^*(x,t))$ *of model* (1) *satisfying condition* (17) *is globally asymptotically stable in* $\mathscr{X}^+$.

Proof. Let $\mathcal{M}(x,t) = M(x,t) - \frac{\alpha}{\gamma_1}$ and $\mathcal{A}(x,t) = A(x,t)$, then system (1) and condition (17) change into

$$\begin{cases} \frac{\partial \mathcal{M}}{\partial t} = d_1\Delta\mathcal{M} - \beta\mathcal{M}\mathcal{A} - \gamma_1\mathcal{M} - (\alpha\beta\gamma_1^{-1} - \delta)\mathcal{A}, & (x,t) \in \Lambda \times \mathbb{R}^+, \\ \frac{\partial \mathcal{A}}{\partial t} = d_2\Delta\mathcal{A} + \beta\mathcal{M}\mathcal{A} + (\alpha\beta\gamma_1^{-1} - \gamma_2 - \delta)\mathcal{A}, & (x,t) \in \Lambda \times \mathbb{R}^+, \\ \frac{\partial \mathcal{M}(x,t)}{\partial \vec{v}} = \frac{\partial \mathcal{A}(x,t)}{\partial \vec{v}} = 0, & (x,t) \in \partial\Lambda \times \mathbb{R}^+, \\ \mathcal{M}(x,0) = \phi_1(x) - \frac{\alpha}{\gamma_1},\ \mathcal{A}(x,0) = \phi_2(x), & x \in \Lambda. \end{cases} \tag{18}$$

Now, it suffices to prove that the traveling wave solution $(\mathcal{M}^*(x,t), \mathcal{A}^*(x,t))$ of (18) is globally asymptotically stable in $\mathscr{X}^+$. To this end, build a functional $V(t) = \int_\Lambda [\mathcal{M}(x,t) + \mathcal{A}(x,t)]dx$. Obviously, $V(t)$ is smooth, $V(t) > 0$ for all $t \neq 0$ and $V(0) = 0$ in

$\mathscr{X}^+$. It follows from [24] that $\{t \in \mathbb{R} : V(t) \leq \mu\}$ is bounded for $\mu \geq 0$. Thus, calculating the derivative of $V(t)$ along (18), we have

$$\begin{aligned}\frac{dV}{dt} &= \int_\Lambda \left[\frac{\partial \mathcal{M}}{\partial t} + \frac{\partial \mathcal{A}}{\partial t}\right] dx = \int_\Lambda [d_1 \Delta \mathcal{M} - \beta \mathcal{M}\mathcal{A} - \gamma_1 \mathcal{M} - (\alpha\beta\gamma_1^{-1} - \delta)\mathcal{A} \\ &+ d_2 \Delta \mathcal{A} + \beta \mathcal{M}\mathcal{A} + (\alpha\beta\gamma_1^{-1} - \gamma_2 - \delta)\mathcal{A}] dx \\ &= \int_\Lambda [d_1 \Delta \mathcal{M} + d_2 \Delta \mathcal{A} - \gamma_1 \mathcal{M} - \gamma_2 \mathcal{A}] dx \\ &= \int_\Lambda [d_1 \Delta \mathcal{M} + d_2 \Delta \mathcal{A}] dx - \int_\Lambda [\gamma_1 \mathcal{M} + \gamma_2 \mathcal{A}] dx. \end{aligned} \tag{19}$$

From the boundary value condition $\frac{\partial \mathcal{M}(x,t)}{\partial \vec{v}} = \frac{\partial \mathcal{A}(x,t)}{\partial \vec{v}} = 0$, we obtain

$$\int_\Lambda \Delta \mathcal{M} dx = \frac{\partial \mathcal{M}}{\partial x}\bigg|_{\partial\Lambda} = 0, \quad \int_\Lambda \Delta \mathcal{A} dx = \frac{\partial \mathcal{A}}{\partial x}\bigg|_{\partial\Lambda} = 0. \tag{20}$$

(19) and (20) yield

$$\frac{dV}{dt} = -\int_\Lambda [\gamma_1 \mathcal{M} + \gamma_2 \mathcal{A}] dx < 0. \tag{21}$$

In view of (21) and [24], we know that $V(t)$ is a Lyapunov function of (18). From the parabolic L^p-theory, the Sobolev Embedding Theorem and the standard compactness argument [25], we conclude that there are some constants $N, t_0 > 0$ such that $\|\mathcal{M}\|_{C^2(\overline{\Lambda})} + \|\mathcal{A}\|_{C^2(\overline{\Lambda})} \leq N, \forall t > t_0$. So, we apply the Sobolev Embedding Theorem [26] to obtain that $(\mathcal{M}, \mathcal{A}) \to (0,0)$ in $L^2(\Lambda) \times L^2(\Lambda)$, as $t \to \infty$. Additionally, $\frac{dV}{dt} = 0$ iff $(\mathcal{M}, \mathcal{A}) = (0,0)$, which leads to $\{(\mathcal{M}, \mathcal{A}) : \frac{dV}{dt} = 0\} = \{(0,0)\}$. Thus, according to Lyapunov stability theory, we conclude that the traveling wave solution $(\mathcal{M}^*(x,t), \mathcal{A}^*(x,t))$ of (18) is globally asymptotically stable in $\mathscr{X}^+$. The proof is completed. □

5. Numerical Simulation

Consider the following non-linear diffusion PDE model of IGD

$$\begin{cases} \frac{\partial M}{\partial t} = d_1 \Delta M + \alpha - \beta M A - \gamma_1 M + \delta A, & (x,t) \in \Lambda \times \mathbb{R}^+, \\ \frac{\partial A}{\partial t} = d_2 \Delta A + \beta M A - (\gamma_2 + \delta) A, & (x,t) \in \Lambda \times \mathbb{R}^+, \\ \frac{\partial M(x,t)}{\partial \vec{v}} = \frac{\partial A(x,t)}{\partial \vec{v}} = 0, & (x,t) \in \partial\Lambda \times \mathbb{R}^+, \\ M(x,0) = \phi_1(x), \quad A(x,0) = \phi_2(x), & x \in \Lambda, \end{cases} \tag{22}$$

where $\mathbb{R}^+ = (0, \infty)$, $\Lambda = (0, 10)$, $\alpha = 10$, $\beta = 6$, $\gamma_1 = 3$ $\gamma_2 = 2$, $\delta = 3$, $d_1 = 0.5$, $d_2 = 0.8$, $\phi_1(x) = 5 + 3\sin(x)$, $\phi_2(x) = 7 + 4\cos(x)$.

A simple calculation gives $5 = \gamma_2 + \delta < \alpha\beta\gamma_1^{-1} = 20$ and $c^* = 2\sqrt{d_2(\alpha\beta\gamma_1^{-1} - \gamma_2 - \delta)}$ = 8. The condition (A) holds. According to Theorem 1 and Theorem 2, for any $c > c^* = 8$, the model (22) has a traveling wave solution $(\widetilde{M}^*(\xi), \widetilde{A}^*(\xi))$, which is globally asymptotically stable.

Figure 2 shows that when the initial conditions are the periodic functions $\phi_1(x) = 5 + 3\sin(x)$ and $\phi_2(x) = 7 + 4\cos(x)$, the system (22) exists as a globally asymptotically stable oscillatory periodic traveling wave solution.

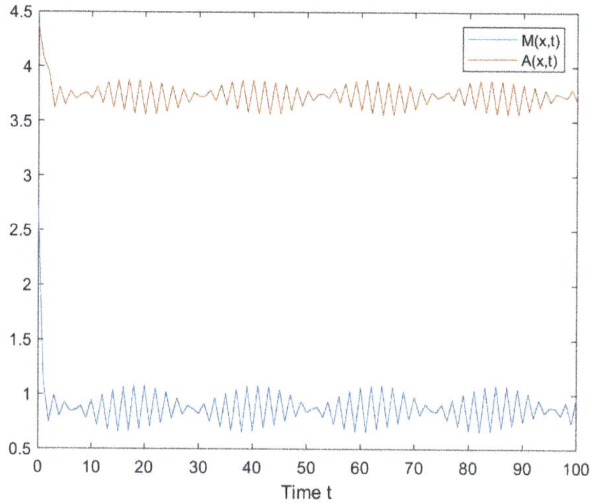

Figure 2. Evolutions of $M(x,t)$ and $A(x,t)$ over time t.

6. Conclusions

In the last decade, with the popularity of the Internet, the number of Internet users has continued to increase. While people enjoy the convenience and benefits brought by the Internet, some disadvantages brought by the Internet also begin to appear gradually. For example, Internet game addiction endangers the physical and mental health of players. In particular, many young addictive gamers are trapped in it. Many scholars, including mathematicians, have begun to pay attention to and study this phenomenon. Through the analysis of the dynamic change process of Internet gamers, we put forward a new non-linear diffusion PDE model (1) of IGD in this paper. By applying fixed point theory and Lyapunov stability theory, we study the existence and asymptotic stability of the traveling wave of model (1). With the help of the MATLAB toolbox, an example is numerically simulated to examine the correctness of our outcomes. The major findings of the paper provide theoretical help for the research and treatment of Internet game addiction. For example, our results show that appropriate treatment can ensure that the number of gamers is bounded without unlimited increase. The population density of gamers will gradually stabilize at $(\frac{\alpha}{\gamma_1}, 0)$, which suggests that we can eventually make the gamers disappear by reducing the number of moderate gamers and strengthening their treatment. Our work provides an example for applying mathematical theories and methods to solve social problems such as Internet game addiction, which makes the study of this kind of problem transform from qualitative research to quantitative research. In addition, recently published papers [27–46] enlighten us to discuss the existence, exponential stability and Ulam–Hyers stability of model (1) in the sense of fractional calculus in the future.

Funding: The APC was funded by research start-up funds for high-level talents of Taizhou University.

Institutional Review Board Statement: Not applicable.

Informed Consent Statement: Not applicable.

Data Availability Statement: Not applicable.

Acknowledgments: The author would like to express his heartfelt gratitude to the editors and reviewers for their constructive comments.

Conflicts of Interest: The author declares no conflict of interest.

References

1. World Health Organization. The 11th Revision of the International Classification of Diseases (ICD-11). Available online: https://icd.who.int/ (accessed on 25 May 2019).
2. Feng, W.; Ramo, D.; Chan, S.; Bourgeois, J. Internet gaming disorder: Trends in prevalence 1998–2016. *Addic. Behav.* **2017**, *75*, 17–24. [CrossRef] [PubMed]
3. *American Psychiatric Association, Diagnostic and Statistical Manual of Mental Disorders (DSM-5)*; American Psychiatric Publishing: Washington, DC, USA, 2013.
4. Paulus, F.; Ohmann, S.; von Gontard, A.; Popow, C. Internet gaming disorder in children and adolescents: A systematic review. *Dev. Med. Child Neurol.* **2018**, *60*, 645–659. [CrossRef] [PubMed]
5. Guo, Y.; Li, T. Optimal control and stability analysis of an online game addiction model with two stages. *Math. Meth. Appl. Sci.* **2020**, *43*, 4391–4408. [CrossRef]
6. Li, T.; Guo, Y. Stability and optimal control in a mathematical model of online game addiction. *Filomat* **2019**, *33*, 5691–5711. [CrossRef]
7. Viriyapong, R.; Sookpiam, M. Education campaign and family understanding affect stability and qualitative behavior of an online game addiction model for children and youth in Thailand. *Math. Meth. Appl. Sci.* **2019**, *42*, 6906–6916. [CrossRef]
8. Seno, H. A mathematical model of population dynamics for the internet gaming addiction. *Nonlinear Anal-Model.* **2021**, *26*, 861–883. [CrossRef]
9. Zhao, K. Global stability of a novel nonlinear diffusion online game addiction model with unsustainable control. *AIMS Math.* **2022**, *7*, 20752–20766. [CrossRef]
10. Murray, J. *Mathematical Biology*; Springer: New York, NY, USA, 1993.
11. Britton, N. *Reaction-Diffusion Equations and Their Applications to Biology*; Academic Press: New York, NY, USA, 1986.
12. Brauer, F.; Castillo-Chavez, C. *Mathematical Models in Population Biology and Epidemiology*; Springer: New York, NY, USA, 2012.
13. Diekmann, O. Run for your life, a note on the asymptotic speed of propagation of an epidemic. *J. Differ. Equ.* **1979**, *33*, 58–73. [CrossRef]
14. Abi Rizk, L.; Burie, J.; Ducrot, A. Travelling wave solutions for a nonlocal evolutionary-epidemic system. *J. Differ. Equ.* **2019**, *267*, 1467–1509. [CrossRef]
15. Zhang, Y.; Xu, Z. Dynamics of a diffusive HBV model with delayed Beddington-DeAngelis response. *Nonlinear Anal. Real World Appl.* **2014**, *15*, 118–139. [CrossRef]
16. Ren, X.; Tian, Y.; Liu, L.; Liu, X. A reaction-diffusion within-host HIV model with cell-to-cell transmission. *J. Math. Biol.* **2018**, *76*, 1831–1872. [CrossRef] [PubMed]
17. Kapel, A. Existence of travelling-wave type solutions for the Belousov-Zhabotinskii system of equations. *Sib. Mat. Zhurnal* **1991**, *32*, 47–59.
18. Trofimchuk, E.; Pinto, M.; Trofimchuk, S. On the minimal speed of front propagation in a model of the Belousov-Zhabotinsky reaction. *Discrete Contin. Dyn. Syst. Ser. B* **2014**, *19*, 1769–1781. [CrossRef]
19. Owolabi, K.; Hammouch, Z. Spatiotemporal patterns in the Belousov-Zhabotinskii reaction systems with Atangana-Baleanu fractional order derivative. *Phys. A* **2019**, *523*, 1072–1090. [CrossRef]
20. Alfaro, M.; Coville, J.; Raoul, G. Traveling waves in a nonlocal reaction-diffusion equation as a model for a population structured by a space variable and a phenotypic trait. *Commun. Part. Diff. Equ.* **2013**, *38*, 2126–2154. [CrossRef]
21. Li, J.; Latos, E.; Chen, L. Wavefronts for a nonlinear nonlocal bistable reaction-diffusion equation in population dynamics. *J. Differ. Equ.* **2017**, *263*, 6427–6455. [CrossRef]
22. Diaz, J.; Vrabie, I. Existence for reaction diffusion systems: A compactness method approach. *J. Math. Anal. Appl.* **1994**, *188*, 521–540. [CrossRef]
23. Mallet-Paret, J. The global structure of traveling waves in spatially discrete dynamical systems. *J. Dyn. Differ. Equ.* **1999**, *11*, 49–127. [CrossRef]
24. Guo, Z.; Huang, L.; Zou, X. Impact of discontinuous treatments on disease dynamics in an SIR epidemic model. *Math. Biosci. Eng.* **2012**, *9*, 97–110.
25. Brown, K.; Dunne, P.; Gardner, R. A semilinear parabolic system arising in the theory of superconductivity. *J. Differ. Equ.* **1981**, *40*, 232–252. [CrossRef]
26. Simsen, J.; Gentile, C. On p-Laplacian differential inclusions-Global existence, compactness properties and asymptotic behavior. *Nonlinear Anal.* **2009**, *71*, 3488–3500. [CrossRef]
27. Zhao, K. Stability of a nonlinear ML-nonsingular kernel fractional Langevin system with distributed lags and integral control. *Axioms* **2022**, *11*, 350. [CrossRef]
28. Zhao, K. Existence, stability and simulation of a class of nonlinear fractional Langevin equations involving nonsingular Mittag—Leffler kernel. *Fractal Fract.* **2022**, *6*, 469. [CrossRef]
29. Zhao, K.; Ma, Y. Study on the existence of solutions for a class of nonlinear neutral Hadamard-type fractional integro-differential equation with infinite delay. *Fractal Fract.* **2021**, *5*, 52. [CrossRef]
30. Zhao, K. Stability of a nonlinear fractional Langevin system with nonsingular exponential kernel and delay Control. *Discrete Dyn. Nat. Soc.* **2022**, *2022*, 9169185. [CrossRef]

31. Zhao, K. Local exponential stability of four almost-periodic positive solutions for a classic Ayala-Gilpin competitive ecosystem provided with varying-lags and control terms. *Int. J. Control* 2022, *in press*. [CrossRef]
32. Zhao, K. Local exponential stability of several almost periodic positive solutions for a classical controlled GA-predation ecosystem possessed distributed delays. *Appl. Math. Comput.* **2023**, *437*, 127540. [CrossRef]
33. Huang H.; Zhao, K.; Liu, X. On solvability of BVP for a coupled Hadamard fractional systems involving fractional derivative impulses. *AIMS Math.* **2022**, *7*, 19221–19236. [CrossRef]
34. Zhao, K.; Ma, S. Ulam-Hyers-Rassias stability for a class of nonlinear implicit Hadamard fractional integral boundary value problem with impulses. *AIMS Math.* **2021**, *7*, 3169–3185. [CrossRef]
35. Zhao, K.; Deng, S. Existence and Ulam-Hyers stability of a kind of fractional-order multiple point BVP involving noninstantaneous impulses and abstract bounded operator. *Adv. Differ. Equ-NY* **2021**, *2021*, 44. [CrossRef]
36. Luo, D.; Tian, M.; Zhu, Q. Some results on finite-time stability of stochastic fractional-order delay differential equations. *Chaos Soliton Fract.* **2022**, *158*, 111996. [CrossRef]
37. Wang, X.; Luo, D.; Zhu, Q. Ulam-Hyers stability of Caputo type fuzzy fractional differential equations with time-delays. *Chaos Soliton Fract.* **2022**, *156*, 111822. [CrossRef]
38. Luo, D.; Zhu, Q.; Luo, Z. A novel result on averaging principle of stochastic Hilfer-type fractional system involving non-Lipschitz coefficients. *Appl. Math. Lett.* **2021**, *122*, 107549. [CrossRef]
39. Luo, D.; Zhu, Q.; Luo, Z. An averaging principle for stochastic fractional differential equations with time-delays. *Appl. Math. Lett.* **2020**, *105*, 106290. [CrossRef]
40. Zhang, T.; Xiong, L. Periodic motion for impulsive fractional functional differential equations with piecewise Caputo derivative. *Appl. Math. Lett.* **2020**, *101*, 106072. [CrossRef]
41. Zhang, T.; Zhou, J.; Liao, Y. Exponentially stable periodic oscillation and Mittag-Leffler stabilization for fractional-order impulsive control neural networks with piecewise Caputo derivatives. *IEEE Trans. Cybernet.* **2022**, *52*, 9670–9683. [CrossRef]
42. Zhang, T.; Li, Y. Exponential Euler scheme of multi-delay Caputo-Fabrizio fractional-order differential equations. *Appl. Math. Lett.* **2022**, *124*, 107709. [CrossRef]
43. Zhang, T.; Li, Y. Global exponential stability of discrete-time almost automorphic Caputo-Fabrizio BAM fuzzy neural networks via exponential Euler technique. *Knowl-Based Syst.* **2022**, *246*, 108675. [CrossRef]
44. Li, Z.; Zhang, W.; Huang, C.; Zhou, J. Bifurcation for a fractional-order Lotka-Volterra predator-prey model with delay feedback control. *AIMS Math.* **2021**, *6*, 675–687.
45. Zhou, J.; Zhou, B.; Tian, L.; Wang, Y. Variational approach for the variable-order fractional magnetic Schrödinger equation with variable growth and steep potential in $\mathbb{R}^{N*}$. *Adv. Math. Phys.* **2020**, *2020*, 1320635. [CrossRef]
46. Zhou, J.; Zhou, B.; Wang, Y. Multiplicity results for variable-order nonlinear fractional magnetic Schrödinger equation with variable growth. *J. Funct. Spaces* **2020**, *2020*, 7817843. [CrossRef]

MDPI
St. Alban-Anlage 66
4052 Basel
Switzerland
www.mdpi.com

Axioms Editorial Office
E-mail: axioms@mdpi.com
www.mdpi.com/journal/axioms